Rethinking Normalcy
A Disability Studies Reader

Edited by
TANYA TITCHKOSKY
and ROD MICHALKO

Foreword by
GEOFFREY REAUME

Canadian Scholars' Press Inc.
Toronto

Rethinking Normalcy
Edited by Tanya Titchkosky and Rod Michalko

First published in 2009 by Canadian Scholars' Press Inc.
180 Bloor Street West, Suite 801
Toronto, Ontario
M5S 2V6

www.cspi.org

Canadian Scholars' Press Inc. gratefully acknowledges financial support for our publishing activities from the Government of Canada through the Book Publishing Industry Development Program (BPIDP) and the Government of Ontario through the Ontario Book Publishing Tax Credit Program.

Library and Archives Canada Cataloguing in Publication

Rethinking normalcy : a disability studies reader / edited by Tanya Titchkosky and Rod Michalko.

Includes bibliographical references.
ISBN 978-1-55130-363-5

1. Disabilities—Textbooks. 2. Sociology of disability—Textbooks.
3. Disability studies. I. Titchkosky, Tanya II. Michalko, Rod

HV1568.2.R48 2009   362.4   C2009-900888-2

Cover design, interior design and layout: Susan MacGregor/Digital Zone

09 10 11 12 13   5 4 3 2 1

Printed and bound in Canada by Marquis Book Printing Inc.

Table of Contents

Foreword

by Geoffrey Reaume

Critical Disability Studies Graduate Program, York University

This volume is a strong, interdisciplinary resource that illustrates the richness of disability studies, the depth and seriousness of the field, and the wide scope from which students can approach this topic. It is well organized and clearly addresses some of the major issues in disability studies that an introductory course needs to offer. It is also essential that it mix the theoretical with personal accounts, thus creating a synthesis between both approaches. This reader is an excellent resource for university undergraduates who want to know what this field is about, for professors to use in their disability studies courses, and for people who work as advocates and researchers in the wider community for whom this book will be a helpful reference text.

It is inspiring and exciting to see so much happening in disability studies in Canada and abroad in recent years. The field is relatively young, and within a decade, it will look radically different. *Rethinking Normalcy: A Disability Studies Reader* illustrates the richness and relevance of disability studies in our everyday lives by covering many of the debates, concepts, and controversies in this field from a primarily Canadian perspective, along with examples from the United States and Britain. It brings together both theoretical and personal accounts from a variety of disciplines, which combine to make an excellent resource for students from all backgrounds.

It is clear that the editors wish to bring critical concepts around disability and what it means to be considered "normal" and "abnormal" to the attention of a wider audience. Their arguments for doing so are compelling and important in enabling a much wider group of people to understand this topic from the point of view of people with disabilities, and allies who support a critical perspective that is different from the mainstream medical model approach. Undergraduate students who are not familiar with the field will have a new world open up to them, and people with disabilities will find this text an empowering resource in their understanding of the world in which we live.

This book will help fill a gap, as there is nothing comparable in Canada and there exists no single source that has such a large selection of Canadian writers in disability studies from such a broad, interdisciplinary approach.

Preface

We want to say from the outset that we are very proud of this collection. Never before has such a book been published in Canada. This book; never before has an anthology dedicated to introducing disability studies has included so many people who are working in Canada. This is also why we are so proud.

In his book, *The Truth about Stories,* Thomas King tells us that "the truth about stories is that that's all we are." This is as true for books as it is for people. As is the case with people's stories, the story of where a book begins is sometimes difficult to say. Did the story of this book begin when we first started to publish and teach in disability studies? Did it begin with our discoveries of our own disabilities? Or, did it begin when we began to reflect upon our disability experiences? Perhaps the story of this book begins in all of these spaces and in many others. What is certain, though, is that this book is now among us and we will tell at least a few stories of its origin.

In the summer of 2006, we moved to Toronto from Antigonish, Nova Scotia, where we had been teaching in the Sociology department of Saint Francis Xavier University. This move marked a return because we had moved to Antigonish from Toronto in the summer of 1997. Nine years later, we returned to begin teaching and writing in the field of disability studies at the University of Toronto. This was, however not the first time we did so—we were teaching disability studies and publishing in the field long before this return. Disability and disability studies was at the heart, or perhaps they were the heart, of our scholarly and activist work for many, many years. What was significant about our return in 2006 was that we embarked on a new journey, a twofold one really, of simultaneously continuing our work and developing disability studies at our new university at both the undergraduate and graduate levels. The pace and significance of how this work has proceeded has surprised even us. Disability studies is attracting much attention and a lively and ever-growing group of students. In some ways this attention is not surprising since disability studies is firmly established at both York University and Ryerson University in Toronto, and thus the ground has already been prepared.

Our experience of returning to Toronto marks one of the places where the story of this book begins. But there is another and even more significant beginning to this story. The story of this book begins in a fundamental sense with our own disability experiences;

Tanya Titchkosky is dyslexic and Rod Michalko is blind. Not only are we colleagues, we are life partners, and we live with and together in disability in many different ways. We live and work in and through dyslexia and blindness, and these too make extremely interesting and intriguing travel companions.

Travelling through our lives in dyslexia and blindness has led to many interesting and surprising experiences. At times the trip has been difficult, at other times it has been humorous, and still at other times the trip has been an occasion to think through the ways our world has been and continues to be put together. There is no doubt that this world has been built on the foundation of some key dominant interests, not the least of which is the often tacit production and maintenance of "normalcy" as the "natural order of things" and "the way things are." It is equally beyond question that dyslexia and blindness, and every other disability for that matter, has not been and is not now figured in the blueprint for the construction of this "normal world."

Our disabilities together with our disability studies perspective have provided the occasion for us to question this otherwise unquestionable sense of a "normal world." And yet, our disabilities represent more than an occasion for us to question and theorize. Our disabilities are our teachers and they have taught us much. They have taught us that the world is put together by dominant ideologies and interests, and it is not just "naturally there" for any "normal" person to experience and participate in fully. Our disabilities have taught us that disability is not a wholly negative experience, but is instead a life, and a valuable one at that. As such, it is a life worth living. They have taught us that far from being a "natural" thing to which everyone ought to aspire, normalcy is a mythical and mysterious human creation, and that disability represents a key to opening the region of this mythical and mysterious realm. Our disabilities have taught us to wander with wonder in the mystery of normalcy and to embark on the mysterious path of unravelling this mystery, at least a little. They have taught us that disabled people are valuable members of our society and that disability can teach us about the inequities of our world, and of its potential for social change. Most importantly, our disabilities have taught us that they will continue to teach and that we should, therefore, remain ever-vigilant and open to learning.

It was with these beginnings that we came to Megan Mueller of Canadian Scholars' Press/Women's Press. The three of us met at a Bloor Street café in Toronto in the summer of 2007. After dealing with the main agenda for our meeting, we began discussing disability studies and how we were engaging with this work. The three of us very quickly began to lament the fact that there was no introductory text in disability studies published in Canada featuring Canadian scholars and activists. Just as quickly, Megan raised the possibility of us putting such a book together and the rest of the story, as the adage goes, is history. This book grew out of our meeting at that Bloor Street café.

There are so many who have assisted us in putting this book together and to whom we owe thanks. There is, of course, Megan Mueller, who was the first to raise the idea of such a book and who encouraged us through all phases of its production, and for this we are grateful. Our Social Sciences and Humanities Research Council (SSHRC) grant provided us with the resources so necessary for bringing this project to fruition. We are indebted to a lively group of students, some who have come before us and some who have now joined us in telling and re-telling the story of disability and disability studies. A particular thanks is due to those students who helped gather materials for this book in 2008. Thus, we thank Katie Aubrecht, Eliza Chandler, Erick Fabris, Energy Manyimo, Jan McDougall, Isaac Stein, Melissa Strowger, Anne McGuire, and Leeanne Whitely. There are two students to whom we owe a special debt of thanks, Laura Thrasher and Katie Aubrecht. Much of what we have written was recorded on a dictaphone. Laura showed extraordinary patience in transcribing the often muffled dictaphone voice. Katie also did some transcription and she edited the chapters in this book, giving them a sense of belonging together. We also thank each of the authors who contributed to this book for their incredible work. The three anonymous reviewers of this book offered insightful comments and we have incorporated many of their suggestions. Finally, we are especially indebted to our disabled colleagues, students, and friends. These people have always been, and continue to be, a rich source of inspiration and encouragement to us and we are forever grateful for the ways in which they exemplify living in and with disability.

Tanya Titchkosky
Rod Michalko
Toronto, 2009

Introduction

Disability Matters

Disability matters and so does the study of disability and so too does *disability studies*. What also matters is that these three phenomena follow one another, not so much in a linear fashion, but in a circular one. They circle round and round, simultaneously leading and following one another, and form a complex circular web of meaning. Where this circle starts is difficult to discern and so too is its end. What matters, though, is that disability matters and the matter of disability finds its expression in the midst of this complex circular web of meaning. It is this web of meaning that we explore here as a way to begin to introduce disability studies as the need to think about disability in new ways, or to think and do disability differently.

The following chapters explore this web of meaning as they themselves emerge from, and find their possibility in, that web. This book intends to introduce readers to the rapidly emerging field of disability studies, particularly as it is starting to make an appearance in the Canadian academy. All of the chapters reveal something about how disability matters to all of us and how we come to think of, speak about, and act upon disability in the ways that we do. The diverse chapters all reflect a fundamental belief shared by those engaged in disability studies, namely, that disability is a social and political construction and we need to address this in our work and in our lives. What is unique about this particular book is its focus on normalcy. Disability studies is a way of knowing that can disrupt the "dangerous illusion about the meaning of normality" itself (Finkelstein, 1998, 30). Thus, the heart of this book is normalcy; the readings attempt, at times implicitly and at other times explicitly, to reveal the meaning of normalcy by asking how it matters to disability and how disability matters to it.

With this understanding of disability studies as a way to question normalcy, we turn to a discussion of what is usually quite opposite, and sometimes even opposed to disability studies, namely, the study of disability.

Normalcy and the Study of Disability

There are many ways to define disability and thus to come to some understanding of what disability is. Any and all definitions and understandings of disability, however, are rooted in the interests of those of us engaged in such definitional work. Such work is not restricted to professionals working in the fields of medicine, rehabilitation, or even in the field of disability studies. Everyone operates with some definition of disability whether we realize it or not. Thus, whatever else disability is, it *is* something that people define, understand, and come to know and live with in particular ways. Virtually no one in contemporary Western culture is without some sense of what disability is; thus, no one is without some thoughts or feelings about it.

Our thoughts and feelings about disability are typically negative in character. It is rare, for example, for anyone who is not disabled to want to become so; in fact, non-disabled people typically do their best to avoid becoming disabled. It is also the case that disability more often than not conjures up sympathy, since disability is usually thought of (defined and understood) as a misfortune. Disability is often defined as an unfortunate tragedy that happens to a few individuals and we almost always hope that such a tragedy will not happen to us. Yet, as Colin Barnes pointedly reminds us,

> The idea that disability is a medical problem affecting a small proportion of the population is no longer sustainable ... Internationally there are about 50 million disabled people in Europe ... and around 500 million world wide. (Barnes, 1998, 65)

Despite the impossible belief that disability is not a broad social issue, there are still people and institutions that begin from the premise that disability is simply a rare and anomalous personal tragedy.

It is precisely this "personal tragedy" conception of disability that acts as the impetus and provides the foundation for the study of disability. Professions such as medicine, rehabilitation, counselling, and special education make up the dominant ways that disability is studied in our society. All of these endeavours have their own ways of defining disability and coming to an understanding of what disability is. What these professions share in common, however, is that disability is a personal tragedy wrought with problems, problems for which solutions *must* be sought. As David Mitchell reminds us,

> Nearly every culture views disability as a problem in need of a solution ... [which] situates people with disabilities in a profoundly ambivalent relation to the cultures and stories they inhabit. (Mitchell, 2002, 15)

That disability is a personal problem of tragic proportions requiring the assistance of the helping professions makes this story the major one that disabled people in Western cultures are forced to inhabit today. This story, moreover, also forces the study of disability to reproduce the belief that disability can be contained and managed by sustaining the one-dimensional definition that it is only a problem in need of a solution.

Given such an understanding of disability, professions such as medicine, rehabilitation, counselling, and special education are committed, first and foremost, to the prevention of disability. If prevention fails and someone becomes disabled, the second commitment of these professions is to cure disability. If cure also fails, the final commitment is to making a disabled person feel and "look" (appear) as normal as possible. This latter commitment is grounded in disability defined and understood as a physical, sensory, emotional, or intellectual "abnormal condition" that happens to a few individuals.

There is a significant consequence that comes from understanding disability as an individual matter, namely, that disabled people represent a random collection of individuals who happen to possess "abnormal" bodily, sensory, emotional, or intellectual conditions. This collection of individuals can then be defined as the rate of disability in a population, or as itself a population within the overall population of a country such as Canada. This consequence is manifested in the Canadian government's understanding of disability:

> Over 12% of Canadians have a disability—that means 3.6 million people … Some people are born with disabilities, while others experience disability later in life, through an accident or because of an illness or disease … Canada's Aboriginal population experiences a particularly high rate of disability—more than one and a half times the rate of the non-Aboriginal population … Nationally, and in every province, the majority of Canadians with disabilities have mild to moderate disabilities … A disability may be mild or profound, temporary or permanent. (Canada: *Advancing the Inclusion of Persons with Disabilities,* 2004, 8, 9, 10, 11)

Some people are regarded by the Canadian government as people "with disabilities," insofar as they are people with an "abnormal condition." Moreover, this condition is understood as a "thing" that happens to some individuals either at birth or later in life because of an accident, illness, or disease. Disability, defined as a thing that happens to some individuals, can now be counted and measured, its causes discerned, and its demographic distribution charted. The Canadian government does not regard disability as a way of life generated through *relations* that cultures, and thus people, have to their histories, their material conditions of life, their ways of understanding what it means to be human, and what it means to live together in a society. Understood as an "abnormal condition," diversity within disability is measured in terms of "severity, longevity, cause and consequence" as this is causally related to "personal, social and economic disadvantages" (Canada: *In Unison: A Canadian Approach to Disability Issues,* 1998, 11). Measuring people's unfortunate problems and ascertaining their location within the social whole in order to address their personal accommodation needs is the kind of work done by those professions committed to the study of disability.

This sort of work seeks to minimize the negative effects of disability and to "help" disabled people "fit" into "normal" society. *Making* disabled people as normal as possible is the goal of the typical ways of studying disability. In fact, what the oft-called "helping professions" stress in relation to disability is the "normal individual" and "normal functioning." Thus, disability is conceived of as an "abnormal" and an "unnatural" condition that attaches itself to a few "normal" persons. What remains for these professions to do, then, is to solve the problem of disability by giving disabled people a variety of ways to cope with and adjust to their unwanted "abnormal" conditions. The study of disability is committed to producing knowledge that might better alleviate the sense in which the disabled person represents a departure from normalcy. These professions, then, are committed to "normalcy" as the only life worth living and thus they are committed to defining disability as a condition that requires adjustment in order to sustain normalcy as the singularly good way of being-in-the-world. This commitment to personal adjustment and to "fitting" disabled people into "normal life" means that the "cultural assumptions that structure the normal remain unquestioned ... [and] disability as a political issue, a social construction ... and a category of inquiry..." remains unacknowledged (Rosemarie Garland-Thomson, 1996, xvii).

It should now be clear that the study of disability is the study of "abnormal" conditions. Disability thus becomes something about which expertise can be developed —expertise in the biomedical nature of disability, in the rehabilitation and counselling of disabled people, and in the "special" ways disabled students must be educated. The study of disability, then, defines and understands disability as an object, as a "thing" that can and should be studied so as to discern its cause, measure its severity and longevity, and predict its consequence—all with the ultimate aim of remedy.

What is disturbing is that "remedy" within the study of disability perspective means ridding society of disability (Michalko, 2002, 73ff; Titchkosky, 2007, 145ff, 177ff). More disturbing still is that all of this expertise is developed and gleaned virtually without participation of disabled people themselves, except as objects of professional study. While this has led to a gigantic "helping" industry (Albrecht and Bury, 2001; Oliver, 1996; Zola, 1982), it has not resulted in changing the marginalization and discrimination faced by disabled people on a daily basis. The unemployment and non-labour force participation rates among disabled people in Canada, and around the globe, remain disturbingly high, education rates disturbingly low, and a full third of people with disabilities report not receiving the assistance and supports they require. (For such information see www.hrsdc.gc.ca/en/cs/sp/sdc/pkrf/publications/research/2001-000123/page00.shtml or www.statcan.ca/english/freepub/89-577-XIE/) But, we do not require statistics to tell us that disability is not a welcome feature of individual and collective life; nor do we need statistics to tell us that disabled people are not regular participants in the realms of daily life. We need only consult our own feelings and thoughts about disability—feelings and thoughts gleaned from our culture—to "know" that disability is a condition of "abnormalcy" that should be removed from both individuals and society; these thoughts and feelings about disability also tell us that if disability cannot be removed, it must be coped with and adjusted to, and that such practices are second-best.

From the framework of the study of disability, then, disability remains essentially abnormal. The commitment to studying disability defined as an "individual abnormality" is always a commitment to normalcy. Bodies, minds, emotions, and senses should be normal, and almost always are, according to those professions that study disability and according even to those people who are not professionally involved in studying disability but who, nonetheless, think of themselves as normal. Those who share this understanding of normalcy do allow for a degree of variation. We operate within an implicit conception of a "normal range" of variation or difference. A little trouble seeing or a little trouble hearing, for example, are usually thought of as normal differences; but blindness or deafness is another matter. They are thought of as far outside, or at the extreme end of the range of normal difference (Davis, 1995). There are normal differences that are not too worrisome since they are, after all, normal, and there are abnormal differences that are worrisome. In the latter instance, this worry is abated somewhat since it is thought that medical, rehabilitation, or other forms of professional intervention can make these abnormalities normal or, at least, as normal as possible.

We can now more fully understand that the commitment to the study of disability is really a commitment to normalcy. Disability matters to the study of disability because normalcy matters. And, normalcy matters because it is understood as the legitimate way of being in the world and the only version of the good life. The study of disability is committed to normalcy insofar as it represents the standard against which any human life is measured; the closer a human being is to normalcy, the closer he or she is to being human.

This is why any professional study of disability is required to define disability in a precise and exact way. When a "successful disabled person" is understood as one who comes very close to the standard of normalcy, measurement and calculation become necessary. The precise definition or measurement of the extent or degree of a disability is crucial if it is to be known and measured against the standard of normalcy. The questions asked by those who study disability, therefore, take the following form: Does a blind person do normal things, even though he or she does them differently from sighted people? Does the person with anxiety control his or her disorder and act normally? Does a dyslexic person develop learning strategies that allow him or her to read and write normally? Does the person with physical impairments make normal and full use of his or her non-impaired body parts? What interventions are necessary in order for "individuals with disabilities" to live as normally as possible? These questions, and others like them, form the basis of the study of disability. But, this is not the only way that disability matters, nor is it the only way that normalcy matters. We turn now to a consideration of how these issues matter differently to disability studies.

Disability Studies and Normalcy

First and foremost, disability does not matter to disability studies in the way that it does to the study of disability and neither does normalcy. This is so insofar as, unlike the study of disability, disability studies does not, strictly speaking, study disability. As a way to address the apparent counterintuitive character of this strange claim, here are some of the ways that disability does not matter to disability studies. Those of us who do disability studies do not conceive of disability as a thing-in-the-world. Disability does not matter to us as an object of inquiry about which expertise can be developed; we do not treat disability as something separate from an individual or from a collective, such as a society. Since disability studies does not study disability as an isolated thing or measure it against the standard of normalcy understood as the "good life," there is no need for us to define it in a precise and exact way. Disability studies does define disability, but it does so in a way that allows disability to be fluid and not restricted in the yoke of a positivist standard of normalcy. Disability is, for disability studies, a "fluid and shifting" set of meanings involved in the greater question of what it means to be human (Shildrick and Price, 1996, 93). Thus, we understand disability as connected to, as well as reflective of, the social scenes of which it is always a part.

Disability matters to disability studies in the sense that it is an integral part of the essential diversity of human life both individually and collectively. Far from being an unfortunate and negative happenstance of human existence, disability is, for disability studies, a way of being-in-the-world, and a legitimate one at that. It is a way of understanding who we are or, at least, a part of who we are. Disability is a cogent and valuable aspect of the array of differences represented in any human and in any human collective. Disability is as legitimate and valuable a part of who we are as is our gender, race, sexuality, ethnicity, and so on. Like any other aspect of our understanding of who we are, disability's significance is caught up and even constituted by the structures of normal life. Even though disabled people are marginalized in a whole host of ways, those processes that make people marginal are also part of what makes disability matter to disability studies. bell hooks (1990, 342) tells us "that … margins have been both sites of repression and sites of resistance." This prompts us to understand that the margins are not a "nowhere" void of life and culture, but are instead related to what is central—related to versions of normalcy, but are not the same versions. bell hooks suggests that respecting the voices, lives, and events found at the margins of a society might be a way to begin to resist and remake the centre's norms. From the perspective of disability studies, studying the centrality of normalcy is a way to know and resist that which makes disability matter as a form of devalued marginality.

Like the study of disability, disability studies too encompasses a relation to normalcy. But, unlike the study of disability, we do not conceive of disability as a problem in need of a solution. Instead, disability studies, in its various expressions, understands disability as a disruption to normalcy and thus as problematizing it; i.e., making the taken-for-granted character of normalcy "visible" and thus open to both exploration and change. Disability, then, becomes the occasion for disability studies to interrogate normalcy, to make *it* an object of study. Disability brings normalcy into view and allows for the possibility of wondering how normalcy came about or how it was constructed in the first place. No one "normally" thinks of "normalcy" (Michalko, see Chapter 6). Everyone does, however, typically take normalcy for granted, thus rarely disturbing its implicit claim as being the good life and the only life worth living. Disability allows not only for the possibility of bringing this normative claim into "view," but also allows for the possibility of critically interrogating this claim.

It should be clear by now that disability studies conceives of disability as a socio-political phenomenon, one that marks an occasion to interrogate what we "normally" think of and experience as "normal life." After all, it is this taken-for-granted character of "normal life" that generates disability in the first place. All of us, including disabled people, live in the midst of others. As marginalized as we disabled people are, we live in and with the cultural understanding that we live on the margins of a centre or on the margins of what we have been calling normalcy. We recognize that the centre builds its environment—both physical and attitudinal—from the blueprint or standard of normalcy, and we recognize that, for the most part, this blueprint does not include us. This blueprint does include lighting for sighted people, stairs for walking people, sounds for hearing people and the like; it rarely includes voice-description for blind people, accessible washrooms for wheelchair users, sign interpreters for D/deaf people, and so on.

Even though disability is largely excluded from the centre, the life in the centre, in normalcy, is sometimes very compelling and even quite seductive to disabled people (Garland-Thomson, 1996, xvii). We sometimes feel compelled to live in the centre and are sometimes seduced by its rhetorical claims to being the only good life and the best way of being-in-the-world. Disabled people fight for access to the centre, for example, and often claim to be "persons with disabilities," or "simply people," or even "just like everyone else." We sometimes stress and privilege our personhood over our disabilities in an attempt to claim a place in the centre. We are sometimes tempted by the desire to belong in the centre, in the social space that "appears" to be so advantageous to so many people. It is ironic that disabled people want so badly to belong to that which makes us marginal and that which excludes and disadvantages so many.

Equally as ironic, the compelling and seductive character of normalcy conceals the compelling and seductive character of the margins, and it conceals this not only from its "view" but from ours as well. Normalcy accomplishes this concealment by conceiving of marginality as a kind of "no-where" and also as a "somewhere" where no one wants to be since it is virtually uninhabitable. From the standpoint of the centre, no one desires to inhabit a disabled body, or disabled senses or minds, since to do so is tantamount to barely living at all. The centre conceives of disability as a devalued life where its only hope for even a semblance of value is to evoke the "human spirit" and to "overcome disability," to adapt, to adjust, and to live as normally as possible. Such a conception of the relation between disability and normalcy holds out only two options for disabled people: we overcome our disabilities and are heroic or we do not and are tragic. Normalcy imagines—"sees"—no other possibility of human life than itself, and thus, ironically, does not "see" itself. The centre understands itself as the only legitimate space of human habitation and, like all spaces, the centre too has its casualties.

But what of the compelling and seductive character of marginality? What is it about marginality that can allow us to resist the temptation to desire normalcy? How can the margins show the centre that its margins are not merely uninhabitable voids, but are instead spaces where it is possible to reveal the otherwise concealed character of the centre, thus uncovering the "fact" that the centre is not natural, but is human-made and can be otherwise? Desiring normalcy, then, is not the problem; the problem is developing a relation to this desire that does not simultaneously reject life on the margins.

In relation to racialized experience, bell hooks speaks powerfully of the conflict between margin and centre. She says,

> When I left that concrete space in the margins, I kept alive in my heart a way of knowing reality which affirms continually not only the primacy of resistance but the necessity of a resistance that is sustained by remembrance of the past, which includes recollections of broken tongues, giving us ways to speak that de-colonize our minds, our very beings. Once mama said to me as I was about to go again to the predominately white university, "You can take what the white people have to offer but you do not have to love them." Now understanding her cultural codes I know that she was not saying to me not to love people of other races. She was speaking about colonization and the reality of what it means to be taught in a culture of domination by those who dominate. She was insisting on my power to be able to separate useful knowledge that I might get from the dominating group from participation in ways of knowing that would lead to estrangement, alienation, and, worse, assimilation and cooption. (bell hooks, 1990, 342)

While there are many intersections and differences between racialized margins and disability margins, they do share a space where reality is experienced and known, a reality different from that of the centre. The centre does, however, produce knowledge about our lives in the margins and posits this knowledge as "more real" than our own. The centre's knowledge dominates, and we must be careful to separate our participation from this domination so that we can avoid being co-opted and assimilated. We can take bell hooks' mother's advice and put it into disability and disability studies terms: "You can take what ... [those who study disability] ... have to offer but you do not have to love them." "Loving them," of course, refers to loving the ways in which the study of disability thinks of, speaks of, and acts on disability. Loving these ways invites estrangement from our own disability experience and it risks the annihilation of disability studies' power to resist the dominant ideology of normalcy. While the margins are spaces of oppression, they are also spaces of resistance, and it is this power to uncover and resist normalcy that makes marginality so compelling and so seductive.

Now Is the Time for Disability Studies

In his *History of Disability*, Henri-Jacques Stiker (1999, 362) tells us that, "Deformity of the body, troubles of the mind, loss of senses, have always worried social groups, just as sex, power, change, death and ancestors have." While there has likely been in every culture and at every time ways dealing with and explaining these worries, there has not always been an established space to critically question how we go about worrying. Since at least the time of the Enlightenment, "… disability has been the province of numerous professional and academic disciplines that concentrate upon the management, repair, and maintenance of physical and cognitive incapacity" (Mitchell and Snyder, 1997, 1). These processes of "management" do not allow for disability to be understood as a space for critical reflection on how the voice of normalcy seeks to dominate by speaking on behalf of disability experience. The busy work of defining disability as a problem for which solutions must be sought has not lent itself to the timely and necessary task of critical reflection. However, the work of the various helping industries has provoked others to question what exactly is being accomplished by managing the experience of disability.

Even before there was a field called disability studies, in whose name we could collect ourselves, there were critiques and contestations of dominant ways of managing, repairing, and maintaining those people conceived of as disabled. Once we begin to understand that disability oppression and marginalization are not caused by the vagaries of the body, the points made by the UK Union of the Physically Impaired Against Segregation (UPIAS) begin to seem obvious. More than thirty years ago, UPIAS wrote:

> In our view, it is society which disables physically impaired people. Disability is something imposed on top of our impairments by the way we are unnecessarily isolated and excluded from full participation in society. Disabled people are therefore an oppressed group in society. To understand this it is necessary to grasp the distinction between the physical impairment and the social situation, called "disability," of people with such impairment. Thus we define impairment as lacking part of or all of a limb, or having a defective limb, organ or mechanism of the body; and disability as the disadvantage or restriction of activity caused by a contemporary social organisation which takes no or little account of people who have physical impairments and thus excludes them from participation in the mainstream of social activities. Physical disability is therefore a particular form of social oppression. (UPIAS: *Fundamental Principles of Disability*, 1975, page 14 in original document, www.leeds.ac.uk/disability-studies/archiveuk/UPIAS/UPIAS.htm)

For disability activists, artists, and scholars, keeping the social character of the production of disability front and centre has been of primary importance. For some this has meant keeping a clear distinction between the idea of impairment and that of disability; for others, it has meant blurring such a distinction (e.g., Oliver, Barnes, Corker, Michalko). Despite these differences, the political and theoretical act of locating disability firmly in the realm of the social remains a fundamental principle of disability studies work around the globe today.

What the "social" means and what is "social" about disability for disability studies has generated a myriad of responses provoking nuanced and invigorating theoretical and political developments. For example, our bodies are not asocial since the social organizes even what can be understood as impairment, lack, defect, or bodily function. Thus, different lessons can be learned from society's failure to respond to impaired bodies, from our experience of embodiment, and from sensing and feeling differently from the norm. Despite how obvious society's imposition of barriers to full participation seems, this imposition persists and is treated as if it is as "natural" as impairment itself. Any use of the idea of natural, then, begs the question of whether the concept of "natural" is itself part of the normative order that reproduces exclusion and oppression. Disability studies promises to complicate our taken-for-granted relations to normal conceptions of body and mind, of impairment and disability, of nature and culture, and even of non-person and person. The diversity of interests found in disability studies can be read as actualizing the promise of complicating our relation to the good of normalcy. The commitments of disability studies scholars, for example, range from materialist Marxism to post-structuralist cultural studies, making this a dynamic field where the assumptions, demands, and meanings of normalcy are being engaged in new ways.

Catherine Kudlicks's characterization (see chapter two) of disability studies provides a way to collect the variety of interests expressed in disability studies. She says,

> Disability studies takes for its subject matter not simply the variations that exist in human behavior, appearance, functioning, sensory acuity, and cognitive processing, but, more crucially, the meaning we make of those variations ... Simi Linton explains in her influential 1998 manifesto *Claiming Disability*. "It is an interdisciplinary field based on a socio-political analysis of disability and informed both by the knowledge base and methodologies used in the traditional liberal arts, and by conceptualizations and approaches developed in areas of the new scholarship." By approaching disability as a social category rather than as an individual characteristic, the field challenges long-held perceptions that relegate it to the unglamorous backwaters primarily of interest to people in rehabilitation, special education, and other applied professional fields. (Kudlick, 2003, 763 [citing Linton, 1998, 2])

The variety of interests in disability studies, according to Kudlick, is due to the interdisciplinary character of disability studies and not to conflicting paradigms and approaches. Indeed, this interdisciplinary variety enhances disability studies by understanding it as necessarily diverse and not as a disparate aggregation of theoretical orientations.

Disability studies scholarship is now emerging globally, including in Canada, in exciting and various ways and, moreover, is beginning to be recognized as a necessary aspect for inclusion in the social sciences, humanities, and health science fields. With the growing recognition that disability touches every aspect of human existence, innumerable topic areas are beginning to emerge and be engaged with from a disability studies perspective. Given that the meaning of our bodies, minds, senses, and emotions are tied up, and made manifest through, every part of social life, disability serves as a prime location to examine all that is social.

We cannot emphasize enough that disability studies requires that we ready ourselves to loosen the hold of the normative demand to fix impairments, and that we begin to learn how to notice and think about social relations we develop with bodies conceived of as different. This reader is oriented to helping accomplish the task of thinking in new ways about disability, the study of disability, and disability studies. The following chapters are animated by the spirit of the resistive power of the margins. All of the chapters represent a critique of, and thus resistance to, the dominant cultural ways of "knowing" disability. We now turn to a brief description of the organization of this book.

Organization

Rethinking Normalcy is divided into six parts. The chapters in Part I, "Disability Studies and the Question of Normalcy," address the founding principles and questions of disability studies. In this way, Part I represents a history of disability studies; not a conventional and concrete historical description of its development, but a depiction of its grounding principles and conceptions. Of key importance is the concept of normalcy and approaching it directly as a concept in need of questioning. This question is raised through narrating and theorizing personal, historical, institutional, and cultural manifestations of the issue of normalcy as it is intertwined with bodies, minds, senses, and emotions. Normalcy is interrogated as a phenomenon that is socially constructed rather than as one that is natural and beyond question.

Even though Part II, "Normalizing Suffering," addresses the idea of suffering, it does not do so through accepting the conventional way that suffering is understood. Instead, the chapters in this part demonstrate that under contemporary conditions disabled people suffer the normative demands of social life, and that social life imposes ways to normatively order this suffering *as if* it is merely an individual issue and not a collective one. Disability studies, then, locates suffering directly in the realm of society and not in the realm of individuals.

Part III, "Institutionalizing Normalcy," exemplifies some of the key ways that the issue of disability is dealt with by social institutions. In the face of the unexamined conceptions that disability is a charity issue, an individual problem, a bureaucratic and institutional problem, we encounter some of the major ways disability is dealt with in contemporary times. The chapters in Part III provide the opportunity to explore some of the many ways we have of reducing disability to the problem of management. Of course, there are many other forms of managing disability, such as eugenic programs that attempt to eliminate disability or educational programs that attempt to control it. Nonetheless, managing disability is one of the dominant ways our society has of thinking about disability and, therefore, acting upon it. Part III introduces the need to disrupt this usual way of understanding disability as it is represented in institutional life.

In Part IV, "Law and Social Space," Canadian policy and legal issues are examined as they relate to the issues of impairment and disability. The chapters in Part IV attest to the complicated political character of disability, even though social institutions appear to be working with clear and certain definitions of it. How disability is defined, whether implicitly or explicitly, governs the way it is acted upon through legislation and in social spaces which, in turn, governs the interaction between disabled and non-disabled people. Moreover, how disabled people interpret and live with legal relations to disability can also provide ways to question normal or expected relations to legal rights.

In Part V, "Education, Technology, and Work," the dynamic interrelation of learning and work as activities and as social spaces ruled by normative expectations are revealed and explored. The question of negotiating a place in activities and spaces that do not normally anticipate the participation of disabled people is exemplified in different ways by all of the chapters in Part V. Their animating question is best captured in this way: "What do we do when the unexpected show up?" (Michalko and Titchkosky, 2001). This leads to a further question: What is it about so-called "normal" educational and work environments that seems not to expect disability to show up?

Finally, Part VI, "Global Interconnections and Local Challenges," provides an occasion to directly address the issues of race, class, gender, sexuality, and nation (Bell, 2006). Even though many of the chapters in this reader touch on these intersecting aspects of social difference, Part VI can be read as an explicit invitation to imagine the future of disability and disability studies in new and less oppressive ways. How we imagine the meaning and constitution of difference in both the global and local arenas of our lives has much to do with the kinds of social and political realities that can be forged in the future. Critically considering what the newly emerging field of disability studies has not yet addressed, or has addressed poorly, is an invitation for readers to pursue these gaps and absences; in thinking about disability studies, we can also rethink its "normal" trajectories and moments of inclusion and exclusion.

This book questions normalcy as it appears in our lives at different times and in different social locations. At times, normalcy appears as a demand on our face-to-face interactions, and at other times it appears as a demand for us to comply with the realities imposed upon us by social structures external to us. Still, at other times, normalcy appears embedded in our ways of knowing ourselves and the world. This reader represents a particular way that the demands of normalcy can be de-centered, thus allowing for its interrogation and ultimate restructuring. At its core, *Rethinking Normalcy: A Disability Studies Reader* is an invitation for you to join disability studies scholars, artists, and activists on the journey to an understanding of disability as a genuine and creative aspect of social life and conceive of it as a crucial space for critically interrogating the ways in which we live together.

References

Albrecht, G. and Bury, M. (2001). "The Political Economy of the Disability Market." In G. L. Albrecht, K. D. Seelman & M. Bury (Eds.), *Handbook of Disability Studies*. Thousand Oaks: Sage Publications, Inc. 585–609.

Barnes, Colin. (1998). "The Social Model of Disability: A Sociological Phenomenon Ignored by Sociologists?" In Tom Shakespeare (Ed.), *The Disability Reader: Social Science Perspectives*. London: Cassell Academic. 66–78.

Bell, Chris. (2006). "Introducing White Disability Studies: A Modest Proposal." In Lennard J. Davis (Ed.), *The Disability Studies Reader* 2nd Edition. New York: Routledge. 275–282.

Canada. (2004). Advancing the Inclusion of Persons with Disabilities. Ottawa: Social Development Canada.

Canada. (2003). *Defining Disability: A Complex Issue*. Office for Disability Issues, HRDC. Ottawa: Human Resources Development Canada. (RH37-4/3-2003 –E).

Canada. (2000). A Visionary Paper of Federal/Provincial/Territorial Ministers Responsible for Social Services (2000). *In Unison 2000: Persons with Disabilities in Canada*. Ottawa: Supply and Service Canada.

Davis, Lennard J. (1995). *Enforcing Normalcy: Disability, Deafness, and the Body*. London: Verso Press.

Finkelstein, Vic. (1998). "Emancipating Disability Studies." In Tom Shakespeare (Ed.), *The Disability Reader*. London: Cassel Academic. 28–49.

hooks, bell. (1990). "Marginality as a Site of Resistance." In Russell Ferguson, Martha Gever, Trinh T. Minh-ha & Cornel West (Eds.), *Out There: Marginalization and Contemporary Cultures*. Boston: MIT Press. 341–343.

Kudlick, C.J. (2003). "Disability History: Why We Need Another 'Other.'" *The American History Review*, 108(3): 763–793. Retrieved June 1, 2003 from www.historycooperative.org/journals/ahr/108.3/kudlick.html

Linton, Simi. (1998). *Claiming Disability: Knowledge and Identity*. New York: New York University Press.

McColl, Mary Ann and Lyn Jongbloed (Eds.). (2006). *Disability and Social Policy in Canada*, 2nd Edition. Toronto: Captus Press.

Michalko, Rod. (2002). *The Difference that Disability Makes*. Philadelphia: Temple University Press.

Michalko, Rod. (2001). "Blindness Enters the Classroom." *Disability & Society*, 16 (3): 349–359.

Michalko, Rod (1998). *The Mystery of the Eye and the Shadow of Blindness*. Toronto: University of Toronto Press.

Mitchell, David T. (2002). "Narrative Prosthesis and the Materiality of Metaphor." In Sharon L. Snyder, Brenda Jo Brueggemann & Rosemarie Garland-Thomson (Eds.), *Disability Studies: Enabling the Humanities*. New York: The Modern Language Association of America. 15–30.

Mitchell, David and Sharon Snyder. (1997). "Disability Studies and the Double Bind of Representation." In David Mitchell & Sharon Snyder (Eds.), *The Body and Physical Difference: Discourses of Disability*. Ann Arbor: University of Michigan Press. 1–31.

Oliver, Michael. (1996). *Understanding Disability: From Theory to Practice*. New York: St. Martin's Press.

Pothier, Diane and Richard Devlin (Eds.), (2006). *Critical Disability Theory: Essays in Philosophy, Politics, Policy, and Law*. Vancouver: UBC Press.

Shildrick, Margrit and Janet Price. (1996). "Breaking the Boundaries of the Broken Body." *Body & Society*, 2(4): 93–113.

Stiker, Henri-Jacques. (1999). *A History of Disability*. William Sayers (Trans). Foreword by David T. Mitchell. Ann Arbor: The University of Michigan Press.

Thomas, Carol. (1999). *Female Forms: Experiencing and Understanding Disability*. Buckingham: Open University Press.

Thomson, Rosemarie Garland. (1997). Extraordinary Bodies: Figuring Physical Disability in American Culture and Literature. New York: Columbia University Press.

Titchkosky, Tanya. (2007). *Reading and Writing Disability Differently: The Textured Life of Embodiment*. Toronto: University of Toronto Press.

Titchkosky, Tanya. (2003). *Disability, Self, and Society*. Toronto: University of Toronto Press.

UPIAS. 1976. *Fundamental Principles of Disability*. London: Union of the Physically Impaired Against Segregation.

Zola, Irving Kenneth. (1993). "Self, Identity, and the Naming Question: Reflections on the Language of Disability." *Social Science and Medicine*, 36(2): 167–173.

Zola, Irving Kenneth. (1982). *Missing Pieces: A Chronicle of Living with a Disability*. Philadelphia: Temple University Press.

PART I

Disability Studies and the Question of Normalcy

Since this book seeks to rethink normalcy, we begin by addressing the connection between disability, disability studies, and normalcy. The chapters in Part I, in their various ways, draw out this connection. Rather than treating normalcy as a taken-for-granted and thus unexamined feature of how we think about and act toward disability, all of the chapters in Part I conceive of normalcy not as a natural phenomenon, but as something that is socially achieved through the ways in which we understand what it means to be human and through the subsequent ways we interact with one another.

In Chapter 1, Michael Oliver introduces the social model of disability. We "normally" think of and experience disability as an individual, biomedical condition. Oliver refers to this understanding as the individual model of disability. He says that not only do we understand disability as an individual, biomedical condition, but we also think of it as a "personal tragedy." Thus, we "normally" think of and experience disability as personal tragedy that happens to a few people. In contrast to the individual model of disability that locates disability in the person, Oliver suggests that disability is actually located in society and this he calls the social model of disability. The social model distinguishes between "impairment" and "disability." Impairments are those conditions that we disabled people have while disability is the result of inappropriate and discriminatory action by society with regard to impairment.

In Chapter 2, Catherine Kudlick takes up the historical development of disability studies as well as the ways in which we have historically understood disability. Like any other academic discipline, disability studies did not emerge in a historical or socio-political vacuum. Kudlick points out how disability studies developed over the last three decades or so as an activist and scholarly response to the ways in which disability was "normally" understood and experienced in our society, including in the academy. She demonstrates how disability studies has emerged as an interdisciplinary endeavour. The development of disability studies challenges how disability is typically conceived of and Kudlick reveals these new conceptions and their influence on the production of knowledge.

Tanya Titchkosky's chapter may be read as a complement to the work of Catherine Kudlick. In Chapter 3, Titchkosky develops a critique of how sociology typically conceives of disability. She shows how sociology conventionally understands disability as a deviation from the norm or as stigma. While Titchkosky does suggest that treating disability as stigma has been useful to the development of disability studies, she vividly demonstrates how both the stigma and deviance conceptions have been detrimental to a more enhanced and richer version of disability studies. A "new" disability studies, Titchkosky argues, would situate disability neither as deviance nor as stigma. Instead, she locates disability as a liminal space, as occupying a space between what we think of as "normal" and "abnormal." From this space, disability represents an opportunity to bring the meaning of normalcy "into view," into conversation. The meaning of normalcy hides from itself, and by revealing it, Titchkosky shows how normalcy acts as a "meaning-maker" of disability. For Titchkosky, bringing normalcy "into view" marks the gift that both disability and disability studies offer.

Rosemarie Garland-Thomson continues the conversation of the connection between normalcy and disability in Chapter 4. Perhaps her greatest contribution to this conversation is the invocation of what she calls the "normate." Like Titchkosky, Garland-Thomson demonstrates how the meaning of disability is made by people and is not something "natural" as we normally think it is. The normate and its ideological twin, normate culture, is the social invention of a mythical "normal" body, senses, mind, and emotions. It is upon this nebulous foundation of the normate that disability and its meaning are made.

We end Part I with a chapter by James Overboe. The concepts of normalcy, abnormalcy, difference, and sameness are ubiquitous in his work and these are concepts with which he creatively engages. Overboe suggests that the concept of normalcy influences our lives in many ways, but that the strongest influence it has is to act as a "benchmark" for deciding which lives are worth living and which are not. The benchmark of normalcy is used in our society to invalidate the lives of disabled people. Rather than treating disability as a valid difference and a life worth living, Overboe demonstrates how the concept of normalcy is used to remove the difference of disability by de-emphasizing its value while emphasizing the value of personhood. In this way, normalcy conceives of disabled people as "just like everyone else" except that we have some unessential difference. In contrast, Overboe argues for validating difference, disability, and disabled people.

CHAPTER 1

The Social Model in Context

Michael Oliver

Introduction

As one of the originators of discussions about disability models, it is important that I clarify some of the issues I intended to raise when I began to write about the individual and social models of disability as I saw them (Oliver 1983). Before so doing, it is necessary to state at the outset, however, that in claiming parental rights to disability models, I am not seeking personal aggrandizement nor indeed to deny the very real contribution that other disabled people have made to opening up the issue, notably Finkelstein (1980).

I originally conceptualised models of disability as the binary distinction between what I chose to call the individual and social models of disability (Oliver 1983). This was no amazing new insight on my part dreamed up in some ivory tower but was really an attempt to enable me to make sense of the world for my social work students and other professionals whom I taught. The idea of the individual and the social model was taken quite simply and explicitly from the distinction originally made between impairment and disability by the Union of the Physically Impaired Against Segregation in the Fundamental Principles document (1976).

I wanted to put this distinction into a framework that could be understood by professionals with a limited though expanding knowledge of disability issues. The individual model for me encompassed a whole range of issues and was underpinned by what I called the personal tragedy theory of disability. But it also included psychological and medical aspects of disability; the latter being what I preferred, and still prefer, to call the medicalisation rather than the medical model of disability (Manning and Oliver 1985). In short, for me, there is no such thing as the medical model of disability, there is instead an individual model of disability of which medicalisation is one significant component.

The articulation of this new view of disability did not receive universal acceptance. Originally, it was professionals, policy makers and staff from organisations for disabled people who, because they had vested interests in maintaining the status quo underpinned by the individual model, questioned the experiential validity and explanatory reliability of the social model. However, we have seen a paradigm shift and many professionals have now come to espouse the social model, in theory at least (DHSS 1988, CCETSW 1992). Whether it has had much impact on practice is another question altogether.

The articulation of the social model was received much more enthusiastically by disabled people because it made an immediate connection to their own experiences. It quickly became the basis for disability awareness and later disability equality training. So successful did it become that we saw a proliferation of other models. No longer did we just have the individual and social models; we had the medical, psychological, charity and later the administrative models. At one point it seemed that we would end up with more models than the Lucy Clayton Modelling Agency. Alongside this proliferation of different models disabled people themselves have begun to question the explanatory power of the social model. I myself questioned the way the social model was becoming a strait jacket for our experience in the original version of this chapter, which was a talk I gave to the annual course for disability equality trainers organised by Jane Campbell and Kath Gillespie-Sells of the Disability Resource Team in 1989.

This aroused a great deal of anger amongst some of the course participants but, quite rightly, the questioning has continued. This questioning has not attempted to deny the value of the social model but rather to suggest that while it may connect with some of the experiences of disabled people, it does not connect with all of them (French 1993). Further, its explanatory power has also been questioned (Morris 1991, Crow 1992); while it may partially explain the social oppression of disabled people, it cannot fully explain it (Finkelstein 1991).

In this chapter, I want to address some of these important issues and question some of the questions that have been raised about the social model. I shall initially restate what I see to be the essential differences between the individual and social models of disability before going on to clarify the fundamental distinction between illness and disability and to suggest that it is crucial that we continue to reject the medicalisation of disability, not just in practice but in theory too. I shall then attempt to engage with some of the important questions disabled people have recently been raising about the social model of disability. Finally, I will suggest that "our child"—the social model—is not yet grown up and that if we turn her out into the world too soon, we do so at both our and her peril.

Individual and Social Models

There are two fundamental points that need to be made about the individual model of disability. Firstly, it locates the "problem" of disability within the individual and, secondly, it sees the causes of this problem as stemming from the functional limitations or psychological losses which are assumed to arise from disability. These two points are underpinned by what might be called "the personal tragedy theory of disability" which suggests that disability is some terrible chance event which occurs at random to unfortunate individuals. Of course, nothing could be further from the truth.

The genesis, development and articulation of the social model of disability by disabled people themselves is a rejection of all of these fundamentals (Oliver 1990). It does not deny the problem of disability but locates it squarely within society. It is not individual limitations, of whatever kind, which are the cause of the problem but society's failure to provide appropriate services and adequately ensure the needs of disabled people are fully taken into account in its social organisation.

Hence disability, according to the social model, is all the things that impose restrictions on disabled people; ranging from individual prejudice to institutional discrimination, from inaccessible public buildings to unusable transport systems, from segregated education to excluding work arrangements, and so on. Further, the consequences of this failure do not simply and randomly fall on individuals but systematically upon disabled people as a group who experience this failure as discrimination institutionalised throughout society.

The social model itself can be located within the original UPIAS definition, which bears repeating here.

> In our view it is society which disables physically impaired people. Disability is something imposed on top of our impairments by the way we are unnecessarily isolated and excluded from full participation in society. Disabled people are therefore an oppressed group in society. (UPIAS 1976, p. 14)

This definition was adopted in modified form by Disabled Peoples International hence ensuring the international influence of the work of UPIAS.

It would be possible to devote the rest of this chapter, and much more, to discussing differences between the individual and social models, but neither time nor space will allow and I have done this elsewhere (Oliver 1983, 1989). Instead, Table 1.1 below summarises some of these differences. It should be noted that, like all tables, this one oversimplifies a complex reality and each item should be seen as the polar end of a continuum. Nevertheless, underpinning it is the fundamental distinction between impairment and disability as defined by UPIAS in the previous chapter.

Questioning the Social Model from the Outside— the Medicalisation of Disability

Central to this issue is the question of whether there is a useful or valid distinction between illness and disability. Certainly a number of people, including medical sociologists and policy researchers, have questioned this distinction suggesting that the two are interrelated. They argue that the concept of "social handicap," which was introduced in the mid-1960s and subsequently incorporated both into the first national survey of disabled people (Harris 1971) and the International Classification of Impairments, Disabilities and Handicaps (WHO 1980), refers to what disabled people call disability. In other words WHO's definition of social handicap is the same as UPIAS's definition of disability.

TABLE 1.1: Disability models

The individual model	The social model
personal tragedy theory	social oppression theory
personal problem	social problem
individual treatment	social action
medicalisation	self-help
professional dominance	individual and collective responsibility
expertise	experience
adjustment	affirmation
individual identity	collective identity
prejudice	discrimination
attitudes	behaviour
care	rights
control	choice
policy	politics
individual adaptation	social change

This claim has not been accepted by disabled people and has led to conflicts between social scientists seeking to classify the disabled population and map the dimensions of disadvantage they face and disabled people struggling to develop a collective identity and overcome the disadvantages they face. Partly as a consequence of these early conflicts, the medical sociology of chronic illness and social theorising about disability developed into two separate and occasionally hostile camps. While each may have influenced the other to some extent, this influence has rarely been acknowledged. Nonetheless, both camps have now produced impressive bodies of work, incorporating both academic scholarship and substantial empirical research.

The two areas where these conflicts have emerged are epistemological and methodological. In epistemological terms, the crucial issue is that of causality. For medical sociologists, what they call chronic illness is causally related to the disadvantages disabled people experience. For the social model, however, there is no causal link; disability is wholly and exclusively social. Hence each side accuses the other of being incorrect in causal terms. It may well be, however, that this debate is in reality the result of terminological rather than epistemological confusion; that the real similarities exist between chronic illness and impairment.

Thus one medical sociologist critically argues:

> Sometimes, in seeking to reject the reductionism of the medical model and its institutional contexts, proponents of independent living have tended to discuss disablement as if it had nothing to do with the physical body. (Williams 1991, p. 521)

Ironically that is precisely what the social model insists, disablement is nothing to do with the body. It is a consequence of social oppression. But the social model does not deny that impairment is closely related to the physical body. Impairment is, in fact, nothing less than a description of the physical body.

This terminological confusion also appeared when a policy analyst attempted to relate her own experience to policy issues in the area of disability.

> I found myself puzzled by arguments that held that disability had nothing to do with illness or that belief in a need for some form of personal adaptation to impairment was essentially a form of false consciousness. I knew that disabled people argue that they should not be treated as if they were ill, but could see that many people who had impairments as a result of ongoing illness were also disabled. My unease increased as I watched my parents coming to terms with my mother's increasing impairments (and disability) related to arterial disease which left her tired and in almost continual pain. I could see that people can be disabled by their physical, economic and social environment but I could also see that people who became disabled (rather than being born with impairments) might have to renegotiate their sense of themselves both with themselves and with those closest to them. (Parker 1993, p. 2)

The social model does not deny that some illnesses may have disabling consequences and many disabled people have illnesses at various points in their lives. Further, it may be entirely appropriate for doctors to treat illnesses of all kinds, though even here, the record of the medical profession is increasingly coming under critical scrutiny. Leaving this aside, however, doctors can have a role to play in the lives of disabled people: stabilising their initial condition, treating any illnesses which may arise and which may or may not be disability related.

The problem arises when doctors try to use their knowledge and skills to treat disability rather than illness. Disability as a long-term social state is not treatable medically and is certainly not curable. Hence many disabled people experience much medical intervention as, at best, inappropriate, and, at worst, oppressive. This should not be seen as a personal attack on individual doctors, or indeed the medical profession, for they, too, are trapped in a set of social relations with which they are not trained or equipped to deal.

The problem is that doctors are socialised by their own training into believing that they are "experts" and accorded that role by society. When confronted with the social problems of disability as experts, they cannot admit that they don't know what to do. Consequently they feel threatened and fall back on their medical skills and training, inappropriate as they are, and impose them on disabled people. They then appear bewildered when disabled people criticise or reject this imposed treatment.

Of course, one could pursue this image of doctors as threatened and bewildered too far. As society's experts, they have a great deal of power and this gives them control over fundamental aspects of peoples' lives and they have not been noticeably reticent about using this power to make decisions about disabled peoples' lives; where they should live, whether they should work or not, what kind of school they should go to, what kinds of benefits and services they should receive and in the case of unborn disabled children, whether they should live or not.

However, it's not just decisions that doctors make about disabled people that are questionable, it's also about what they do to them. The whole medical and rehabilitation enterprise is founded upon an ideology of normality and this has far-reaching implications for rehabilitation and treatment. Its aim is to restore the disabled person to normality, whatever that may mean. Where that is not possible, the basic aim is not abandoned; the goal is to restore the disabled person to a state that is as near normality as possible. So, surgical intervention and physical rehabilitation, whatever its costs in terms of the pain and suffering of disabled individuals, is always justified and justifiable—the ideology of normality rules.

Further, the medical profession, because of its power and dominance, has spawned a whole range of pseudo-professions in its own image: physiotherapy, occupational therapy, speech therapy, clinical psychology; each one geared to the same aim—the restoration of normality. And each one of these pseudo-professions develops its own knowledge base and set of skills to facilitate this. They organise their interventions and intrusions into disabled peoples' lives on the basis of discreet and limited knowledge and skills.

The reality, of course, is that disabled peoples' lives cannot be divided up in this way to suit professional activity and increasingly, disabled people, individually and collectively, are coming to reject the prescriptions of the "normalising" society and the whole range of professional activities which attempt to reinforce it.

Instead, we are increasingly demanding acceptance from society as we are, not as society thinks we should be. It is society that has to change, not individuals, and this change will come about as part of a process of political empowerment of disabled people as a group and not through social policies and programmes delivered by establishment politicians and policy makers, nor through individualised treatments and interventions provided by the medical and para-medical professions. This is the core of the social model and its message should not be mystified by conceptual misunderstandings about the meanings of terms like illness and disability.

Criticising the Social Model from within

A major criticism that some disabled people have made of the social model concerns the way it connects, or rather doesn't connect, with the experience of impairment. French

(1993), for example, argues that her visual impairment imposes some social restrictions which cannot be resolved by the application of the principles of the social model. She cites as examples her inability to recognise people and read or emit non-verbal cues in social interactions.

Clearly, most disabled people can come up with similar examples. As a wheelchair user, when I go to parties I am more restricted than some other people from interacting with everyone else and what's more, it is difficult to see a solution—houses are usually crowded with people during parties and that makes circulation difficult for a wheelchair user. But other people may find circulation difficult as well but for other reasons; they may simply be shy. The point that I am making is that the social model is not an attempt to deal with the personal restrictions of impairment but the social barriers of disability.

Other disabled people have criticised the social model for its assumed denial of "the pain of impairment," both physical and psychological. In many ways some of these criticisms mirror those made from without although they are not beset by the same terminological confusion between illness and impairment.

> ... there is a tendency within the social model of disability to deny the experience of our own bodies, insisting that our physical differences and restrictions are entirely socially created. While environmental barriers and social attitudes are a crucial part of our experience of disability—and do indeed disable us—to suggest that this is all there is to it is to deny the personal experience of physical or intellectual restrictions, of illness, of the fear of dying. (Morris 1991, p. 10)

This denial of the pain of impairment has not, in reality, been a denial at all. Rather it has been a pragmatic attempt to identify and address issues that can be changed through collective action rather than medical or other professional treatment.

> If a person's physical pain is the reason they are unhappy then there is nothing the disability movement can do about it. All that BCODP can do is facilitate the politicisation of people around these issues. Of course this politicisation is fairly difficult to make practical progress with—much easier to achieve anti-discrimination legislation than a total review of how society regards death and dying, I imagine. This might explain why these subjects haven't been made a priority, but their day will come. (Vasey 1992, p. 43)

These criticisms are taken further by Crow (1992) who argues that the way forward for the social model is to fully integrate the experience of impairment with the experience of disability. However, up to now and for very important reasons, the social model has insisted that there is no causal relationship between impairment and disability.

> The achievement of the disability movement has been to break the link between our bodies and our social situation, and to focus on the real cause of disability, i.e. discrimination and prejudice. To mention biology, to admit pain, to confront our impairments, has been to risk the oppressors seizing on evidence that disability is "really" about physical limitation after all. (Shakespeare 1992, p. 40)

A further internal criticism comes from other oppressed groups who feel that these other oppressions such as racism (Hill 1992), sexism (Morris 1991) and homophobia (Hearn 1991) have not been incorporated into the social model. Again, it is certainly true that the social model has not explicitly addressed the issue of multiple oppression but then such issues are only just beginning to be explored both in respect of disability (Zarb and Oliver 1993) and race and gender.

This dissatisfaction, then, has been expressed not simply because the social model does not adequately reflect experience of oppression of all disabled people but also because it may "oversimplify" some of the issues raised in Disability Equality Training.

> For some time I have been dissatisfied with the oversimplified "social model" of disability we are obliged to use in Disability Equality Training and have read with interest the recent arguments re-introducing "impairment" into that model.
>
> Although the "social model" has for some time served us well as a way of directing attention away from the personal to the political, I feel now that the debate has been hampered by the rather rigid genealogy of disability thinking. My own literary, linguistic and therapeutic background led me to post-modernist thinkers such as Foucault, Derrida, Barthes and Lacan in an attempt to make sense of the personal and political aspects of the disability debate. (Cashling 1993, pp. 199–200)

It is undeniably true that some trainers may have used the social model in an overly rigid way, and as I have already argued, I made a similar point in 1989. Those like myself who draw on Marxist rather than post-modernist thinking call this reification, a not uncommon phenomena in late capitalist society. Such criticism, however, raises questions about the way the model is used, rather than the model itself; although, as I have already suggested, models are merely ways to help us to better understand the world, or those bits of it under scrutiny. If we expect models to explain, rather than aid understanding, they are bound to be found wanting. And it remains to be seen if post-modernist thinking, as Cashling suggests it might, ends up explaining the oppression of disabled people as simply a manifestation of society's hatred of us, whether this will take us as far as the social model in challenging that oppression.

A final criticism comes from another of the founding fathers of the social model, Vic Finkelstein. Recently (Finkelstein 1991) he has questioned the ability of the social model to fully explain the social position of disabled people in modern society, and suggests that there are at least two variants: the social death model and the social barriers model. He then goes on to suggest that the administrative model is the only one which has sufficient scope to fully explain societal responses to disabled people.

> In my view administrative approaches dominate all forms of helping services for disabled people in the UK, whether these are provided by statutory agencies or voluntary bodies, or demanded by pressure group organisations. The cure or care forms of intervention are administered within the rehabilitation and personal-care services respectively. (Finkelstein 1993, p. 37)

Thus, for him, the administrative model subsumes both the medical and welfare (care) approaches to disability and is centrally concerned with controlling disabled people. For me, the administrative model is similar to the position I took in trying to locate disability historically within the rise of capitalist society.

> As the conditions of capitalist production changed in the twentieth century, so the labour needs of capital shifted from a mass of unskilled workers to a more limited need of skilled ones. As a result of this, the Welfare State arose as a means of ensuring the supply of skill, and in order to "pacify" the ever increasing army of the unemployed, the under-employed and the unemployable. (Manning and Oliver 1985, p. 102)

While I think Finkelstein and I are basically saying the same thing, for me it is important not to stretch the explanatory power of models further than they are able to go. For me the social model of disability is about personal experience and professional practice but it is not a substitute for social theory, a materialist history of disability nor an explanation of the welfare state.

Conclusions

My argument in this chapter has centred on two key points. Firstly, we must not assume that models in general and the social model in particular can do everything; that it can explain disability in totality. It is not a social theory of disability and it cannot do the work of social theory. Secondly, because it cannot explain everything, we should neither seek to expose inadequacies, which are more a product of the way we use it, nor abandon it before its usefulness has been fully exploited.

The social model does connect with the experience of disabled people as the following quote illustrates.

> The second flash on this road to Damascus as a disabled person came when I encountered the disability movement. I had learnt to live with my private fear

and to feel that I was the only one involved in this fight. I had internalised my oppression. As a working class son of Irish immigrants, I had experienced other struggles but, in retrospect, I evidently saw epilepsy as my hidden cross. I cannot explain how significantly all this was turned around when I came into contact with the notion of the social model of disabilities, rather than the medical model which I had hitherto lived with. Over a matter of months, my discomfort with this secret beast of burden called epilepsy, and my festering hatred at the silencing of myself as a disabled person, "because I didn't look it," completely changed. I think I went through an almost evangelical conversion as I realised that my disability was not, in fact, the epilepsy, but the toxic drugs with their denied side-effects; the medical regime with its blaming of the victim; the judgement through distance and silence of bus-stop crowds, bar-room crowds and dinner-table friends; the fear; and, not least, the employment problems. All this was the oppression, not the epileptic seizure at which I was hardly (consciously) present. (Hevey 1992, pp. 1–2)

While it has the power to transform consciousness in the way described above, its demise is surely premature.

In addition it continues to serve as a means for getting professionals to reflect on their own practice.

It was during this period that I discovered the writings of disabled people on the broader nature of disablism and the "social model of disability"—which provided a theoretical model that was more meaningful to me. (Stevens 1993, p. 33)

Finally, the continuing use and refinement of the social model can contribute to rather than be a substitute for the development of an adequate social theory of disability. And as both Abberley (1987) and myself (1990) have argued, an adequate social theory of disability must contain a theory of impairment. But they are not interchangeable and should not be treated as such as one recent commentator does.

The social model of disability appears to have been constructed for healthy quadriplegics. The social model avoids mention of pain, medication or ill-health. (Humphrey 1994, p. 6)

The social model of disability does, indeed, avoid mention of such things, not because it was written by healthy quadriplegics, but because they properly belong within the social model of impairment. So let's develop a social model of impairment to stand alongside a social model of disability but let's not pretend that either or both are social theory.

References

Abberley, P. (1987) "The Concept of Oppression and the Development of a Social Theory of Disability," *Disability, Handicap and Society*, vol. 2, no. 1, 5–19.

Campbell, J. and Gillespie-Sells, C. (1991) *Disability Equality Trainers Training Guide* (London: CCETSW).

Cashling, D. (1993) "Cobblers and Song-birds: the Language and Imagery of Disability," *Disability, Handicap and Society*, vol. 8, no. 2, 199–206.

Crow, L. (1992) "Renewing the Social Model of Disability," *Coalition*, July 1992.

Finkelstein, V. (1980) *Attitudes and Disabled People: Issues for Discussion* (New York: World Rehabilitation Fund).

Finkelstein, V. (1991) "Disability: An Administrative Challenge? The Health and Welfare Heritage" in Oliver, M. (ed.), *Social Work, Disabled People and Disabling Environments* (London: Jessica Kingsley).

Finkelstein, V. (1993) "Disability: A Social Challenge or an Administrative Responsibility?" in Swaine, J., Finkelstein, V., French, S., and Oliver, M. (eds.), *Disabling Barriers—Enabling Environments* (London: Sage).

French, S. (1993) "Disability, Impairment or Something in between?" in Swaine, J., Finkelstein, V., French, S. and Oliver, M. (eds.), *Disabling Barriers—Enabling Environments* (London: Sage).

Harris, A. I. (1971) *Handicapped and Impaired in Great Britain. Part I*. London, Office of Population Censuses and Surveys.

Hearn, K. (1991) "Disabled Lesbians and Gays are Here to Stay" in Kaufman, T. and Lincoln, P. (eds.), *High Risk Lives: Lesbian and Gay Politics After the Clause* (Bridport: Prism Press).

Hevey, D. (1992) *The Creatures Time Forgot: Photography and Disability Imagery* (London: Routledge).

Hill, M. (1992) "Conference Address" in *Race and Disability: A dialogue for action* (London: Greater London Association of Disabled People).

Humphrey, R. (1994) "Thoughts on Disability Arts," DAM, vol. 4, no. 1.

Manning, N. and Oliver, M. (1985) "Madness, Epilepsy and Medicine" in Manning, N. (ed.), *Social Problems and Welfare Ideology* (Aldershot: Gower).

Morris, J. (1991) *Pride against Prejudice* (London: Women's Press).

Oliver, M. (1983) *Social Work with Disabled People* (Basingtoke: Macmillan).

Oliver, M. (1989) "Social Work and the Social Model of Disability: Some Current Reflections" in Carter, P., Jeffs, T. and Smith, M. (eds.), *Social Work and the Social Welfare Yearbook* (Milton Keynes: Open University Press).

Oliver, M. (1990) *The Politics of Disablement* (Bakingstoke: Macmillan and St. Martin's Press).

Parker, G. (1993) *With this Body: Caring and Disability in Marriage* (Milton Keynes: Open University Press).

Shakespeare, T. (1992) "A Response to Liz Crow," *Coalition*, September 1992.

Stevens, A. (1993) "Communicating with Users: Learning a User Led Perspective through Reflective Practice" in Stevens, A. (ed.), *Back from the Wellhouse: Discussion Papers on Sensory Impairment and Training in Community Care* (London: CCETSW, Paper 32.1).

UPIAS. (1976) *Fundamental Principles of Disability* (London: Union of the Physically Impaired Against Segregation).

Vasey, S. (1992) "A Response to Liz Crow," *Coalition*, September 1992.

Williams, G. H. (1991) "Disablement and the Ideological Crisis in Health Care," *Social Science and Medicine*, vol. 33, no. 4, 517–24.

World Health Organization (WHO). (1980) International Classification of Impairments, Disabilities and Handicaps: A Manual of Classification Relating to the Consequences of Disease (Geneva, Switzerland: WHO).

Zarb, G. and Oliver, M. (1993) *Ageing with a Disability: What Do They Expect after All These Years?* (London: University of Greenwich).

CHAPTER 2

Disability History:

Why We Need Another "Other"

Catherine J. Kudlick

Not Since Joan Wallach Scott heralded a new age with her "Gender: A Useful Category of Historical Analysis" have historians faced such an exciting time to rethink what we do.[1] Over the past two decades, our cousins in anthropology and literature have produced essays and monographs dealing with disability as a historical subject.[2] The fields that blazed the trail for studying race, gender, and sexuality while introducing postmodernism and the linguistic turn have provided valuable analytic and theoretical tools for exploring this new Other.[3] Now the work of more and more historians—some who have been studying disability for decades, others who have been doing it without consciously describing it this way, still others recently inspired by different disciplines—is beginning to bear fruit in the form of a fresh area of inquiry that could well reshape our scholarly landscape.[4] One need not identify oneself as disabled in order to reap the benefits of this up-and-coming field. Rather, [Disability Studies] help historians ask and attempt to answer the overarching questions central to our mission as scholars and teachers in a humanistic discipline: what does it mean to be human? How can we respond ethically to difference? What is the value of a human life? Who decides these questions, and what do the answers reveal?

Much of the new work springs from disability studies, an interdisciplinary field dating from the mid-1980s that invites scholars to think about disability not as an isolated, individual medical pathology but instead as a key defining social category on a par with race, class, and gender.[5] "Disability studies takes for its subject matter not simply the variations that exist in human behavior, appearance, functioning, sensory acuity, and cognitive processing, but, more crucially, the meaning we make of those variations," Simi Linton explains in her influential 1998 manifesto *Claiming Disability*. "It is an interdisciplinary field based on a socio-political analysis of disability and informed both by the knowledge base and methodologies used in the traditional liberal arts, and by conceptualizations and approaches developed in areas of the new scholarship."[6] By approaching disability as a social category rather than as an individual characteristic, the field challenges long-held perceptions that relegate it to the unglamorous backwaters primarily of interest to people in rehabilitation, special education, and other applied professional fields.

Seen in this way, disability should sit squarely at the center of historical inquiry, both as a subject worth studying in its own right and as one that will provide scholars with a new analytic tool for exploring power itself. Indeed, [disability studies] will reveal disability as crucial for understanding how Western cultures determine hierarchies and maintain social order as well as how they define progress. For the United States and Western Europe—the most widely studied areas in this very new field—it might even be argued that hierarchy depends on the threat of disability always lurking as the ultimate living catastrophe. How else might we account for the prevalence of so many metaphors across times and places that derive rhetorical force from disabling conditions? For example, in 1558, John Knox's "First Blast of the Trumpet against the Monstrous Regiment of Women" (a pamphlet containing sixteen references to blindness and numerous others to madness, along with the ubiquitous "monstrous") drew on ancient scriptures to inform the English-speaking world that women should not rule.[7] Two and a half centuries later, writers with opinions as diverse as Edmund Burke and Tom Paine would rely on often identical monstrous metaphors to malign those they wished to attack.[8] Even the most basic look at narratives of modern European history conveys notions of degeneracy, defectiveness, and decline steeped in images of idiocy and deformity attributed to crowds, anarchists, mass democracy, Jews, women, homosexuals, corrupt politicians, the French, the English, the Germans, the Italians ...[9] With a slight twist, Europeans used similar images to allege their superiority over what would become known as "lesser-developed" nations.[10]

Such condemnations were more than mere rhetoric; oppressors used them and their implicit threat of incapacity to wield power, while the oppressed themselves appropriated negative views of disability to fight back. Disability worked as a critique of the social body in large part because classical thinkers such as Aristotle had established a particular understanding of the perfect human body. This father of Western taxonomy and later political thought saw "imperfect bodies"—notably women's but also those of "anyone who does not take after his parents"—as "deformed," "mutilated," "monstrous," "deviant," all synonyms for disability today.[11] The specter of disability also came through in religious writings and eventually would underpin scientific notions of progress and evolution's "survival of the fittest."[12] Moreover, Western nations embraced capitalism, a system predicated on able-bodied ideals of independence, strength, control, self-mastery, and struggle. Douglas Baynton's pathbreaking essay, "Disability and the Justification for Inequality in American History," shows how in the United States opponents of suffragists, abolitionists, and immigration all used disability to discredit undesirable groups' claims to citizenship, while women, African Americans, and immigrants bristled at being associated with disability.[13] The centrality of this concept to power, hierarchy, and social order raises intriguing comparative questions for cultures outside the United States and Europe, especially in light of initial research that suggests that not all cultures have seen the same impairments as disabling.[14]

Viewed in such protean terms, the field offers possibilities for intellectual exploration that will appeal to a variety of scholarly tastes. For political and policy historians, disability is a significant factor in the development of the modern state, by raising questions of who deserves the government's assistance and protection, what constitutes a capable citizen, and who merits the full rights of citizenship. For labor historians, it suggests ways of exploring assumptions about work, strength, productivity, and tensions between solidarity and individuality. Anyone interested in subjects as diverse as war, the body, the senses, aging, medicine, beauty, aesthetics, or technology will find ways of making the familiar refreshingly unfamiliar again. Just as gender and race have had an impact well beyond women and people of color, disability is so vast in its economic, social, political, cultural, religious, legal, philosophical, artistic, moral, and medical import that it can force historians to reconsider virtually every concept, every event, every "given" we have taken for granted.

The breadth of this new field—indeed, the problem that makes it so rich and interesting—stems from the fact that the term "disability" defies easy definition.[15] No clear consensus has emerged perhaps because human bodies and the societies they live in are by nature unstable. As numerous court battles have shown, even the 1990 Americans with Disabilities Act (ADA), designed to be multivalent, leaves intentional room for interpretation: "The term 'disability' means, with respect to an individual: (A) a physical or mental impairment that substantially limits one or more of the major life activities of such individual; (B) a record of such an impairment; or (C) being regarded as having such an impairment."[16] Making an observation that could prove useful to historians, activist Mary Johnson emphasizes the subjectivity inherent in such a definition, explaining that "'disabled' is in the final analysis a political or a moral judgement, based not on anything about the individual in question so much as the viewer's own perception and attitudes about the way society should function."[17] [Disability Studies] will thus introduce readers to blind and deaf people, freak show performers, wounded veterans, patients with Tourette's Syndrome and autism, and users of artificial limbs. We also meet teachers, researchers, bureaucrats, journalists, physicians, artists, clerics, anthropologists, advertisers, and activists, each striving to change the lives of the above groups in some way, and therefore inadvertently working to define disability in a collective sense. Here we have an impressive variety of topics and approaches as well as a category that in essence is commonplace, even seen as natural, yet treated as inherently abnormal. Thus its very ambiguity and changing meanings open up uncharted areas of research and modes of analysis, which in turn will bring about a greater understanding of disability and its repercussions.

In light of these sweeping implications, it is curious that disability did not capture historians' attention sooner. Certainly, in terms of raw numbers and lived experience, it occupies a place comparable to gender and race in defining the human condition. According to the University of California San Francisco's Disability Statistics Center, at present nearly one fifth (19.7 percent) of Americans qualify as people with disabilities, while some sources place the number even higher.[18] Ironically, the ranks of disabled people will grow further as medicine advances, because, as more people will be able to survive longer, they can be expected to acquire impairments that worsen with age. Meanwhile, in the past decade, researchers have been discovering and labeling new conditions with astonishing speed.[19] Even those who do not have a disability know relatives, friends, or colleagues who do. Moreover, we all encounter or think we encounter disability at some point in our lives because we acquire temporary impairments or have experiences described as "disabling." To be sure, such visits only scratch the surface of living with a chronic condition and fail to introduce people to the real problems posed by social and economic environments that compound, often even outweigh, the physical challenges. Still, they alert us to the porous boundaries between disability and apparent health. More significant, disability cuts across all races, classes, genders, nationalities, and generations because it can potentially happen to anyone at any time; an accident, a degenerative disease of the limbs, eyes, ears, or nervous system, can instantly transport someone into a new category of existence, a fact some activists underscore by referring to non-disabled people as "temporarily able bodied" or "TABS."[20]

The field of disability studies faces hurdles—some of them personal, some intellectual, some institutional—that could prompt historians to explore the roots and mechanisms of how societies function in new ways. Unlike racial, ethnic, and sexual minorities, disabled people experience attacks cloaked in pity accompanied by a widely held perception that no one wishes them ill. Yet while people in many other marginal groups have campaigned with some success to change their public image, disability carries a negative social charge still supported by dominant cultural assumptions across the economic, political, and intellectual spectrum.[21] The demeaning ideas and representations are everywhere: from the media's emphasis on normality, youth, and bodily perfection and its feel-good holiday stories about blind people getting guide dogs to everyday expressions such as "a crippled/paralyzed economy," "blind obedience/rage/ambition," "that's so lame/idiotic/dumb," "her suggestion fell on deaf ears," or in admonitions to "stand up for yourself."[22] My point here is not to call out the language police but rather to underscore the impulse and the significance behind disability being represented in such trivializing, negative ways within so many diverse contexts. Indeed, one of the most challenging aspects of disability is to convince non-disabled people that even when it involves pain and hardship, disability is not always a tragedy, hardship, or lack but in fact often provides much of value.[23] This helps explain why, like the pioneers in gay and lesbian history, many disabled scholars try to "pass," worrying that "coming out" will lead to stigma and isolation as long as our culture consciously or subconsciously equates dis-ability with in-ability.[24] Compounded by disability's absence from diversity discussions, the resulting invisibility of disabled colleagues reinforces the idea that the topic remains marginal to academic inquiry, being instead a condition to be fixed by installing ramps and special mechanisms on doors. But, in fact, the study of disability offers the conceptual tools for exploring the underlying assumptions beneath modern Western societies' creation of the very environments where historians work—environments built on the assumption that everyone is young, strong, tireless, healthy, of similar size and shape, independent, and with all physical and mental components and in perfect working order.

Endnotes

1 Joan Wallach Scott, "Gender: A Useful Category of Historical Analysis," in *Gender and the Politics of History* (New York, 1999), 28–52; originally published in AHR 91 (December 1986): 1053–75.

2 Although the quality of the historical scholarship varies, these works offer important insights and leads. Moshe Barasch, *Blindness: The History of a Mental Image in Western Thought* (New York, 2001); Lennard J. Davis, *Enforcing Normalcy: Disability, Deafness, and the Body* (New York, 1995); Lennard J. Davis, ed., *The Disability Studies Reader* (London, 1997); David T. Mitchell and Sharon L. Snyder, eds., *The Body and Physical Difference: Discourses of Disability* (Ann Arbor, Mich., 1997); Peter W. Graham and Fritz H. Oehlschlaeger, *Articulating the Elephant Man: John Merrick and His Interpreters* (Baltimore, 1992); Nora Groce, *Everyone Here Spoke Sign Language* (Cambridge, Mass., 1985); Diane Price Herndl, *Invalid Women: Figuring Feminine Illness in American Fiction and Culture, 1840–1940* (Chapel Hill, N.C., 1993); Mary Klages, *Woeful Afflictions: Disability and Sentimentality in Victorian America* (Philadelphia, 1999); Susan Plann, *A Silent Minority: Deaf Education in Spain, 1550–1835* (Berkeley, Calif., 1997); Rosemarie Garland-Thomson, ed., *Freakery: Cultural Spectacles of the Extraordinary Body* (New York, 1996); Nicholas Mirzoeff, *Silent Poetry: Deafness, Sign, and Visual Culture in Modern France* (Princeton, N.J., 1995); Allen Thiher, *Revels in Madness: Insanity in Medicine and Literature* (Ann Arbor, 2000).

3 Erving Goffman, *Stigma: Notes on the Management of Spoiled Identity* (New York, 1963), is the most widely cited early book to theorize the issue of disability, although an impressive group of earlier works that explored disability as a minority status would be well worth resuscitating, both as primary and secondary sources: Roger G. Barker, "The Social Psychology of Physical Disability," *Journal of Social Issues* 4 (1948): 4; Roger G. Barker, Beatrice A. Wright, and Mollie Gonick, *Adjustment to Physical Handicap and Illness* (New York, 1946). Georges Canguilhem, *The Normal and the Pathological* (1966; rpt. edn., New York, 1989), provides a perspective on medicine's normalizing tendencies. For more recent discussions of disability and theory, see Rosemarie Garland-Thomson, *Extraordinary Bodies: Figuring Physical Disability in American Culture and Literature* (New York, 1997); Lennard J. Davis, *Bending over Backwards: Disability, Dismodernism, and Other Difficult Positions* (New York, 2002); David T. Mitchell and Sharon Snyder, *Narrative Prosthesis: Disability and the Dependencies of Discourse* (Ann Arbor, Mich., 2000); Tobin Siebers, ed., *The Body Aesthetic: From Fine Art to Body Modification* (Ann Arbor, 2000); Rod Michalko, *The Difference That Disability Makes* (Philadelphia, 2002); Susan Wendell, *The Rejected Body: Feminist Philosophical Reflections on Disability* (London, 1996); Sharon L. Snyder, Brenda Jo Bruggemann, and Rosemarie Garland-Thomson, eds., *Disability Studies: Enabling the Humanities* (New York, 2002), esp. Part 1, "Enabling Theory," 15–106.

4 The field is now established enough to have its own electronic discussion group, H-Disability. For subscription information, go to http://www2.h-net.msu.edu/. Three excellent books from the mid-1990s helped launch the field in its current direction: Douglas C. Baynton, *Forbidden Signs: American Culture and the Campaign against Sign Language* (Chicago, 1996); Martin Pernick, *The Black Stork: Eugenics and the Death of "Defective" Babies in American Medicine and Motion Pictures since 1915* (Oxford, 1996); James W. Trent, *Inventing the Feeble Mind: A History of Mental Retardation in the United States* (Berkeley, Calif., 1994). They in turn built on earlier scholarship: Hugh Gregory Gallagher, *FDR's Splendid Deception* (1985; rpt. edn., Arlington, Va., 1999); William O. McCagg and Lewis Siegelbaum, eds., *The Disabled in the Soviet Union: Past and Present, Theory and Practice* (Pittsburgh, 1989); William R. Paulson, *Enlightenment, Romanticism, and the Blind in France* (Princeton, N.J., 1987); Harlan L. Lane, *When the Mind Hears: A History of the Deaf* (New York, 1984); Robert K. Scotch, *From Good Will to Civil Rights: Transforming Disability Policy* (Philadelphia, 1984, 2001). Paul K. Longmore has just published a collection of his scholarly and activist writings as *Why I Burned My Book and Other Essays* (Philadelphia, 2003); also see his important article with David Goldberger, "The League of the Physically Handicapped and the Great Depression: A Case Study in the New Disability History," *Journal of American History* 87, no. 3 (December 2000): 888–922; and his "Conspicuous Contribution and American Cultural Dilemmas: Telethon Rituals of Cleansing and Renewal," in Mitchell and Snyder, *Body and Physical Difference*, 134–58. A number of scholars have also unwittingly touched on the disability paradigm. See, for example, Lorraine Daston and Katharine Park, eds., *Wonders and the Order of Nature, 1150–1750* (New York, 1998); Sander Gilman, *Difference and Pathology: Stereotypes of Sexuality, Race, and Madness* (Ithaca, N.Y., 1985); Stephen Jay Gould, *The Mismeasure of Man* (1981; rpt. edn., New York, 1996). Books on psychiatry and mental illness proved to be early trailblazers for disability history. See, for example, Michel Foucault, *Madness and Civilization: A History of Insanity in the Age of Reason*, Richard Howard, trans. (New York, 1965); Jan Goldstein, *Console and Classify: The French Psychiatric Profession in the Nineteenth Century* (Cambridge, 1987); Michael MacDonald, *Mystical Bedlam: Madness, Anxiety, and Healing in Seventeenth-Century England* (Cambridge, 1981); David Rothman, *Conscience and Convenience: The Asylum and Its Alternatives in Progressive-Era America* (Boston, 1980); David Rothman, *The Discovery of the Asylum: Social Order and Disorder in the New Republic* (Boston, 1971).

5 Simi Linton, *Claiming Disability: Knowledge and Identity* (New York, 1998), offers an indispensable, cogent overview. The Society for Disability Studies hosts an annual interdisciplinary conference that attracts a wide spectrum of several hundred scholars, activists, and policy makers. Its initials—SDS—were chosen deliberately to mirror the activism of Students for a Democratic Society from the 1960s. For information on the society, go to www.uic.edu/orgs/sds. A chapter called "Scholars" in Andrew Potok's rich and engaging book *A Matter of Dignity: Changing the World of the Disabled* (New York, 2002), 159–89, explores this academic world. Syllabi, bibliographies, and a treasure trove of other information can be found at the DISC (Disability Studies Academic Community) web site: http://mith2.umd.edu8080/disc/index.html, as well as at www.georgetown.edu/crossroads/interests/ds-hum/index.html. A lively virtual community of scholars exploring this issue and others can be found on the DS-HUM (Disability Studies in the Humanities) electronic discussion group: www.georgetown.edu/crossroads/interests/ds-hum/dshowto.html.

6 Linton, *Claiming Disability*, 2.

7 John Knox, "The First Blast of the Trumpet against the Monstrous Regiment of Women," 1558.

8 Douglas C. Baynton, "Disability and the Justification for Inequality in American History," in Paul K. Longmore and Lauri Umansky, eds., *The New Disability History: American Perspectives* (New York, 2001), 34–35. An intellectual historian, Baynton offers the best blend of history and theory to explore disability's place within larger historical contexts, and I owe much of this discussion to what I have learned from him. His book *Forbidden Signs* also explores valuable "cross-over" ground between disability and concepts more familiar to non-disability historians. In addition, I have greatly benefited from the insights of Rosemarie Garland-Thomson in her *Extraordinary Bodies*, esp. 5–51.

9 Since the number of works is too exhaustive to cite in full, I offer a few examples: J. Edward Chamberlin and Sander L. Gilman, eds., *Degeneration: The Dark Side of Progress* (New York, 1985); Daniel Pick, *Faces of Degeneration: A European Disorder, 1848–1914* (Cambridge, 1989); Robert A. Nye, *Crime, Madness, and Politics in Modern France: The Medical Concept of National Decline* (Princeton, N.J., 1984); William H. Schneider, *Quality and Quantity: The Quest for Biological Regeneration in Twentieth-Century France* (Cambridge, 1990); Walter L. Adamson, *Avant-Garde Florence: From Modernism to Fascism* (Cambridge, Mass., 1993); Carl Ipsen, *Dictating Demography: The Problem of Population in Fascist Italy* (Cambridge, 1996); Michael Burleigh, *The Racial State: Germany, 1933–1945* (Cambridge, 1991).

10 Consider the case of footbinding, a subject often invoked in Western writings about China. Where the Chinese saw beauty and status, Europeans found yet another place to condemn a civilization that "crippled" its women. This divergence of opinion reached a climax in the nineteenth century with the increasing influence of medicalization in the West. As Patricia Ebrey points out, "empathizing with the weak and unfortunate within a society is implicitly a critique of its power structure." "Gender and Sinology: Shifting Western Interpretations of Foodbinding, 1300–1890," *Late Imperial China* 20, no. 2 (December 1999): 1–34. For a more general overview of how Western cultures depicted outsiders, see Gustav Jahoda, *Images of Savages: Ancient Roots of Modern Prejudice in Western Culture* (London, 1999).

11 Robert Garland, *The Eye of the Beholder: Deformity and Disability in the Greco-Roman World* (Ithaca, N.Y., 1995); Garland-Thomson, *Extraordinary Bodies*, 19–20.

12 On religion, see Nancy L. Eiesland, *The Disabled God: Toward a Liberatory Theology of Disability* (Nashville, Tenn., 1994), 70–75. For a discussion of evolutionary theory and disability, see Baynton, *Forbidden Signs*. Gould, *Mismeasure of Man,* and Gilman, *Difference and Pathology*, offer but two of the most striking examples of scientific thought and disability.

13 Baynton, "Disability and the Justification for Inequality," 33–57.

14 Michael Oliver, *The Politics of Disablement* (London, 1990), 14–17.

15 For an excellent discussion of definitions and their implications, see Wendell, *Rejected Body*, 11–33.

16 U.S. Department of Justice, Americans with Disabilities Act of 1990: www.usdoj.gov/crt/ada/pubs/ada.txt.

17 Mary Johnson, *Make Them Go Away: Clint Eastwood, Christopher Reeve, and the Case against Disability Rights* (Louisville, Ky., 2003), 46.

18 Disability Statistics Center, UCSF, http://dsc.ucsf.edu/UCSF/pub.taf?. The data is corroborated by the U.S. Census, which further states that one in eight—33 million—reported they had a severe disability, according to a report released on March 16, 2001. See the Department of Commerce Census Bureau web site at www.census.gov/Press-Release/www/2001/cb01-46.html. A higher figure averaging 40 percent can be found in Barbara M. Altman, "Definitions of Disability and Their Operationalization and Measurement in Survey Data: An Update," in Sharon N. Barnartt and Barbara M. Altman, eds., *Research in Social Science and Disability*, Vol. 2: *Exploring Theories and Expanding Methodologies* (New York, 2001), 77–100.

19 Consider new learning disabilities such as Attention Deficit Disorder (ADD), Attention Deficit Hyperactivity Disorder (ADHD), and Asperger's Syndrome. Even if such diagnoses have proved controversial, they reveal much

about American society's coming to terms with defining disability and responding to it, a fact that will surely interest future historians.

20 As Susan Wendell and others have made clear, factors such as race, class, gender, nationality, and age can have a significant impact on the experience of living with an impairment and its disabling consequences. Her book *The Rejected Body* carries on a sensitive, thought-provoking discussion of these congruences throughout.

21 Trying to explain why even those who champion the causes of most marginal groups have trouble viewing disabled people as an oppressed minority, Mary Johnson boils it down to the false perception that "'no one is against the handicapped.' The phrase says there is no animus against disabled people—even though they are segregated and kept from full access to society, even though the special programs society affords them make for a much circumscribed life." Johnson, *Make Them Go Away,* 44. These issues also come up in Linda Hamilton Krieger, ed., *Backlash against the Americans with Disabilities Act: Interdisciplinary Perspectives* (Ann Arbor, Mich., 2002). In light of these observations, we need more scholarship that explores how disability intersects with other identities in the past.

22 On disability and language, see Irving Kenneth Zola, "Self, Identity, and the Naming Question: Reflections on the Language of Disability," *Social Science and Medicine* 36, no. 2 (1993): 167–73; Wendell, *Rejected Body*, 77–81.

23 As physical and/or mental outsiders, disabled people offer a valuable critique of a world that non-disabled people take for granted. "When people cannot ground their self-worth in their conformity to cultural body ideals or social expectations of performance," Wendell explains, "the exact nature of those ideals and expectations and their pervasive, unquestioning acceptance becomes much clearer." *Rejected Body*, 69. Profiling various people both disabled and not who have worked with disability in some way, Andrew Potok, *A Matter of Dignity: Changing the Lives of the Disabled* (New York, 2002), offers perhaps the most compelling, unsentimental case for finding beauty, wonder, and imagination in the challenges disability brings. As he explains in the introduction, "some say that being different means being less, others that it has within it the possibility of a new synthesis, a new paradigm. And it can provide the joys that attend transformation" (8). Georgina Kleege's unorthodox memoir *Sight Unseen* (New Haven, Conn., 1999) uses her partial blindness to explore visual culture, providing a fine example of how a disability can enhance perspectives. Some credit Dr. Oliver Sacks for doing something similar, albeit from the perspective of a person without a disability, a topic explored by Leonard Cassuto, "Oliver Sacks and the Medical Case Narrative," in Snyder, Bruggemann, and Garland-Thomson, *Enabling the Humanities*, 118–30. An increasingly vocal group of disabled people has begun to celebrate difference in ways comparable to the cultures of ethnic minorities. On the topic of a broader disability culture, see Susan Crutchfield and Martha Epstein, *Points of Contact: Disability, Art, and Culture* (Ann Arbor, Mich., 2000), 1–20. For disability and popular culture, see *The Ragged Edge Magazine* (formerly *The Disability Rag*), www.ragged-edge-mag.com; and *The Mouth: Voice of the Disability Nation*, www.mouthmag.com.

24 Goffman, *Stigma*, 73–91, offers a valuable framework for thinking about issues related to passing and disability. Also see Brenda Jo Bruggemann, "On (Almost) Passing," in her *Lend Me Your Ear: Rhetorical Constructions of Deafness* (Washington, D.C., 1999), 81–99. On "coming out," see Georgina Kleege, "Disabled Students Come Out: Questions without Answers," in Snyder, Bruggemann, and Garland-Thomson, *Enabling the Humanities*, 308–16.

25 On teaching disability studies, see Snyder, Bruggemann, and Garland-Thomson, *Enabling the Humanities*, Part 4, "Enabling Pedagogy," 283–336. In 2002, a new discussion group, "DS-Teaching," began. For information, see http://faculty.washington.edu/dlang/ds-teaching.html. For information to use in teaching disability history at all grade levels, visit the Disability History Museum at www.disabilitymuseum.org.

26 For example, I did not include the two recent biographies about Laura Bridgman: Ernest Freeberg, *The Education of Laura Bridgman: First Deaf and Blind Person to Learn Language* (Cambridge, Mass., 2001); and Elizabeth Gitter, *The Imprisoned Guest: Samuel Howe and Laura Bridgman, the Original Deaf-Blind Girl* (New York, 2001). They have been extensively reviewed together in both the mainstream and academic press. Historians will gain much by reading Douglas C. Baynton's discussion in "Laura Bridgman and the History of Disability," *Reviews in American History* 30, no. 2 (June 2002).

27 For simplicity, I use small d "deaf" rather than capital D "Deaf" throughout this essay.

CHAPTER 3

Disability Studies:

The Old and the New

Tanya Titchkosky

Disabled people are, as Abberley (1998:93) points out, often "only relevant as problems," and are thus excluded from the making of the cultural, political, and intellectual world. "Problem" is the definition of the situation of disability. (Thomas, 1971 [1923]:276). Such an understanding does not arise simply because our bodies give us troubles; disability as a problem is presented to people through interaction, with the social and physical environment, and through the social production of knowledge. The over-determined sense in which our culture gives us disability as a problem is shared by the discipline of sociology in that social scientific research, textbooks, and course offerings in, for example, Deviance, represent disability as a "problem" of the body gone wrong. This problem obtrudes into the social world and is studied by sociologists as such, thus representing disability as a social problem.

In his discussion of social representation, Dyer (1993:3) says that a culture's representation of its people is not a mirror reflection of reality in that "reality is always more extensive and complicated than any system of representation can comprehend." Still, Dyer insists that there is something very real about a culture's representation of its people, especially its "problem" people. The reality which is of concern to Dyer (1993:3) lies in this:

> ... representations here and now have real consequences for real people, not just in the way they are treated but in terms of the way representations delimit and enable what people can be in any given society.

The fundamental social character of representation lies in its ability to present a version of reality and not necessarily in its ability to "get it right." Representations have real consequences for real people, but these consequences go beyond the people being represented, since there are consequences for those who make these representations as well. The most authoritative representations of disabled persons arise from medical and/or therapeutic disciplines, and the social sciences. Anyone who is to be regarded as "in the know" about disability must show that they know that it is a problem and the more details they possess of the problem, the better. This is the "official textbook" of disability represented in our culture.

What Smith (1999:73–95) calls the "official text producers" of a society rely upon and enhance the ideological constructs of people and things that already circulate within a culture. These producers have more resources, institutional support, and authority to "put the word out," and even claim to have the most important word to put out, more important even than the words of the subjects of these texts. Such official definers of disability have usually come from medical jurisdictions, but sociologists, too, have a long history of producing textual knowledge on and about disabled people. The latter has typically treated disabled people as expressions of the problem of involuntary deviance, subject to processes of stigmatization who employ a variety of techniques and technologies in order to manage, cope with, or hide the problems that impaired senses, minds and/or bodies are assumed to generate. (Davis, 1961; Jones, et al., 1984)

Still, "problem" is not the final word on the social significance of disability, since other representations of it also arise. There is a "new" Disability Studies. It argues that traditional sociological research, and the curriculum which has developed from it, "... strengthens the control that the rehabilitation/medical industry and the special education system have over disabled people" and that it has served to keep disability research "... isolated in the applied fields." (Linton, et al., 1995:8) The rapidly growing body of "new" Disability Studies research highlights the oppressive character of much of the traditional sociological research. Yet, according to some, there is nothing new to be found in the study of disability.

In this paper, I do not seek to establish whether Disability Studies is truly new or not. Instead, I aim to uncover what the gloss "new" means in relation to mainstream sociology's rejection of such a claim and Disability Studies repetitive articulation of it. This paper uncovers the values and epistemological assumptions that lie behind the social act of conceptualizing Disability Studies as a "new" field of inquiry. I contrast this with more traditional sociological studies of disability which flow from the premise that there is little new in the study of disability beyond the generation of more information about particular types of disabilities in particular social contexts and in particular times and places. I show that the concept of a "newly emerging" field of inquiry is symbolic of a critical relation to much of the social scientific research on disability. "New" is also symbolic of an affirmation of inquiry into able-bodiedness as itself a culture in need of critical engagement, as well as a way to articulate the standpoint of disability as an opportunity to provoke such inquiry. "New" is also a rhetorical device to highlight the idea that the traditional ways to study disability are underdeveloped. I hope, of course, that my examination of the academic discourse surrounding the study of disability serves to draw out the importance of Disability Studies ... in general.

The Problem of Meaning

"Disability Studies should not be considered as a newly emerging field": this was one of the reasons a mainstream American "social problems" journal gave for rejecting the paper that I had submitted to them [...] The reviewers claimed that Disability Studies was at least 30 years old, citing the work of Goffman as proof. Of course, the reviewers could have gone as far back as Durkheim (1915) for an example of "the disabled" conceived of as an object for sociological inquiry. Or, back even farther, we could turn to the Enlightenment where "the disabled" first became an [...] category, bureaucratically tracked, counted, managed, and subsequently evocative of a peculiar fascination for thinkers of the time (Davis, 1997c:9–28; 1997d:110–127). The development of the concept of the "deserving poor," as well as the industrial revolution, wars, and medical advancements have also coincided with an ongoing concern with disability as a social problem (Russell, 1998; Shapiro, 1993; Jones, 1994; Liachowitz, 1988; Stone, 1984).

There is nothing new; disability *is* a problem and it is one of the many problems sociologists have studied, for some time. Involuntary deviance, stigmatized master status, management of a spoiled identity, passing, coping, etc., are some of the most systematic representations of disability as a problem produced by sociologists. I agree—there *is* nothing new about treating disability as a problem. Manifestations of the problem of disability and even institutional processes of its amelioration and control are things which sociologists have studied for many years.[1]

But, there are many who publish within the field of Disability Studies and who claim that they are engaged in a "new" area of inquiry. Simi Linton et al. (1995:8), in their discussion of Disability Studies curriculum, claim that it began "some fifteen years ago." In a recent *Disability Studies Reader*, Lennard Davis (1997b:1) claims that

> This reader is one of the first devoted to disability studies. But it will not be the last. Disability studies is a field of study whose time has come ... People with disabilities have been isolated, incarcerated, observed, written about, operated on, instructed, implanted, regulated, treated, institutionalized, and controlled to a degree probably unequal to that experienced by any other minority group. As fifteen percent of the population, people with disabilities make up the largest physical minority within the United States—One would never know this to be the case by looking at the literature on minorities and discrimination.[2]

Shelly Tremain (1993:131) says that "There is, to be sure, a substantial corpus of clinical, empirical, and demographic work on disability," yet Tremain also says that she is "... keenly aware of the dearth of critical academic work done under the rubric of the 'socio-political construction of disability.'" Since 1995, there have been a number of readers and individual studies of disability, almost all of which make similar claims (Ingstad and Whyte, 1995; Hales, 1996; Thomson, 1996; Mitchell and Snyder, 1997; Jenkins, 1998; Shakespeare, 1998; Barnes, et al., 1999; Corker and French, 1999).

There are very few academic conferences devoted to, or that even include, Disability Studies, especially in Canada. Unlike Women Studies, Race Relations or Minority Studies, Disability Studies is not (yet?) regarded as a hiring, research, or curriculum interest within sociology—at best there are research areas such as deviance, health and illness, or aging.

From my personal experience as an academic, I know that there are otherwise politically astute academics who are not aware that it is illegal to decide against hiring a disabled person solely on the grounds that the institution would have to provide some sort of "reasonable accommodation." Insofar as disabled people are still discriminated against in practical matters such as hiring and promotion, imagine the status or stigma of an academic field dedicated to disability. If Disability Studies has been around for more than thirty years in the university system, it appears to have exercised very little influence upon the day-to-day decision making processes of academic departments, conference organizers, and journal editorial boards [...] I had assumed that the exclusion, oppression, and devaluation of disabled persons had, in the last ten years or so, become obvious to most wide awake sociologists.

However, sociologists *have* studied "the disabled," have done so for many years, and have not made any claim of participating in a new field of inquiry. Many mainstream deviance textbooks (Clinard and Meier, 1998; Rubington and Weinberg, 1998; Heitzeg, 1996; Dellos, 1996; Pontell, 1996) include such phenomena as deafness, blindness, wheelchair use, stuttering, and physical "deformities" as topic areas for the sociological study of deviance. Disability is also likely to be included as a research area in considerations of health and illness and of gerontology. Yet, it is rare that mainstream introductory sociology textbooks include disability as a distinct topic area, often only dedicating a page or two to "disability rights."[3]

Thus, there are two different claims: first, disability has been an object of sociological study for a very long time and, second, disability has just recently become a site of critical inquiry. "How can the conflict of rival interpretations be arbitrated?" (Ricoeur, 1974:10) One way to arbitrate these conflicting interpretations of disability, within the academy, is to "settle accounts." Settling accounts means to prove one side as mostly true and the other as mostly false. It is, for example, true that the discipline of Sociology has, since its inception, treated disabled persons as an object of inquiry. Perhaps, or so the argument could go, people working within the field of Disability Studies are unaware of this fact. Thus, the conflict could be settled if one side is proven correct and the other wrong, misguided, or misinformed.

[...] If we do not rely on the true/false dichotomy, and its necessary assumption that one side is mystified by its own ignorance, what other possible ways come to the fore in order to arbitrate these conflicting interpretations of the study of disability? By side-stepping the "settling of accounts," the language through which the study of disability is represented, and the resulting conflicts, can themselves become an object of inquiry [.... W]e could ask, "What meaning do these conflicting interpretations of the study of disability point to?"

Such questioning would allow us to treat the conflicting arguments as documents (Schutz, 1973:208–234; Garfinkel 1967:9–34; Smith, 1990:61ff) of the way our culture and its "learned people" interpret, and thereby represent, disability. As Ricoeur (1974:11) says, "Is it not once again *within language* itself that we must seek the indication that understanding is a mode of being." Disability Studies' "mode of being," its particular interpretation of disability and how it ought to be studied, can come to light through an examination of the field's claim of newness as this stands in relation to mainstream sociological ways of speaking about disability. In this way, it becomes possible to think about the "actual" (Smith, 1999:6) language used to articulate disability as a field of inquiry. Focusing on the academic language surrounding disability allows us to develop an understanding of how disability has been made an object for research. Such a focus requires that I regard my "preliminary assumptions" (Arendt, 1994:310), and how they are rejected by others, as food for thought and not simply as an occasion to argue about truth or falsehood.

Disability: Nothing's New

Respecting the position of those who reject the notion of a new Disability Studies, I turn now to Goffman's work. Within more traditional sociological examinations of disability, Goffman's work is cited, used, critiqued, revisited, and revised extensively (Jones, et al., 1984; Geyla, 1988; Herman and Miall, 1990; Manning, 1992; Susman, 1994; West, 1996; Norwich, 1997; Nijhof, 1998). Following a brief explication of his conceptualization of disability, I will analyze a text that is typical of the kind of sociological research that has flowed from Goffman's insights. I am concerned here with drawing out the concrete ways that disability has been conceived, worked on, and represented within sociological research.

Goffman's *Stigma* (1963:4) makes disability a sociological topic in that he speaks of societal reactions to "abominations of the body." He speaks of stigma as a "special kind of relationship between attribute and stereotype." (Ibid.) "Stigma" is a social phenomenon for Goffman in that the meaning of a mark of difference (attribute) is generated *between* people. The mark *becomes* a stigma through interaction, thus marks of difference are not treated by Goffman as *ipso facto* leading to stigma. Depending on context and its interactants a mark of difference is regarded by others as a stigma which can eventually lead to the social construction of stigmatized people.

A stigmatized person is a blemished, not quite human person. "By definition, of course, we believe the person with a stigma is not quite human" (Ibid.:5). A stigma is used by others to define a blemished person as different from other humans, thus making them not quite human. Stigma itself comes in three basic types or forms: 1.) abominations of the body or "various physical deformities," 2.) blemishes of character or "weak will, domineering or unnatural" beliefs, values and attitudes, and 3.) tribal stigma or "race, nation and religion" (Ibid.:4). Thus many different aspects of human practices and appearances fit under the umbrella concept of stigma. This means that many different humans are regarded by others as not quite human. For example, stigma can be attached to visible and non-visible disabilities, physical abnormalities, unusual body shape or marks, interactional quirks, mental illness, and depending on the context, aspects of gender, sexuality, race, and class.

Regardless of such a multitude of specific differences, Goffman says that any stigmatized person:

> .... possesses a trait that can obtrude itself upon attention and turn those of us whom he meets away from him, breaking the claim that his other attributes have on us. He possesses a stigma, an undesired differentness from what we had anticipated. We and those who do not depart negatively from particular expectations at issue I shall call the *normals* (Ibid.:5, italics his own).

Potentially stigmatized people interact with others who can potentially stigmatize them. The others who possess the potential to stigmatize people are referred to as the "normals." Normals are those who have many different attributes but who do not, in the interactional situation in question, have an attribute of difference. Normals are those who, at least in the face of some individuals and within some interactional situations, do not represent "undesired differentness." The many different attributes that make up the appearance and the behavior of any normal person are regarded as desired differences. Normals, at the same time, do not possess an obtrusive difference from humanity ... thus they are normal. Moreover, it is normal for normals to notice those who are endowed with an undesired difference.

In Goffman's delineation of the social construction of stigma, "normalcy" is the standpoint which does not obtrude but, rather, *allows* for the recognition of who or what is stigmatized. Normalcy is the unmarked site from which people view the stigma of disability. Goffman anticipates that both reader and researcher are "normals." Normals are a "we" that includes Goffman, his imagined readers, and all others who do not depart negatively from normalcy.

Normals do not depart from their sense of being connected to normalcy. *They* do not depart, according to Goffman, because they do not possess the condition of bearing a mark of difference. The normals do not possess a stigmatized or stigmatizing attribute which will obtrude upon others and force them into an interactional relation with an undesired differentness. Insofar as Goffman conceives of some human attributes as conditions of differentness and conceives of the stereotypes which surround such attributes as social phenomena produced through interaction, he can regard encounters between normals and stigmatized as "... one of the primal scenes of sociology." (Goffman, 1967:13)

"Primal scene" is a term that Goffman has borrowed from Freud (1978 [1917]) which refers to formative traumatic encounters, such as a child witnessing his/her parents having sex. When we encounter such traumas, according to Freud, we come to recognize our difference from others (I am not my father) and we make something of that difference (I am inadequate, I lack). Such scenes give us an initial or primal sense of self. Just as Freud aimed to return his patients to such primal scenes in order to unwrap the mystery of their psychological problems, Goffman suggests that sociologists need to return to the primal scene of interactions between the normals and the stigmatized in order to unwrap the mystery of the genesis of social identity and difference.

Interactions with disabled others are, for Goffman, one such primal scene. Through his theory of the processes of stigmatization, Goffman unwraps the disturbing character of disabled persons whom are found in the midst of the normals. At the same time, interactions with people whose bodies are an abomination to the normals' sense of the normal body serve Goffman as a way to highlight the concrete interactional processes of stigmatization. Thus, in both theory and content, Goffman studies disability. "Abominations of the body" are, after all, one of Goffman's key types of stigma, and a major source of data throughout his work. It is easy to understand that disability certainly can be conceived of as an interaction between attribute and stereotype, resulting in a discredited, discreditable, failed, or not quite human person. Disability can be regarded as a powerful and obtrusive trait, a master status, marking all of the other attributes a person possesses. All of this helps to explicate the *problem* of disability.

Goffman's research consequently represents disability both as a "thing," a problematic attribute, and also as an "occasion." Disabled people occasion a trauma of recognition which obtrudes upon a normal's sense of normalcy as an expected feature of daily life. Thus, disability is highlighted in Goffman's work as an occasion that has led to a consolidation of the "we-the-normals" experience, as well as to the possibility of unpacking the normal/disabled interactional scene. Disability as an occasion to unpack the meaning of normalcy is explicitly articulated by Goffman in his final two chapters of *Stigma*. He provides for, and thus prefigures, the necessity of unpacking norms of identity and he posits the general impossibility of normalcy's achievement even if one is "... a young, married, white, urban, northern, heterosexual, Protestant father of college education, fully employed, of good complexion, weight and height, and a recent record in sports" (Goffman, 1963:128).

Disability-Knowledge

Today, many stigmatized persons have secured their status as "human" in law. Disability was, for example, categorically included in the Canadian Charter of Rights and Freedoms in 1985, and in 1981 "handicap" was excluded as a valid ground of discrimination in the Human Rights Code of Canada, initially introduced 1962 (Jones, 1994:91–92). In 1992, the Americans' with Disabilities Act (ADA), signed into law in 1990, took effect and began to offer legal protections against discrimination, just as women and minorities had begun to secure such protection through the 1964 Civil Rights Act (Shapiro, 1993:105–141).

While legally "persons," disabled people are still treated as deviating from normal representations of normal people and disabled persons have thus been studied as such. In sociology, disability is often represented as the social problem of deviance. The primal scene of interaction with disabled others has served as data for the study of the social construction of deviance, especially what some sociologists call, "involuntary deviance" (Sagarin, 1975:201–213). What knowledge have we sociologists typically gleaned from this primal scene? In order to consider this, I turn to an exemplary representation of disability-knowledge that flows from a traditional way of conceptualizing disability within the social sciences. I chose this text, in part, because it is published by a major mainstream publishing company, has been deemed to be re-printable at least nine times, because it cites and makes use of a vast quantity of mainstream sociological work on disability published from 1960 to 1995, and because the book's web page advertisement highlights the text's disability chapter and claims that it is "updated." (This text, however, is not an anomaly.) Written initially in 1957, and revised and updated numerous times, here is what this deviance text book has to say about disabled persons in its 1998 edition [and 2007, 12th edition]:

> The central difference between a physical disability and another form of deviance is its identity as a condition rather than a behavior; a disabled person exerts no control over this condition.... Society considers both visible disabilities, like those caused by physical disfigurements, and less evident ones, like mental retardation, as deviance because they depart from normative conceptions of "normal" conditions, and affected people experience sanctioning processes that lead to social stigmas (Clinard and Meier, 1998:482).

It would appear that the primal scene is truly a traumatic one (Freud, 1978 [1917]:308) for the normals: in the last thirty odd years, some normal sociologists have lost any sense of a disability as a "stigma*tized*" attribute." Disability is treated as a "condition" interpreted as a "given." Disability is the condition of having a body that is a problem. Thus, disability is stripped of any social location or social significance. It simply is. As "objectively given" (Goode, 1996), it becomes the material made use of in "sanctioning processes" and social stigma.

In the face of the asocial condition of disability taken as a given, "society considers...." The first thing society considers is that it has nothing to do with noticing disability-as-a-condition and is unrelated to making *it* meaningful as such. The next thing society considers is that disabled persons are just like able-bodied persons in the (mystified) sense that both "exert no control over this condition." Beyond the common and shared conception of disability as a problem condition, other similarities between able-bodied and disabled people disintegrate or disappear in the primal scene of interactional engagement with disabled persons.

Following the lead of society's consideration of disabled persons, the work of some sociologists begins. Society considers disabled persons as deviant and sociologists study disability as "... deviance because they [disabled persons] depart from normative conceptions of 'normal' conditions." The conditions the text highlights include blindness (Ibid.:487–489), mental retardation (Ibid.:489–490), physical handicaps, referred to throughout as "crippled people," (Ibid.:490–492), and obesity and eating disorders (Ibid.:492–500).

With these abnormal bodies, sociologists can thus study normal reactions to deviant conditions taken as a given. For example:

> People have long recognized the blind as one of the most conspicuous groups of disabled people in society. Because the eyes communicate much human expression, some feel extremely disturbed when they confront blind people. A blind person's gaze does not transmit the same psychological or emotional cues as that of a sighted person. Facial expressions provide less information to others. Various behavioral mannerisms and other visible clues increase the social conspicuousness of the blind, including odd postures, rocking of the head or tilting it at odd angles, and touching objects in a groping manner, as well as distinctive paraphernalia, such as thick glasses, white canes, and guide dogs (Clinard and Meier, 1998:488).

Along with sheer offensiveness to blind people, the phrase "Because the eyes communicate much ..." communicates the understanding that sight too is seen, by normals, as a condition interpreted as a given. However, eyesight is not a *problem* condition. Those with the condition of eyesight are disturbed when they see blindness "because" they see that the other does not. Sighted others observe the blind person's gaze and find lack, difference, anomaly, and conspicuous oddness. Eyesight is the condition of normalcy, the expected, communicative, and yet non-obtrusive fact of normal life. Indeed, the "condition" of eyesight is only brought to awareness in the face of the "conspicuousness of the blind," e.g., odd postures, rocking, tilting, angling, touching, groping, and stigmatized paraphernalia that signifies blindness.

Despite the fact that the face of blindness has communicated the obtrusive, conspicuous, disturbing condition of blindness, and has brought the normalcy of sight to mind, the face of blindness is still interpreted as one which "... provides less information to others." The lesser kind of information blind persons provide seems to be that "the blind" are a representation of deviance *par excellence*. What appears as both primary and as a greater kind of information is the face of normalcy.

It is difficult, however, to come face-to-face with normalcy. The text encodes (Smith, 1995:23ff) normalcy as the expected but taken-for-granted ground for the "we-the-normals" experience, an experience that does not usually obtrude upon one's consciousness. Instead, normalcy is the unmarked viewpoint from which deviance is observed. Normalcy is typically only indirectly available to human experience as an unobtrusive background expectation. Unless we are oriented to avoiding stigmatization, we do not usually attend to the fact of "being normal." Yet, the odd postures, rocking, tilting, angling, touching, groping, and stigmatized paraphernalia of disability functions to bring normalcy to consciousness. This information, however, is evaluated as "lesser."

That this kind of information is "lesser" is ascertained quickly and before the text displays any kind of awareness of its use of blindness to reconstitute the unquestioned, hegemonic normalcy of sight and able-bodiedness. Understood as lesser to the extent that blind persons lack sight, the blind person implicitly functions in the text as a kind of tribute to the greatness of normalcy. Blindness is used to make a spectacle of that which is normally the unseen taken-for-granted "condition" of sight and able-bodiedness.

It appears as if the sociological study of disability is, as with medicine, the study of problem conditions: those who possess a body in normal working condition notice those who do not possess such a body and what "naturally" obtrudes are disabled persons' deviation from the normative order of normalcy. Medicine studies pathology, sociologists study deviance, and both begin with a similar conception of the disabled body—the condition of having, and thus being, a problem.

A consequence of all this is that normal sociologists have generated disability-knowledge as to why it is normal, but perhaps not necessary, to feel "extremely disturbed" in the face of disabled persons. Note the detailed focus on the features which are assumed to deviate from the normal features of the able-bodied. This deviant-detail "obtrudes," that is, is focused on, to such an extent that any interaction between attribute and stereotype is made almost invisible. Perhaps, as Goffman (1963:126–39) mentions in his discussion of the "unblushing American male" and "normal deviance," the primal scene would be better understood as the interaction between culture's dominant and unquestioned representations of difference as these interact with normal's perception and treatment of difference[....] I turn now to a discussion of the consequences of the traditional production of disability-knowledge.

Real Consequences for Real People

Disability-knowledge, along with recounting the details of the disturbing character of blindness or disability in general, teaches much to the "normals."[4] In this case, it teaches much to normal teachers and normal students in the sociology of deviance. It teaches normals to attend to the primal scene *as if* the discomfort they hold in the face of disability can be attributed to disabled people alone. It teaches normals to act *as if* this uneasiness is simply one more condition that comes from disability itself and is somehow unrelated to interpretation and interaction. It also teaches professors and their students that it is normal to act *as if* no one in their classroom, and no reader of this 1998 [or 2007] deviance textbook, belongs to the identity category of disability. In general, this traditional sociological approach to disability teaches normals many ways to confound the relation between normalcy/deviance, disability/able-bodiedness, and knowledge/unexamined common-sense conceptions. The mainstream approach reproduces the illusion that disability is far removed from normal life and does so, in part, by communicating the improbable belief that disability is *not* a real possibility for everyone. The text makes disability "far out," in every sense of that term.

Disability as the type of deviance taken as a given, about which we can do nothing ("no control"), has allowed sociologists to study the exact way the appearance of deviance obtrudes. While "Some people live with visible physical handicaps" (Clinard and Meier, 1998:490) the text concludes that

> contemporary attitudes still tend to regard people with visible physical handicaps as being apart from other human beings; many people today look on them with pity or avoid them all together (Ibid.:491).

Given that disability is formulated as a type of person, steeped in the condition of lack, that no one, including the disabled person, would want to be, sociology proceeds to study how the disabled self and others "manage" this obtrusive, worthless, unexpected, unintended deviation from normalcy. The text turns to an explication of various forms of management, e.g., rehabilitation and role socialization (Ibid.:500–506), passing (Ibid.:508), normalizing and coping (Ibid.:509), dissociation or avoidance, denial and retreat (Ibid.:510).[5]

Such a textual rendering of disability constructs disabled persons as unexpected and unintended persons and it constructs normal persons as, indeed, quite normal when they understand disabled persons as such (Michalko and Titchkosky, 2000:304). As unintended, unexpected conditional beings, this sociological textbook (discourse) also constructs disability as something a disabled person can do nothing about, cannot exert control. Of course, such an understanding of disability flies in the face of the growing disability movement and consequent legislative changes in, for example, Canada, the US, and UK. Nonetheless, with this conception of disability sociologists may learn many details about how people become disabled, are isolated and institutionalized, how blind people are trained to make eye contact and deaf people to speak, how disabled people are shocked, watched, beat up, operated on, regularized, medicated, put into therapy, locked up, controlled, helped, measured, raped, unemployed, counted, evaluated, documented and ... studied by sociologists. Insofar as disabled people are understood as unintended and unexpected people conditioned by their lack of normalcy in regards to which s/he exerts no control, much of what is done to disabled persons, including sociological research, seems rational and sensible. This way of studying disability has generated a body of knowledge that tacitly functions as a form of maintenance for the status quo while providing exotic details on disabled people's lives.

While this may strike some of us as a social scientific version of the "freak show" (Thomson, 1997), there is no indication of such a concern. At the same time, the text does not provide an argument for its version of disability and does not introduce any alternative versions. The text obliterates all signs of interpretation *as if* interpretation is not part of the experience of disability, as if disabled people are not surrounded by conflicting interpretations of their identity. (Michalko and Titchkosky, 2000:292) Not only does this way of conceptualizing disability occlude the possibility of any alternative sociological views regarding it, it also denies a disability politics. Thus,

> Unlike homosexuals and other identified groups, however, they have not yet
> established common a [sic] sociological identity ... As a result, they have not
> successfully pressed for political power to remedy common concerns and problems
> (Clinard and Meier, 1998:482).

(Recall that the Americans with Disability Act was passed in 1990.) Curiously, the asocial and apolitical character of disability that the text relies upon in order to produce its disability-knowledge is not attributed to the authors of the text, nor to sociological research. Instead, it is *they*, disabled people alone, who are held to be responsible for *their* asocial and apolitical position in society.[6]

From the standpoint of conformity with the dominant point of view on disability as simply an undesired condition of lack and inability, sociologists working in the area of disability need not consider alterity (Titchkosky, 1998). For example, crime and most other topic areas in the introductory level deviance textbook are presented in relation to competing sociological theories and debates regarding the social significance of deviant phenomena. Disability, however, is not. It simply is ... and what disability *is* is an indirect spectacle of the power of normalcy. Like the normals who are full of pity and avoidance, sociology, too, often avoids disability as a phenomenon in its own right. Such a hegemonic presentation of disability is a sign of the kind of tyranny that surrounds disability as a sociological topic. There *is*, sadly, nothing new about this. Nor is there anything new about interpreting tyranny as humanistic social scientific knowledge.

The prevalence of the sociological representation of disability as a mere spectacle in service of normalcy, stripped of any understanding of its social production, is certainly open to debate. What is not open to debate is that this is one way that academics produce disability-knowledge. It is also beyond question that since the category "the disabled" entered Western culture, there have been researchers and theorists that have resisted conformity to the dominant ideologies of their day (e.g., Zola, 1982; Scott, 1969) and, of course, others who have not. There are many empirical questions which could be raised at this point: just exactly how dominant is this dominant ideology? Who has succumbed and who has not? How many researchers are searching for an alternative representation of disability and how many are stuck in a freak show mentality? What version of disability are funding agencies, publishers, or hiring committees supporting and who is getting funded, published, hired and who is not? Not only the answering but the *very asking* of any of these questions would require that we possess some sense of the alternative representations of disability currently being proposed and employed. However, such alternatives are typically excluded by the sociological research on disability. I turn now to alternative conceptions of disability represented by those researchers who claim that there is a "new" approach to the study of disability.

Disability: What's New?

Those who claim to be involved in the "new" Disability Studies do not do so by enumerating and criticizing those who claim Disability Studies is "old." Instead, like many other pronouncements of newness in our culture, Disability Studies articulates itself as qualitatively different from that which came before. For example, Simi Linton (1998:1) begins her book by claiming that

> It was at one time seamless. There were no disjunctures between the dominant cultural narrative of disability and the academic narrative. But in the past 20 years.... Enter disability studies: a location and a means to think critically about disability, a juncture that can serve both academic discourse and social change ...

No one is named. Whatever is new about Disability Studies is not expressed as a reaction to others nor derived from a particular person, a founding mother or father. Yet, the nature of the mainstream approach to the study of disability is characterized: it provided a seamless narrative that fit into, and reflected, taken-for-granted cultural assumptions of disability. Linton's pronouncement of newness refers to some kind of recent juncture in, or gap between, the way disability is conceived academically as opposed to common-sensically.

Still, her pronouncement is not an argument regarding the number of years Disability Studies has been around, for Linton (1998:3) goes on to say:

> Despite the steady growth of scholarship and courses, particularly in the past five years, the field of disability studies is even more marginal in the academic culture than disabled people are in the civic culture. The enormous energy society expends keeping people with disabilities sequestered and in subordinate positions is matched by the academy's effort to justify that isolation and oppression.

Linton passes from twenty years to five, without much hesitation. Whatever is deemed "new" about Disability Studies is not attached to a concrete historical moment of birth, and is not due to a single transformative moment in time.[7] Instead, new appears to mark a movement, a movement from a seamless unified concept of disability to disjunctive and multiple conceptions of disability. This movement is spoken of in spacial terms and not only in temporal ones. The central conception of disabled people as justifiably positioned on the margins, oppressed and sequestered, gives rise to a seamless relation between everyday conceptions of disabled people and academic ones. The claim to newness is a reference to an alternative way to move within the topic of disability. Thus disability is described both as a *location*, albeit marginal, and as a means to critically analyze the mainstream academic and cultural narratives that already surround disabled people. In Linton's

(1998:4) words "... now it behooves us to demonstrate how knowledge about disability is socially produced to uphold existing practices."

At "one time" there was a dominant way to work on disability that was shared by sociologists, psychologists, medical practitioners, rehabilitators, and special educators. As deviance textbooks demonstrate, this time has not left us—it is present, prevalent, and powerful. For example, Oliver (1990:x–xi) says,

> As a disabled sociologist, my own experience of marginalization has been more from the sociological community than from society at large. A sociologist having either a personal or a professional interest in disability will not find disability occupies a central or even a marginal place on the sociological agenda. And even where it does appear, sociology has done little except reproduce the medical approach to this issue. In recent years medical sociology has grown faster than most other areas, but even within this sub-division, medical sociologists have been unable to distinguish between illness and disability and have proceeded as if they are the same thing.

Disability is still viewed as an unexpected, undesired, asocial, apolitical, bodily condition. Both Oliver and Linton articulate the academy's current role in seamlessly stitching together disabled people's oppression and the knowledge which justifies this state of affairs. Thus, the gloss *new* does not refer to a "paradigm shift" (Kuhn, 1962). New is not a metaphoric device to refer to some kind of progress of, or evolution within, the production of disability-knowledge.

So far, we should posses the sense that whatever the claim to newness means, it is not an announcement of an individual's crowning achievement, nor is it a coded reference to a discipline's birth date, nor is it symbolic of a paradigmatic shift within the academy as a whole. Still, the claim to newness is articulated poignantly and often. For example,

> *Disability studies* is a relatively recent rubric that seeks to group research that focuses upon the historical, political, social and professional meanings ascribed to disability and disabled populations.... Disability studies takes the medicalized model of disability as its primary object of critique (Mitchell and Snyder, 1997:24n2, italics their own)

and

> Historically, disability has been the province of numerous professional and academic disciplines that concentrate upon the management, repair, and maintenance of physical and cognitive incapacity.... We rarely consider that the continual circulation of professionally sponsored stories about disabled people's limitations, dependencies, and abnormalities, proves necessary to the continuing existence of these professional fields of study (Ibid.:1).

What is articulated as recent, is a rubric of critique. Part of that which the new Disability Studies has to offer is a critique of professionally generated disability-knowledge. It is a critique aimed at those forces and traditions which have functioned as the primary producers of the ascription of meaning to (representations of) the lives of disabled people. The primary object of critique is the body of knowledge and practices which constitute disability as an asocial and apolitical condition of lack and inability, i.e., the discourses which shape the meaning of disability in conformity with the medical model's version which holds that disability is primarily a problem condition located in an individual's body, mind, or senses. It is a critique aimed at *normal* conceptions of disability that help to constitute and sustain normate culture. (Thomson, 1997)[8] The relatively recent rubric of Disability Studies understands disability as the location and the space in which to engage in such critique.

The qualitative move to which the term "new" implicitly refers, announces the fact that the kind of disability-knowledge which is generated has much to do with our conception of disability. In so doing, the importance of perspective is asserted. Still, referring to Disability Studies as new is not necessarily a code word for the glorification of perspectivism or relativism. Rather, the conflict between the mainstream sociological perspective and the new Disability Studies' perspective is treated as "really Real," especially in regards to the shaping of disabled people's lives and the knowledge formed from this shaping (Bickenbach, 1993; Michalko, 1998). One would be hard pressed to find a Disability Studies text that does not begin from the assumption that there are conflicting interpretations surrounding disability and that these conflicts are of essential importance.

What is new is that Disability Studies focuses on these conflicting interpretations and in so doing attests to the understanding that disability can be conceptualized and researched in at least two ways. That there are at least two ways to conceive of disability *performs* the understanding that disability is a social and not a natural category of persons. Disability Studies exemplifies what Berger (1963:23) calls the first wisdom of sociology, namely, things could be otherwise, and exemplifies Simpson's (1995:94) principle that "pluralism is important in countering domination ..." Consider, for example, how alternative and multiple conceptions of disability are being performed and brought to attention in the following:

> So, this reader appears at the moment that disability, always an actively repressed *memento mori* for the fate of the normal body, gains new, nonmedicalized, and positive legitimacy both as an academic discipline and as an area of political struggle. As with any new discourse, disability studies must claim space in a contested area, trace it[s] continuities and discontinuities, argue for its existence, and justify its assertions (Davis, 1997b:1).

Davis asserts that the denial of the political and social constitution of disability is, nonetheless, a political and social act.... This commitment to the social character of disability leads Davis to show how disability is regarded by some as not normal and how disability is the normal fate for the normal body, how disability is conceived of as a medical phenomenon and how disability's social significance is repressed when regarded as simply bodily impairment, how disability is not regarded as a socio-political phenomenon and how those engaged in Disability Studies must engage in the social and political work of arguing and justifying their engagement in a legitimate area of inquiry. Through these contrasting interpretations of disability, Davis asserts disability *as* a location and a means of social research and political action. Thus, disability is conceived of as a confrontation with society's ways of making up the meaning of its people. These contrasting ways of speaking and gaining disability-knowledge *are* our ways of making up the meaning of people.

As does the mainstream account of disability, Davis' text shows a growing awareness of the normative order of the normal body when in the presence of disability. But, unlike the mainstream account, becoming aware does not entail spectacular justifications for treating the standpoint of normalcy as the only place from which disability should be observed, researched, judged, evaluated, treated, and examined sociologically. While tacitly referring to the domination of the standpoint of normalcy in previous disability research, Davis also makes explicit the alternative view that such "normal" research is engaged in the activity of repression. He suggests that others research disability so as to re-establish the primacy of normalcy while repressing the common (and normal) fate of all of us in our move toward and within disability.

If mainstream life is to remain beholden to the ideal of normalcy as the organizing standard of life and knowledge, it will require that we forget that the disabled body is the fate of the body, that the disabled body brings to mind the death, vulnerability, and the mythic quality of the body conceived of as normal.

The communication of disability-knowledge through texts written *as if* no writer and no researcher, no teacher and no student is or will ever become disabled, can now be understood as one way of repressing the profound social significance of disability. All of us in all probability will spend part or all of our lives as disabled people. (Zola, 1982:246) Disability, as Gadacz (1994:ix) says, "... is a social category whose membership is always open...." But what is new is more than the mere debunking of the mythic quality of normalcy. The critique of the ideal of normalcy, and what Thomson (1997:8ff) calls "normate culture," serves to open the way to understanding that something is

> to be gained by all people from exploring the ways that the body in its variations is metaphorized, disbursed, promulgated, commodified, cathected, and de-cathected, normalized, abnormalized, formed, and deformed.... What is more representative of the human condition than the body and its vicissitudes? (Davis, 1997b:2)

What is new is that disability is being regarded by some researchers as a place from which to speak and learn about the human condition. For example, speaking from the standpoint of blindness, Rod Michalko (1998:4) says "It [blindness] has something to tell us about the human community and about what we value as individuals and as a collective." Disability Studies refutes the sense that disability is only and merely a condition to be spoken *about*. Thus Michalko (1999, 1998) gives analytic attention to ophthalmologists, rehabilitators, guide dog trainers, and blind people as various voices involved in making up our culture's story of blindness, and does so as a blind sociologist. Regarding disability as a space to speak from allows entry of another interlocutor into the conversation of the cultural constitution of the meaning and significance of disability (Frank, 1998; 1995; 1990). Disability here gains meaning as a place to reflect upon interpretive relations to the human condition.

Disability as Conversation

Giving shape to disability as a space to speak from and as a new legitimate speaker among all the others who have attributed meaning to disability leads to formulations of disability which are steeped in dialogue. For example,

> Although the disabled people's movement in Britain dates from the 1970's, the development of disability studies, as an academic discipline, really took off during the 1990's ... the theme of this book establishes disability as a major and neglected area of human social experience, to which it is essential and timely to devote scholarly attention. The dialogue of the collection is between the new researchers in disability studies; the political disability community; and the traditional academic approaches to disability (Shakespeare, 1998:1).

Or,

> This book thus begins what I hope will be a lively conversation within the Humanities not only about the construction of disability through representation but also about the attendant political consequences (Thomson, 1997:18).

Thus, there is a new and growing sense that whatever disability is, its meaning is born of our conversations with it. These conversations, Thomson insists, have real consequences.

Again, this more conversational view of disability stands in contradistinction to mainstream sociological approaches which have typically treated most of what disabled people have had to say and live, not as speech and life, but instead as *symptom*. Disabled people speak, engage in socio-political action, and have done so for a very long time. Nonetheless, sociology (when it functions as a representative of normate culture) has readily regarded all such speech and action as a kind of symptomatology, as signs of adjustment to, coping with, management and acceptance of, disability. Thus it is possible to interpret any or all aspects of a disabled person's life as a series of signs and symptoms, e.g., Is the disabled person avowing their deviance or disavowing it? Is the disabled person adjusting to *their* bodily condition or not? Are *they* overcoming or succumbing to the condition of disability? Everything disabled people say and do, from political action to putting on make-up, from writing books to dropping out of school, from laughter to tears, has been read as symptom. Under the hegemonic control of the medical model, disabled persons are deciphered but not understood. Starting from the taken-for-granted singular sense that disability is a bodily condition of lack and inability unchosen and despised, all speech and action can be regarded as merely symptomatic of the disabled person's healthy or ill relation to such a "condition." In standard and routine ways, the lived experience of disability becomes encoded as a series of signs and symptoms in need of deciphering by normate culture.

The act of regarding speech and action as symptomatic of relations to a condition may be a useful sociological technique for uncovering interpretative relations to any given phenomenon. But it is curious how rarely the "normal" researchers of disability have turned this technique on to their own inquiry (certainly a form of speech as well as a course of action). More curious still is how this technique, which officially claims to uncover the meaningful interpretive relations people develop to the conditions of their lives, can in fact be regarded, at least in the case of disability, as a means to constitute disabled people as speechless. By claiming that there is a new Disability Studies, research-ers are asserting that the experience of disability, the actual speech and actions of disabled people, no longer needs to be read as mere symptom.

> With word and deed we insert ourselves into the human world, and this insertion is like second birth, in which we confirm and take upon ourselves the naked fact of our original physical appearance ... its impulse springs from the beginning which came into the world when we were born and to which we respond by beginning something new on our own initiative.... This beginning is not the same as the beginning of the world; it is not the beginning of something but of somebody ... (Arendt, 1958:176–177).

There is a common character to each and every person's first birth, including those of us who are disabled. We are brought into the world as the consequence of other people's words and deeds and our beginning in the world is marked first and foremost with what those others have already begun, already thought, and have already understood. We come into the world as subjects of others' interpretations of our naked physical existence. The meaning and sig-nificance of our race, class, gender, and disabilities are inscribed and re-inscribed by others from the moment of our birth and forever onwards. Thus, our naked physical appearance is interpreted, treated, trained, and acted upon. In all these ways, our physical existence is a social one. With our first birth, the *meaning* of our physical self is given to us.

At various points, and hopefully over and over again, we go through a second birth. Conformity with the understandings given to our first birth can be a laborious process, especially in the case of the naked fact of our physical existence as disabled. But conformity is not the kind of labor which gives rise to the travail of our second birth. Nonetheless, Arendt suggests that what comes with our first birth needs to be "*confirmed*" so as to allow for the second. Disability Studies does just this. Disability Studies has taken it upon itself to confirm the exact character of that which is given to disabled people at birth. Such confirmation, Arendt suggests, is like a second birth inasmuch as it requires words and deeds that insert the self into the world of ascribed meanings that were begun before and will continue after the birth and death of disabled people. With word and deed we insert our self into the meanings already provided to us. We insert our self in relation to the history of disability. In these ways, we insert into the world the possibility of beginning something new.

Interpreting everything disabled people say and do as nothing but a symptom or measure of their conformity to the established meaning of disability, given by normate culture, certainly does seem to eliminate the understanding that disabled people are actors and speakers. However, even if every word and deed of the new Disability Studies and of disabled people is taken as mere symptom of the first birth into disability, the phenomenon of confirmation and insertion remains. There is, after all, a growing sense among Disability Studies researchers and disabled people that the beginning of something new has been inserted into the world, most notably a confirmation and critique of normate culture. What Disability Studies offers the academy is a disciplined way to study and confirm normate culture, and it puts forward the possibility that the values and epistemological assumptions of "normalcy" can be inserted into the world in a new way.

Still, I do not want to underestimate the ever present power of normate culture to arrange the life and death of the development of selfhood, and to arrange the life and death of the concrete physical existence of disabled people, as well as to arrange the life and death of any knowledge which does not originate from a standpoint of normalcy. We should recall that the act of confirmation now needs to be achieved within an academic environment that includes philosophers who argue for the non-human status of some disabled people, as well as genetic researchers, engineers, ethicists, and counselors who (on national television) speak of the "social obligation" to eliminate "expensive" or "hopeless" bodily conditions.[9] The act of confirmation also needs to be achieved within an academic environment where special educators, rehabilitators, and occupational therapists can "reasonably" speak of the problem of disability as locatable in disabled individuals alone, who are regarded as destined to suffer not only from bodily conditions but also from a lack of assertiveness or lack of self-esteem. The act of confirmation needs to be accomplished in relation to journalism, creative writing, and policy analysis courses that stipulate, under the guise of political correctness, that disabled people must be referred to as "people with disabilities" (PWDs) thus reproducing the taken-for-granted sense that disabled people are "normal" people who just happen to be troubled by an add-on condition, taken as a given. This act of confirmation also needs to be achieved among social theorists, including cultural studies and women studies theorists, who continue, to this day, to use disability only as a metaphor to express cultural inequality and processes of marginalization, while continuing to exclude disability as a social and political issue. Many different contemporary ideologies and ideals inscribe themselves onto the issue of disability and the task and the promise of Disability Studies is to confirm and insert these disability issues into the world in a new way. This paper has been written in light of this principle of "confirmation."

Endnotes

1   Nonetheless, I had assumed that it is common knowledge that much of the social scientific research *on* disability has supported disabled persons' oppression as well as the ideological tyranny of the bio-medical model. (Oliver 1996, 1990; Shakespeare and Watson, 1997; Barnes and Oliver, 1995; Gadacz, 1994) I had assumed that the academy's participation in this oppression was obvious and required critical engagement.

2   In Canada, the official rate of disability among the working age (16–65) population is 17.7%, or well over two million persons. (Gadacz, 1994:27–33) The unemployment rate, which includes the under-employed and the officially unemployed, among disabled persons is 48%—this means that over one million working age adults with disabilities in Canada are not in the labor force. (Statistics Canada, 1991, 1995) A recent report released from the Canadian Human Rights Commission (CHRC, March 23, 1999:1) states that "The Commission welcomed the latest amendments to the Canadian Human Rights Act recognizing that accommodation, short of undue hardship, is a right, not a privilege." Yet, despite this legal support, the report went on to say that, "... the situation of people with disabilities in the workforce is abysmal. 'It is most disturbing that the already deplorable situation of people with disabilities has further deteriorated,' stated the Commission. In the federally-regulated private sector, their representation deteriorated from 2.7 per cent in 1996 to 2.3 per cent in 1997 ..." (Ibid.) The U.S. Department of Commerce, Economics, and Statistics Administration (1997:1) brief on disability states: "About 1 in 5 Americans have some kind of disability, and 1 in 10 have a severe disability." As in Canada, the U.S. rate of unemployment and labor force non-participation among disabled persons is huge. The United Nations (1996) says that "More than half a billion persons are disabled as a result of mental, physical or sensory impairment and no matter, which part of the world they are in, their lives are often limited by physical or social barriers." The United Nations (Ibid.) calls the state and fate of disabled persons world wide a "silent crisis." These numerical depictions of disability are startling, just as startling is the obvious absence of disability as a major social issue within the discipline of sociology.

3   At the introductory level, an example of a Canadian exception is Anderson (1996) and an American exception is Cahill (1998). In *Deviance*, Schissel and Mahood (1996) provide a section that deconstructs taken-for-granted conceptions of "health."

4   In this context, I use "normal" to refer to readers of the deviance text book who accept, or conform to, the text's positioning of them as such.

5   There is a massive body of literature that exists in regards to these topic areas which can be found referenced in most deviance text books.

6   Bauman (1990:37–53) discusses the "us/them" dichotomy as it is used in everyday life. In his introductory sociology text, he presents this theme as a topic area for sociological research. It is curious that while first year students may be introduced to sociological thought on the us/them dichotomy, deviance research and texts often pay no attention to their own employment of it in the production disability-knowledge.

7   In the UK there is another story of the development of Disability Studies. The story does have founding fathers, Michael Oliver (1996, 1990) and Vic Finkelstein (1998), and it does have a birth date, 1973 with the Union of the Physically Impaired Against Segregation (UPIAS) document that delineates the "Social Model of Disability." The Social Model is understood by some to represent a paradigmatic shift in that it is taken as a rejection of the World Health Organization's (WHO) medicalized conception of impairment/disability/handicap. (For a discussion of the WHO model see, Ingstad and Whyte, 1995:5–7 and Wendell, 1996; Chapter 2) The Social Model claims that while there is the problem of bodily impairment best managed by medicine and technology, the focus of disability research should be on how societies disable their impaired members. This genesis story is also repeated in Canada with the founding of the Independent Living Movement and the establishment of the Coalition of Provincial Organizations of the Handicapped (COPOH) in 1976. (Driedger, 1989:22) In this case, the founding father is Henry Enns. These interpretive takes on disability were instrumental in the establishment of Disabled Person's

International (DPI) in 1980. The UK model has led to much research regarding the isolation and oppression of disabled people usually published by Open University Press and in the journal of *Disability and Society*. The Canadian model has led to research that often begins from a "consumeristic" slant (see, Gadacz, 1994) and has led recently to the establishment of the Canadian Center for Studies in Disability (CCSD, formally established in 1995). COPOH, DPI, CCSD headquarters are located in Winnipeg.

8   "Normate" is a term that makes reference to unmarked categories of persons that are culturally regarded as "definitive human beings" (Thomson, 1997:8, see also Goffman, 1963:128), e.g., white, able-bodied, average height, white teeth, unblemished, athletic, married with one or two children, employed, heterosexual, male, etc., wielding authority and power and generally intended and expected by the normal order of interaction, the physical environment, and the structures of knowledge production. "Normate" is also a term made use of to bracket the taken-for-granted status of normalcy and to highlight normalcy as an ideological construct. *Insofar as normalcy is more of an ideological code than actual embodied beings*, "normate culture" is a way to refer to how this ideology works to exclude, oppress, and remove definitional power from so many different types of people.

9   I am referring here to the recent outbreak of eugenic discourse into popular culture.

References

Abberley, Paul. 1987. "The Concept of Oppression and the Development of a Social Theory of Disability." *Disability, Handicap, and Society*. 2(1): 5–19.

Anderson, Karen. 1996. *Sociology: A Critical Introduction*. Toronto: Nelson Canada.

Arendt, Hannah. 1994. *Arendt: Essays in Understanding: 1930–1954*. New York: Harcourt Brace and Company.

——. 1958. *The Human Condition*. Chicago: The University of Chicago Press.

Barnes, Colin. 1998. "The Social Model of Disability: A Sociological Phenomenon Ignored by Sociologists?" Ed. Tom Shakespeare. *The Disability Reader: Social Science Perspectives*. London: Cassell Academic: 66–78.

Barnes, Colin, Geof Mercer, Tom Shakespeare. 1999. *Exploring Disability: A Sociological Introduction*. Cambridge: Polity Press.

Barnes, Colin and Mike Oliver. 1995. "Disability Rights: Rhetoric and Reality in the UK." *Disability and Society*. 10(1): 111–116.

Bauman, Zygmunt. 1990. *Thinking Sociologically*. Oxford: Blackwell Publishers.

Berger, Peter. 1963. *Invitation to Sociology: A Humanistic Perspective*. New York: Doubleday and Company, Incorporated.

Bickenbach, Jerome. 1993. *Physical Disability and Social Policy*. Toronto: University of Toronto Press.

Cahill, Spencer E. and Robin Eggleston. 1998. "Wheelchair Users' Interpersonal Management of Emotions." Ed. Spencer Cahill. *Inside Social Life: Readings in Sociological Psychology and Microsociology*. Los Angeles: Roxbury Publishing Company.

CHRC—Canadian Human Rights Commission. 1999. "Canadians with Disabilities Still Denied Equal Opportunities" [on line] March 6. http://www.chrc-ccdp.ca/ar-ra/ar98-ra98/nrdis-cpdef.asp

Clinard, B. Marshall and Robert F. Meier. 1998. *Sociology of Deviant Behaviour*, Tenth Edition. Fort Worth: Harcourt Brace College Publishers. [1957]

Corker, Marian and Sally French (Eds.). 1999. *Disability Discourse*. Buckingham: Open University Press.

Davis, Fred. 1961. "Deviance Disavowal: The Management of Strained Interaction by the Visibly Handicapped." *Social Problems*. 9: 120–132.

Davis, Lennard J. 1997a. *The Disability Studies Reader*. New York: Routledge. 1997b. "The Need for Disability Studies." *The Disability Studies Reader*. New York: Routledge: 1–6. 1997c. "Constructing Normalcy: The Bell Curve, the Novel, and the Invention of the Disabled Body in the Nineteenth Century." *The Disability Studies Reader*. New York: Routledge: 928. 1997d. "Universalizing Marginality: How Europe Become Deaf in the Eighteenth Century." *The Disability Studies Reader*. New York: Routledge: 110–127. 1995. *Enforcing Normalcy: Disability, Deafness, and the Body*. London: Verso Press.

Delos, Kelly. 1996. *Deviant Behavior: A Text-Reader in the Sociology of Deviance*. New York: St. Martin's Press.

Driedger, Diane. 1989. *The Last Civil Rights Movement: Disabled People's International*. New York: St. Martin's Press.

Durkheim, Emile. 1915. *The Elementary Forms of Religious Life*. New York: George Allen and Unwin, Ltd.

Dyer, Richard. 1993. *The Matter of Images: Essays on Representations*. London: Routledge.

Finkelstein, Vic. 1998. "Emancipating Disability Studies." Ed. Tom Shakespeare. *The Disability Reader*. London: Cassell: 28–49.

Frank, Arthur W.. 1998. "Enacting Illness Stories: When, What and Why." Ed. Hilde L. Nelson. *Stories and Their Limits: Narrative Approaches to Bioethics*. New York: Routledge: 31–49. 1995. *The Wounded Storyteller: Body, Illness, and Ethics*. Chicago: University of Chicago Press. 1990. "Bringing Bodies Back in: A Decade in Review." *Theory, Culture, and Society*. 7(1): 131–162.

Freud, Sigmund. 1973. *I. Introductory Lectures on Psychoanalysis*. London: Penguin Books. [1915–1917]

Gadacz, Rene. 1994. *Re-Thinking Dis-Ability: New Structures, New Relationships*. Edmonton: The University of Alberta Press.

Garfinkel, Harold. 1967. *Studies in Ethnomethodology*. New Jersey: Prentice-Hall, Incorporated.

Geyla, Frank. 1988. "Beyond Stigma: Visibility and Self-Empowerment of Persons with Congenital Limb Deficiencies." *Journal of Social Issues*. 44(1): 95–115.

Goffman, Erving. 1963. *Stigma: Notes on the Management of Spoiled Identity*. Englewood Cliffs: Prentice-Hall, Inc.

Goode, Erich (Ed.). 1996. *Social Deviance*. Boston: Allyn and Bacon.

Hales, Gerald. 1996. *Beyond Disability: Towards an Enabling Society*. London: Sage Publications and Open University Press.

Heitzeg, Nancy A. 1996. *Deviance: Rulemakers and Rulebreakers*. Minneapolis: West Publishing Company.

Herman, Nancy and Charlene Miall. 1990. "The Positive Consequences of Stigma: Two Case Studies in Mental and Physical Disability." *Qualitative Sociology*. 13(3): 251–269.

Hillyer, Barbara. 1993. *Feminism and Disability*. Norman: University of Oklahoma Press.

Ingstad, Benedicte and Susan Reynolds Whyte (Eds.). 1995. *Disability and Culture*. Berkeley: University of California Press.

Jenkins, Richard (Ed.). 1998. *Questions of Competence: Culture, Classification, and Intellectual Disability*. Cambridge: Cambridge University Press.

Johnstone, David. 1998. *An Introduction to Disability Studies*. London: David Fulton Publishers Ltd.

Jones, Edward, Amerigo Farina, Alberta Hastorf, Hazel Markus, Dale Miller, Robert Scott. 1984. *Social Stigma: The Psychology of Marked Relationships*. New York: W. H. Freeman and Company.

Jones, Ruth J. E. 1994. *Their Rightful Place: Society and Disability*. Toronto: Canadian Academy of the Arts, Inc.

Kuhn, Thomas S. 1962. *The Structure of Scientific Revolutions*. Chicago: University of Chicago Press.

Liachowitz, Claire H. 1988. *Disability as a Social Construct: Legislative Roots*. Philadelphia: University of Pennsylvania Press.

Liggett, Helen. 1988. "Stars Are Not Born: An Interpretive Approach to the Politics of Disability." *Disability, Handicap & Society*. 3(3): 263–275.

Linton, Simi. 1998. *Claiming Disability: Knowledge and Identity*. New York: New York University Press.

Linton, Simi, Susan Mello, John O'Neill. 1995. "Disability Studies: Expanding the Parameters of Diversity." *Radical Teacher*. 47: 4–10.

Manning, Philip. 1992. *Erving Goffman and Modern Sociology*. Stanford: Stanford University Press.

Michalko, Rod. 1999. *The Two-in-One: Walking with Smokie, Walking with Blindness*. Philadelphia: Temple University Press. 1998. *The Mystery of the Eye and the Shadow of Blindness*. Toronto: University of Toronto Press.

Michalko, Rod and Tanya Titchkosky. 2001. "Putting Disability in Its Place: It's Not a Joking Matter." Eds. Wilson and Lewicki-Wilson. *Embodied Rhetorics: Disability in Language and Culture*. Carbondale and Edwardsville: Southern Illinois University Press: 200–228.

Minnich, Elizabeth Kamarck. 1990. *Transforming Knowledge*. Philadelphia: Temple University Press.

Mitchell, David T. and Sharon L. Snyder. 1997. "Disability Studies and the Double Bind of Representation." Eds. Mitchell and Snyder. *The Body and Physical Difference: Discourses of Disability*. Ann Arbor: University of Michigan Press: 1–31.

Nijhof, Gerhard. 1998. "Heterogeneity in the Interpretation of Epilepsy." *Qualitative Health Research*. 8(1): 95–105.

Norwich, Brahm. 1997. "Exploring the Perspectives of Adolescents with Modern Learning Difficulties on Their Special Schooling and Themselves: Stigma and Self-Perception." *European Journal of Special Needs Education*. 12(1): 38–53.

Oliver, Michael. 1999. "Final Accounts and the Parasite People." Eds. Marian Corker and Sally French. *Disability Discourse*. Buckingham: Open University Press: 183–191. 1996. *Understanding Disability: From Theory to Practice*. New York: St. Martin's Press. 1990. *The Politics of Disablement*. Hampshire, London: The MacMillan Press, Ltd.

Pontell, Henry N. (Ed.). 1996. *Social Deviance: Readings in Theory and Research*. Upper Saddle River: Prentice-Hall, Inc.

Ricoeur, Paul. 1974. *The Conflict of Interpretations: Essays in Hermeneutics*. Evanston, Illinois: Northwestern University Press.

Rubington, Earl and Martin S. Weinberg (Eds.). 1999. *Deviance: The Interactionist Perspective*, Seventh Edition. Boston: Allyn and Bacon.

Russell, Marta. 1998. *Beyond Ramps: Disability at the End of the Social Contract*. Monroe: Common Courage Press.

Sagarin, Edward. 1975. "The Disabled as Involuntary Deviants." *Deviants and Deviance: An Introduction to Disvalued People and Behaviour*. New York: Praeger: 210–213.

Schissel, Bernard and Linda Mahood (Eds.). 1996. *Social Control in Canada: Issues in the Social Construction of Deviance*. Toronto: Oxford University Press.

Schutz, Alfred. 1973. *Collected Papers I: The Problem of Social Reality*. The Hague: Martinus Nijhoff.

Scott, Robert A. 1969. *The Making of Blind Men: A Study of Adult Socialization*. New Brunswick: Transaction Books, Inc.

Shakespeare, Tom (Ed.). 1998. *The Disability Reader: Social Science Perspectives*. London: Cassell Academic.

Shapiro, Joseph P. 1993. *No Pity: People with Disabilities Forging a New Civil Rights Movement*. New York: Time Books.

Simpson, Murray. 1996. "The Sociology of 'Competence' in Learning Disability Services." *Social Work and Social Sciences Review*. 6(2): 85–97.

Smith, Dorothy E. 1999. *Writing the Social: Critique, Theory, and Investigations*. Toronto: University of Toronto Press. 1995. "Politically Correct An Ideological Code." Eds. Stephen Richer and Lorna Weir. *Political Correctness: Toward the Inclusive University*. Toronto: University of Toronto Press: 23–50. 1990. *The Conceptual Practices of Power: A Feminist Sociology of Knowledge*. Toronto: University of Toronto Press.

Stone, Deborah A. 1984. *The Disabled State*. Philadelphia: Temple University Press.

Statistics Canada. 1995. *A Portrait of Persons with Disabilities: Target Groups Project*. Statistics Canada Housing, Family, and Social Statistics Division. Ottawa: Minister of Industry, Science, and Technology.

Statistics Canada. 1991. Census Disability Rates in Canada and by Province. [on line] http://www.statcan.ca/english/Pgdb/People/Health/health12a.htm and http://www.hrdc-drhc.gc.ca/sommon/news/982 1b3.html

Susman, Joan. 1994. "Disability, Stigma, and Deviance." *Social Science and Medicine*. 38(1):15–22.

Thomas, W. I. 1971. "On the Definition of the Situation." Ed. Marcello Truzzi. *Sociology: The Classical Statements*. New York: Random House: 274–277. [1923]

Thomson, Rosemarie Garland. 1997. *Extraordinary Bodies: Figuring Physical Disability in American Culture and Literature*. New York: Columbia University Press. 1996. *Freakery: Cultural Spectacles of the Extraordinary Body*. New York: New York University Press.

Titchkosky, Tanya. 1998. "Women, Anorexia, and Change." *Dharma: The Changing Faces of Femininity*. XXIII(4): 479–500.

Tremain, Shelly. 1993. "Book Reviews: *Feminism and Disability* by Barbara Hillyer." *Canadian Women Studies: Women and Disability*. 13(4): 131–132.

United Nations. 1996. *Information Note Prepared by the United Nations Secretariat*. [on line] Gopher://gopher.un.org/00/sec/dpcsd/dspd/disabled/DIS96 or http://www.un.org/dpcsd/

U.S. Department of Commerce, Economics, and Statistics Administration. 1997. *Census Brief: Disabilities Affect One-Fifth of All Americans*. Bureau of Census: Dec. Cenbr/97–5.

Wendell, Susan. 1997. "Toward a Feminist Theory of Disability." Ed. Lennard J. Davis. *The Disability Studies Reader*. New York: Routledge: 260–278. 1996. *The Rejected Body: Feminist Philosophical Reflections on Disability*. New York: Routledge.

West, Candace. 1996. "Goffman in Feminist Perspective." *Sociological Perspectives*. 39(3): 353–369.

Zola, Irving Kenneth. 1982. *Missing Pieces: A Chronicle of Living with a Disability*. Philadelphia: Temple University Press.

CHAPTER 4

Disability, Identity, and Representation: An Introduction

Rosemarie Garland-Thomson

The Disabled Figure in Culture

In its broadest sense, this chapter investigates how representation attaches meanings to bodies. Although much recent scholarship explores how difference and identity operate in such politicized constructions as gender, race, and sexuality, cultural and literary criticism has generally overlooked the related perceptions of corporeal otherness we think of variously as "monstrosity," "mutilation," "deformation," "crippledness," or "physical disability."[1] Yet the physically extraordinary figure these terms describe is as essential to the cultural project of American self-making as the varied throng of gendered, racial, ethnic, and sexual figures of otherness that support the privileged norm. My purpose here is to alter the terms and expand our understanding of the cultural construction of bodies and identity by reframing "disability" as another culture-bound, physically justified difference to consider along with race, gender, class, ethnicity, and sexuality. In other words, I intend to introduce such figures as the cripple, the invalid, and the freak into the critical conversations we devote to deconstructing figures like the mulatto, the primitive, the queer, and the lady. To denaturalize the cultural encoding of these extraordinary bodies, I go beyond assailing stereotypes to interrogate the conventions of representation and unravel the complexities of identity production within social narratives of bodily differences. In accordance with postmodernism's premise that the margin constitutes the center, I probe the peripheral so as to view the whole in a fresh way. By scrutinizing the disabled figure as the paradigm of what culture calls deviant, I hope to expose the assumptions that support seemingly neutral norms. Therefore, I focus here on how disability operates in culture and on how the discourses of disability, race, gender, and sexuality intermingle to create figures of otherness from the raw materials of bodily variation, specifically at sites of representation such as the freak show, sentimental fiction, and black women's liberatory novels. Such an analysis furthers our collective understanding of the complex processes by which *all* forms of corporeal diversity acquire the cultural meanings undergirding a hierarchy of bodily traits that determines the distribution of privilege, status, and power.

One of this chapter's aims is to challenge entrenched assumptions that "able-bodiedness" and its conceptual opposite, "disability," are self-evident physical conditions. My intention is to defamiliarize these identity categories by disclosing how the "physically disabled" are produced by way of legal, medical, political, cultural, and literary narratives that comprise an exclusionary discourse. Constructed as the embodiment of corporeal insufficiency and deviance, the physically disabled body becomes a repository for social anxieties about such troubling concerns as vulnerability, control, and identity. In other words, I want to move disability from the realm of medicine into that of political minorities, to recast it from a form of pathology to a form of ethnicity. By asserting that disability is a reading of bodily particularities in the context of social power relations, I intend to counter the accepted notions of physical disability as an absolute, inferior state and a personal misfortune. Instead, I show that disability is a representation, a cultural interpretation of physical transformation or configuration, and a comparison of bodies that structures social relations and institutions. Disability, then, is the attribution of corporeal deviance—not so much a property of bodies as a product of cultural rules about what bodies should be or do.

This socially contextualized view of disability is evident, for example, in the current legal definition of disability established by the Americans with Disabilities Act of 1990. This landmark civil rights legislation acknowledges that disability depends upon perception and subjective judgment rather than on objective bodily states: after identifying disability as an "impairment that substantially limits one or more of the major life activities," the law concedes that being legally disabled is also a matter of "being regarded as having such an impairment."[2] Essential but implicit to this definition is that both "impairment" and "limits" depend on comparing individual bodies with unstated but determining norms, a hypothetical set of guidelines for corporeal form and function arising from cultural expectations about how human beings should look and act. Although these expectations are partly founded on physiological facts about typical humans—such as having two legs with which to walk upright or having some capacity for sight or speech—their sociopolitical meanings and consequences are entirely culturally determined. Stairs, for example, create a functional "impairment" for wheelchair users that ramps do not. Printed information accommodates the sighted but "limits" blind persons. Deafness is not a disabling condition in a community that communicates by signing as well as speaking.[3] People who cannot lift three hundred pounds are "able-bodied," whereas those who cannot lift fifty pounds are "disabled." More-over, such culturally generated and perpetuated standards as "beauty," "independence," "fitness," "competence," and "normalcy" exclude and disable many human bodies while validating and affirming others. Even though the law attempts to define disability in terms of function, the meanings attached to physical form and appearance constitute "limits" for many people—as evidenced, for example, by "ugly laws," some repealed as recently as 1974, that restricted visibly disabled people from public places.[4] Thus, the ways that bodies interact with the socially engineered environment and conform to social expectations determine the varying degrees of disability or able-bodiedness, of extra-ordinariness or ordinariness.

Consequently, the meanings attributed to extraordinary bodies reside not in inherent physical flaws, but in social relationships in which one group is legitimated by possessing valued physical characteristics and maintains its ascendancy and its self-identity by system-atically imposing the role of cultural or corporeal inferiority on others. Representation thus simultaneously buttresses an embodied version of normative identity and shapes a narrative of corporeal difference that excludes those whose bodies or behaviors do not conform. So by focusing on how representation creates the physically disabled figure in American culture, I will also clarify the corresponding figure of the normative American self so powerfully etched into our collective cultural consciousness. We will see that the disabled figure operates as the vividly embodied, stigmatized other whose social role is to symbolically free the privileged, idealized figure of the American self from the vagaries and vulnerabilities of embodiment.

One purpose of this chapter, then, is to probe the relations among social identi-ties—valued and devalued—outlined by our accepted hierarchies of embodiment. Cor-poreal departures from dominant expectations never go uninterpreted or unpunished, and conformities are almost always rewarded. The narrative of deviance surrounding bodies considered different is paralleled by a narrative of universality surrounding bodies that correspond to notions of the ordinary or the superlative. Cultural dichotomies do their evaluative work: this body is inferior and that one is superior; this one is beautiful or per-fect and that one is grotesque or ugly. In this economy of visual difference, those bodies deemed inferior become spectacles of otherness while the unmarked are sheltered in the neutral space of normalcy. Invested with meanings that far outstrip their biological bases, figures such as the cripple, the quadroon, the queer, the outsider, the whore are taxo-nomical, ideological products marked by socially determined stigmata, defined through representation, and excluded from social power and status. Thus, the cultural other and the cultural self operate together as opposing twin figures that legitimate a system of social, economic, and political empowerment justified by physiological differences.[5]

As I examine the disabled figure, I will also trouble the mutually constituting figure this study coins: the normate. This neologism names the veiled subject position of cultural self, the figure outlined by the array of deviant others whose marked bodies shore up the normate's boundaries.[6] The term *normate* usefully designates the social figure through which people can represent themselves as definitive human beings. Normate, then, is the constructed identity of those who, by way of the bodily configurations and cultural capital they assume, can step into a position of authority and wield the power it grants them. If one attempts to define the normate position by peeling away all the marked traits within the social order at this historical moment, what emerges is a very narrowly defined profile that describes only a minority of actual people. Erving Goffman, whose work I discuss in greater detail later, observes the logical conclusion of this phenomenon by noting wryly that there is "only one complete unblushing male in America: a young, married, white, urban, northern, heterosexual, Protestant father of college education, fully employed, of good complexion, weight and height, and a recent record in sports."[7] Interestingly, Goffman takes for granted that femaleness has no part in his sketch of a normative human being. Yet this image's ubiquity, power, and value resonate clearly. One testimony to the power of the normate subject position is that people often try to fit its description in the same way that Cinderella's stepsisters attempted to squeeze their feet into her glass slipper. Naming the figure of the normate is one conceptual strategy that will allow us to press our analyses beyond the simple dichotomies of male/female, white/black, straight/gay, or able-bodied/disabled so that we can examine the subtle interrelations among social identities that are anchored to physical differences.

The normate subject position emerges, however, only when we scrutinize the social processes and discourses that constitute physical and cultural otherness. Because figures of otherness are highly marked in power relations, even as they are marginalized, their cultural visibility as deviant obscures and neutralizes the normative figure that they legitimate. To analyze the operation of disability, it is essential then to theorize at length about the processes and assumptions that produce both the normate and its discordant companion figures.

The Disabled Figure in Literature

The discursive construct of the disabled figure, informed more by received attitudes than by people's actual experience of disability, circulates in culture and finds a home within the conventions and codes of literary representation. As Paul Robinson notes, "the disabled, like all minorities, have ... existed not as subjects of art, but merely as its occasions." Disabled literary characters usually remain on the margins of fiction as uncomplicated figures or exotic aliens whose bodily configurations operate as spectacles, eliciting responses from other characters or producing rhetorical effects that depend on disability's cultural resonance. Indeed, main characters almost never have physical disabilities. Even though mainstream critics have long discussed, for example, the implications of Twain's Jim for blacks, when literary critics look at disabled characters, they often interpret them metaphorically or aesthetically, reading them without political awareness as conventional elements of the sentimental, romantic, Gothic, or grotesque traditions.[8]

The disparity between "disabled" as an attributed, decontextualizing identity and the perceptions and experiences of real people living with disabilities suggests that this figure of otherness emerges from positioning, interpreting, and conferring meaning upon bodies. Representation yields cultural identities and categories, the given paradigms Alfred Schutz calls "recipes," with which we communally organize raw experience and routinize the world.[9] Literary conventions even further mediate experience that the wider cultural matrix, including literature itself, has already informed. If we accept the convention that fiction has some mimetic relation to life, we grant it power to further shape our perceptions of the world, especially regarding situations about which we have little direct knowledge. Because disability is so strongly stigmatized and is countered by so few mitigating narratives, the literary traffic in metaphors often misrepresents or flattens the experience real people have of their own or others' disabilities.

I therefore want to explicitly open up the gap between disabled people and their representations by exploring how disability operates in texts. The rhetorical effect of representing disability derives from social relations between people who assume the normate position and those who are assigned the disabled position. From folktales and classical myths to modern and postmodern "grotesques," the disabled body is almost always a freakish spectacle presented by the mediating narrative voice. Most disabled characters are enveloped by the otherness that their disability signals in the text. Take, as a few examples, Dickens's pathetic and romanticized Tiny Tim of *A Christmas Carol*, J. M. Barrie's villainous Captain Hook from *Peter Pan*, Victor Hugo's Gothic Quasimodo in *The Hunchback of Notre Dame*, D. H. Lawrence's impotent Clifford Chatterley in *Lady Chatterley's Lover*, and Tennessee Williams's long-suffering Laura Wingfield from *The Glass Menagerie*. The very act of representing corporeal otherness places them in a frame that highlights their differences from ostensibly normate readers. Although such representations refer to actual social relations, they do not of course reproduce those relations with mimetic fullness. Characters are thus necessarily rendered by a few determining strokes that create an illusion of reality far short of the intricate, undifferentiated, and uninterpreted context in which real people exist. Textual descriptions are overdetermined: they invest the traits, qualities, and behaviors of their characters with much rhetorical influence simply by omitting—and therefore erasing—other factors or traits that might mitigate or complicate the delineations. A disability functions only as visual difference that signals meanings. Consequently, literary texts necessarily make disabled characters into freaks, stripped of normalizing contexts and engulfed by a single stigmatic trait.

Not only is the relationship between text and world not exact, but representation also relies upon cultural assumptions to fill in missing details. All people construct interpretive schemata that make their worlds seem knowable and predictable, thus producing perceptual categories that may harden into stereotypes or caricatures when communally shared and culturally inculcated.[10] As Aristotle suggests in the *Poetics*, literary representation depends more on probability—what people take to be accurate—than on reality. Caricatures and stereotypical portrayals that depend more on gesture than complexity arise necessarily out of this gap between representation and life. Stereotypes in life become tropes in textual representation. For example, Marianna Torgovnick describes the trope of the primitive as a discursive construct in the broadest sense, a "world" that has been "structured by sets of images and ideas that have slipped from their original metaphoric status to control perceptions of [actual] primitives."[11] Such portrayals invoke, reiterate, and are reinforced by cultural stereotypes. A highly stigmatized characteristic like disability gains its rhetorical effectiveness from the powerful, often mixed responses that real disabled people elicit from readers who consider themselves normates. The more the literary portrayal conforms to the social stereotype, the more economical and intense is the effect; representation thus exaggerates an already highlighted physical difference. Moreover, Western tradition posits the visible world as the index of a coherent and just invisible world, encouraging us to read the material body as a sign invested with transcendent meaning. In interpreting the material world, literature tends to imbue any visual differences with significance that obscures the complexity of their bearers.

Besides stripping any normalizing context away from disability literary representation sets up static encounters between disabled figures and normate readers, whereas real social relations are always dynamic. Focusing on a body feature to describe a character throws the reader into a confrontation with the character that is predetermined by cultural notions about disability. With the notable exception of autobiographical texts, representation tends to objectify disabled characters by denying them any opportunity for subjectivity or agency. The plot or the work's rhetorical potential usually benefits from the disabled figure remaining other to the reader—identifiably human but resolutely different. How could Ahab operate effectively if the reader were allowed to see him as an ordinary fellow instead of as an icon of monomaniacal revenge—if his disability lost its transcendent meaning? What would happen to the pure pity generated for Tiny Tim if he were portrayed as sometimes naughty, like a "normal" child? Thus the rhetorical function of the highly charged trait fixes relations between disabled figures and their readers. If disabled characters acted, as real people with disabilities often do, to counter their stigmatized status, the rhetorical potency of the stigma would be mitigated or lost. If Hawthorne's Chillingworth made many friends, for instance, or appeared lovable to Hester, his role in *The Scarlet Letter* would be diminished. If Flannery O'Connor's Hulga Hopewell were pretty, cheerful, and one-legged instead of ugly and bitter, "Good Country People" would fail. So, like *tableaux vivants*, beauty pageants, and freak shows—all related forms of representation grounded in the conventions of spectacle—literary narratives of disability usually depend on the objectification of the spectacle that representation has created.

The Gap between Representation and Reality

Whether one lives with a disability or encounters someone who has one, the actual experience of disability is more complex and more dynamic than representation usually suggests. Just one example illustrates the skill disabled people often must learn in managing social encounters. Initial or casual exchanges between normate and disabled people differ markedly from the usual relations between readers and disabled characters. In a first encounter with another person, a tremendous amount of information must be organized and interpreted simultaneously: each participant probes the explicit for the implicit, determines what is significant for particular purposes, and prepares a response that is guided by many cues, both subtle and obvious. When one person has a visible disability, however, it almost always dominates and skews the normate's process of sorting out perceptions and forming a reaction.[12] The interaction is usually strained because the nondisabled person may feel fear, pity, fascination, repulsion, or merely surprise, none of which is expressible according to social protocol. Besides the discomforting dissonance between experienced and expressed reaction, a nondisabled person often does not know how to act toward a disabled person: how or whether to offer assistance; whether to acknowledge the disability; what words, gestures, or expectations to use or avoid. Perhaps most destructive to the potential for continuing relations is the normate's frequent assumption that a disability cancels out other qualities, reducing the complex person to a single attribute. This uncertainty and discord make the encounter especially stressful for the nondisabled person unaccustomed to disabled people. The disabled person may be anxious about whether the encounter will be too uncomfortable for either of them to sustain and may feel the ever-present threat of rejection. Even though disability threatens to snap the slender thread of sociability, most physically disabled people are skilled enough in these encounters to repair the fabric of the relation so that it can continue.

To be granted fully human status by normates, disabled people must learn to manage relationships from the beginning. In other words, disabled people must use charm, intimidation, ardor, deference, humor, or entertainment to relieve nondisabled people of their discomfort. Those of us with disabilities are supplicants and minstrels, striving to create valued representations of ourselves in our relations with the nondisabled majority. This is precisely what many newly disabled people can neither do nor accept; it is a subtle part of adjustment and often the most difficult.[13] If such efforts at reparation are successful, disabled people neutralize the initial stigma of disability so that relationships can be sustained and deepened. Only then can other aspects of personhood emerge and expand the initial focus so that the relationship becomes more comfortable, more broadly based, and less affected by the disability. Only then can each person emerge as multifaceted, whole. If, however, disabled people pursue normalization too much, they risk denying limitations and pain for the comfort of others and may edge into the self-betrayal associated with "passing."

This is not to suggest that all forms of disability are interchangeable or that all disabled people experience their bodies or negotiate their identities in the same ways. Indeed, it is precisely the variation among individuals that cultural categories trivialize and that representation often distorts. Disability is an overarching and in some ways artificial category that encompasses congenital and acquired physical differences, mental illness and retardation, chronic and acute illnesses, fatal and progressive diseases, temporary and permanent injuries, and a wide range of bodily characteristics considered disfiguring, such as scars, birthmarks, unusual proportions, or obesity. Even though the prototypical disabled person posited in cultural representations never leaves a wheelchair, is totally blind, or profoundly deaf, most of the approximately forty million Americans with disabilities have a much more ambiguous relationship to the label. The physical impairments that render someone "disabled" are almost never absolute or static; they are dynamic, contingent conditions affected by many external factors and usually fluctuate over time. Some conditions, like multiple sclerosis or arthritis, are progressive and chronic; others, such as epilepsy can be acute. Even seemingly static disabilities like amputation affect activities differently, depending on the condition of the rest of the body.

Of course, everyone is subject to the gradually disabling process of aging. The fact that we will all become disabled if we live long enough is a reality many people who consider themselves able-bodied are reluctant to admit.[14] As physical abilities change, so do individual needs, and the perception of those needs. The pain that often accompanies or causes disability also influences both the degree and the perception of impairment. According to Elaine Scarry, because pain is invisible, unverifiable, and unrepresentable, it is often subject to misattribution or denial by those who are not experiencing it.[15] Disability, then, can be painful, comfortable, familiar, alienating, bonding, isolating, disturbing, endearing, challenging, infuriating, or ordinary. Embedded in the complexity of actual human relations, it is always more than the disabled figure can signify.

That anyone can become disabled at any time makes disability more fluid, and perhaps more threatening, to those who identify themselves as normates than such seemingly more stable marginal identities as femaleness, blackness, or nondominant ethnic identities.[16] In addition, the time and way in which one becomes disabled influence its perception, as do the ways one incorporates disability into one's sense of self or resists it. For instance, the gradual disablement of aging or a progressive illness may not be considered a disability at all. In contrast, a severe, sudden impairment, as from an accident, is almost always experienced as a greater loss than is a congenital or gradual disability which does not demand adjustment so abruptly. A disability's degree of visibility also affects social relations. An invisible disability much like a homosexual identity always presents the dilemma of whether or when to come out or to pass. One must always anticipate the risk of tainting a new relationship by announcing an invisible impairment or the equal hazard of surprising someone by revealing a previously undisclosed disability. The distinction between formal and functional aspects of a disability affects its perception as well. People whose disability is primarily functional but not visible often are accused of malingering or of disappointing expectations about their physical capabilities. Yet those whose disabilities are largely formal often are considered incapable of things they can easily do. Furthermore, formal conditions such as facial disfigurement, scarring, birthmarks, obesity, and visual or hearing impairments corrected with mechanical aids are usually socially disabling, even though they entail almost no physical dysfunction. Moreover, no firm distinction exists between primarily formal disabilities and racial physical features considered atypical by dominant, white standards.

Although categories such as ethnicity, race, and gender are based on shared traits that result in community formation, disabled people seldom consider themselves a group. Little somatic commonality exists among people with different kinds of disabilities because needs and situations are so diverse. A blind person, an epileptic, a paraplegic, a deaf person, and an amputee, for example, have no shared cultural heritage, traditional activities, or common physical experience. Only the shared experience of stigmatization creates commonality. Having been acculturated similarly to everyone else, disabled people also often avoid and stereotype one another in attempting to normalize their own social identities. Moreover, many disabled people at one time considered themselves nondisabled and may have had very limited contact with disabled people before joining their group. As with all culturally imposed categories extrapolated from biological differences, the identity has a forced quality that levels intragroup variations. For example, the now crumbling institution of "special" education enacts this cultural impulse toward ghettoization by segregating people with disabilities from nondisabled students regardless of individual needs. Finally most disabled people are surrounded by nondisabled families and communities in which disabilities are unanticipated and almost always perceived as calamitous. Unlike the ethnically grouped, but more like gays and lesbians, disabled people are sometimes fundamentally isolated from each other, existing often as aliens within their social units.[17]

Yet representation frequently obscures these complexities in favor of the rhetorical or symbolic potential of the prototypical disabled figure, who often functions as a lightning rod for the pity, fear, discomfort, guilt, or sense of normalcy of the reader or a more significant character. I intend here to shift from this usual interpretive framework of aesthetics and metaphor to the critical arena of cultural studies to denaturalize such representations. By examining the "disabled figure," rather than discussing the "grotesque" or "cripple" or "deformed," I hope to catapult this analysis out of a purely aesthetic context and into a political one. By opening up a critical gap between disabled figures as fashioned corporeal others whose bodies carry social meaning and actual people with atypical bodies in real-world social relations, I suggest that representation informs the identity—and often the fate—of real people with extraordinary bodies.

Endnotes

1   For example, two recent books that analyze "race" and "gender," respectively, as historical, ideological constructions legitimated by physical differences are Thomas Laqueur, *Making Sex: Body and Gender from the Greeks to Freud* (Cambridge: Harvard University Press, 1990), and Kwame Anthony Appiah, *In My Father's House* (New York: Oxford University Press, 1992), an exploration of "the idea of the Negro, the idea of an African race" (p. x). Disability has been acknowledged in American studies by Douglas C. Baynton's study of the metaphorical construction of deafness in the nineteenth century, "A Silent Exile on This Earth: The Metaphorical Construction of Deafness in the Nineteenth Century" in *American Quarterly* 44 (2): 216–43; by David A. Gerber, "Heroes and Misfits: The Troubled Social Reintegration of Disabled Veterans in *The Best Years of Our Lives*" in *American Quarterly* 46 (1994): 545–74; and by Martin Norden in *The Cinema of Isolation: A History of Physical Disability in the Movies* (New Brunswick, N.J.: Rutgers University Press, 1994). Disability studies is a recognized and articulated subfield of sociology that tends to emphasize medical anthropology, social policy, and rehabilitative medicine, although the voices of cultural critics are emerging here as well. Several important studies of the social, political, and legal history of disabled people treat disability as a social construction; for example, see Deborah Stone, *The Disabled State* (Philadelphia: Temple University Press, 1984); Richard Scotch, *From Good Will to Civil Rights: Transforming Federal Disability Policy* (Philadelphia: Temple University Press, 1984); Nora Groce, *Everyone Here Spoke Sign Language: Hereditary Deafness on Martha's Vineyard* (Cambridge: Harvard University Press, 1985); Stephen Ainlay et al., eds., *The Dilemma of Difference: A Multidisciplinary View of Stigma* (New York: Plenum Press, 1986); Robert Bogdan, *Freak Show: Presenting Human Oddities for Amusement and Profit* (Chicago: University of Chicago Press, 1988); David Hevey, *The Creatures That Time Forgot: Photography and Disability Imagery* (New York: Routledge, 1992); Claire Liachowitz, *Disability as a Social Construct: Legislative Roots* (Philadelphia: University of Pennsylvania Press, 1988); Iris Marion Young, *Justice and the Politics of Difference* (Princeton: Princeton University Press, 1990): Martha Minow, *Making All the Difference: Inclusion, Exclusion, and American Law* (Ithaca: Cornell University Press, 1990); Robert Murphy, *The Body Silent* (New York: Holt, 1987); Lennard J. Davis, *Enforcing*

Normalcy: Disability, Deafness, and the Body (New York: Verso, 1995); and Joseph Shapiro, *No Pity: People with Disabilities Forging a New Civil Rights Movement* (New York: Times Books/Random House, 1993). Many theorists and historians come close to confronting disability as a cultural product, but they do not question the category, perhaps because disability is so widely naturalized in Western culture. This omission has motivated my own study. See, for example, Michel Foucault, *Birth of the Clinic: An Archaeology of Medical Perception*, trans. A. M. Sheridan-Smith (New York: Pantheon, 1973); Mary Douglas, *Purity and Danger: An Analysis of Concepts of Pollution and Taboo* (New York: Praeger, 1966); Geoffrey Galt Harpham, *On the Grotesque: Strategies of Contradiction in Art and Literature* (Princeton: Princeton University Press, 1982); and David Rothman, *The Discovery of the Asylum: Social Order and Disorder in the New Republic* (Boston: Little, Brown, 1971).

2   U.S. Congress, The Americans with Disabilities Act of 1989, 101st Cong., 1st sess., S. Res. 933 (Washington, DC: GPO, 1989), p. 6.

3   See Nora Groce's study of the prevalence of hereditary deafness on Martha's Vineyard (*Everyone Here Spoke Sign Language*).

4   Marcia Pearce Burgdorf and Robert Burgdorf Jr., "A History of Unequal Treatment: The Qualifications of Handicapped Persons as a 'Suspect Class' under the Equal Protection Clause," *Santa Clara Lawyer* 15 (1975): 863.

5   My repeated use of the term "figure" is meant to indicate an important distinction between actual people with disabilities and the subject positions "disabled" and "able-bodied" that culture assigns and that must be negotiated in lives and relationships. As products of cultural representation, figures reveal attitudes and assumptions about disability that make up the ideological environment. As I suggest later, there is always a gap between the subjective experience and the cultural identity of having a disability, between any actual life and any imposed social category. From this gap arises the alienation and sense of oppression with which people labeled as different must contend. It should be clear that this study focuses on the representations of disability that yield stigmatized collective identities, not the histories of actual people who have physical disabilities.

6   This term was suggested in jest by my colleague, the sociologist Daryl Evans, in an informal talk given at the 1989 Society for Disability Studies Annual Conference in Denver.

7   Erving Goffman, *Stigma: Notes on the Management of Spoiled Identity* (Englewood Cliffs, N.J.: Prentice-Hall, 1963), p. 128.

8   Paul Robinson, "Responses to Leslie Fiedler," *Salmagundi* 57 (Fall 1982): 78. For an example of disability analyzed as an apolitical metaphor, see Peter Hays, *The Limping Hero: Grotesques in Literature* (New York: New York University Press, 1971).

9   Schutz is quoted in Ainlay et al., eds., *The Dilemma of Difference*, p. 20.

10 Ainlay et al., eds., *The Dilemma of Difference*, p. 20; Sander Gilman, *Difference and Pathology: Stereotypes of Sexuality, Race, and Madness* (Ithaca: Cornell University Press, 1985), p. 16.

11 Marianna Torgovnick's discussion of Homer's Polyphemus as one of the earliest Western tropes of primitivist discourse is suggestive here (*Gone Primitive: Savage Intellects, Modern Lives* [Chicago: University of Chicago Press, 1990], p. 8). According to Torgovnick, Odysseus becomes a kind of founding father of ethnography by reading the Cyclops's otherness as uncivilized and savage. Grounded in physiognomy, Polyphemus's otherness is figured as the monstrous state of being cycloptic (cycloptic fetuses are always stillborn). Torgovnick does not note that Polyphemus's aberrant physical form, not simply his foreignness, determines his otherness. In fact, this visible physical stigma is perhaps the most salient feature of the story. Moreover, Polyphemus's treatment by Odysseus seems to be justified because the Cyclops is inhuman, and he is inhuman because he is physically different from Odysseus. I would add to Torgovnick's observation, then, that the representation of Polyphemus can also be read as an early and definitive instance of physical disability as a sign of inhumanness.

12 Because most disabilities in literature are necessarily manifest, I discuss here visible disabilities. However, hidden disabilities present somewhat different and in some ways more stressful social encounters. The person with the disability controls the exposure of the disability in order to avoid undue surprise. Furthermore, a nondisabled person may reveal prejudices or expectations before he or she is aware of the disability, making both people feel uncomfortable later. A hidden disability simply introduces more unpredictability into an encounter. Sometimes a person will actually announce a hidden disability to avoid this uncertainty. For a discussion of interactions between the disabled and nondisabled, see Fred Davis, "Deviance Disavowal: The Management of Strained Interaction by the Visibly Handicapped," *Social Problems* 9 (1961): 120–32.

13 Murphy, *The Body Silent*, chapters 4 and 5.

14 A term that has much currency in the disability rights movement brings this point home nicely: people who consider themselves to be nondisabled are often called TABS, an acronym that stands for the label "temporarily able-bodied."

15 Elaine Scarry, *The Body in Pain: The Making and Unmaking of the World* (New York: Oxford University Press, 1985), pp. 3–10.

16 The cultural propensity to further mark and bound such classifications testifies to their fluidity and socially constructed character. Miscegenation laws, legal definitions of slaves, laws that defined disability for economic assistance, gendered dress codes, and customs such as branding slaves, criminals, and paupers erect boundaries around social categories in order to maintain and enforce distinctions purported to inhere in the body. The yellow star and the scarlet letter are familiar socially mandated marks of deviance that witness the need to absolutely mark what is in fact biologically unstable.

17 The important exceptions to this generalized portrayal of disabled people's situations are the communities that arise from institutionalization. Like ethnic ghettoes, these communities are often sites of both solidarity and exclusion. Deaf schools and their surrounding communities, based on common language, seem to function more like ethnic communities in building positive identities and self-concepts. Perhaps this is due to the difference between the profound isolation deaf signers experience in a speaking population and the contrasting opportunities available in a community of signers. For discussions of disability communities, see Irving Kenneth Zola, *Missing Pieces: A Chronicle of Living with a Disability* (Philadelphia: Temple University Press, 1982); Oliver Sacks, *Seeing Voices: A Journey into the World of the Deaf* (Berkeley: University of California Press, 1989); Tom Humphreys and Carol Paden, *Deaf in America: Voices from a Culture* (Cambridge: Harvard University Press, 1998).

References

Ainlay, Stephen, Gaylene Becker, and Lerita M. Coleman (Eds.). (1986). *The Dilemma of Difference: A Multidisciplinary View of Stigma*. New York: Plenum Press.

Appiah, Kwame Anthony. (1992). *In My Father's House*. New York: Oxford University Press.

Aristotle. (1971). "The Poetics." In Hazard Adams, ed., *Critical Theory Since Plato*. New York: Harcourt Brace Jovanovich. 48–66.

Baynton, Douglas C. (1994). "A Silent Exile on This Earth: The Metaphorical Construction of Deafness in the Nineteenth Century." *American Quarterly* 46 (2): 216–43.

Bogdan, Robert. (1988). *Freak Show: Presenting Human Oddities for Amusement and Profit*. Chicago: University of Chicago Press.

Burgdorf, Marcia Pearce and Robert Burgdorf Jr. (1975). "A History of Unequal Treatment: The Qualifications of Handicapped Persons as a 'Suspect Class' under the Equal Protection Clause," *Santa Clara Lawyer* 15: 855–910.

David, Fred. (1961). "Deviance Disavowal: The Management of Strained Interaction by the Visibly Handicapped." *Social Problems* 9: 120–32.

Davis, Lennard J. (1995). *Enforcing Normalcy: Disability, Deafness, and the Body*. New York: Verso.

Davis, Lennard J. (1996). *The Disability Studies Reader*. New York: Routledge.

Douglas, Mary. (1966). *Purity and Danger: An Analysis of Concepts of Pollution and Taboo*. New York: Praeger.

Foucault, Michel. (1973). *The Birth of the Clinic: An Archaeology of Medical Perception*. A. M. Sheridan (trans.). New York: Pantheon.

Gerber, David. (1994). "Heroes and Misfits: The Troubled Social Reintegration of Disabled Veterans in *The Best Years of Our Lives*." *American Quarterly* (46): 545–74.

Gilman, Sander. (1985). *Difference and Pathology: Stereotypes of Sexuality, Race, and Madness*. Ithaca: Cornell University Press.

Goffman, Erving. (1963). *Stigma: Notes on the Management of a Spoiled Identity*. Englewood Cliffs, N.J.: Prentice Hall.

Groce, Nora. (1985). *Everyone Here Spoke Sign Language: Hereditary Deafness on Martha's Vineyard*. Cambridge: Harvard University Press.

Harpham, Geoffrey Galt. (1982). *On the Grotesque: Strategies of Contradiction in Art and Literature.* Princeton: Princeton University Press.

Hevey, David. (1992). *The Creatures That Time Forgot: Photography and Disability Imagery.* New York: Routledge.

Humphreys, Tom and Carol Paden. (1988). *Deaf in America: Voices from a Culture.* Cambridge: Harvard University Press.

Laqueur, Thomas. (1990). *Making Sex: Body and Gender from the Greeks to Freud.* Cambridge: Harvard University Press.

Liachowitz, Claire. (1988). *Disability as a Social Construct: Legislative Roots.* Philadelphia: University of Pennsylvania Press.

Minow, Martha. (1990). *Making All the Difference: Inclusion, Exclusion, and American Law.* Ithaca: Cornell University Press.

Murphy, Robert. (1987). *The Body Silent.* New York: Holt.

Norden, Martin. (1994). *The Cinema of Isolation: A History of Physical Disability in the Movies.* New Brunswick, N.J.: Rutgers University Press.

Robinson, Paul. (1982). "Responses to Leslie Fiedler." *Salmagundi* 57: 74–78.

Rothman, David. (1971). *On the Discovery of the Asylum: Social Order and Disorder in the New Republic.* Boston: Little, Brown.

Sacks, Oliver. (1989). *Seeing Voices: A Journey into the World of the Deaf.* Berkeley: University of California Press.

Scarry, Elaine. (1985). *The Body in Pain: The Making and Unmaking of the World.* New York: Oxford University Press.

Scotch, Richard. (1984). *From Good Will to Civil Rights: Transforming Federal Disability Policy.* Philadelphia: Temple University Press.

Shapiro, Joseph. (1993). *No Pity: People with Disabilities Forging a New Civil Rights Movement.* New York: Time Books/Random House.

Stone, Deborah. (1984). *The Disabled State.* Philadelphia: Temple University Press.

Torgovnick, Marianna. (1990). *Gone Primitive: Savage Intellects, Modern Lives.* Chicago: University of Chicago Press.

U.S. Congress. The Americans with Disabilities Act of 1989, 101st Cong., 1st sess., S. Res. 933 (Washington, DC: GPO, 1989).

Young, Iris Marion. (1990). *Justice and the Politics of Difference.* Princeton: Princeton University Press.

Zola, Irving Kenneth. (1982). *Missing Pieces: A Chronicle of Living with a Disability.* Philadelphia: Temple University Press.

CHAPTER 5

"Difference in Itself":

Validating Disabled People's Lived Experience

James Overboe

Massumi (1993: 23) argues that each person has a limited range of characteristics that he or she broadcasts through his or her body which then is either visually or aurally received by others. These aural or visual images are filtered through the receiver's preconceived categories of identity. Thus the body is a medium that helps people define each other's identity.

I believe that these preconceived categories of identity devalue both a disabled embodiment and sensibility. For example, Adrienne Asch (1976: 28) argues that disability is not part of her self-definition or "lived experience," but it is the basis of most other people's definition of her. Therefore I call for the validation of disabled people[1] by recognizing their lived experience. In this article I begin by examining Leder's (1990) distinction between a *korper* (categorization) and a *leib* (lived experience) consideration of the body.

Within the realm of the hyperreal world I next illustrate how a korper interpretation of the body continues to devalue the experience of disability. My analysis of a play called *Creeps* demonstrates that for the audience a simulation of disability was "more real than real" and was given precedence over the "lived experience" of disability. Sobchack's (1995) experience of using a prosthesis and Clark's (1995) observations about media representations of embodiment illustrate how the techno-body and cyberbody of the hyperreal world continue to negate a disabled embodiment by relying upon residual ableist interpretations of what is acceptable and visually desirable in contemporary bodies. I next examine how Deleuze's (1994) concept of "difference for itself" could validate the lived experience of disabled people.

A Korper or Leib Interpretation of Embodiment

The notion of a distinction between leib and korper interpretation of embodiment originates in works in phenomenology and physical anthropology. Physical anthropologist Gehlen (1988: 252) believes the korper body exists independent of its surroundings while the leib is the aspect of the body which interacts with its surroundings. Phenomenologist Maurice Merleau-Ponty (1962: 283) believes that the korper interpretation of the body reduces it to an organism that merely exists. The leib interpretation of the body comprehends the body as a knowing essence with a soul.

Similarly, Leder (1990) maintains that a korper interpretation of the body reduces it to a classification, whereas a leib interpretation considers the body to be an entity which experiences itself and its environment. According to Leder (1990: 5), since the time of Descartes people have interpreted the body as korper rather than leib, which has resulted in a rationalization that views the physical body only as an object to be classified like any other thing. Leder (1990: 6) equates a lived body with an embodied self that lives and breathes, perceives and acts, speaks and reasons. For Leder (1990: 6) the korper body is an aspect of the leib bodily experience.

The Korper Interpretation of the Disabled Body

I agree with Leder who argues that the body should be interpreted as a lived experience.[2] Nevertheless, the korper interpretation of body is the norm as it lends itself easily to demarcating categories of identity. For example, the identity of disabled people who experience cerebral palsy is reduced to their appearance that is, according to Young (1990: 124), the antithesis of the controlled being associated with rationality, linearity, productivity and normality.

Generally speaking, the devaluation of disabled people's lived experiences has a long history. Lennard Davis (1997: 1) writes, "People with disabilities have been isolated, incarcerated, observed, written about, operated on, instructed, implanted, regulated, treated, institutionalized, and controlled to a degree probably unequal to that experienced by any other minority group." Thus, our lived experiences are reduced to a classification or korper reading which demands that the able-bodied take some sort of action that implicitly or explicitly controls our lives.

Theorists concerned with disability (Bedini, 1991: 62; Keith, 1996: 71–2; Lonsdale, 1990: 95; Morris, 1991: 35; Wendell, 1996: 60–1) assert that most non-disabled people feel disabled people symbolize, among other things, imperfection, failure to control the body and everyone's vulnerability to weakness, pain and death. So pervasive are these projected ableist attitudes that many disabled people also internalize them and replicate a scale of disabilities. Wendell (1989: 116) points out that some people have transformed their disability from a perceived detriment to cultural capital by becoming "disabled heroes."

Wendell (1989: 116–17) believes, "While disabled heroes can be inspiring and heartening to the disabled, they may give the able-bodied the false impression that anyone can 'overcome' a disability." Paradoxically, the image of the disabled hero validates the lived experience of a few disabled people and invalidates the lived experience of the majority of disabled people because they cannot meet such expectations. I would agree with Michael Oliver (1990: 91) who writes, "Throughout the twentieth century ... disabled people continue to be portrayed as more than or less than human, rarely as ordinary people doing ordinary things."

Baudrillard's Simulation:
Through Foucault the Broadcasting of the Korper Disabled Body

A few years ago I was a technical adviser for the play called *Creeps*,[3] which focused on the problems faced by institutionalized disabled people. This play illustrates both Foucault's concept of disciplining of the body and Baudrillard's concept of simulation. In Foucauldian terms, through functional, continuous and hierarchical surveillance (Foucault, 1984: 192), Tom McCamus, who played a person with cerebral palsy, had to discipline his body in order for him to mirror the spasms that are inherent in people who experience spastic cerebral palsy. For Tom these disciplining techniques became all-encompassing and pervasive as they permeated his body and caused him to experience pain which, ironically, is similar to that felt by many disabled people as they contort their bodies in an attempt to appear normal.

Often audience members stated that they had a better appreciation of cerebral palsy because of the play. At first I thought this was only natural as the play concentrated on the discrimination against disabled people. However, these same people always remarked on Tom's disabled/non-disabled persona. Both Tom and I felt others were losing a sense of us as individuals in their appreciation of this simulated disabled/non-disabled persona.

For Baudrillard (1988: 20–1) appearance is the only thing that matters in the realm of hyperreality. In short, the concept of representation is no more, it's been replaced by simulation that is reality. Baudrillard (1988: 16) asserts that in the era of hyperreality we no longer exist as playwrights or actors on the world's stage, but as terminals of multiple networks. Tom was no longer an actor on stage portraying a person who experiences cerebral palsy. He had become a terminal that broadcast disabled and non-disabled networks. Tom's simulation had become "more real" than "real."

Tom had become a vulnerable, non-threatening person who had the strength to overcome any (imagined? or real? perhaps simulated?) disability. Agreeing with Linda William, Norden (1994: 6) believes that disabled people embody the paradoxical objectification of being both an object of desire and an object of horror for non-disabled people. Whenever the audience found his disability repugnant or grotesque they easily perceived Tom as having a non-disabled identity.

Within the hyperreal world the audience "desires" the exotic, but only if such observations take place in an environment that is safe for them. For example, in his discussion about the San Diego Zoo, Umberto Eco (1983: 51) argues that in the world of hyperreality one can witness savagery in a fabricated jungle setting while still feeling safe and secure.

In the same manner, I argue that the audience with an able-bodied sensibility satisfies their "desire" for the exotic "disabled" by witnessing the simultaneous "absolutely fake but real" spectacle of Tom's wild and savage disability within a safe environment. They could be immersed in the experience of disability and feel the heightened titillation of the exotic without risk. To speak with disabled people the audience risks having to confront their own fear of disability as it manifests itself in our experience.

77

I believe that the audience's reaction to both Tom and his performance typifies what Derrida calls:

> ... the theological stage [that] comports a passive seated public, a public of spectators, of consumers, of "enjoyers" ... attending a production that lacks true volume or depth, a production that is level, offered to voyeuristic scrutiny. But what is this God who not only controls the audience but is also simultaneously "nowhere" and "everywhere"? (Derrida, 1978: 235)

The audience that attended the play *Creeps*, in Derridean terms, "defers" (perhaps unwittingly and without awareness) to an able-bodied sensibility. This non-disabled sensibility in fact is a "God" that is both "everywhere" and "nowhere," it is so pervasive that it permeates every pore of their being and in doing so is "naturalized" and "normalized."

The Continuation of the Negation of a Disabled Presence in the Techno/Cyber World

Baudrillard (1988) predicts that disabled people and their sensibilities will have a pivotal role in this hyperreal world. Baudrillard writes,

> Such are the blind, and the handicapped; mutant figures, because mutilated and hence closer to commutation, closer to this telepathic, telecommunicational universe than we others: humans all-too-human, condemned by our lack of disabilities to conventional forms of work.
>
> By the force of circumstance the disabled person is a potential expert in the motor or sensorial domain. And it is not by chance that the social is aligning itself more and more with the handicapped, and their operational advancement: they can become wonderful instruments because of their handicap. They may precede us on the path towards mutation and dehumanization.

While I admire his intent I feel Baudrillard's position is marred by his negation of disabled people's presence, bodies and their flesh.

Vivian Sobchack (1995), who is disabled, makes some interesting observations about embodiment and flesh within our techno-body world. At first she is enamoured by her prosthetic which is aesthetically pleasing with its lack of cellulite. Sobchack (1995: 208) admits, "The truth of the matter is that I feel more, not less, attractive than I used to. Hard body (however partial) that I am, I feel more erotically distracting and distracted than I have in years."

Although Sobchack (1995) celebrates her prosthesis she understands that it must be incorporated into her embodiment. While she realizes the limits of both her flesh and her prosthetic Sobchack gives preference to her flesh over her prosthetic tool. Sobchack (1995: 213) writes:

> Living—rather than writing or thinking—my "newly extended body of technological engagement," I find the fragility of my flesh significantly precious. While I am deeply grateful for the motility my prosthetic affords me (however much in a transformation that is perceptually reduced as well as amplified), the new leg is dependent finally upon my last leg. Without my lived-body to live it, the prosthetic exists as part of a body without organs—techno-body that has no sympathy for human suffering, cannot understand human pleasure and, since it has no conception of death, cannot possibly value life.

Ironically, her prosthetic allowed Sobchack (1995) to conform more closely to an embodiment and mobility that has become normalized as the prototype for what is human. But this prosthetic solution that offered her "normalization" proved unsatisfactory for Sobchack because it failed to meet the requirements of her lived experience.

Many advocates of the cyberworld contend that the future seamless post-human body of the cyborg will be free from oppression. Thus cyberworld bodily differences are situated knowledges located as sites on the equal textual plane of postmodernity (Caddick, 1995: 159). Caddick (1995: 159–61) points out these situated knowledges—such as body-image— are not equal sites on the playing field because these new technologies are concerned only with the surface of the body (in essence its image) and negate its visceral depth. Caddick (1995) contends that the difference between the ugliness and beauty is not diminished but heightened by a greater fetishism of a particular body—the body beautiful.

Similarly, Nigel Clark (1995) argues that the notion that we are on the verge of a new age society is premature because the cyberworld relies on prior beliefs about what constitutes desirable bodies. Clark (1995: 125) argues that "the focus of contemporary digital body construction seems to lie neither in an unembellished 'naturalism' nor in the unconstrained mutability of forms." Instead digital body construction defers to the past by resurrecting images of dead film stars such as Marilyn Monroe, James Dean and Elvis Presley.

Yet these spectacular digital bodies prove inadequate for this cyberworld and have been eclipsed by a constellation of still more spectacular bodies epitomized by the steroid and silicon enhanced physiques of human actors (Clark, 1995: 125). Clark (1995: 126) adds, "What we seem to be dealing with here is not the ultimate in cybernetic bodies, but a recursive corporeality which arises out of the transition from one generation of mediated affects to another." With its emphasis on "spectacular bodies" this new generation of mediated affects continues the devaluation of disabled bodies. Thus, the oppression of disabled people extends from the analogue period to this post-analogue period.

Difference in Itself and Repetition in Itself

Baudrillard (1988) and Deleuze (1994) both use the term "dehumanization" to denote a shift to the hyperreal or cyberworld. However, the term "dehumanization" has often been evoked as a justification for the eradication of disabled people. For example, the government of Nazi Germany began the annihilation of disabled people by socially constructing their dehumanization (Proctor, 1995). More recently, under the auspice of "caring for his child," Robert Latimer argued successfully that he was justified in killing his disabled daughter because her existence was "less than human."[4]

In spite of my reservations I agree with both Baudrillard (1988) and Deleuze (1994) in their rejection of the restrictive aspects of humanity. Perhaps one could escape the shackles of this restrictive humanism by incorporating the sensibility of disability as it manifests itself in the lived experience of disability. Kroker and Kroker (1997: 24) have argued that the postmodern body is not as unsettling for women because their bodies have often been reduced to visual texts. In the same manner I argue that the notion of simulacra or "difference in itself" has been an unrecognized part of disabled people's existence. Deleuze (1994: 262) argues that difference has been thought of solely in terms of representation: identity in the concept; opposition in the predicate; analogy in judgement; and resemblance in perception.

Identity of the concept derives from the formation of the thinking subject which desires through memory, recognition and self-consciousness not only to make common sense of the world but to tame it. From the perspective of disabled people "identity in concept" has meant the negation of a disabled presence. The desire to tame the world points to an extreme independent liberalism that negates the lived experience of many disabled people who are interdependent on others. This exclusion of disabled people can be traced to the fact that dependency has been, and continues to be, devalued and attributed to persons perceived as inadequate (Siegal, 1988: 113–14).

Cheryl Wade (1994) argues this emphasis on independence created a new image for disabled people—the able-disabled. Wade (1994: 35) writes, "What was missing in the political identity, able–disabled crip identity was a true esteeming of the Cripple body." Agreeing with Wade, De Felice notes:

> The disabled movement has purchased political visibility at the price of physical invisibility. The cripple and the lame had bodies, but the handicapped, or so the social workers say, are just a little late at the starting gate. I don't like that; it's banal. When we speak in metaphorical terms we deny physical reality. The further we get from our bodies the further we get from the body politic. (De Felice, 1986: 13)

The rhetoric of equality of rights is a cornerstone of identity politics movements with its liberal individualistic embodiment. By arguing that disabled people must demand equality of rights for themselves, supporters of "equality of rights" deny the "lived experience" of disabled people. For example, Bickenbach (1993: 163) argues that disabled people may have the "equal right" to enter government offices, but if these offices are not accessible then many of us cannot exercise our "equal rights." The obtaining of equal rights that maintains the systemic discrimination against disabled people does not resolve problems for us. It only exacerbates them.

In respect of "identity in concept" Deleuze (1994: 266) writes, "To restore difference in thought is to untie this first knot which consists of representing difference through the identity of the concept and the thinking subject." Applying Deleuze's insights to disability I believe that by untying this knot that garrottes our lived experience and imposes an identity on us, we can begin to rid ourselves of the twin concepts of ableism and extreme liberal individualism that often lead others to see us as an abomination.

Rather than an "equality of rights" based on identity politics, I call for an "equality of condition" that validates both a disabled embodiment and sensibility. Our physical, mental and emotional manifestations of disability as well as the social, political, moral and physical environment will continue to have an impact upon us. But shifting the notion of an identity which is devalued to a lived experience that is validated causes a change in approach.

No longer would we be "done to," and "done for," or even "done with" as so often within non-disabled and extreme liberal individualism parameters and with the restrictions of an ableist sensibility. The shedding of the illusion of identity allows for our "lived experience" to come to the forefront. Thus our "lived experience" would be an integral part of the atmosphere and tone for any change within our lives and our interaction with others, whether they be disabled or non-disabled.

The second concept is the subordination of difference to resemblance. Deleuze (1994: 266) believes that "difference" necessarily tends to be cancelled in the quality of the concept which covers it, while at the same time inequality tends to be equalized within the extension in which it is distributed. Thus "difference" that reveals itself in the embodiment and sensibility of disabled people is cancelled (as the prefix "dis" designates) in favour of an able-bodied corporeality and "common" sense.

When we overcome our disabilities, as in the case of "disabled heroes" (Wendell, 1989: 116), we necessarily feed back into this loop by not validating our previous sensibility and by accepting the great equalizer—normality, the benchmark for humanity. I believe that the term "person with a disability" demonstrates and is underscored by a "normative" resemblance that we can attain if we achieve the status of being deemed "people first" (with the term's emphasis on independence and extreme liberal individualism) in the eyes of an ableist-centred society.

But our negation or inequality is equalized and extended because other disabled people fail to meet normative expectations and are deemed "damaged goods" (Bauman, 1988). For those disabled people who fail to achieve this status there is a legitimization of their position because of the fairness of distribution. One has failed because one does not meet the legitimized basic standards required for acceptance into the "people first" circle. The decision is not based on a discrimination against this particular person but a matter of "objective fact."

The "naturalness" of the notion of the able-bodied liberal individual coupled with the negation of a disabled sensibility makes many disabled people queue for the chance to be anointed as "people first," while simultaneously disavowing their previous embodied positions as "gimps" and "cripples." Ironically, disabled people who achieve "people first" status are not achieving full normative status but are only legitimizing an able-bodied resemblance through their desire for normality. Moreover, they reinforce an extension of the legitimacy of this resemblance by validating a continuum of disabled persons ranging from the successful "people first" to the pitiful "gimps" and "cripples" who are deemed worthless failures.

To facilitate a notion of "difference" that validates a disabled embodiment as well as a disabled sensibility I prefer the term "disabled persons" because it implies that their disabilities not only inform their lives but may also be a positive factor in many aspects of their lives. Employing the term "disabled people" allows for the "leib" experience of all "gimps" and "cripples" to come to the forefront. If we accept the notion of "difference in itself" then we do not have to accept the normative benchmark and its reliance on resemblance which sets the parameters of what constitutes a favourable difference. Disabled people may or may not choose to reject the notion of resembling a liberal individualistic able-bodied template. Hopefully, they will find desire in their own embodiment and sensibility "in and of itself," as well as when it interacts with others.

According to Deleuze (1994:266) difference has been represented as opposition and limitation, which has led to hierarchical levels that have been counterproductive for people. For example, in his discussion about opposition and revolution Deleuze (1994: 268) writes, "Contradiction is not the weapon of the proletariat but, rather, the manner in which the bourgeoisie defends and preserves itself, the shadow behind which it maintains its claim to decide what the problems are."

Similarly, by framing the argument within a non-disabled/disabled restriction the able-bodied have been able to preserve and defend their superior position because their normalized embodiment and sensibility sets not only the parameters of "what the problem is," but also the limits of the discussion and the type of communication required to take part in the dialogue. Thus, an able-bodied sensibility often excludes a disabled embodiment (such as a spastic embodiment), which is interpreted by others as conveying that this individual lacks the intelligence to partake in a discussion in any "meaningful" or "appropriate" manner.

Disabled people may want to problematize the ableist assumptions that underscore their interaction or meetings with able-bodied people. But we are unable to articulate or communicate our position because often we have to attend to our disability rather than voice our opinion. At other times we are too tired.

Given our subordinate position in our interaction with the non-disabled we might fear the negative consequences of "speaking our mind." Or a disabled person may not want to speak because the lines of communication may not be open to them. For example, the linear rationality of the able-bodied subject has difficulty in understanding a somewhat chaotic communication that is informed by the "disruptive" embodiment of a disabled person. In any case, others interpret disabled people's silence as tacit agreement.

Instead of hierarchy of levels, Deleuze (1994: 267) calls for a "diagonal" approach that recognizes difference without negation. A diagonal approach would allow a disabled embodiment and sensibility to be perceived as one way of being without its automatic negation, or without inversely giving it prominence over non-disabled continuance. For example, disabled people have a sense of time which is informed by our embodiment. If we were to look at difference as "diagonal" rather than "hierarchical" then disabled people's embodied sense of temporality and thinking would be neither valued nor devalued but only exist.

I illustrate a diagonal approach by explaining how my lived experience of cerebral palsy informs my thinking. In my brain linear thought-process pathways have been damaged which requires an alternative route for my thoughts. An unintended consequence of this meandering through various avenues is the possibility of exposing the obscure. My spasms part of my embodiment informs this meandering method.

On a personal level I read an able-bodied sensibility diagonally through my experience of cerebral palsy. Generally, a diagonal approach would allow for able-bodied and disabled narratives to be read across and against each other. Reading both embodied narratives in this way allows for origins or "originary experience" not in the sense of either an essential disability or ability, "but as a continuous generative source" as Ann Game (1991: 47–8) suggests. Thus as Deleuze (1994) and Game (1991) argue, moments of difference that inform each other may bring about other origins.

According to Deleuze (1994), difference has been relegated to the separation of "this" from "that" according to the need to categorize. There is a distribution of difference that is entirely dependent on representation. For example, most disabled people would be primarily classified as disabled persons, which separates them from others with the exception of other disabled people. Although they would also be cross-referenced under the terms sex, race, age, education, employment and familial position the category of disability overshadows all other categories that are indexed.

Yet sometimes disabled people do not fit neatly into these categories. For example, initially I was judged to be abnormal in comparison to the able-bodied population (Foucault, 1980). In some ways I could accept this designation because I was classified (albeit negatively) as having cerebral palsy which gave me a sense of "identity" (albeit devalued) and "place" (albeit marginal).

However, after an incident in my life I began questioning the classification of people. While undergoing a physical examination the head orthopaedic surgeon told the observing medical students that I failed to reach the recovery levels expected of cerebral palsy patients. I was shattered because not only was I not "normal" but now I was also judged to be a "freak" among people who experience cerebral palsy.

In terms of cerebral palsy or able-bodied embodiment there was no prior template from which I came. It could be argued that I was born into a family that through genetics and socialization left me with some sort of "blueprint" to follow. But, as I have argued, the representation of disability often negated my lived experience that includes my genetic background as well as my familial influence. Moreover, it is not a given that a family will provide a supportive environment for disabled people, as the Latimer case illustrates. The difference between my upbringing and that of Tracy Latimer stems from my family's willingness to validate my lived experience.

The classification of disability and, more specifically, cerebral palsy derived from the "desire" of society to impose a category upon me. After I overcame the uncertainty and the fear of being "different for itself" (to use Deleuze's term) with no category with which to anchor my existence or no place to belong, I felt a sense of freedom because I was released from the restrictions of the ability/disability categories. It was only then that I was able to validate my experience of cerebral palsy (I realize that the term "cerebral palsy" is a restrictive category itself, but presently I do not have a language that adequately describes my experience).

But no matter how detrimental the devaluation of a disabled sensibility, the temptation to be safe and fall back on the familiar ability/disability continuum and its understandings is seductive. Thus for me there is an on-going struggle to escape these understandings that to some extent are embedded in my lived experience. I feel the risk in applying "difference in itself" will be beneficial to myself and others in my interaction with them. Hopefully, both myself and others will be able to shed our preconceived notions about ableism.

Perhaps Nietzsche was right. Speaking of the notion of "Eternal Recurrence," Philip Kain (1996: 138–9) argues that the "new heaven" is not an escape from the suffering of this world. You must see and interpret the world in a different way. Based on his own experience, Nietzsche believes that we need to embrace illness and have it no other way. Through illness Nietzsche hopes to create new meaning.

While I do not necessarily associate disability with illness I realize that both physical manifestations are considered to be negations of able-bodiedness. Therefore, I feel that Kain's (1996) interpretation of Nietzsche has pertinence for validating a disabled sensibility. No longer will we be considered the negation of a "quality" life. No longer will we be considered heroic representations to be put on a pedestal. Nor will we be vilified or pitied as representations of what can go wrong with humanity's fragile existence. Our experience of disability must be embraced in order for there to be the creation of a new meaning of life.

Endnotes

1   In this article I follow the lead of Michael Oliver (1990) who prefers the term disabled persons. For Oliver: "It is sometimes argued, often by able-bodied professionals and some disabled people, that 'people with disabilities' is the preferred term, for it asserts the value of the person first and the disability then becomes merely an appendage. This liberal and humanist view flies in the face of reality as it is experienced by disabled people themselves who argue that far from being an appendage, disability is an essential part of the self. In this view it is nonsensical to talk about the person and the disability separately and consequently disabled people are demanding acceptance as they are, as disabled people" (1990: xiii). Moreover I argue that a person's disabled embodiment not only informs an individual's life but also can be a positive factor in one's life.

2   Although I am using Leder's (1990) notion of leib bodily experience to help refigure the notion of disability, Leder himself employs a korper interpretation when he considers a disabled embodiment. He reduces disability to a dysfunctional state.

3   While I advised all the actors, most of my time was spent with the lead actor.

4   In October 1993, Robert Latimer admitted to murdering his daughter, Tracy, who experienced cerebral palsy (Jenish, 1994: 16). In his first trial Mr. Latimer was convicted of second-degree murder, which carries a mandatory sentence of 10 years without parole. On appeal his conviction was overturned because the prosecution had screened the jurors for their views on "mercy killing."

   In his second trial, Latimer was convicted of second-degree murder on 5 November 1997 for killing 12-year-old Tracy by carbon monoxide gas in 1993. Latimer then applied for a constitutional exemption from the minimum sentence of life imprisonment with no chance of parole for 10 years. Justice Noble granted the exemption and ruled that Latimer killed Tracy out of mercy and the minimum sentence would be cruel and unusual punishment. Noble then sentenced Latimer to two years less a day, with half to be served in a provincial jail and half on his farm (O'Hanlon, 1997: A1, A14). A higher court in the province of Saskatchewan "struck down" Judge Noble's provision for a constitutional exemption and restored minimum sentence of life imprisonment. Nevertheless, most Canadians believe Latimer deserves leniency.

References

Asch, Adrienne (1976) "Adrienne Asch: Civil Rights Investigator," pp. 19–30 in Harilyn Rousso, Susan Gunshee O'Malley and Mary Severance (eds) *Disabled, Female and Proud!* Boston, MA: Exceptional Parent Press.

Baudrillard, Jean (1988) *The Ecstasy of Communication*, trans. Bernard Schultze and Caroline Schultze. New York: Semiotext(e).

Bauman, Zygmunt (1988) *Freedom.* Markham: Fitzhenry and Whiteside.

Bedini, Leandra A. (1991) "Modern Day 'Freaks'? The Exploitation of People with Disabilities," *Therapeutic Recreational Journal* 4: 61–70.

Bickenbach, Jerome E. (1993) *Physical Disability and Social Policy.* Toronto: University of Toronto Press.

Caddick, Alison (1995) "Making Babies, Making Sense: Reproductive Technologies, Postmodernity, and the Ambiguities of Feminism," pp. 142–67 in Paul A. Komesaroff (ed.) *Troubled Politics: Critical Perspectives on Postmodernism, Medical Ethics, and the Body.* Durham, NC: Duke University Press.

Clark, Nigel (1995) "Rear-View Mirrorshades: The Recursive Generation of the Cyberbody," pp. 113–31 in Mike Featherstone and Roger Burrows (eds) *Cyberspace/Cyberbodies/Cyberpunk: Cultures of Technological Embodiment.* London: Sage.

Davis, Lennard (1997) "Introduction," pp. 1–6 in Lennard Davis (ed.) *The Disability Studies Reader.* New York: Routledge.

De Felice, R. J. (1986) "A Crippled Child Grows up," *Newsweek* 3 Nov: 13.

Deleuze, Gilles (1994) *Difference and Repetition*, trans. Paul Patton. New York: Columbia University Press.

Derrida, Jacques (1978) "The Theatre of Cruelty and the Closure of Representation," pp. 232–50 in *Writing and Difference*, trans. Alan Bass. Chicago, IL: University of Chicago Press.

Eco, Umberto (1983) "Travels in Hyperreality," pp. 3–58 in *Travels in Hyperreality*, trans. William Weaver. New York: Harcourt Brace.

Foucault, Michel (1980) "The Politics of Health in the Eighteenth Century," pp. 166–82 in Colin Gordon (ed.) *Power/Knowledge*. New York Pantheon.

Foucault, Michel (1984) "The Means of Correct Training," pp. 188–205 in Paul Rabinow (ed.) *The Foucault Reader*. Toronto: Random House.

Freeman, David (1972) *Creeps*. London, Canada: Theatre London, March 1983.

Game, Ann (1991) *Undoing the Social: Towards a Deconstructive Sociology*. Toronto: University of Toronto Press.

Gehlen, Arnold (1988) *Man: His Nature and Place in the World*, trans. Clare McMillan and Karl Pillemer. New York: Columbia University Press.

Jenish, D'Arcy (1994) "What Would You Do?", *Maclean's Magazine* 28 Nov.: 16–20.

Kain, Philip J. (1996) "Nietzschean Genealogy and Hegelian History in the Genealogy of Morals," *Canadian Journal of Philosophy* 26(1): 123–48.

Keith, Lois (1996) "Encounters with Strangers: The Public's Responses to Disabled Women and How That Affects Our Sense of Self," pp. 69–88 in Jenny Morris (ed.) *Encounters with Strangers: Feminism and Disability*. London: The Women's Press.

Kroker, Arthur and Marilouise Kroker (1997) "Theses on the Disappearing Body in the Hyper-Modern Condition," pp. 10–34 in Arthur Kroker and Marilouise Kroker (eds) *Body Invaders: Panic Sex in America*. Montreal: New World Perspectives.

Leder, Drew (1990) *The Absent Body*. Chicago, IL: University of Chicago Press.

Lonsdale, Susan (1990) *Women and Disability: The Experience of Physical Disability among Women*. Hampshire: Macmillan Education.

Massumi, Brian (1993) "Everywhere You Want to Be: Introduction to Fear," pp. 3–37 in B. Massumi (ed.) *The Politics of Everyday Fear*. Minneapolis: University of Minnesota Press.

Merleau-Ponty, Maurice (1962) *Phenomenology of Perception*, trans. Colin Smith. London: Routledge and Kegan Paul.

Morris, Jenny (1991) *Pride against Prejudice: Transforming Attitudes towards Disability*. Gabriola Island: New Society Publications.

Norden, Martin E. (1994) *The Cinema of Isolation: A History of Physical Disability in the Movies*. New Brunswick, NJ: Rutgers University Press.

O'Hanlon, Martin (1997) "Latimer Decision Being Appealed," *London Free Press* (London, Canada) 18 Dec.: A1, A14.

Oliver, Michael (1990) *The Politics of Disablement: A Sociological Approach*. New York: St. Martin's Press.

Proctor, Robert N. (1995) "The Destruction of 'Lives Not Worth Living'," pp. 170–96 in Jennifer Terry and Jacqueline Urla (eds) *Deviant Bodies: Critical Perspectives on Difference in Science and Popular Culture*. Indianapolis: Indiana University Press.

Siegal, Josefowitz Rachel (1988) "Women's 'Dependency' in a Male-Centred Value System: Gender-Based Values Regarding Dependency and Independence?", *Women and Therapy* 7(1): 113–23.

Sobchack, Vivian (1995) "Beating the Meat/Surviving the Text, or How to Get out of This Century Alive," pp. 205–14 in Mike Featherstone and Roger Burrows (eds) *Cyberspace/Cyberbodies/Cyberpunk: Cultures of Technological Embodiment*. London: Sage.

Turner, Bryan S. (1984) *The Body and Society*. Oxford: Basil Blackwell.

Wade, Cheryl Marie (1994) "Identity," *The Disability Rag and ReSource* Sept./Oct.: 32–6.

Wendell, Susan (1989) "Toward a Feminist Theory of Disability," *Hypatia* 4(2): 104–28.

Wendell, Susan (1996) *The Rejected Body: Feminist Philosophical Reflections on Disability*. New York: Routledge.

Young, Iris Marion (1990) *Justice and the Politics of Difference*. Princeton, NJ: Princeton University Press.

PART II

Normalizing Suffering

The three chapters in Part II are dedicated to raising the connection between disability and suffering. Such a connection is not only often made, the connection is also normalized and thus it appears almost natural to link disability with suffering. We often "hear" remarks such as, "She suffers from Cerebral Palsy," or "He suffers from blindness." In fact, the connection between disability and suffering is so "normal" and thus so strong that we find it extremely difficult to separate the two. We think of disability or we "see" a disabled person and suffering almost always springs to mind.

In Chapter 6, Rod Michalko topicalizes the connection between disability and suffering in order to come to an understanding of how the two are intertwined so tightly that they seem to be inseparable companions. By making use of the work of Emmanuel Levinas, Michalko demonstrates that when we come face-to-face with disability we face suffering as well. He then raises the question of whose suffering we face when we come face-to-face with disability. Michalko develops a response to this question by addressing the murder of Tracy Latimer by her father Robert Latimer.

Chapters 7 and 8 continue the exploration of the connection between disability and suffering by invoking the lived experience of disability. First, Diane Driedger speaks of her own disability and her own pain. For her, pain marks a protest by her body. This protest, in turn, generates Driedger's disability activism. Second, Tanis Doe and Barbara Ladouceur bring death into the disability/suffering connection. Like suffering, death too is often and "normally" connected to disability. We often wonder whether the life of disability is one worth living. We wonder too how much suffering someone or we should endure. "To be or not to be" is often genuinely the question. In a moving and revealing conversation, Doe and Ladouceur address this very difficult but crucial question. Combined, these chapters represent an opportunity to question what normally remains unquestioned, namely, the connections made between disability and suffering.

CHAPTER 6
Coming Face-to-Face with Suffering

Rod Michalko

One of the most "abnormal" things about being "normal" is attending to its production. Once this is done, normalcy loses its self-proclaimed status of unreflexive naturalness. Normalcy blends into what is conceived of as "naturally given" and the only way to sustain this camouflage is for it to avoid any attention, especially its own. The humanities and social sciences have a long and well-known history of attending to the normal. The animating question for sociology since the time of Saint-Simon and Comte, for example, has been, how is society possible? Philosophers of the modern age asked a similar question. René Descartes wondered what counts as indubitable knowledge. Nietzsche, and later postmodern philosophers, raised the question of perspective in human life. Until recently, however, this attention has restricted itself to human action and has excluded the body,[1] as in Max Weber's famous distinction between "behavior and action" (1947). This ilk of attention to normalcy as human action assumes a taken-for-granted-ness of the body as a relatively stable set of unstable physiological processes. Thus, the study of the body was left to the "natural sciences" while the humanities and social sciences focused on human action in relation to nature.

Through the conception of "social construction" the latter focus included the constant of the natural body by suggesting that its meaning flows from human interpretation. Beautiful and ugly bodies, ill and well bodies are matters connected to the social construction of nature. The body thus is understood as a constant set of building blocks upon which such interpretations are constructed. Even the natural body is sometimes seen as an exclusively human phenomenon in that it, too, is the "script of culture."

That we interpret our bodies and those of others is undoubtedly true. As the social model of disability so poignantly points out, impaired bodies are given negative interpretations by contemporary society. But, like much of the humanities and social sciences, this model also suggests that impairment (the body) resides in the domain of nature and that the negative interpretations of such bodies (disability) are the domain of the social. A "disability consciousness," then, is located in the social and not in the natural region of impairment. Whether there is "no natural body," as Susan Bordo (1993) says, or whether there is one, as the social model of disability says, the consequence for disabled people is the same: we must focus, or refocus, as Colin Barnes (1995) says, our gaze on what culture and society make of our impairments.

Making something of the body is an activity conducted in the confusing space between nature and culture. The confusing space between the normal and the abnormal is similarly the "work place" in which "societal stuff" is made of our impairments. It is within this space that concepts of disability are developed by society. Now developed, however, disability remains in this confusing space and disabled people are forced to live a life in this space, between nature and culture, normal and abnormal. Is it I who am abnormal or is it my impairment, my body that is? Or, is (n)either abnormal? Certainly something abnormal is going on since I am raising such questions. What sort of a consciousness is this? I rarely hear sighted people raising such questions. To borrow from Martin Milligan's "brilliantly clear vision," sighted people simply "live in their eyes" (Magee and Milligan 1995, 45). Their life is in their eyes; they see themselves in one another's eyes (Cooley 1909). Their identities are in their eyes; their world comes into their eyes; they "live in their eyes." They construct a world, natural and otherwise, taken for granted, "in their eyes." The confusing space between nature and culture is "cleared up" and fused in the distinction between the two that exists "in their eyes."

But the confusing space between the abnormal and the normal remains for disabled people.

> The disabled person always fuses the physically typical with the physically atypical. The disabled body is also often merged with prosthetics such as wheelchairs, hearing aids, or white canes. Disability is also sometimes experienced as a transformation, or a violation, of self, creating classification dilemmas, ambiguous status, or questioning assumptions about wholeness. All persons with physical disabilities thus embody the "illegitimate fusion" of the cultural categories "normal," which qualifies people for human status, and "abnormal," which disqualifies them. Within this liminal space the disabled person must constitute something akin to identity. (Thomson 1997, 114)

The elusive "figure of difference" resides in this liminal space. Out of the complex fusion of typicality and atypicality, as well as of normalcy and abnormalcy combined with the transformed and often violated self, the disabled person must carve an identity. Moreover, this identity is constituted within the nature/culture and the subsequent impairment/disability split, which suggests that the experience of impairment (the body) is existentially different from that of disability (society). Thus, who I am is what is made of my impairment.

But if, as Milligan says, sighted people "live in their eyes," where do blind people live? Common sense along with science tells us that blindness is the negation or lack of sight. Much of what we experience and know, they argue, comes from the sense of sight. These two perspectives make a distinction between the world and the sense-perception of it, and thus they would never answer the question of where blind persons live since they would never pose it in that way. Disagreeing with Milligan, common sense and science would say that sighted persons "live through, and not in, their eyes." Their question would be, "Through what do blind persons live?" And predictably, their answer would be, "Through hearing, through touching, through their remaining senses." This reasoning presupposes a clear distinction between the world and the body connected by the thread of the subject/object dichotomy—the world is a common object perceivable and knowable by a subject through the "common senses."

But these distinctions are not as clearly given as common sense and science would have it. The distinction between the world and the perceiving subject as well as the one between the body and the self are not so separable and are actually quite blurry. Arthur Frank (1998, 209) says, "Culture inscribes the body, the body projects itself into social space, and the boundary of these reciprocal movements is in flux." Culture inscribes my blindness in the script of disability but my blindness (my body) projects itself into the social space of such inscribing activity. The boundaries of this space are in flux.

"Bodies are in," says Frank (1990, 131), and by particularized extension I would say, "so are eyes." Like bodies, eyes are in, "in academia as well as in popular culture" (131). The academy has developed an interest in the "place of the eyes" in contemporary society (Foster 1988; Jay 1993; Jenks 1995; Mirzoeff 1998) and popular postmodern culture, with its character of the simulacrum, privileges the "image as visual" (Baudrillard 1990).[2] It is not difficult to "see" that our contemporary society "lives in its eyes" as well.

I too live in my eyes, albeit differently at different times, and these differences are what blur any distinction between my impairment and my disability and also are what keeps the boundaries between them in flux. Like anyone else who is sighted, I lived the first ten or eleven years of my life in my eyes. But then I experienced a dramatic "loss of sight." I could still see, but not much. I lived in "partial sight" and, for many years, relied on this partiality as well as on memory to "live in the eyes" of my world. "Life in my eyes" certainly characterized my years of passing as fully sighted. I live now with almost no sight (light perception) and I move in the world with my guide dog, Smokie.

Living "in eyes that do not work" does not mean that I do not live in my eyes, for I still do. My identity resides in my eyes, despite, or perhaps because of, their nonworking status. I live disjointedly as an instrumental actor trying to "see" a world with these eyes. The world comes to me as "dysappearance."[3] "Life in my eyes," ensconced in the blurry memory of appearances, transmogrifies these appearances into the dysappearances of "what I see."

My eyes, in contact with Smokie's eyes, guide me across the border into the "world of appearances." We are cautious; we are vigilant; we walk with a precision known only to us. We walk, blind man and dog, culture and nature, through a world from which we are ordinarily estranged and yet through a world with which we are extraordinarily familiar (Michalko 1999). Smokie and the life in my eyes have both been "domesticated" in and by this world of appearances. This is our domicile, our homeland, and yet our life in it resonates with the trepidation felt by those who move through a land to which they no longer and not yet belong (Arendt 1955, 4).

I move through the world with my eyes, with the memories of eyes from another time, and with Smokie. Much of my movement is instrumental; after all, the "eyes of my homeland" are watching. Will I make a mistake? Will I get disoriented, or worse still, lost? Will I bump into one of the homeland's many appearances? The homeland is concerned and watches to make sure that I have "figured out" its intricate arrangement of appearances. Most important, the homeland watches to make sure that I do not mistake my dysappearances for its "real appearances." I too am familiar with these appearances and I am also watchful of any mistakes I might make. Everything becomes a "cue" for appearances and everything, including appearances themselves, signifies appearances. Whatever appears to me in the "world of the normal" does so as a signifier of "what is really there." I see a wisp of cloud pass by me on the sidewalk; but not really, since I immediately begin to "look" for what it signifies: Is it a person, a post, a no-parking sign? Is it a telephone booth? These are the things that belong on a sidewalk, not clouds, and when I see a cloud, I look for these other things.

Sounds, smells, my "distant sense" (Howes 1991) of touch from my six points of contact with my world (my two feet and Smokie's four paws)—all of this floods through me as I move through the world. This experience comes to me not so much as a smooth flow of sensibility but as a kaleidoscope of sensation, a kaleidoscope made up of all of the senses, not just sight.

With Smokie and with the memories of the eyes of another time, I have sorted out many of these kaleidoscopic dysappearances. Many of my wisps of clouds have taken on the shape of other significations. The thin, tall, and darker clouds are posts of one type or another ... usually. The ones that are not so tall that move with a more erratic wisp are people ... usually. A darting movement to the side from Smokie and then back again tells me we have just moved around something—perhaps a sandwich board advertisement or a person standing still or an open car door or perhaps just a piece of paper or a twig Smokie thought I might trip on. A sudden and sometimes barely perceptible flow of air and we have reached the end of the buildings on a sidewalk and in a few feet Smokie will stop at the curb of an intersecting street. The wisps of clouds are now cloud formations and the kaleidoscope of dysappearances take on an order, an apparent one.

Still, my kaleidoscope retains some of its kaleidoscopic character. Some of the clouds remain cloudy and mysterious. "What was that?" I ask Smokie as we pass one of them. "What could that be?" I wonder as another "cloud of mystery" makes an appearance on my horizon while we stand waiting at an intersection for the traffic light to turn in our favor. "Who was that?" I ask Smokie, as we pass by a "Hi" emanating from a group of wispy clouds. Smokie sometimes unravels the mystery of clouds, especially the clouds he likes. He sometimes moves gradually, almost hesitating, to the edge of the sidewalk and stops in front of a low and dark cloud. I reach and touch the stretch of shrubbery he has found there. Laughing, I remove his harness and, while I hold only his leash, Smokie sniffs, pees, and takes a respite from his work of moving me among and through the clouds.[4]

Sounds, smells, and the ever-present "feel" of Smokie in his harness as he extends my sense of touch—all of this is my world. But it is not the world of my homeland—that I need to "figure out" from my world conceived of by me as a kaleidoscope of cues and signs. My world is the signifier, my homeland the signified.

There is a temptation, one to which I often succumb, to conceive of my environment instrumentally and to treat it almost exclusively in that way. It is tempting for me to "see my seeing" as a world of dysappearances that, although themselves not real, point to the real ones and thus to the "real world." This temptation does have its drawbacks, because in the process of "figuring out" what is "really there," I am in the constant presence of potential mistakes, some of which represent potential danger to both Smokie and me. But there is the other side; it is fun to figure things out and my environment often comes to me as the most complicated of all puzzles with Smokie, my memories, and stock of commonsense knowledge and my "kaleidoscopic seeing" as clues. Either way, I am instrumentally involved in piecing the puzzle of my environment together.

The most salient feature of this puzzle and of my figuring it out is blindness. I move through the world "blind-ly." I am with and in blindness as I move (Michalko 1998, 1999). I insert blindness into the world as yet one more piece of the complicated puzzle. But Smokie and I (as blind) never enter a world bereft of blindness. Blindness is always-already in the world in the form of cultural representation. This cultural representation is also in me. As Frank suggests, culture is inscribed on my body—my blindness—and I project this "body of blindness" into social space. My culture, together with Smokie and me, reflexively inscribes blindness on and into social space.

This activity, too, has its drawbacks; some cultural representations of blindness make moving through the world quite arduous. There is the ever-present ethos of "help" and the equally ubiquitous sentiment of "pity" that greets Smokie and me as we enter the world. People often grab my arm and offer me help in crossing a street, more often than not a street I do not wish to cross; a few people have offered me money; others offer prayers; still others speak of the good fortune of their "gift of sight"; and some, of how they have been graced by God, saying, "There but for the grace of God go I," and they say these things in a stage whisper as Smokie and I pass by; a few even express their amazement at Smokie's prowess at guiding. All of this encompasses the social identity "ready-made" (Taylor 1989) for me as Smokie and I enter social space. This is the identity I suffer daily.

But there is also a humorous side to "walking into" such an identity. After all, identities can be ironically mirrored and reflected back to the world. There are times when I meet a person for the first time or speak with a stranger on the street that my blindness becomes a topic. Some will ask me about my "eye condition" and once in a while, but often enough to make me "blink" with wonder, some ask whether I have "seen an eye doctor." Irony comes in very handy in these situations. I tell them "No, I've never thought of it!" Inevitably, they laugh, apologize, and chide themselves for asking such a question.

But what remains? What is left unspoken and unseen in this story of figuring out the "real world" and of suffering a pregiven marginal identity? What is this story about? Is it a parable? A fable? Does it bear a message, itself to be figured out? Is living in the clouds merely living in the literal difference between sight and blindness? Is this difference only physical? Or does it bear a metaphysical mark? What of the freedom from signposts, from curbs, and from the body itself, which is "seen" only when one is in the clouds? Can freedom from the hegemonic hold of the natural body be secured by anything other than disability? Disability is not merely a reminder of the fragility and mortality of the body; it is the standpoint from which we are free to view the body as the multitude, diversity, and possibility of movement; it is the view that sees the restricted and limited version of movement that springs from the impairment of "body natural." Physical movement is cloaked in the mystery of clouds. Let me now demonstrate what happens when such mystery is removed, when disability is ignored.

Facing Suffering

The beginning is a good place to start and this story begins with the hard fact of eyesight and the equally hard fact of the physical and social environment. It turns out, though, that the "fact of eyesight" is not all that firm. It happens, so the story goes, that some of us actually lose it. Eyesight is very fragile and is vulnerable to disease, flawed genes, and accident. It is a gift, and if we are not careful, we can lose this "gift of sight" (Levin 1988, 56). This story begins, then, with the loss of this gift.

And what of the hard fact of the environment? It is very hard, harder than eyesight, and even harder than it appeared at "first glance." No fragility here, and the environment, especially the social one, does not seem to be vulnerable to anything, or so the story goes. Enter blindness. And with it the return to the hard fact of eyes, but this time to the incurable hardness of eyes that do not work ... naturally. So there we have it, the two protagonists of this story; on one side, the hard and immutable social world and on the other, the hard and immutable fact of blindness. And, oh, how they suffer each other.

This suffering takes the form of the superior/inferior relation. The facticity of the physical and social environment is taken for granted and is understood as "just there" for anyone to "see." The "just there-ness" of the environment is achieved through what Hans-Georg Gadamer (1975, 19–28) calls "*sensus comunus,*" a combination of the common senses of the body and the common stock of knowledge of culture. Thus, the environment is not only understood as a hard fact, it is also "seen" as a "true thing." As a true thing, the environment is itself "true." It does not lie; it presents itself truly to those with naturally (true) working senses and with a common (true) stock of cultural knowledge.

Blindness, however, presents a threat and a challenge to the superiority of this true thing, the environment. While the environment is just there for anyone to see, it is only truly "just there" for those who "can see." It can make an appearance only when appearances can be "commonly sensed." Blindness generates only dysappearances and, from the point of view of sight, blindness cannot "see" the "truth" of appearances. Blindness is a reminder to sight of the fragile vulnerability of eyes and, since blindness is typically conceived of as happenstance, it also reminds sighted people of the risk of going blind. Blindness is a threat to both seeing and appreciating the world decked out in its true-thing-ness splendor.

But the threat runs a bit deeper than this; what if blind people actually believed what they saw? What if we thought we were actually seeing the true thing? Then there would be two true things—one "seen" by common senses and another "seen" by uncommon senses. The world would appear in one way to sighted people and in another way to blind people and, as radically different as these two worlds would be (are?), they would both be true things. But our society, steeped in Aristotelian logic and the philosophy of the Enlightenment, will have no such thing: "You cannot have A and not A at the same time," and "You cannot have a sighted world and a nonsighted one at the same time either." Modernity conceives of the idea of multiple realities in terms of opposition as well as in terms of contradiction; reality is one and only one true thing. There is no blending or synthesis of multiple realities for modernity, since reality is a monologue and not a dialogue.

The challenge that blindness presents to the commonsensically organized social world is to convince its members, including its blind ones, that the essence of blindness is nothing other than biology "gone wrong." This demonstrates that, far from being *sensus comunus*, blindness is "really" *sensus privatus*, a pseudo reality generated by the private experience of blindness. The concept invoked as a way to signify this state of "biology gone wrong" is impairment, which is understood, even by the social model of disability, as an individual and not a collective "problem." This understanding is rooted in the biological gloss "human biology" that defines the "human condition" as the shared condition of nature expressed in the naturally occurring biology of any human.[5]

Any individual or group differences in this shared condition can also be accounted for biologically. A shared biological condition conceived of as "normal" is not understood as having a "cause" since it is understood within the paradigm of "nature," and, from an empirical point of view, a phenomenon cannot cause itself. The cause of nature thus cannot be located in nature. But differences in biology have a quite different biological frame. Human difference such as that found in height, hair color, and eye color are seen as quite "normal" and as part of the "normal variation" of human beings. But other differences are not so "normal." They are biologically framed within the "abnormal"—as disease and mutation. Unlike "normal biology" and its "normal variation," these differences are conceived of as caused. Nonimpaired biology "happens" and, depending on one's perspective, it happens usually either naturally or supernaturally. Either way, modern science cannot attribute cause to either of these two perspectives because they too would have to be caused and this would lead to the unfathomable sense of infinite regress. Thus, even though modern science is animated by the understanding that the workings of nature can be understood, the causes of such workings cannot be definitely established. "Normal human biology," "normal biological variation," and even "nature" itself, then, are interpretive, metaphoric representations of the Realness of human life and for the understanding that while the "workings" of this Realness can eventually be understood, its cause and "nature" cannot.

This depiction of the paradigm of human biology is undoubtedly overly simple. My purpose, however, is to deconstruct the "natural body" and thus to provide grounds for understanding the "impaired body." This deconstruction suggests that while impairment can also be framed within the concept of "biological difference," it is certainly not an aspect of "normal biological variation" as is eye color, for example. Variation in eye color does not represent an impairment as long as the color falls within the spectrum of what biology understands as "normal biological difference." Typically, however, eye color does not make a "social difference." Of course, when eye color is combined with skin color and when these traits are combined with some genetic or supernatural sense of who counts as human and who does not, a social difference is made—racism. But in terms of the five senses and the natural way of seeing the world, eye color makes no difference. In contrast, a significant variation in the number of rods in the retina or the presence of pigmentation on the macula, for example, does make a difference. The difference is that, unlike eye color, these conditions often cause blindness.

A different set of appearances appears to people with these "eye conditions" than to those without them. This difference amounts to living in the same world as everyone else but "seeing" it differently. I am not using the term *seeing* metaphorically here; I am not suggesting some ocular centric notion that generates contradictions in knowing and believing. I am not speaking of hegemonic visual metaphors, such as, "I see your point, but I disagree." Or, "From my point of view, I see a completely different reality than you do." Instead, I am speaking about the differences in the sort of "vision" that different eye physiologies permit. That I "see" clouds where others "see" people or sign posts is not a reflection of differences in our standpoints or even of our social location. When I "see" clouds, I "know" and "believe" that I am "looking" at something else. I am looking at what everyone else is looking at, but I am not seeing what everyone else is seeing.

The question now becomes, what difference does this difference make? What difference does it make to me when I see clouds where others see sign posts and what difference does it make to them and what difference does it make to us? The common sense of sight along with commonsense knowledge permits people to see sign posts while the uncommon sense of blindness, together with the same commonsense knowledge, permits the same sight. In this, there is no difference between blind and sighted people. When I see a cloud, I know I am looking at a sign post, or at "some such thing," and herein lies the difference. When I see, I know I am looking at "some such thing" yet to be determined, figured out, whereas when sighted people see, they know they are looking at "some particular thing" always-already determined and without the requirement of "figuring out."

Still, we are looking at the same thing and the difference is that we are "seeing it" differently. But, this difference is more radical; while we see things differently, I am wrong and "they" are right. The difference our difference makes is that *I am different.* Even though "we" claim to see differently from one another, only my difference counts as such.

The difference I experience in the context of blindness and sightedness is not that of the one between points of view. We can rationalize our points of view and argue for their superiority over others. We hold opinions and beliefs that may differ from those of others. Despite these differences, and despite arguments we may have with others regarding these differences, we continue to hold opinions, points of view, and beliefs and we may even change them from time to time.

The difference my blindness presents to me and to the rest of the world, however, is a different matter. When I say I see clouds on the street, for example, I am not starting a discussion or inviting an exchange of opinions. I do not expect to hear in response, "No, Rod, I think that's dust being blown up by the wind." My seeing clouds is neither spoken nor heard as opinion, belief, or point of view. The speech genre (Bakhtin 1986) of discussion or exchange of opinions does not mark the social occasion of my difference. But, what does mark it?

Useless-Difference

The difference of blindness is located in the understanding that blindness resides in the genre of difference that does not make a difference. It is not the insertion of a new (different) point of view, belief, or opinion into the world. The world remains the same, it is no different now that blindness is in it. Blindness merely conjoins with the already existing genre of the possibility of distortion. The world is "just there" for anyone to "see" and this "seeing" is predicated upon a perceptual apparatus that does not produce a "distorted look." The biomedical version of blindness—the "look" that blindness has of (on) the world—is not new and different; it is the "distorted look" or, more poignantly, the "look of distortion."

There are no clouds on the street, standing still, moving, or speaking. There is no almost imperceptible breeze between the end of a row of buildings on a street and an intersection. These are only distortions, for there are only sign posts and people on the street and only buildings and intersections. My blindness and thus "my look" does not make a difference; there are no clouds on the streets for others, now that I am looking. Neither a different aesthetic nor a different utility are inserted into the world when I look since what I "see" comes from the "look of distortion." Despite the radical differentness of my "look," no difference is made; the world remains the same. Blindness is thrown on the heap of "useless-difference."

In the "face-to-face" (Levinas 1969) of blindness and the world, there is no essential difference, since blindness is distortion. The modern world is open to, and welcomes, new discoveries and new perspectives, but it is not open to and does not welcome differences that distort.[6] This is what grounds the suffering that blindness engenders and, perhaps, what grounds the suffering of all disabilities. We (disabled people) suffer our difference in the face of the Other as a difference that does not make a difference; we suffer our useless-difference.

Suffering, says Emmanuel Levinas (1988, 156), "is at once what disturbs order and this disturbance itself." Disability is much the same. It certainly does disturb order represented as the physical and social environment, including those for whom this environment is intended. This "order" is the imaginary of, in Irving Zola's terms (1982), the "world of the normal," where what is imagined is an edifice conceived of as the "normal world" constructed by and for "normal people." Since it cannot, this world does not imagine disability as an integral part of itself, and when disability shows up, not only is it unexpected but also it disturbs the "world of the normal" at all levels of its consciousness.

Disability is certainly disturbing at the level of individual consciousness, both for those who are disabled and for those who are not. It is disturbing to be marginalized in a world in which your heart is firmly entrenched, in a world you experience as your homeland. It is more disturbing still to realize that your sensorium or your body "sees" differently or "looks" different from what is expected, including from what you expect.

Nondisabled people are disturbed by disability. It reminds them of the fragility and vulnerability of their existence and reminds them of their mortality as well. Furthermore, nondisabled people are often very uncomfortable in the presence of those of us who are disabled. They patronize, pity, and even ignore us. Many times Smokie has guided me to the door of a public building where I have "groped" for the handle of a door being held open for me by a silent someone doing a "good deed." Of course, this good deed effectively achieves and perpetuates the disturbing character of "the groping blind." It is disturbing to watch a blind man approaching a door and it is disturbing to "know" that he will "grope" for the handle and it is disturbing (somehow) to tell him that you have opened the door for him. To open the door or not to open the door; both are disturbing, for the man is blind. Asking him whether he would like you to open the door may be disturbing to the blind man, but a closed door may be disturbing to him as well since he will have to grope for the handle. Ignore the blind man: let him, or better still, someone else, deal with the door. Still, you are right here, you should hold it open. What to do? This is all very disturbing.

At a more collective level of consciousness, things were going along quite well, at one time. Sure people had accidents or contracted diseases, and sure, some people were disabled by these things and there were some who were even born disabled. But there were "special places" where *they* could live, "special schools" that *they* could attend, "special places" where *they* could work and all kinds of "special stuff" that *they* could do. Now, this was not disturbing to anyone, well, maybe to *them*, but *they* were already disturbed. It was not as though *they* were not being taken care of; *they* were with *their* own kind and, moreover, with our help *they* are living the best kind of life *their* limitations allow. This is the best situation for all concerned.

But then, someone, somewhere had the bright idea that *they* should live in the "world of the normal." Some even said that *they* had a "right" to do so.[7] And things got really disturbing. The disturbance was in the disability itself. Disability reminds people of something they already know about but would rather act as though they do not—their mortality. What is disturbing about disability, then, is that it disrupts this "acting as if" by reminding people of the fragility of their existence. Furthermore, people know that the membership category "disability" is always open and is open to anyone. The presence of disability reminds people of this fact and this, too, is disturbing.

Since disability is so tightly bound to the biomedical model of the body in contemporary society, it is almost impossible to conceive of it as a category of societal membership. Like Emmanuel Levinas's conception of suffering, disability is understood and experienced as nothing other than a disturbance to the "normal" biology of the body. It is conceived of not as a collective matter but as an individual one. This reasoning holds that disability is collected under the category of "population," not of "people" (Foucault 1980, 25). There is a "disabled population" and not a "disabled people."

Thus, disability conventionally represents a disturbance to individuals and to a population. Individuals take precautions against becoming disabled and populations take precautions against having a "high rate" of disability. To both groups disability is a disturbance to be avoided and, as such, it is usually not thought of as a category of societal membership with "human rights." Instead, disability is often conceived of as a strictly biological matter that results in negative consequences for an individual, requiring the consequential act of "humane treatment" rather than "human rights." This is why the fight for disability rights has taken so long and why legislated disability rights are so often not enforced.

What the nondisabled Other suffers in the face of disability, then, is the suffering that comes from being present to one experienced as a "victim of misfortune." The difference of disability thus becomes the useless-difference borne by anyone victimized (disturbed) by misfortune. Individual strength and the degree of humane treatment exercised by a society toward misfortune become the only measures of how well either individuals or a society lives with disability. This provides at least a partial response to Zola's question regarding why society excludes so many of its members.

> Suffering, in its hurt and its in-spite-of consciousness, is passivity.... Is not the evil of suffering—extreme passivity, impotence, abandonment and solitude—also the unassumable and thus the possibility of a half opening, and, more precisely, the possibility that wherever a moan, a cry, a groan or a sigh happen there is the original call for aid, for curative help, for help from the other ego whose alterity, whose exteriority promises salvation? It is the original opening toward what is helpful, where the primordial, irreducible, and ethical, anthropological category of the

medical comes to impose itself—across a demand for analgesia, more pressing, more urgent in the groan than a demand for consolation or a postponement of death. (Levinas 1988, 157, 158)

Thus,

The inter-human lies also in the recourse that people have to one another for help, before the marvellous alterity of the Other has been banalized or dimmed in a simple exchange of courtesies which become established as an "inter-personal commerce" of customs. (Levinas 1988, 165)

The "extreme passivity" by which Emmanuel Levinas characterizes useless suffering may also be located in the difference of disability. What difference, for example, does someone's blindness make—to that someone or to how that blindness is "seen" by others in the world? Is blindness "seen" as a "unique look"? Or, what difference does wheelchair use make? How is someone in a wheelchair "seen"?

If blindness and wheelchair use are "seen" strictly and only as deviations from "normal seeing" and "normal mobility," then the ground for useless-difference and thus passivity is laid. Those who are blind and those who use wheelchairs are "restricted" to the difference-of-deviance and need only fit into, or be fit into, the identity and life ready-made for them in and by the world of the normal (Titchkosky 2000). The passivity of this "fitting into" is found in the fact that a place has been ready-made for disability in this world. The difference-of-disability makes no difference to the world of the normal and the quintessential place of this world remains, despite disability, the hegemonic ideology of "normalcy." The "view" from blindness or from a wheelchair makes no difference since it has no value as a view. The "sighted world" sees blindness as distortion and the "walking world" sees wheelchair use as confinement. Both are seen as misfortune. Blindness is understood as "impotence" with respect to "normal seeing" and the same holds true for wheelchair use with respect to "normal walking." Both are seen as the misfortune of solitude conceived of as confinement—the one bound to "not seeing" (*sensus privatus*), the other "wheelchair bound" (*corpus privatus*).

The ideology of nondisability as normalcy symbolically constructs disability as, to continue with Levinas, "abandonment." Some "natural" ability or function has abandoned someone; eyesight has abandoned the now-blind person and the "natural" ability to walk has abandoned the person now "bound" to a wheelchair. The former is "confined" by a "distorted look" and the other is confined by useless legs. What remains is a life conceived of as the "task," often thought of as a laborious one, of living with confinement. The difference-of-disability is thus understood as a useless-difference—living with useless eyes, with useless legs.

But then there is Levinas's sense of the Other, of alterity, of exteriority; there is the sense of the other to disability that is clearly nondisability—useful eyes, useful legs. This

Other is not confined to those others concretely seen as nondisabled people. While it includes these types, the Other is given birth and informed by the ideology of nondisability, of the "natural body." It is the inscription, to return to Foucault, of culture writ large on all of our bodies. But this inscription is easily erased. Disability itself, as Lennard Davis (1995) suggests, is a reminder of the fallibility of culture's inscription; it is erased as easily as it is written. But the script cannot be erased. The cultural script of the "natural body" remains indelibly with us regardless of and in spite of the particular condition of our bodies. The "natural" (nondisabled) body is with us, one and all, disabled and nondisabled. Naturalness is not to be found in any particular body; it is the exterior, alter (body), the Other found written on every particular body.

The moans, cries, groans, and sighs of suffering to which Levinas refers are heard emanating from those whose inscription of naturalness (of humanness) has been erased. In the face of this erasure stands the exteriority and alterity of the Other holding out the "promised salvation" of "aid and curative help." Face-to-face, disability and nondisability "stand" opposed, the latter suffering the useless-difference of the former. The difference-of-disability makes no difference to the "natural Other" except to remind it of the fragility of life and the need to end the "useless-suffering of useless-difference" with aid and curative help. Thus, disability is an "unworthy difference" that generates both the meaninglessness of useless-suffering and the ethical requirement to remedy it. The contemporary biomedical response to disability is not only grounded in this version of the difference-of-disability, it also perpetuates this difference and produces the disability/suffering connection as a "natural" one.

The biomedical ethics of remedy ("curative help") represents a "bad will" toward the recognition of any meaningful difference that disability might make. "This bad will," Levinas (1988, 158–59) writes, "is perhaps only the price which must sometimes be paid by the elevated thought of a civilization called to nourish persons and to lighten their suffering." Levinas conceives of this bad will as the "uncertainty" of modernity in the face of suffering. The opening of an ethics of the "inter-human," according to Levinas, originates in the "suffering of suffering" where one "justifiably suffers" the useless, and thus unjustifiable, suffering of the Other. Thus, "the very phenomenon of suffering in its uselessness is, in principle the pain of the Other" (163).

The pain (suffering) of disability can now be seen as socially located in the Other. It is nondisabled others who suffer the difference-of-disability. Disability, understood as useless-difference and unjustifiable suffering is what generates both the biomedical ethics of remedy and the commonsense response of pity. Understanding the idea of suffering a disability, therefore, requires us to interrogate the scene in which disability appears. This scenography (Butler 1993) does not seek to dismiss or destroy the notion of "suffering a disability"; instead, as I try to show, it aims to deconstruct this notion, thereby laying out the scene that provides for the possibility of any connection between suffering and disability.

This deconstruction brings to the fore a more social sense of "suffering a disability." Some disabilities include the suffering of physical pain but all disabilities include an orientation to and, in many instances, a suffering of "the suffering of suffering." This means that disability is understood in contemporary society as an "unjustifiable condition" of which some people are "victims." Disabled people thus suffer the social category and orientation of victim. This suffering expresses itself most often in the response of pity experienced by disabled people in the face-to-face interaction with nondisabled others. It generates clichés, such as, "I've still got all of my senses; knock on wood," or "Be thankful for what you have because that can happen to anyone." Disability as memento mori springs from this version of "suffering a disability," and thus disability becomes a reminder both of the fragility of the human body and of how fortunate or graced are those who are not disabled.

This version of "suffering a disability" not only "hears" disability as a "cry for help" but also yields a particular orientation to what counts as "help." Recall Levinas (1988, 165): "The inter-human lies also in the recourse that people have to one another for help, before the marvellous alterity of the Other has been banalized or dimmed in a simple exchange of courtesies which become established as an 'inter-personal commerce' of customs." Understood as victimage, disability becomes, as Michael Oliver (1996) says, an individual or personal matter. It becomes a matter of finding a cure, of adjusting, and of coping, a matter of all the techniques and technologies so "customary" to the disciplines of medicine and rehabilitation. It becomes a matter, too, of the form and content of interaction between disabled and nondisabled people. "Common courtesy" is one such interactional form. "Don't stare, it's not nice." "Just be lucky *you* can walk." "See, that man is blind; that dog is helping him." Comments such as these, by parents to their children, mark both the beginning and the perpetuation of the banal courtesies that characterize the interpersonal commerce of the customary face-to-face of disability and nondisability. Turning to the Other, what Levinas refers to as the "inter-human recourse" that we have to one another for help, disabled people find a "face" but usually one "dimmed" with the conception of disability as misfortune. The trope that brings disability face-to-face with nondisability is framed within the ideological superiority of the latter and is thus "seen" as a "cry for help." The appearance of disabled people in the public realm is directed by this framing, and thus interaction between disabled and nondisabled people is often animated by an obligation to "help the unfortunate."

The relationship between disability and nondisability depends not only on the two categories being understood as binary opposites but also on the body being conceived of as "natural," as "given." But, as Judith Shklar (1990, 5) says, "We must recognize that the line of separation between injustice and misfortune is a political choice, not a simple rule that can be taken as a given." The line that separates disability from nondisability is understood as a given, drawn once and traced over and over again with the indelible pencil of nature. The scenography of human life is sketched with this imagined pencil of nature, marking a complex network of distinctions between what we choose and what is a given. But these lines of demarcation, as Frank (1998, 209) suggests, are "blurred" (in flux) and remain so despite the continuous tracing. Ironically, it is the blurriness of these lines of demarcation that calls for such continuous tracing.

Humanity is constantly involved in this act of demarcation; we trace lines, for example, between nature (what is given to us) and nurture (what we make of what is given to us), contextualizing human life by making distinctions also between nature and society, sex and gender, health and illness, disability and nondisability. Human life is played out in the scene of this network of distinctions. Our treatment of one another is enmeshed in this complex network. Complex as this network is, however, the "rule of the given" of which Shklar speaks clarifies any "blurriness" between misfortune and injustice and prevents any recognition of the politics (choice) of such a distinction. This results in the "pencil of nature" being equated with the "pencil of normalcy"; thus, able-bodiedness is "natural/normal," disability is not. Neither is political, since the one is nature, the other is "nature gone wrong." There is nothing just or unjust here, there is merely nature and misfortune. This presupposition of the "body as nature" grounds the "naturalness" of thinking of, and even experiencing, disability as "misfortune." "To call a presupposition into question is not the same as doing away with it; rather, it is to free it from its metaphysical lodgings in order to understand what political interests were secured in and by that metaphysical placing, and thereby to permit the term to occupy and to serve very different political aims" (Butler 1993, 30).

The presupposition that the matter (materiality) of the body, either the disabled one or the nondisabled one, is nature—the one normal, the other not—is itself not made by the "matter-of-nature." That the body can be spoken of as "natural" and that disability can be "prefigured" by impairment, also thought of as "natural," does not mean that these distinctions need necessarily be treated as a "given" and, therefore, as a "rule." To do so presupposes a politics of the body and is thus to invoke a language in which is embedded a hegemonic ideology of an either/or dichotomy recommending that you either have a "normal body" or you do not. This hegemonic ideology remains "lodged" in the perpetuation of this dichotomy for, as Butler (1993, 35) suggests, "When this material effect is taken as an epistemological point of departure, a *sine qua non* of some political argumentation, this is a move of empiricist foundationalism that, in accepting this constitutive effect as a primary given, successfully buries and masks the genealogy of power relations by which it is constituted." The constitutive power relations of disability resides in what I call "useless-difference." Thus, disability does not, and should not, make a difference in the world. The idea of useless-difference suggests that disability makes a difference only to the individual and it does so in two important ways: it engenders "suffering" in the Other and it has a psychological effect. The individual who now finds himself or herself disabled, or the one who is born so, will be traumatized to some degree and will now have to "accept" the disability, "cope" with it, and "adjust" to it. This difference, in its twofold character, is useless insofar as it is "passive," to borrow from Levinas, and inserts nothing essentially different into the world. Everything remains the same—the world still sees, despite blindness; the world still hears, despite deafness; the world still has places accessed only by stairs, despite people in wheelchairs; and parents still count the fingers and toes of their newborn. Blindness, deafness, and paraplegia are still unfortunate conditions that some of us have to suffer and are not (yet?) worthwhile and legitimate alternatives. They are not alternative ways of sensing the world and moving through it. Thus, disability becomes a difference that should be prevented, not "lived in." We should see clouds for what they are, posts and people; we should not live in clouds, let alone be intrigued by their mystery. The political aim of privileging normalcy, expressed in the language of the body as natural and conditional, is what lies buried beneath and is masked by the empirical distinction between disability and nondisability.

This distinction, which renders disability as useless-difference and as a personal problem burdensome to both the individual and society, commingles with a specific version of "help." It expresses itself in the "inter-personal commerce" of which Levinas speaks and can be found in the banalized courtesies and customs that often mark the interaction between disabled and nondisabled people in contemporary society. But, the useless-difference of disability can also derive an extreme version of help that goes far beyond this customary courtesy even though it is equally banalized. I end this chapter with a brief example of such "help," which springs from the "natural" sense that clouds are indeed not clouds—that freedom is not disability.

Tracy Latimer: Our Problem

On October 24, 1993, Robert Latimer, a Saskatchewan farmer, killed his twelve-year-old daughter, Tracy.[8] Tracy was born with cerebral palsy and as she grew older, Tracy experienced physical pain, described as severe by her parents as well as by physicians. Tracy had surgery to correct the abnormal formation of her hips and to alleviate some of her pain. Her father, no longer able to witness the pain of his daughter, or so his defense lawyer claimed, killed her.

Robert Latimer confesses: "I took her in the truck, took her to the shed, closed both doors, hooked up a hose to the exhaust pipe and put it in the cab" (Eckstein 1995, 6). Tracy died of carbon monoxide poisoning. This was not the first time that Latimer thought of killing his daughter: "I don't know what day it was. I was combining. I thought I'd give her some Valium.... I was going to shoot her in the head and burn her in a fire" (6).

This time, however, Latimer did not merely think of killing Tracy, he actually did. Tracy's pain was too much for him. For Latimer, killing her was an "act of mercy" and not a criminal act. In a CBC interview, Latimer said, "I honestly don't believe there was ever any crime committed here" (6). Responding to the court after his second-degree murder conviction, Latimer said, "I still feel I did what was right" (6).

As can be expected, the Latimer case has been embroiled in legal appeals. In 1994, Robert Latimer was convicted of second-degree murder and was sentenced to life imprisonment with no parole for a minimum of ten years. The conviction was appealed in 1995 and the 1994 decision was upheld. Another appeal granted Latimer a new trial and in 1997 he was retried. He was once again convicted of second-degree murder but with a new twist; Latimer's sentence of life imprisonment with no parole for a minimum of ten years was reduced to two years, only one of which had to be served in a prison. In an unprecedented action, the judge invoked Latimer's constitutional rights under the Canadian Charter of Rights and Freedoms and ruled that the ten-year minimum sentence was "cruel and unusual punishment." This decision was overturned by the Supreme Court of Canada and the initial sentence of a minimum of ten years in prison was upheld early in 2001.

The rationale for Latimer's appeals was that his killing of his daughter was an "act of mercy." The court, the media, and physicians, as well as Tracy's parents described her cerebral palsy as a "severe disability" causing Tracy to experience "severe pain" (Enns 1999, 9–47). The media depicted Tracy not only as suffering from severe pain but also as "helpless" both physically and mentally. Thus, her father was behaving "mercifully" when he killed her and life imprisonment with no parole for a minimum of ten years was seen as cruel and unusual punishment. The idea that he behaved "mercifully" represented the whole of Latimer's defense in court and represented, in part, the grounds of his appeal. This aspect of the appellant's factum reads as follows: "Trial judge erred ... in not charging the jury that they could find that Robert William Latimer had the legal right to decide to commit suicide for his daughter, by virtue of her complete absence of physical and intellectual abilities ... judge erred in law in not holding that the minimum sentence for murder on the facts of this case is a cruel and unusual punishment, contrary to S.12 of the Charter" (Eckstein 1995, 1).

Latimer was certainly not alone in his understanding that killing his daughter was necessary and that it was an act of mercy. In fact, Latimer has received wide support for both his action and his appeal. In a May 1999 CTV, News 1 interview, Latimer said, "One of the most important things to mention is all the people all across the country that have sent some really good letters and things like that, and over 175,000 to try and beat the government off on this one, ... they are powerful letters. There's a professor from Saskatoon who said he was ashamed to be a Canadian when the first verdict was announced" (*Canadian News Bulletins*, May 6,1999).

I want, finally, to speak of what Laura Latimer, Tracy's mother, thought of her daughter's murder. Laura Latimer and Tracy's siblings were at church at the time of Tracy's murder. Here is a portion of how Laura Latimer responded to defense questioning during her husband's trial.

Defense lawyer: As Tracy developed in her first year, was there any suggestion that Tracy would not live at home?

Laura Latimer: No.—when she was born? No.

Defense lawyer: What were your hopes for her at that stage?

Laura Latimer: When we very first took Tracy home we knew that she had brain damage but they said it might be very mild or it might be worse. We ... had every hopes that ... she would be able to go to school but would just be maybe slow in school.... We tried to treat her like a normal child ... we tried to make her life as normal as we could.

Defense lawyer: How did you feel after Tracy died?

Laura Latimer: When I found Tracy I was happy for her ... I was happy because she didn't have to deal with her pain anymore. After she died ... I don't even know if I cried. Tracy's her birth was way, way sadder than her death ... we lost Tracy when she was born and ... that's when I grieved for her ... I did all my grieving when she was little. We lost her then. (Quoted in Eckstein 1995, 6–7)

After killing his daughter, Robert Latimer removed her body from the truck and placed it back in bed. This is where Laura Latimer, returning from church, found Tracy and "discovered" that she was dead.

Latimer was faced with a daughter whom he "saw" as suffering from a severe disability and from severe pain. Despite the fact that he withheld pain medication from Tracy and one surgical procedure for her and despite the fact that he refused a permanent replacement home for Tracy (Eckstein 1995), he killed her because the pain was too much for him; he decided to put Tracy "out of her misery" and to perform the ultimate act of mercy. But, as Cheryl Eckstein (1995, 1) asks, "And whose pain are we really talking about?"

Clearly, Tracy was not the only one suffering from severe pain. This point brings us back to Levinas and "useless-suffering." Latimer was suffering and the source of his suffering was Tracy's suffering; he was, as Levinas puts it, suffering suffering. To him, Tracy's disability was nothing other than the moans, groans, and sighs of suffering of which Levinas speaks. Tracy's disability was "heard" (interpreted by Latimer) as a "cry for help" and he responded by silencing her cry once and for all.

Extreme as it is, death is the practical consequence of Latimer's version of "help." In the face of suffering, Latimer responds with help and this "help" takes the form of eliminating the suffering. And by eliminating Tracy's suffering, he eliminated his own suffering as well. The elimination of one is simultaneously the elimination of the other. It is useless to suffer the suffering of another when both can be eliminated.

Contrary to all opinion about the Latimer case—that of the media, of the courts, and of Latimer himself—his problem is not born of suffering. Latimer "knows" suffering all too well and he can recognize it when he "sees it." For him, no mistake, Tracy was suffering. Latimer was equally firm in his knowledge of what to do about suffering—eliminate it. For him, "do the right thing," eliminate Tracy's suffering through the only available means—eliminate Tracy. Latimer had resolved the question of suffering, and what to do about it, long before Tracy's birth. The only dilemma Latimer faced for years before the murder was whether to do it now or put it off. He was not vexed by Tolstoy's question, about how to live or by the question of what counts as life presupposed by this question. Latimer's resolution of such questions was both expressed and affirmed in his "practical ethics," which called for nothing other than the elimination of suffering.

Even though the professor from Saskatoon, and others, support Latimer's decision to eliminate his daughter's suffering and his own suffering of her suffering, how are disabled people to interpret these "practical ethics"? Ruth Enns (1999, 26) wonders, "If the facts could clearly establish the guilt of a murderer but the victim's disabilities could cloud the judgement of the media, the public and those representing the law, where could disabled people turn for protection and justice?"

In the face of disability, as I show in a previous discussion, suffering finds its place within a "seeing" that depicts disability as useless-difference. The appearance of blindness in the world, for example, is signified as the useless-difference of "abnormalcy," "defect," and "distortion," and thus is a difference that makes no difference to the "normal percep-tion" of the world. But because blindness contributes nothing to "normal perception" does not mean that it is a "neutral" difference. After all, blindness contributes a great deal to the conventional understanding of the "normalcy of normal perception," according to which blindness is the sheer negation of sight and thus the opposite of all that is signified by sight—normalcy, knowledge, accuracy of perception. These qualities (and many oth-ers like them) are far removed from any empirical account or descriptive fidelity regarding the sense of sight. The same is true for blindness insofar as it does not empirically represent the lack of such qualities. It is not an "either/or" issue (Butler 1993, 254), specifying that either you can see and, therefore, have knowledge and accurate perception or you are blind and you do not. This either/or reasoning is borne of the understanding that sight and blindness are opposites and that they are opposed to one another in terms of these qualities. When qualities such as knowledge and accurate perception are connected to Enlightenment versions of empiricism, rationality, and reality, it is an almost impercep-tible move to conceive of sight as a "powerful sense" and of blindness as the negation of such power. Far from being self-evident, therefore, the oppositional relation between sight and blindness is steeped within the power relations at play within the ideological struggle over what counts as reality and what counts as "seeing" and "knowing" it.

This rationality of opposites often governs conceptions and evaluations of the lives of disabled people. Thought of as the opposite of able-bodiedness, disability, and the lives of its people, is judged second-rate at best and unworthy at worst. This is the sort of "best of times and worst of times" sentiment that Tracy Latimer's mother, Laura Latimer, expressed during her husband's trial. Second-rate was the best that Laura Latimer could "see" in her daughter who had "brain damage" and there was the "hope" that Tracy would stay home and go to school even though a "little slow" in school was the best that could be expected. As she said, Laura Latimer "tried" to treat Tracy "like a normal child" and she and her husband "tried to make her life as normal as we could." Some semblance of normalcy was the best that could be hoped for, for a brain-damaged child. Expressions such as "normal treatment" and "normal as we could" are intelligible and even understandable when spoken of an "abnormal" (brain-damaged) child but not so intelligible and understandable when spoken of a "normal" child. Hopes and desires for "normalcy" are spoken and heard only within a context that signifies "abnormalcy." Without such a context, it is difficult to imagine Laura Latimer expressing these hopes for her "normal" (non-brain-damaged) children or to imagine any parent expressing any such hopes. Either a child is "abnormal" and must be "treated as normal" or a child is "normal" and no such "treatment" is necessary.

Tracy's mother "lost her" when she was born not only with "brain damage" but also with "normalcy damage." There was no need for tears when Laura Latimer found her daughter, dead, in her bed where Robert Latimer placed her after killing her. When she "found" her daughter's body, Tracy's mother was "happy for her." She was happy "because she [Tracy] didn't have to deal with her pain any more." Crying was unnecessary because Tracy's birth "was way sadder than her death." "We lost Tracy when she was born"; for Laura Latimer, that was the time for grieving. All grieving for Tracy was done when she was "little"; "we lost her then."

Laura Latimer's account involves at least two versions of "loss." There was, of course, the loss of her twelve-year-old daughter: Tracy was killed. But this loss did not necessarily call for grieving because Tracy was always-already lost to her parents. Tracy was dead from the moment she was born. Unlike the other Latimer children, Tracy was born without the prerequisite condition of normalcy (nondamaged brain). What is more, Tracy was born with the condition of physical pain—again not, for the Latimers, a prerequisite condition of normalcy. This was barely the birth of a human, let alone a normal, child.

There was no celebration of Tracy's birth; there were only tears, only grieving; they "lost her then." Tracy's birth held no promise for the Latimers. This brain-damaged infant the Latimers called Tracy would never develop into a normal child, a normal adolescent and would certainly never achieve even a semblance of what the Latimers conceived of as independence or adulthood. All of this—life—was lost to the Latimers "back then," when Tracy was born.

What was lost to the Latimers was personhood; Tracy's birth did not manifest any precondition for such a status and thus personhood was an impossibility. The Latimers saw no condition that would allow them to see her as cerebral palsy, or as a disabled child; they did not even see her as a child with a disability. Since personhood was impossible for Tracy, so was "seeing" her as a person with a disability. As the Latimers' "scene of life" spread out before them, they saw no frame for the possibility of the lived experience of cerebral palsy. There were only "persons with ———" in the Latimers' scene of life and since Tracy was born without the preconditions for "person," the Latimers could not see Tracy in their scene. "I believe that the term 'person with a disability' demonstrates and is underscored by a 'normative' resemblance that we [disabled people] can attain if we achieve the status of being deemed 'people first' (with the term's emphasis on independence and extreme liberal individualism) in the eyes of an ableist-centred society" (Overboe 1999, 24). Thus, we accept "the great equalizer—normality, the bench mark for humanity" (24). Despite losing Tracy at birth, Laura Latimer did see the possibility of Tracy's resembling normalcy. The possibility was slim, however, and Tracy would be "slow," at best, in school. Her parents would treat Tracy as "normal" as possible, as normal as one could treat a "brain-damaged" child. This was the best that could be "hoped" for her. But that "great equalizer—normality" was only a hope for the Latimers. The loss of normalcy and personhood—the loss of Tracy—occurred at her birth and her actual death was inevitable and anticlimactic. Robert Latimer killed his *already dead* daughter. As he said, no crime was committed; he did the right thing.

Robert Latimer's act of murder reflects the view that normalcy is the bench-mark for measuring humanity. To be human is to be normal, average, and just like everyone else; it is to be without the requirement of "normal treatment." "Normal treatment" is restricted to those who, although they are like everyone else, have a useless-difference. Privileging personhood and devaluing the lived experience of disability (Overboe 1999) is the register known as "normal treatment." The Latimers could not conceive of Tracy as a "person with a disability" since they could not see any person in her. They could see only disability (cerebral palsy and physical pain) in Tracy and this was death for the Latimers, not merely the reminder of it (Davis 1997, 1) but death itself. The Latimers could not conceive of the possibility of living disability and since it was impossible for Tracy to be a "person with a disability" it was equally impossible for Tracy to be.

The case of Tracy Latimer involves far more than the life and death of a child and whether a parent, the courts, or practical ethicists can and should decide when an "extreme case of disability" is too extreme. Tracy Latimer is a problem for all of us. She reminds us of what we all face when, at birth, we are inserted into ready-made social identities. What is given to us when we are given birth? What is given when disability is given birth? What choices (politics) are involved in the "birthing of disability"? What politics places disability on one side or the other of the line between misfortune and injustice?

Endnotes

[1]   An exception to this is the work of Georg Simmel (see Stewart 1999). For recent examples, see Featherstone, Hepworth, and Turner 1991; Frank 1995; Howes 1991; O'Neil 1985; Shilling 1993; Synnott 1993; Turner 1996. For an excellent review of this development of the interest in the body see Frank 1990. However, various feminisms are arguably the chief originators of such an interest. See Bordo 1993; Butler 1993; Smith 1987, 1990, 1999; Wendell 1996.

[2]   I am referring here to the postmodern contention that social reality is bereft of origin and essence and consists only of image. Of course, postmodernism privileges vision and the visual image.

[3]   I follow the work of Drew Leder. He suggests that when the body is working properly it "disappears." Leder 1990, 83–84, contrasts this with the dysappearance of the nonworking body, "that is, the body appears as thematic focus, but precisely in a dys state." I am suggesting that when eyes "do not work," not only do they represent

Leder's sense of dysappearance but the appearances of the world are also "dysappearance"—they too are in a dys-state. This, of course, comes about only when the body is conceived instrumentally, "as a tool."

4 Since Smokie's death, I have a new blindness—one with a white cane as my guide. Yet, I still talk to Smokie, silently now, as I move through the world. It seems as though there is more to figure out now, probably because the cane can never replace Smokie's guidance.

5 I rely heavily on Canguilhem 1991 and Merleau-Ponty 1962 for what follows. The concept "normal human biology" is not as simple and as neutral as it appears. For an excellent analysis of how this concept fluctuates in the ongoing dialectic of normalcy/abnormalcy and of how the biological and medical sciences invoke the tacit sense of "typical functioning" as a way to privilege normal human biology as natural, see Silvers 1998.

6 For an excellent discussion about the modern version of the environment as "neutral," see Sennett 1990, especially pages 41–68. Distortion is located in the subject since the object (environment) is neutral.

7 This sardonic and even flippant micro analysis of the development (techniques) of a self and of the social identity "disability" reveals a macro development of such a self and of such an identity. Michel Foucault (1978) provides the basis for a macro analysis in his understanding of governmental transformations of "people" into "populations." "Movements of life" (25), such as disability, are thus transformed into rates as well as into a population with rights. But such a transformation brings with it a version of a "disabled self" (social identity) that must conform to surveillance and to the proof that one belongs in this population, thereby having rights. Such an analysis is beyond the scope of this chapter since my intention is to unravel the phenomenological dilemma of suffering that presents itself in the face of disability. It is necessary for this sort of analysis to be conducted in order to reveal the governmental and institutional "techniques" involved in the development of a Self.

8 I rely heavily on Enns 1999 in the following discussion. My point in this section is not to provide a descriptive account of the Latimer case but to explicate the social consequences of understanding disability as useless-difference.

References

Arendt, Hannah. 1955. *Men in Dark Times*. San Diego: Harcourt Brace Jovanovich.

Bakhtin, Mikhail Mikhailovich. 1986. Edited by Caryl Emerson and Michael Holquist. Translated by Vern W. McGee. *Speech Genres and Other Late Essays*. Austin: University of Texas Press.

Barnes, Colin. 1995. "Visual Impairment and Disability." In *Beyond Disability: Towards an Enabling Society*, edited by Gerald Hales. Thousand Oaks, Calif.: Sage. 37–44.

Baudrillard, Jean. 1990. *Seduction*. Translated by Brian Singer. Montreal: New World Perspectives.

Bordo, Susan. 1993. *Unbearable Weight: Feminism, Western Culture, and the Body*. Berkeley and Los Angeles, Calif.: University of California Press.

Butler, Judith. 1993. *Bodies that Matter*. New York: Routledge.

Canguilhem, Georges. 1991. Reprint. *The Normal and the Pathological*. Translated by Carolyn R. Fawcett in collaboration with Robert S. Cohen. With an Introduction by Michel Foucault. New York: Zone Books. Original edition, *Le Normal et le Pathologique*. Paris: Presses Universitaires de France, 1966.

Cooley, Charles Horton. 1909. *Social Organization*. New York: Schocken Books.

Davis, Lennard J. 1995. *Enforcing Normalcy: Disability, Deafness and the Body*. London: Verso.

Eckstein, Cheryl. 1995. "Tracy Latimer, Better Off Dead? A Breach of Compassion." Compassionate Healthcare Network, March. http://www.chninternational.com/tracybod.htm

Enns, Ruth. 1999. *A Voice Unheard: The Latimer Case and People with Disabilities*. Halifax: Fernwood.

Featherstone, Mike, Mike Hempworth, and Bryan S. Turner, eds. 1991. *The Body: Social Process and Cultural Theory*. Newbury Park, Calif.: Sage.

Foster, Hal, ed. 1988. *Vision and Visuality: Discussions in Contemporary Culture*. Seattle: Bay Press.

Foucault, Michel. 1980. *Power/Knowledge: Selected Interviews and Other Writings, 1972–1977*. Edited by Colin Gordon. Translated by Colin Gordon, Leo Marshall, John Mepham and Kate Soper. New York: Pantheon.

Frank, Arthur W. 1990. "Bringing Bodies Back in: A Decade in Review." *Theory, Culture, and Society* 7(1): 131–62.

———. 1995. *The Wounded Storyteller: Body, Illness and Ethics*. Chicago: University of Chicago Press.

———. 1998. "From Dysappearance to Hyperappearance: Sliding Boundaries of Illness and Bodies." *The Body and Psychology*. Edited by Henderikus J. Stam. London: Sage. 205–32.

Gadamer, Hans-Georg. 1975. *Truth and Method*. New York: Crossroad.

Howes, David, ed. 1991. *The Variety of Sensory Experience: A Sourcebook in the Anthropology of the Senses*. Toronto: University of Toronto Press.

Jay, Martin. 1993. *Downcast Eyes: The Denigration of Vision in Twentieth Century French Thought*. Berkeley and Los Angeles, Calif.: University of California Press.

Jenks, Chris, ed. 1995. *Visual Culture*. New York: Routledge.

Leder, Drew. 1990. *The Absent Body*. Chicago: University of Chicago Press.

Levinas, Emmanuel. 1969. *Totality and Infinity: An Essay on Exteriority*. Translated by Alphonso Lingis. Pittsburgh, P.A.: Duquesne University Press.

———. 1988. "Useless Suffering." Translated by Richard Cohen. In *The Provocation of Levinas: Rethinking the Other*, edited by Robert Bernasconi and David Wood. New York: Routledge. 156–67.

Levin, David Michael. 1988. *The Opening of Vision: Nihilism and the Postmodern Situation*. New York: Routledge.

Magee, Bryan and Martin Milligan. 1995. *On Blindness: Letters between Bryan Magee and Martin Milligan*. Oxford: Oxford University Press.

Merleau-Ponty, Maurice. 1962. *Phenomenology of Perception*. Translated by Colin Smith. New York: Humanities.

Michalko, Rod. 1998. *The Mystery of the Eye and the Shadow of Blindness*. Toronto: University of Toronto Press.

———. 1999. *The Two-in-One: Walking with Smokie, Walking with Blindness*. Philadelphia: Temple University Press.

Mirzoeff, Nicholas, ed. 1998. *The Visual Culture Reader*. New York: Routledge.

Oliver, Michael. 1996. *Understanding Disability: From Theory to Practice*. New York: St. Martin's.

Overboe, James. 1999. "'Difference in Itself': Validating Disabled People's Lived Experience." *Body and Society* 5(4): 17–29.

Sennett, Richard. 1990. *The Conscience of the Eye: The Design and Social Life of Cities*. New York: W.W. Norton.

Shilling, Chris. 1993. *The Body and Social Theory*. Newbury Park, Calif.: Sage.

Shklar, Judith N. 1990. *The Faces of Injustice*. New Haven: Yale University Press.

Silvers, Anita. 1998. "A Fatal Attraction to Normalizing: Treating Disabilities as Deviations from 'Species-Typical Functioning.'" In *Enhancing Human Traits: Ethical and Social Implications*, edited by Erik Parens. Washington, D.C.: Georgetown University Press. 95–123.

Smith, Dorothy E. 1987. *The Everyday World as Problematic: A Feminist Sociology*. Toronto: University of Toronto Press.

———. 1990. *The Conceptual Practices of Power: A Feminist Sociology of Knowledge*. Toronto: University of Toronto Press.

———. 1990. *Writing the Social: Critique, Theory, Investigations*. Toronto: University of Toronto Press.

Stewart, Janet. 1999. "Georg Simmel at the Lectern: The Lecture as Embodiment of Text." *Body and Society* 5(4): 1–16.

Synnott, Anthony. 1993. *The Body Social: Symbolism, Self and Society*. New York: Routledge.

Taylor, Charles. 1989. *Sources of the Self: The Making of the Modern Identity*. Cambridge, Mass.: Harvard University Press.

Thomson, Rosemarie Garland. 1997. *Extraordinary Bodies: Figuring Physical Disability in American Culture and Literature*. New York: Columbia University Press.

Titchkosky, Tanya. 2000. "Disability Studies: Old or New?" *Canadian Journal of Sociology and Anthropology* 25(2): 197–224.

Turner, Bryan S. 1996. *The Body and Society: Explorations in Social Theory*. Thousand Oaks, Calif.: Sage.

Weber, Max. 1947. *The Theory of Social and Economic Organization*. Translated by Talcott Parsons. New York: Free Press.

Wendell, Susan. 1996. *The Rejected Body: Feminist Philosophical Reflections on Disability*. New York: Routledge.

Zola, Irving. 1982. *Missing Pieces: A Chronicle of Living with a Disability*. Philadelphia: Temple University Press.

CHAPTER 7

When the Body Protests:

New Versions of Activism

Diane Driedger

To me, participating in society has always meant being active and being activist. I have always liked to see the TV footage of the U.S. black civil rights movement and the women's movement from the 1960s. In the early 1980s, I found a social movement—the disability rights movement—and proceeded to work with these organizations as a non-disabled ally. I was 20 and was enjoying seeing people who had felt disenfranchised grab hold of the tools of participation. People with disabilities were organizing to have their own voices heard.

By 1992 I had worked with the disability movement at the provincial, national, and international levels, through organizations such as the Manitoba League of Persons with Disabilities, Council of Canadians with Disabilities (CCD), and Disabled Peoples' International (DPI). At this juncture, I started having mysterious muscle aches and mounting fatigue that I brushed off to continue working in international projects with the Council of Canadians with Disabilities. I found that I was spending more time alone in my apartment recuperating after work and that I was not able to participate in as many volunteer activities. I wondered if I was getting lazy, if I had lost my zeal for causes, if it was all in my head.

Ultimately, I was diagnosed with fibromyalgia in 1996, after four years of floundering in the chronic illness wasteland of doubting myself. Fibromyalgia is a kind of arthritis of the muscles characterized by widespread muscle pain throughout the body and bone crushing fatigue. By this time, my preferred location in the house was the bed or the couch as sitting and standing and doing any prolonged physical activity was excruciatingly painful and debilitatingly tiring. All of my advocacy activities involved just those physical activities. And the Winnipeg winters were piling up in my body—my muscles did not like being cold and my limbs did not traverse snow banks gladly. My body was having a protest—something had to change.

I decided to move to Trinidad and Tobago, where I had been traveling with CCD in the past, to work with the disabled peoples' organizations there and where I had helped in the formation of the Disabled Women's Network (DAWN) of Trinidad. I thought, "I will continue to advocate for change in what little way I can, while I get well." I volunteered to teach a self-esteem and body image course at DAWN once a week. This experience was life-changing for me, as I learned so much from the women with disabilities who came to the class, who ranged in age from 12 to 80. I learned about being a woman, being a woman with a disability, and still retaining the dignity of who I was. Who I had been as a non-disabled woman was just part of the continuum of me, the making of me, a process. The DAWN women acted out scenes of the discrimination they had faced in their society and they discovered that they had hidden talents for performing.

We wrote poems, stories, and essays about being disabled and being a woman. In the end, I edited a small collection of these writings and we launched *From Hibernation to Liberation: Women with Disabilities Speak out* in 1999 (Driedger). This book was launched at the prestigious Central Bank in Port of Spain and cabinet ministers and the national media attended. The women read and felt empowered in the process. One woman actually became known as "the author" in her small village, rather than that "lady who walks with a cane" as she had always been known.

I knew that writing one's story had power, as I had been writing my own poetry since the early 1990s. I saw a new kind of activism—it was writing your way into people's consciousness, not marching in the streets. I decided to return to Canada and pursue this further. I needed to know more about literacy and theories of writing. I started a Ph.D. in Education in Language and Literacy in 2001 at the University of Manitoba. I wanted to study how writing and publishing one's work led to empowerment. I wanted to document this process of empowerment in a systematic way. I began to study and now I had no time to be involved in any community groups for change. My relationship to the disability movement was now at arm's length, as my arms couldn't carry any more responsibilities. I slugged it out course by course and did a lot of work lying down on my couch. I had started out feeling quite well after I returned from the sunny winters of Trinidad, but now, again, the cold and snow began to take its toll on my body. I meted out energy as best I could.

Now, in 2006, I am finishing research for my creative writing, publishing, and empowerment project in Baker Lake, Nunavut. I was in Nunavut on a short stint doing research on disability for the J. A. Hildes Northern Medical Unit at the University of Manitoba in 2001. I saw that the idea of writing and empowerment would work very well in the North, a place where orality had been the modus operandi for centuries. And now how did writing fit in to this society where they were looking to combine the traditional and the contemporary ways of life? People in Nunavut were keen to participate in my project.

Again, I packed up and this time went North for a month's time to teach a course with the Elders using traditional songs as our basis to encourage the adult students to write. Everyone produced several pieces of writing and the book, *The Sound of Songs* (Utatnaq), was born. In a few weeks I will return to investigate whether the students felt empowered by seeing their words in print—do they feel that people in the community view them differently now, and does that matter to them?

I see print as a way of extending the little energy I have into the "noosphere," as Pierre Teilhard de Chardin called the amorphous soup of ideas and consciousness that whirls around the world. My body does not need to be physically present at all times to be an activist body. Other ways that I have begun to project my physical body is through visual art. In the last year, I have created two pieces that use my image, in the way that the painter Frida Kahlo used hers. In fact, I see her as my twin activist, as she dealt with chronic pain and disability for most of her life. From her often-prone position in bed, she painted the subject she knew best—the reality of her body and how it appeared to her. Often, these images are raw, stark, and scary. The body is laid bare in all its weakness and despair. Yet, in the process of painting this reality, Kahlo took her body back and propelled it into the world, where it has demanded attention ever since.

I decided to paint myself into Frida's reality—in *Me and Frida Kahlo* I have mimicked her painting, *The Two Fridas*. I have become the Frida on the left, where she had painted

FIGURE 7.1

Diane Driedger, "Me and Frida Kahlo," watercolour on paper, 19" x 20", 2006.

herself in a white dress. In this painting, Frida and I are connected by the arteries of pain, by the blood of being women whose bodies are in protest. In protest of what, we are still unsure. Is it the stress of our societies, is it the disadvantaged position of women, which we rail against, is it the disadvantage of having a weak body in our work-obsessed society, is it the weight of global environmental degradation that has caused our bodies to revolt? In painting myself into Kahlo's picture, I continue to struggle with all these questions thinking perhaps I can find an answer in watercolour.

In my second piece of visual art, entitled, *My Will Remains*, I have created a small installation based on Kahlo's painting, "The Dream." In this painting, Frida lies in her four-poster bed, sleeping, with vines growing over her. On top of her bed's canopy lies a skeleton. Drawing on my interest in handmade rag dolls, I fashioned one of Frida and one of myself. Then, I had Frida's four-poster bed, measuring around two feet by three feet, built by a carpenter friend. Frida is placed in bed, with her easel on her lap, as she often painted, and I am on top of the canopy of the bed, lying down and reading. Next to me is a skeleton that is reaching down to Frida. This skeleton presents the "Judas figure" that was exploded at Easter

FIGURE 7.2

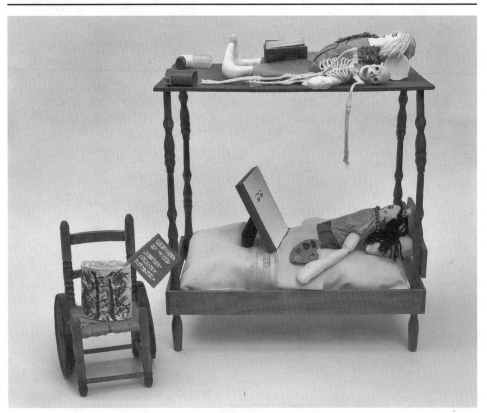

Diane Driedger, "My Will Remains," mixed media, 3' x 4', 2006.

time in Mexico and it is a symbol of suicide (Kettenmann). I see it as a symbol of death and the lines of life with chronic pain and immobility as blurred—death waits around the corner. After completing these two pieces, I learned I had breast cancer.

Premonitions. The artery link between Frida and I in my painting *Me and Frida Kahlo* reminds me of the PICC line that I now have implanted in my right arm to deliver chemotherapy. The plastic line goes up inside my arm and into a main artery of my heart. As for *My Will Remains*, this is a partial quote from Frida Kahlo who wrote, "My will is great. My will remains" (qtd. in Herrera 226). I continue to work lying down, and chemo is almost finished. My prognosis is good—but I must do six weeks of radiation yet. Indeed, my will remains.

References

Driedger, D., ed. *From Hibernation to Liberation: Women with Disabilities Speak out*. Port of Spain: Disabled Women's Network of Trinidad and Tobago, 1999.

Herrera, H. *Frida Kahlo: The Paintings*. New York: HarperCollins, 1993.

Kettenmann, A. *Frida Kahlo 1907–1954: Pain and Passion*. Koln: Taschen, 2000.

Teilhard de Chardin, P. *The Future of Man*. London: Collins, 1964.

Utatnaq, A., ed. *The Sound of Songs: Stories by Baker Lake*, Nunavut: Nunavut Arctic College. A collection.

CHAPTER 8

To Be or Not to Be? Whose Question Is It, Anyway?

Two Women with Disabilities Discuss the Right to Assisted Suicide

Tanis Doe and Barbara Ladouceur

Women with disabilities have been assaulted not only by individuals in their lives but also by a legal system and mass media that claims authority over their physical bodies as well as their minds. Women with disabilities of all types have had their bodies measured, altered, and judged by medical professionals, policy makers, and the general public. The question of whether to live or die must come back to the individual woman with a disability. The following dialogue is one that does not only take place in faculty rooms or at conferences, but also in living rooms, bedrooms, and sometimes hospitals. To be or not to be. Whose choice is it anyway?

Tanis

I wanted to die. I know I wanted to die. I wanted life to end as much as I wanted suffering to stop. I was not terminally ill. I was not even severely disabled in a medical sense. I was chronically ill and felt that my own depression was worse than any possible disease or disability. But I am alive to talk about it and glad that I am alive. I can honestly say that I am happy to have survived depression and that others like me are still alive. Some of us were rescued by friends or crisis lines and others just didn't succeed at getting dead. But we are only one side of the story. How can we ask the women who were actually able to die? Why do we assume that all the women who failed at suicide are the successful ones?

I do not want to debate the afterlife or the ethics of dying. I want women to enjoy living, and to participate in a satisfying life, but I also want to ensure that suicide is a choice for us.

Barbara

You say you wanted to die because you were chronically ill and depressed; I can relate to your situation because twenty years ago I was depressed and deeply dissatisfied with myself as a mother shortly after my daughter was born—it was probably tied in with post-partum depression. I remember how real my feeling was that everybody including my daughter would be better off if I was dead. But I'm glad I didn't "succeed." My failure at suicide felt like a "success" because afterwards I saw my attempt as a cry for help which I couldn't overtly articulate at the time. Fortunately, I did receive counselling which helped me build up the self-esteem and confidence that I needed in order to regard my life as worthwhile and fulfilling. Since then, whenever I contemplate others' failed or successful suicide attempts, I think of them as desperate cries for help, and thus if the woman fails at suicide I do think of her situation as more positive or successful than if she dies. I do think there is a reality that there are many people who killed themselves who could have gone on to live out their natural lives if their suicide had failed and intervention had taken place. I do think of people who are in a suicidal frame of mind as being emotionally disabled. In your case, did you actually attempt suicide or did you seek help beforehand?

Tanis

For me it was actually both. I did ask for help, and [I did] get some help before I tried. I attempted suicide by over-dosing on medication given to me by a doctor, combined with alcohol.

I remember waking up thinking I was once again a failure and couldn't even kill myself properly, but that seems to be common. It is actually difficult to know how to die safely. By "safely," I mean finding a way that will end your life rather than result in permanent brain damage or further disability. Women tend to attempt suicide more often than men, although men are more likely to actually die during their attempts. I think many women are medically treated or restricted during their expression of suicidal thoughts, which makes it very difficult for them to complete their wishes.

Barbara

You make an interesting point in saying that women are more medically treated or restricted, and thus less successful in their suicide attempts. The two most famous cases in the Canadian "right-to-die" movement were initiated by women with disabilities, Nancy B and Sue Rodriguez. I don't think either of them thought of their legal battles as gender-based. However, if we acknowledge that women in general and women with disabilities in particular tend to have less control over their lives than their male counterparts, it does seem most appropriate that it *is* women leading the fight for the ultimate choice: to be or not to be.

Tanis

I feel very strongly about the right to commit suicide because I know that it was a choice for me. When I hear that for some people it is not a choice because of disability, it scares me. Women with disabilities are not able to make their choices because society legally takes away their rights. Does this mean that as women, we are devalued by society, labelled by medical professionals and marginalized from the mainstream, and yet refused this final dignity of choice? They try very hard to prevent fetuses with disabilities from being born, yet once we are alive they won't let us take our own lives?

It has a rather paradoxical ring to it: we don't really want you here but we won't let you leave either. And this is important because there are many ways to address the issue of wanting to die.

Barbara

I agree with you that women with disabilities are especially devalued and marginalized by mainstream society, including the health care professionals to whom they go for service. When you point to the issue of choice, it seems to come down to the ongoing issue of women's control over their bodies, again.

I see parallels with the abortion issue—anti-abortion groups wish to deny all women the choice to terminate pregnancy, yet they do not on the other hand support every child's welfare after birth. There are not large-scale efforts by society in general to show that we value the lives of all children, or to alleviate their problems.

So the message seems to be that all children are valued until they are born, when they have to contend with mainstream society's hierarchy of rights and privileges. Children are certainly not born equal when there is still such deeply entrenched sexism, classism, racism, and ableism in society.

Tanis

If everyone wanted us to be part of society, if all access questions were already dealt with, and perhaps integration was commonplace, would some women with disabilities still want to die? Yes.

We still might want to die the same way thousands of non-disabled women want to die, and their situations are often very different from the lives of women with disabilities. The complexity and diversity of motivations must be considered because disability is not the only "justifiable reason" for wanting to die.

Should it matter if you want to die because of Alzheimer's or because of a personal crisis? In fact, it is silly that if someone is not fatally ill but physically able enough to end her own life we allow this, but if the person is so ill or incapacitated that she requires assistance, then we don't allow it.

Barbara

You are saying that we should separate the issue of disability as the motivation for women committing suicide. We are getting into another paradox because the right-to-die movement is based on the person having a "justifiable reason" for ending their life. It is argued that if a person is terminally ill and/or permanently and severely disabled, they have the right to end their lives because their suffering has become unbearable or the quality of their lives is non-existent. Women with disabilities understandably feel devalued when the degree of physical disability is put forward as justification for suicide. When I follow your line of thinking to put aside motivation and focus solely on the concept of every person having the right to decide when and how they will die, I feel comfortable in saying that I agree with this idea. If a woman kills herself then she has successfully exercised this right. But I am still haunted by the possibility that she was in a temporary state of mind—suffering an emotional disability that could have been alleviated by intervention.

Tanis

Intervention that might be drugs? Or maybe electroshock therapy or restraints and isolation? It is difficult to condemn women's choices when their alternatives seem so poor. So there are two questions about women with disabilities choosing death that need to be thought through—one is their motivation and the other is their ability to follow through with their ideas.

Barbara

You are so right. Given the reality of women's lack of self-esteem and/or lack of "success" in life being rooted in concrete prescribed codes of behaviour according to gender which already restrict their life choices, how can others tell us that we are mentally incompetent if we want to die? Perhaps the opposite is true.

Tanis

Motivation for death is not always due to one specific issue. Some older women want to die to avoid wasting away or suffering unnecessary and intrusive medical procedures. Some people feel that pain is unbearable and prefer the shelter of death over drugs to resolve their pain. Other women may want to die because life has become so emotionally and spiritually empty that life is of no value. The discussion about suicide usually ends up with the issue of disability not being considered worth dying over. In fact, it is not always their disability that motivates women to want to die. In any event, the reasons women choose to die should not affect the judgement of others in power.

Barbara

When I contemplate the overwhelming problems of our world—hunger, war, environmental devastation—and when I visualize the huge number of people, especially women and children, trapped in oppressive and violent situations, it seems clear that a right-minded person would certainly be justified in wanting to make a final exit. I would still prefer to achieve more options and control over our lives for all women, so that less lives are "emotionally and spiritually empty," but such a revolution is not likely to be achieved in the near future.

The right to die is such a complex issue, I have conflicting ideas within me. Yes, I can agree that all women should have total control over their lives including whether to end them but if it was my daughter or friend who successfully committed suicide, I'd be devastated and definitely regret that I hadn't been able to intervene. I guess you could say that sometimes the political conflicts with the personal. So let's move on to the second issue.

Tanis

The second issue is being able to carry through wishes. Searching out and being able to administer a method of death is problematic for women with disabilities. Often the difficulty is finding one that is fatal enough that one can be sure of death and not another version of existence which could possibly be worse than the current situation. But women with severe physical disabilities who need assistance with daily chores and personal care may be dependent on others for several types of assistance. In fact it is the issue of assistance that is almost more contentious than that of choice. Once a woman with a disability who is dependent on others has made the choice to die, who will help her? Can she ask her friends or doctors to do this? If she asks and they refuse, what action can she take? It seems almost cruel to deny a person who normally receives assistance without question this final assistance. Can I have a glass of water please? Can you move my left arm onto my lap? If an assistant ignored these requests and continually denied the woman food or comfort it would be criminal. In fact, it would be considered abuse and neglect if it continued.

Barbara

Yes, it may be that relatives of caregivers are just not emotionally or morally capable of enabling a woman with a disability to end her life. Perhaps our society will have to support more doctors like Kavorkien who are physically and emotionally removed from such situations. They are perhaps in a better position to "objectively" and non-exploitively agree to assist people to die. If we put aside the potential for exploitation and the issue of motivation in order to morally and legally recognize the right to die, then maybe we need "death doctors" just as there are abortion doctors and still others who won't participate.

Otherwise we run into another tragic paradox. I can agree with a woman's right to choose death, but I also think whoever is requested to assist her death has the right to say no for whatever moral or emotional reasons they may have. Following this logic, it is unfortunately quite possible that although women with disabilities may have the legal right to die, there will be no one in her life who can or will assist her to die. Because no one should be forced to help someone die, we are possibly moving towards the ultimate conflict of interests.

Tanis

But women with disabilities who are asking not to be fed, or not to be connected to machines or even to be given medication that would result in death, are not being helped. The helpers themselves are not necessarily making these judgements. There are countless situations that have never been publicized in the media in which women had their friends help them make the final exit without much attention. However, once the public sphere is involved, once there are media, courts, and politicians, death no longer becomes a choice. Death becomes a legal debate, an ethical question, and a political issue.

In many cases women with disabilities have had their rights taken away by the medical system which labels them as incompetent. An insidious legal technique is to institutionalize and medicate her; this process also dehumanizes the woman. Judges look favourably on a medical doctor's opinion regarding the mental competency of a patient, particularly suicidal ones.

In fact, even a layperson would agree that no one in their right mind would want to die. Ergo, suicidal women are mentally incompetent, with legal and medical procedures to support this. But the politicians have a hand in this too.

Barbara

I like your point that it is only when the issue of suicide becomes public that choice is eliminated and suddenly strangers are given the right to tell us whether or not we can choose to die. But I do think it is more a question of the final and irreversible consequences of assisted suicide rather than the apparent inequality of rights we see when we acknowledge the ability of an able-bodied woman to kill herself versus the inability of a woman with a disability to kill herself due to lack of assistance. If a person assists a suicide, then they may wonder if the suicidal person might have later changed their minds about wanting to die. They may question themselves as to whether they made a correct assessment as to whether the assisted suicide was actually in the suicidal person's best interests. In any other "helping" situation, you can still see and communicate with the assisted person and evaluate how they are doing in order to adjust or change strategies accordingly.

At an abstract level, I agree with the right-to-die concept, but when I visualize concrete situations, I start having doubts because once the person has died, they can't come back and assure you that the right decision was made. It's one thing to decriminalize suicide when a person commits the act on their own, but when other people become involved, the issue becomes much more complicated with a wider range of circumstances and variables to be assessed.

Tanis

Suicide has been decriminalized as an act, and yet assisting or encouraging suicide is still against the law. It seems quite discriminatory that this law about suicide was made by able-bodied people who would be able to take their own lives without assistance if need be. However, if a woman with a disability makes the choice to die on her own, and needs help to carry it out, is she a criminal? More specifically is her assistant a criminal? The injustice is obvious: there are two types of equality— equality for those who are able-bodied, and equality for those who are different. Women are already subject to many kinds of violence and control over their bodies. Women are raped, assaulted, battered, stalked, and robbed by people who have power over them. Suicide is a way for women to have control over their own lives.

Barbara

Yes, women with disabilities must have the right to refuse care or treatment. However, the ending of life-support efforts does appear more feasible in terms of merely requiring the cessation of intervention by health-care professionals. But actually *taking* action to kill a person, even when the person has requested death, is more problematic. There is always the legitimate concern that caregivers who are already powerful forces in the lives of women with disabilities could exploit a woman's right to die in the interests of the caregiver and not the woman. So I can only agree that on the one hand women with disabilities must have their choice to die respected and, if necessary, assisted, but as long as society builds in safeguards to assure that the woman with a disability herself has decided to die and that no one coerced them into their decision in order to exploit her.

Tanis

The question of abortion, of fetal testing, or genetic manipulation is not being debated in this case. It is adult women, not science that is being discussed. Some women have become disabled, and generally feel it is tragic that their lives have changed. Some women have had disabilities throughout their lives and continue to lead happy, productive lives. Regardless of their status in life, all women must have death as an option. Not because society wants them to die, but because it is a legal and moral obligation of society to allow the dignity and security of the person. Choice.

Choosing death over life is not a decision made hastily. In fact, there are probably many women who have regretted attempted suicides and are now leading fulfilling lives after treatment or life situation changes. But there will always be women who do want to die and do need help in order to kill themselves. If you are so physically dependent on others for assistance that you need to ask to eat, then you should also have the right to not eat. Forced tube feedings and intrusive operations against personal wishes seem far more criminal than the issue of assisting a choice of a woman.

Questions are raised about abuse, or rather overuse, of this process should it be legalized. Too many people would "help" others die, and there would be ulterior motives in assisting suicides, issues of living wills, estate, inheritance, and burden would come up. There are equally large numbers of violent crimes that now occur, particularly against women, which are not being adequately addressed by the existing laws. In fact, there may eventually be a long list of situations which allow for assistances and others which preclude it. Yet this again avoids the question of choice.

Barbara

Just as outside parties such as police, lawyers, and judges often have to enter an abused woman's life situation in order to assess the appropriate action to protect her against her abuser (such as issuing a restraint order) which guarantees her right to life, so too should there be outside parties involved in the process of facilitating a woman's right to die and to assure that it is in her *own* best interests and not someone else's.

Women with disabilities are not supported in their choices to die, to live, or to procreate, because a system of legal and medical procedures is in place to make decisions for women. But non-disabled women, and to an even greater degree, able-bodied men, are given better choices because of the lack of restraints in their lives. If they choose to die, it is a private matter and their decision. Women with disabilities lack this freedom of choice in death.

Remember that women with disabilities are not asking *only* for the right to die. Women with disabilities want to live, and live happily and with positive results, but they cannot do that without control over their bodies. It does come back to the role of women's bodies in society. Women in general are seen as baby-makers, life givers, and service providers.

Tanis

Lawyers and medical professionals are paid well for their work but women with disabilities, for the most part, are poor, and they are not able to spend their last dollars on hiring specialists to defend or evaluate them, and often would be unwilling to use their time and money for this. The issue of choice must be a personal one, and that choice should be legalized so that no procedures are initiated once the choice is made.

The trouble that some disabled women have with this issue relates to quality of life. Women with disabilities suffer higher rates of sexual and physical abuse, live with psychological abuse, and generally are mistreated by society. Some women with disabilities advocate for better education, safety, and employment while others work for better personal assistance, transportation, and housing. Regardless of the status of women with disabilities in general, a woman with a disability can personally make a choice to die. The issue of birth and death is also tied in with the issue of choice—thousands of women have taken their own lives because of inaccessible abortions. Thousands of women have died because of illegal and unsafe abortions. Choice is a matter of life and death for all women. But even if the situation for all women with disabilities was horrible and painful, each woman would still have to make the personal choice. There is no general rule or procedure because it is a matter of choice. If everything in this complicated world was perfect and accessible to women with all disabilities, some women as individuals would still need the right to make the choice to live or die. It is my life, and my choice to make.

Barbara

But women with disabilities challenge that role and confuse the everyday assumptions about the role of women. As a result, there are endless possibilities for debate: Can women with disabilities reproduce normal healthy babies and do we want these women to be mothers? Should we allow a fetus with an obvious disability to be brought to term? Which disabilities are considered severe enough to terminate pregnancy and which disabilities in adult women should preclude her from being allowed to have children? Can a child or woman with a disability experience any quality of life beyond that of mere existence? If she wants to die should we let her? Should we help her? Who are we to decide for her, whether she is to be or not to be? Whose question is it anyway?

Institutionalizing Normalcy

One common, but nonetheless powerful, way that normalcy arises in the life of disability is through the organization of those institutions that aim to help, manage, contain, or control disabled people. Not only do unquestioned conceptions of normalcy support the ways in which disability makes an appearance in contemporary institutions, but these institutions also help to reproduce these conceptions. The chapters in Part III are an opportunity to explore the role normalcy plays in ordering disability as an institutional matter.

Established institutions for fundraising have been a "normal" part of Western society's conception of disability for a long time. These events always rely on a "charity" orientation to disability and always promote the hope of preventing and curing disability. In Chapter 9, Paul Longmore addresses these issues. Longmore shows how charity fundraisers conceive of people as being either "givers" or "takers." He demonstrates how this dichotomy is used by charities to show how people are either compassionate, and thus "givers," or selfish, and thus "takers." Longmore's analysis shows how charities promote a morality that emphasizes that disability is a tragedy requiring charitable responses and that, while "givers" represent the compassionate part of America, "takers" represent the irresponsible or selfish aspect of America. Of course, in the middle of this institutionalized dichotomy and moral lesson are disabled people. Longmore shows how charities treat disabled people as "recipients" not only of the "good work" of charities, and thus as people who must be grateful, but also as people who are themselves used as examples in order to teach America the moral lesson of being compassionate. Longmore demonstrates that this conception of disability has implications for the careers of disabled people as well as for disability identity.

How we are known to others and to ourselves is steeped in the history of how we are referred to or what we are called. In Chapter 10, Geoffrey Reaume addresses this history as it pertains to people who are referred to as "mentally ill" by conducting an analysis of their labour. What people do or are forced to do can be studied in order to reveal a society's historical response to difference. Reaume shows how patients' work in the last half of the 19th century in Canada enforces a particular understanding of mental illness. The institutionalization of people serves to institutionalize our conceptions of normalcy and abnormalcy. This permits us to understand how mental illness lives through social activities such as work.

In Chapter 11, Claudia Malacrida takes a similar approach in her analysis of "total institutions." Malacrida examines the narratives of people who are survivors of the Michener

Centre. The Michener Center is a total institution in Alberta that opened its doors in 1923. A total institution is one organized to have complete control over the lives of the people contained within it. Such total institutional control makes use of severe forms of discipline and punishment on those "inmates" who are understood to deviate from the normative demand to be "at one with" institutional orders regarding, for example, eating, sleeping, walking, cleaning, or even talking. Malacrida's analysis addresses how total institutions discipline the disabled body and she demonstrates this by focusing on "time-out rooms." In 1923, this Centre called the people they were treating "mental defectives" and this conception of disability influenced how people were disciplined within the institution. Even though Malacrida focuses on one particular institution, institutional life is not a stranger to disability; in fact, it is one of the "normal" ways we think of disabled people. We often think that disabled people should have a "special place" or that they have "special needs" that must be addressed institutionally. Malacrida also demonstrates how total institutions rely on other normative discourses in relation to disability, such as science and eugenics. These discourses influence the lives of disabled people insofar as they determine who is "normal" and who is "abnormal" and who should be institutionalized and who should not.

CHAPTER 9

Conspicuous Contribution and American Cultural Dilemmas:

Telethon Rituals of Cleansing and Renewal

Paul K. Longmore

On the 1989 Muscular Dystrophy Association (MDA) Telethon, the president of the firefighters association declared: "There are givers and there's takers in this world. Firefighters are givers. All those people who can hear me out there can be givers too." This differentiation, which recurs implicitly on all telethons, is more than a ploy to prod donations. It draws an important moral boundary. It contrasts humane concern for one's neighbors with selfish preoccupation with one's private interests. It distinguishes those who personally shoulder responsibility for the civic welfare from those who indulge in self-centered irresponsibility. This marking off of "givers" and "takers," a separation of sheep from goats, is a central symbolic task of telethons.

But as they draw the dichotomy between the compassionate and the selfish, telethons symbolically define not just two but three types of persons. There are not only givers and takers. It is necessary that there also be recipients of "giving." Invention of the third category is indispensable to creation and maintenance of the first two. These classifications have far-reaching consequences for the social identities and social careers of people with disabilities. They are the ones ceremonially defined as the natural objects of charity because, according to the telethons, they have been socially invalidated by disability. Telethons offer occasions for individuals to act upon genuinely compassionate regard for their fellow human beings, but this "caring" is inextricably intertwined with the social stigma inscribed on people with disabilities.

It is important to examine how and why these rites frame opportunities for interwoven compassion and contempt in the particular ways they do. The telethon, a late-twentieth-century American cultural invention, expresses distinctively American values and addresses peculiarly American concerns. It attempts to resolve a variety of historic and ongoing dilemmas within American culture. The telethon is, on one level, a response to a number of deep-rooted American cultural, ultimately moral, predicaments.

Beginning with the era of the Revolution, the founding moment when Americans set into orbit the constellation of values that compose their cultural universe, they have declared and celebrated the right of individuals to pursue their own personal happiness, their own private interests. The dynamic of individualism has functioned as one of the most powerful forces shaping American society, for good and for ill. It claims for each citizen the twin rights to equality of opportunity and equality of esteem.[1]

Yet individualism also has often seemed to Americans to eat away at the bonds of their community by setting individuals above that community and against it. From the beginning, Americans have feared this centrifugal effect of their commitment to an individualistic ethos. Their celebration of the value of the individual and their liberation of individual potentialities has simultaneously given free rein to privatistic and self-centered impulses. As American society emancipated individuals to advance their personal welfare, it also implicitly permitted them to ignore the public weal—and to feel justified in doing so.[2]

In response to this moral and political peril, Americans, throughout their history, have warned themselves that the success of their democratic experiment rests on the public virtue of the people at large. If citizens voluntarily put the common good above their private interests, free democratic society will flourish. But if they set selfish concerns ahead of the general welfare, democracy inevitably will fail. This belief in the necessity of public virtue has operated in tension, and even in competition, with the devotion to individualism.

In historical moments when self-centered, rather than public-minded, individualism seemingly has overtaken them and their society, Americans, with a tone of alarm, have preached to themselves the imperative practicing public virtue. That sense of alarm has grown acute in the late twentieth century as self-maximization seems to have become the credo of American culture. Pop psychologists and self-help gurus proclaim that individuals have first of all to take care of themselves. Social critics decry this as narcissism that spurns true human connection and communal responsibility. They charge that it teaches individuals to aggrandize themselves in disregard of authentic attachments and at the expense of other selves. In particular, some assert, the philosophy of capitalistic individualism teaches that one realizes one's self most fully through consumption. "Capitalism tells us that the meaningful life is the life that maximizes the self," writes Joel Kovel. "Whatever is 'me' has more, does more, achieves more; such is the good life, whether measured in terms of compact disks, muscles, orgasms, publicity, or cash."[3] Heeding such critics, many Americans fear that in getting and spending, buying and consuming, they have become takers, severed from any authentic community by an insatiable, self-centered pursuit of material possessions. At the least, they fear they may be accused of that sort of selfishness.

On one level of cultural meaning, telethon donation is a collective rite designed to enable Americans to demonstrate to themselves that they still belong to a moral community, that they have not succumbed to materialism, that they are givers who fulfill their obligations to their neighbors. The electronic display of charity is a communal response to the moral and social dangers of narcissism and materialism. The vast American audience uses telethon donation to reassure itself, individually and collectively, of *its moral health*.

As with Ebenezer Scrooge, Dickens's symbol of rapacious nineteenth-century capitalism, aiding Tiny Tim, the literal embodiment of neglected human need, telethon poster children are made the means by which nondisabled people can prove to themselves that they have not been corrupted by an egocentric and materialistic capitalist order. People with disabilities are ritually defined as being dependent upon the moral fitness of nondisabled people. While takers repudiate their duty to these helpless neighbors, the compassion of givers toward "the less fortunate" publicly verifies the givers' moral standing. Telethon giving demonstrates the persistence of public virtue. It confirms to individual donors their possession of that virtue by distinguishing them from both takers and the invalidated. It ritualistically enacts a reversal of everyday reality. The ceremonial counterimage to conspicuous consumption is conspicuous contribution.

The telethon ritual also proclaims as an important fact that givers practice their virtue voluntarily. This liturgy rests on the assumption that moral voluntarism, the decisions of individuals, freely and privately made, verifies the reality of public virtue, thus reassuring Americans of the viability of their democratic political order and capitalist economic system. Americans define these "free" choices of each particular donor to give for the common good as morally more laudable than a collective decision to provide for that common good by taxing themselves. The communal commitments of Western European societies to maintain comprehensive national health insurance systems implicitly seem to many Americans not only politically undesirable but morally suspect. Rather than regard such policies as implementing collective moral choices to ensure the common weal, Americans scorn them as state intrusion. Americans, among the most antistatist of peoples, gauge their devotion to the common good far less by the activities they require of their government "to promote the general welfare" than by the volume of their individual donations to private charities. The antistatism, individualism, and privatism so powerfully at work in American culture define the vigor of nongovernmental endeavors as the indicator of Americans' dedication to the general weal. Thus personal moral voluntarism and individual community volunteerism are made measures of the condition of American civic virtue.

From time to time, telethon participants, playing the role of moral leader, spell out this message of the telethon ritual. They proclaim that these efforts vindicate the moral superiority of American voluntarism and volunteerism. Year after year on the United Cerebral Palsy (UCP) Telethon, veteran national emcee Dennis James recites a poem about the special place in heaven reserved for volunteers. In 1993, Jerry Lewis proclaimed his "great pride" that MDA is not "government-oriented ... We've never been subsidized by the government. We have done this ourselves, between you and me." On the 1994 Easter Seals Telethon, cohost Robb Weller introduced someone who literally embodied American values, "the stunning young woman who will be representing the United States at the Miss Universe pageant, ... Miss U.S.A." She would offer "some patriotic words about Easter Seals." Miss U.S.A. then delivered this "patriotic" homily: "Easter Seals typifies what America is all about: hard work, independence, and generosity. Generosity fills the heart of America, because when tragedy strikes, from Mississippi floods to California earthquakes, we Americans come together in the spirit of volunteerism, willing to give whatever we can to help our neighbors get back on their feet. But smaller tragedies happen every day. An auto accident costs a young mother her ability to walk. A stroke paralyzes a middle-aged father of three. A stray gunshot causes a high school senior to lose her sight ... Easter Seals does all it can to help turn tragedy into triumph. So please, reach into your hearts and feel that truly American spirit of generosity."

The "generosity," the moral voluntarism, of charity volunteers aims to restore the "independence" of other individuals whose own competency for moral voluntarism has been compromised by "tragedies," physical and economic limitations resulting from natural catastrophes or physiological disabilities. The capacity to function as a true American, an independent moral agent, is predicated upon physical and economic self-sufficiency. Givers act to revalidate fellow Americans who have been rendered socially illegitimate by disability.

As ceremonies to certify the vitality of moral voluntarism, of public virtue, telethons are rites of American nationalism. In a centrifugal pluralistic society, the broadcasts are designed, in part, to fortify the national identity. Charity giving has long functioned to bolster patriotic Americanism.[4] In a sense, the only thing Americans have held in common, the only glue that has held them together, is a shared allegiance to what is regarded as a distinctive set of "American" values. The nationalistic telethon ritual marks off individuals who practice those values from those who fail to do so. It distinguishes "good," which is to say authentic, Americans from both bad ones and inauthentic ones, which is to say, from takers and those invalidated by disability.

Telethons sometimes convoke themselves as nationalistic ceremonies by stirring viewers with patriotic anthems. On the 1990 MDA extravaganza, live on stage, the venerable pop singer Ray Charles sang "America the Beautiful," and his young counterpart Michael Bolton, on tape at (perhaps predictably) a softball game, trumpeted "The Star-Spangled Banner." Sometimes the patriotic fervor turns militant. The 1992 Easter Seals rally heard country singer Eddie Rabbit proclaim in the song "I'm an American Boy": "I buy American. / I'll die an American." The 1991 UCP pageant occurred during the Persian Gulf War, so opera star Robert Merrill and the American Pilgrim Chorus offered a medley of patriotic songs that included "America the Beautiful" and "God Bless America," and a few minutes later that nationalistically named choir intoned "This Is My Country." A few weeks later on the Easter Seals spectacle, Bobby Vinton sang "I'm Proud to Be an American."

Telethons are a combination of patriotic rally and religious revival. And so, a local Easter Seals host harangued viewers to phone in and make the light circle go all the way around. She proclaimed that Easter Seals was giving disabled people "a chance to step up and out and be a part of life like you and me! We take life for granted! Don't! These people don't!" Like a preacher in a tent meeting, she went on for several minutes, exhorting at the top of her voice. Some of the operators whose phones sat silent started to clap in unison. One of the male hosts also began preaching. The two hosts exhorted simultaneously. "We've got to do it!" they shouted. "I know you can do it! I know we can do it! I believe!"[5] Local hosts on some telethons entreat viewers to make the circle of lights go all the way around. They press watchers to call in so that the telephone operators can sit down. UCP emcee Dennis James will say: "I checked on the phones, and the phones are a hundred percent busy right now." It is a ritual exhortation to demonstrate commitment to moral community in a public way, to display civic virtue conspicuously.

Each year telethon hosts exhort viewers to help them top last year's total. "We have no goal," affirmed Dennis James on the 1993 UCP show and then proceeded to announce their goal. "We want to make as much or more than we made last year." "No telethon has ever gone lower than the year before," he explained significantly. "That's our measure of success. So I know that you're not going to let us down." Jerry Lewis agrees. He always declares his intention to get at least one dollar above the year before.

When the pace of pledge making lags, telethon hosts chide viewers, reminding them of their moral duty. "Sometimes we get to a point like this where I've got to be your conscience," James admonished the audience in a slack moment in 1994. "I've been saying that now for forty-three years on this telethon. I've got to be your conscience." "I hate to pound you," he said, "but I don't want to go off with any less than we had last year ... It's your telethon. You're the ones who make the calls." During one pledge match on the 1989 Arthritis Telethon, cohost Larry Van Nuys exhorted: "You have to decide who you are and what you want to represent."

The annual increases in telethon donations are taken as another sign of the maintenance of public virtue. If the final totals dropped—or even stayed at the same level as the year before—it would evidence a decline in public virtue. Americans are legendary scorekeepers. They rate everything they do with numerical records. They measure their achievements by the stats. Telethon hosts note that many pledge makers like to phone in near the end of these protracted broadcasts. Telethon donation thus becomes a kind of competition, a sport, a game of reaching a new statistical high point. Are Americans more caring or less? More compassionate or more selfish? The figures flashing on the electronic tote boards will tell the tale of success or failure, of moral improvement or moral decline. To everyone's reassurance, the telethons' final totals are above last year's pledges. The numbers confirm that Americans still practice public virtue. "The generosity we're seeing tonight again proves that Americans are loving, caring people," affirmed John Ritter on the 1995 UCP rally. "Let's see how loving, how caring," urged his co-host Henry Winkler. "Let's see the results." The two turned to the tote board. "We are a marvelous country of terrific people," declared Jerry Lewis on the 1989 MDA ritual, pointing to his telethon's tote board, "proof positive, people that care."

Contrary to gloomy social critics, American public virtue, according to the telethons, is not in decline. In 1992, Easter Seals national cohost Mary Frann countered the Jeremiahs: "You know, we hear so much about the problems that we're facing as a society. Our economy is stalled. People are losing their jobs. And people say our values are declining. But I guess any one of those factors would seem like a reason to put off giving to Easter Seals. But thank goodness you decided that the reasons to give outweighed the ones not to. And that tremendous outpouring of goodwill says more about us as a society than any column or poll could ever say." UCP national cohost Nancy Dussault offered identical reassurance in 1994: "If we look at the headlines today, we are misled to believe that America is a nation of heartless, uncaring cynics. Nothing could be farther from the truth," she rebutted. "America is a land of thoughtful, caring, giving people, who do indeed love each other."

Easter Seals enlisted newly inaugurated President Bill Clinton in 1993 to proclaim the same comforting message from the "bully pulpit." The president told telethon viewers that there is "a new spirit" in the land. "There's a new sense of possibility," he claimed, "a new willingness to take on challenges, a new willingness to contribute, I think, a clear new understanding that we have to make strength and unity out of our many diversities as a society. We do have to go back to a community, to know that together we can do more than we ever can separately. So I want to congratulate the Easter Seals on its back-to-community movement. It's an important part of rebuilding the American community and securing the future for all of our people."

America, the historian Sidney Mead wrote, is "a nation with the soul of a church." Telethons are rituals of America's civic religion. They are moral allegories of cleansing and renewal. They symbolically represent individual and collective turning away from the self-centered conduct that is perceived as having undermined or ruptured the community. Although they ostensibly seek the physical repair of those socially invalidated by disability, they are more importantly rituals of moral restoration for nondisabled communicants. Telethons offer donors a momentary sense of the wholeness that comes with membership in a moral community. The broadcasts project a brief annual apparition of that community in a materialistic, competitive, atomized society.

All telethon hosts proclaim that their particular charity restores the sense of "caring" and "community." They call viewers to commit themselves to the telethon's mission. The hosts are not merely emcees but are, more importantly, moral preceptors. And the ministry is the same for all the telethons: to help the needy, to aid "the less fortunate." "The Easter Seals way of caring," said one host in 1990, "is ... one heart reaching out in love to another heart in need of compassion."

Giving to Get

In fact, of course, this "reaching out" of "one heart ... to another" takes place only symbolically. The phone-in pledge makers do not directly come to know any particular person with a disability. The "caring" are connecting only with an image on their TV screens. It is a representation carefully fashioned within the telethon system and bearing little relation to the actual lives of people with disabilities. But this fictive reaching out to a contrived image is necessary to complete the verification of moral voluntarism and personal volunteerism on the part of givers. To function efficaciously, the ritual requires a class of persons defined as "needy," as socially invalidated.

In addition, the actual proportion of viewers phoning in pledges undercuts the claim that conspicuous telethon contribution demonstrates the vitality of American public virtue and community. Dennis James reported on the 1995 UCP Telethon that only two telethon watchers out of ten make pledges. It seems unlikely that other telethons induce much more than 20 percent of their audiences to respond. No more than a righteous remnant of the American people prove themselves to be givers.

Most important, a troubling feature of the telethon system subverts the self-proclaimed restoration of American community and sullies the vaunted virtue of givers. Telethons instantly taint the civic-mindedness they seek to renew by promoting the very materialism and self-centeredness they promise to exorcise. Even while telethon preceptors purport to call on viewers' sense of empathy, they often deliberately appeal to their avarice and self-aggrandizement.

During the 1980s and 1990s, telethons have drawn donations by offering bonuses and discounts, by putting up prizes and "free" gifts. The corporate sponsors of the telethon system promote a wide array of consumer products through special sales linked to the charities. Companies tell potential customers that they will be contributing to help the "less fortunate," even as those businesses urge individual donors to pursue personal economic advantage. A bold-lettered headline in Easter Seals' 1989 Sunday newspaper supplement urged consumers to join self-interest to condescension: "Save up to $8.00 and help us open doors for special people." In 1991, cohost Mary Frann counseled viewers: "You'll get a twofold benefit. You're gonna save lots of money, and you'll also help Easter Seals too by simply using these coupons." Telethons enable not just businesses to gain by giving but individual donors as well. The telethons and the manufacturers encourage consumers to profit under the guise of helping disabled people.

Hungry viewers can get discount coupons on food. In 1993, the marketing director of Little Caesar's Pizza, an Easter Seals corporate sponsor, described their two national promotional campaigns, a calendar and a coupon book available at Little Caesar's outlets. Customers would save money "on select Little Caesar's menu items." In 1994, a spokesman again touted the coupon books: "This is a great way for customers to save money on their favorite foods and help out this great cause." Friendly's Restaurants invites customers to give a dollar to Easter Seals and get something for themselves: a "free" ice cream cone or a discount coupon toward a meal. Consumers who aren't in the mood for pizza or ice cream can go to Wienerschnitzel. On the San Francisco Easter Seals broadcast (1991), a spokesperson announced the fast food chain's promotion: $5 coupon books for those who gave a dollar to Easter Seals. A local host immediately coined a sales slogan: "Eat a corn dog, help Easter Seals."

Local telethon segments offer most of the prizes. Viewers of one cutaway to the 1992 San Francisco Bay Area Easter Seals show could win a large floral bouquet if they were the eighth caller. Later in the broadcast, the first twenty callers would get a cookbook. And if they came down to the site of a remote telecast at a Safeway store in the East Bay, they might win prizes in several draws: backyard barbecues, a set of roller blades, or hats. In 1994 and 1995 during various hours, anyone pledging fifty dollars or more would get a "free," San Jose Sharks hat, a San Francisco 49'ers cap, or an Oakland A's or San Francisco Giants cap. And for a $75 donation, viewers got a Giants cap plus four tickets to a Giants game. During each hour, a different incentive lured pledges. On mid-1990s Easter Seals Chicago segments, a woman from the Honey Bear Ham Company was accompanied by "Mama and Papa Bear," two people wearing bear costumes. The first twenty callers pledging $100 would get Honey Bear's Easter basket with a glazed ham in it.

Younger philanthropists can profit too. MDA's "hop-a-thons" offer nondisabled school-children a selfish incentive. They can earn prizes while they hop "for those who can't."[6]

By using prizes and gifts and discount coupons to draw donations, telethons train non-disabled children and adults to regard people with disabilities not only as objects of their charity but as means for their personal aggrandizement. On the San Francisco portion of the 1994 Easter Seals Telethon, a local host asked one of the telephone operators about the caller she had just spoken with on the phone. "Somebody wants to know when the big screen TV is going to be raffled off," she explained. "Ah, well," said the emcee, a bit embarrassed, "they'll just have to wait on the big screen TV."

The offer of incentives exposes a selfish motive behind the boasted public virtue. It reveals telethon donation as, for many givers, just one more means of personal gain, little different from buying a lottery ticket. Rather than being an American back-to-community effort, telethons often seem to be charity versions of another late-twentieth-century broadcast phenomenon, the home shopping networks.

The Sound of Trumpets

Even when the incentive is nonmaterial, the motive for giving promoted by telethons is still often self-centered.

Jesus Christ taught: "When you give alms, sound no trumpet before you, as the hypocrites do ... that they may be praised by men ... But when you give alms, do not let your left hand know what your right hand is doing, so that your alms may be in secret; and your Father who sees in secret will reward you."[7]

Andy Warhol foretold: "In the future everyone will be famous for fifteen minutes."[8]

Rather than follow the commandment of the Israelite teacher, telethons fulfill the prediction of the American prophet. Every donor gets a shot of celebrity. The national and local broadcasts feature an endless parade of check presenters. They represent labor unions and fraternal orders, schools and sororities, small businesses, and, most visibly, large corporations. On national segments, corporate executives appear in the spotlight more frequently than any other type of check presenter. On some telethons, they display oversized mock "checks," and on all telethons corporate sponsors present their donations in several installments rather than one lump sum. All of this is designed to make the giving even more conspicuous. Sometimes corporate heads and union chiefs introduce employees, distributors, retailers, or members from around the country who have racked up the most pledges. The camera pans down the line, and the telethon hosts greet them. On the local segments, hosts call to center stage representatives of local companies, agencies, and service organizations who report how they raised the funds and present their checks.

Local telethon segments give particular recognition to donors pledging larger amounts. MDA has its "Star Patrons," Easter Seals its "Angel Boards," and the Arthritis Telethon has its "VIP Salutes." As the San Jose MDA segment host explained the Star Patron program in 1994, silver and gold stars were superimposed on the screen. Above the dollar value of each star was the phrase, "Your Name Here."

But even the smallest contributors can get a few seconds of TV fame. Callers can hear their names and the amounts they have pledged read on the air or can see them roll across the bottom or top of the screen. On the national Arthritis, MDA, and UCP telecasts, hosts read the names of pledge makers from all over the country, giving their hometowns and the sums promised.[9] During the 1991 national MDA segments, the San Jose affiliate superimposed the following announcement: "If You Pledge $25 or More, Your Name Will Be Read in the Next Local Segment!" The 1993 Chicago-area Easter Seals broadcast made the same guarantee. The telethons' local hosts often promise to announce pledge makers' names no matter what the amount. As the phones ring, local emcees grab handfuls of pledge cards and reel off names and numbers: "Allen Baumann from West LA, $20. Mr. and Mrs. Gibbs from Reseda, $25. Joseph Withers in Long Beach, $15." And on and on. "Would you call now? We will read your name as fast as we possibly can."

How many viewers, one wonders, would phone in a pledge if their names would not be announced? How many others would give if they could win no prizes or bonuses? How many fund-raisers would organize charity events if they could not present checks on camera? How many corporations would donate if their giving yielded no PR (Public Relations) benefit or additional profits? The telethon makers make plain their answers to these questions.

Alluding to the prescient Andy Warhol, MDA's San Jose host pointed out in 1991: "We often talk about people having their own fifteen minutes of glory. You can have a moment of glory if you make that telephone call right now." Telethons encourage conspicuous charity partly because it stimulates donations. Americans will give if they know it will get their names or faces on the screen. A few dollars buys a few moments of celebrity.

Conspicuous contribution has a long history. Some early-twentieth-century immigrants found it a dismaying feature of American culture. For instance, a 1923 editorial in Chicago's *Sunday Jewish Courier* took the city's Jewish community to task for having adopted American ideas of "charity." Entitled "Too Much Charity—Too Little Tzdokoh," the column reminded readers that "tzdokoh means to give anonymously; charity is a matter of publicity ... One can live in a large Jewish community in Europe for twenty years, and not hear a word about charity and institutions, but one can live no more than three days in a Jewish community in America without hearing a great to-do about charitable affairs, drives, institutions, etc."[10]

On the Los Angeles segment of the 1990 Easter Seals telethon, the hosts reported a surprising act. A man had called up and said he wanted to donate $10,000. He came over to the studio and wrote out a check but said he wanted to remain anonymous. He said to say it was "a gentleman from the Philippines." The hosts marveled at this secret act of generosity. The donation was unusual because one aspect of the Americanization of immigrants has been to teach them to authenticate their "American" identities by highly public charitable donation. To prove one's Americanness, to verify one's social legitimacy, one must publicize one's giving.

The traditional Jewish and Christian injunctions to give secretly have been supplanted by public and publicized donations. The transformation began in the 1920s and 1930s as a new brand of professional fund-raiser converted private and individual charity into public and mass philanthropy and made it a business. "What the scriptures had commanded to be done in secret," said one observer, "would before long be celebrated in public and shouted from the rooftops by a different name: philanthropy." "And the shouting would in time become shrill and incessant as it sought billions of dollars for welfare needs," wrote a historian of modern American fund-raising. "In this profound change from charity to public philanthropy the skilled fund-raiser and high-pressure methods played a key role." Giving was made "a matter of published performance ... a virtual tax with social penalties." Some donors, clinging to the traditional moral economy, objected, but publicity, as carrot and stick, as both personal incentive and social coercion, became established as a powerful central feature of fund-raising.[11]

But the professionalization of fund-raising is inadequate alone to explain the importance of publicity in twentieth-century American mass philanthropy and on telethons in particular. More is going on here than the showy display of generosity or the chance for charity volunteers to take a bow. There are deeper reasons that telethons parade donors across their stages and proclaim their names on the air. Telethons and other professional fund-raisers use the tactic so successfully because it touches upon dilemmas of fundamental concern to Americans. Conspicuous contribution ritually resolves distinctly American predicaments about virtue and community.

What strikes a late-twentieth-century observer is the earnest and unflagging energy with which Americans publicize their "giving." On the annual broadcasts and at fund-raising events throughout the year, they not only constantly put their charitable activities on display, they endlessly congratulate themselves for their generosity and seek public credit for it. They are, they proclaim, the most generous people on earth.

The purpose of conspicuous contribution is in part to reassure givers that they are not avaricious but altruistic, not materialistic but humane. They prove that they have escaped the taint of a culture of conspicuous consumption, that they have retained the public virtue necessary to maintain a democratic community. "It shows you care," declared an

Easter Seals host in 1989. "It shows you want to help other people." "Let us read your name on the air," urged another local Easter Seals host in 1990, "so the rest of the world knows about it." The ritual display of charity verifies the social and moral validity of individual givers and the moral *health* of American society by dramatizing compassion toward those who are socially invalidated by disability or disease.

Predicaments of Identity and Status

Besides confirming the continuance of public virtue, conspicuous contribution helps symbolically to resolve other American dilemmas. It symbolically untangles predicaments of identity and status.

Conspicuous contribution bolsters the myth that America is a classless society that guarantees equal opportunities to all its members. The historian David Brion Davis noted that "beginning in the so-called Age of Jackson, white Americans of diverse backgrounds have anxiously tried to cast off any characteristics identifying them as members of a 'lower' class than the one with which they identify, precisely because they have believed in America as a land of opportunity—a land in which no fixed barriers prevent one from acquiring the skills, tastes, and demeanor, as shown in one's behavior as a consumer, that denote success."[12] Thus, even as they have denied the reality of class, Americans have unflaggingly practiced conspicuous consumption to demonstrate their upward mobility, socioeconomic success, and rising social status.

The fact of class has also been cloaked by the issue of race. Davis noted that one function of the American racial caste system has been to obscure the actual inequalities of class among whites, as well as the reality of disjunctures of class among America's racial groups. "The unacknowledged privileges and benefits most Americans derive from having white skin," wrote Davis, in part grew out of "the dialectical and historical connections between American slavery and American freedom, between the belief in an inferior, servile race and the vision of classless opportunity."[13]

Conspicuous contribution has functioned not only as the obverse of conspicuous consumption but also in a way similar to racial caste. The "dependent" are deemed another naturally servile caste. Even as charitable giving to aid the "less fortunate" marks class standing, it helps mask class distinctions. Philanthropy ascribes the distribution of good and ill fortune to personal effort, providence, or luck. The system of voluntary private charity helps camouflage the web of class by disguising it with myths of personal misfortune.

This fictionalization of life fortunes occurs where Americans least recognize it: in the tales they tell about individuals who become sick or disabled. Because disease and disability seem so self-evidently matters of biology, rather than sociology or public policy, the disadvantaging social and economic consequences endured by sick or disabled individuals are perceived as "natural," the inevitable social outcomes of biological "facts." But much of what Americans think of as the natural results of illness or disability are social and political artifacts.[14] This social construction is especially powerfully present in societal arrangements to provide financial aid to those who become sick or disabled. Establishment of universal, comprehensive health insurance and health care as social rights could prevent much of the financial and emotional devastation visited on American families, many times destroying them. Perpetuation of the system of private charity not only has proved inadequate to meet those needs, more pertinent to the point being made here, it helps sustain the American mythology of personal misfortune. This in turn upholds the corollary myth of classlessness.

Yet charity donation also silently fortifies class boundaries by serving as a visible symbol of status. Those who have succeeded register their upward mobility by giving to "help" the invalidated. The wealthiest and most successful give the most conspicuously at black-tie banquets honoring ones of their own. The second largest MDA fund-raising event (after the telethon itself) is the annual Mary and Harry Zimmerman dinner in Nashville sponsored by the Zimmerman-founded Service Merchandise Company. Each year a celebrity is given the Harry Zimmerman Award, and a million dollars is raised. A video report on this particular dinner is, of course, prominently featured on each year's telethon. Charity banquets such as this are staples of newspaper columns, with names like "The Social Scene," through which America's upper crust displays itself.

In other ways, telethons diagram the American class hierarchy. Though telethon hosts emphasize that even the smallest pledges matter, the extra attention given to what a 1993 Chicago Easter Seals host referred to as "heavy hitters" makes plain that some donors matter more than others. Instead of *answering* calls from would-be pledge makers, corporate executive VIP volunteers exhibit their clout by *making* calls to friends and colleagues, soliciting larger donations and reading the names and amounts on the air. "Business and community leaders" in MDA lockups strut their status by phoning acquaintances to raise the $2,500 that will bail them out. UCP cofounder Jack Hausman reads the names of wealthy New Yorkers and of transplanted New Yorkers in Florida and Hollywood, his personal friends, who donate $3,000, $5,000, $10,000, $25,000, $50,000. Every year on the night before the telethon, Hausman hosts a party for VIPs. At various times throughout each telethon, Dennis James refers to these parties and to some of the wealthy and important persons who attend. Hausman himself says his dinners included a "who's who of America" and mentions a couple of ambassadors. James chimes in with the names of bankers and philanthropists. All of this conspicuous charity by high-status donors charts and bolsters the American social hierarchy.

The telethon system urges average Americans to identify with these big givers by purchasing smaller scraps of the same status. The UCP Telethon's New York segment features a "Labor Cares" panel of union officers who read the names of individual donors and of locals and companies that have made contributions. The panel is the blue collar counterpart to Jack Hausman reading the names of his wealthy friends. And if middle class Americans cannot afford black-tie banquets, they can attend dinner dances, silent auctions and wine-tasting parties. Philanthropy to aid people with disabilities thus helps obscure class lines. Small or big, all contributors are invited to place themselves symbolically on the validated side of a great social divide.

Telethons replicate the class structure in another way. The families affected by disability or disease who are exhibited on telethons are usually not poor and they are certainly not rich. They are middle class. They are overwhelmingly white, but whatever their ethnicity, they are middle class. That implicitly makes them, as one local Easter Seals host put it in 1992, "very deserving." MDA makes a point of announcing that it provides its services to families without requiring a means test. American public and private welfare has long operated on the premise that middle class families in crisis are morally worthy of aid. Means tests and moral evaluations are for the poor, who are inherently suspect and probably undeserving of assistance.[15] Emcees locate telethon families in the social hierarchy by indicating to the vast, middle class audience, "[t]hey're just like your friends, your family, your neighbors."[16] One aim of the telethon ritual is to rescue middle class families from social invalidation.

Thus in several ways, conspicuous contribution buttresses, even as it helps to blur, the reality of social class. It disguises the socially and politically constructed causes of alleg-edly "natural" personal misfortunes. It facilitates display of the superior status of the most advantaged, thereby reinforcing their social power. It encourages ordinary middle class Americans to disregard the disadvantages and dangers to them under the private charity and for-profit health insurance system. Instead, middle class folks are prompted to identify with those who are wealthy enough that they will never need telethon charity.

But the American experience has involved more than a denial of the reality of class. It is much more complicated than that. The disavowed fact of social class is invisibly braided with the much noted fact of social fluidity. That intertwining has had profound and problematic consequences for American identities. Americans have celebrated the fluidity of their society without usually examining the specific nature of that fluidity. Fluidity is not the same thing as social and economic mobility, though for many white Americans it has included the possibility of such mobility. But that mobility might be downward as well as upward.

More troublesome, throughout much of American history the fluidity of American society has produced a disorienting shapelessness. Hurtling expansion, swift and ceaseless change, the relative newness of all institutions, and the ideology of egalitarian individual-ism together generated not only an exhilarating sense of boundless individual possibilities but sometimes a terrifying lack of personal and social boundaries. While the fluidity of the social structure opened enormous possibilities for individual development, it has also left a great many Americans adrift about who they are or what they should become. Americans have fashioned for themselves a society "in which," observed James Baldwin, "nothing is fixed and in which the individual must fight for his identity."[17] Liberated from rigid traditional social hierarchies, many white Americans have also felt dubiously emancipated from any clearly defined identity.

With every prospect seemingly available, no goal has seemed enough, and many Americans have found themselves drawn into an endless competition for status with no finish line, no resting place. As early as 1774, an observer noted that Americans were running "one continued race, in which everyone is endeavoring to distance all behind him, and to overtake or pass by, all before him; everyone flying from his inferiors in pursuit of his superiors, who fly from him with equal alacrity."[18] "People are not ... terribly anxious to be equal," remarked Baldwin almost two centuries later, "but they love the idea of being superior. And this human truth has an especially grinding force here, where identity is almost impossible to achieve and people are perpetually attempting to find their feet on the shifting sands of status."[19] "There are no longer any universally accepted forms or standards," he pointed out, "and since all the roads to the achievement of an identity had vanished, the problem of status in American life became and it remains today acute. In a way, status became a kind of substitute for identity."[20]

In a society that vaunted itself as mobile, fluid, and egalitarian, how would individuals establish their personal identities and social status? And what criteria would the community—which is to say, those who labeled themselves "respectable"—use to measure the eligibility of individuals and groups for membership in that community for equal citizenship? How would the majority simultaneously confirm their own validity, bar those they defined as socially invalid and therefore could justifiably exclude, and yet assure themselves of the openness and fairness of their society? How would dominant groups decide, as the historian Robert H. Wiebe noted, who was "qualified to participate in a democracy of free choices"?[21]

Between the Revolution and the Civil War, Americans devised answers to these questions. To solve the problems of selection and status, to gauge worthiness of social inclusion and attainment of social respect, they sketched a new picture of the social order. Doing away with the traditional conception of an organic hierarchy of stair-step ranks, they substituted "a simple separation," an uncomplicated "division between ins and outs."[22] They reduced the measurement of social validity—and thus of entitlement to equal citizenship—to a stark dichotomy.

That dichotomy grew out of the fluidity of American society, the individualistic ethos of Americans, and Americans' belief in the necessity of public virtue. Those features converged to define an authentic American as a person who was not subject to or dependent upon the will of another. A valid American was a property-holding and therefore economically, morally, and politically independent adult, white, able-bodied male. He was seen as economically and physically self-sufficient. Only a self-contained, self-sustaining person was capable of acting responsibly enough to uphold public virtue. Only such a person possessed the moral and political independence that would make the American democratic experiment viable.[23] Only such an individual was competent to claim and to realize the promise of democratic individualism. Only he qualified for inclusion and equality.

This myth of personal autonomy asserted the sovereignty of the individual over his destiny. Within acceptable society, it was claimed, each individual stood on an equal basis with every other individual, enjoying the same privileges and opportunities. The myth claimed that "everyone achieved a success equivalent to merit." And in a fluid, expanding economy, "enough abrupt falls and dramatic rises in fortune occurred to support the impression of a characterological justice in the world of affairs."[24]

Thus, individual character and status in large part came to be appraised according to personal economic success, a success mostly reckoned by conspicuous consumption. The capacity to consume served as a yardstick of who was in. Monetary income and the material possessions and extraoccupational activities purchased by that income became primary measures of personal achievement, social standing, and qualification for inclusion. "Because money and the things money can buy is the universally accepted symbol here of status," said Baldwin, "we are often condemned as materialists. In fact, we are much closer to being metaphysical because nobody has ever expected from things the miracles that we expect."[25] With one another as audience, Americans have earned, spent, and consumed, endlessly striving to verify their inner worth and social validity.

Conspicuous *contribution* has also served to verify one's place among the validated. Institutionalized charities manufacture "the less fortunate" as status-enhancing commodities. Telethon giving, like all charitable donation and volunteerism, is on one level a corrective of the morally and communally corrosive effects of individualistic consumerism. But the charities have also made donation a consumable product that is guaranteed to boost the buyer's social status and self-worth. "You're going to feel really good about yourself." If conspicuous contribution ritualistically reverses the consequences of consumerism, it simultaneously serves as another form of conspicuous consumption.

Putatively independent Americans have thus employed those they label "dependent" as a negative reference group against which to define themselves. Giving proves that the allegedly self-sufficient belong on the upper side of a great social divide that separates those designated autonomous from those branded dependent. Anyone resorting to public welfare or private charity is regarded as neither fully a person, nor legitimately a citizen. The price of such societal aid in America is social invalidation.

The Sovereignty of the Self versus the Human Condition

But individual autonomy has meant more than exercising the capacity to get and spend and donate. Sovereignty over one's personal destiny came to include dominion over one's body, command of one's health. *Good* health and physical and mental fitness have been made measures of moral and social validity.

Traditional Western Judeo-Christian cultures attributed health or disease to divine power. God punished or purified individuals with sickness or disability, or allowed Satan to momentarily to hold sway over them. Whatever the physiological and moral outcome, the entire course of events was determined by the inscrutable will of the sovereign deity. The human condition ultimately lay beyond the ken or control of finite creatures.

As Western societies modernized themselves, they inverted the order of the universe, commanding God to hew to rational laws that made sense to human beings and proclaiming the capacity of those humans not only to know the operating rules of the universe but increasingly to work the levers themselves. This transformation advanced most rapidly and most thoroughly in America, a society virtually born modern. Socially fluid, sloughing off "the dead hand of the past," future-oriented, American society proclaimed the competency of its people, collectively and individually, to shape human destiny.

Reflecting this long-term process, health reformers and fitness experts from the 1830s onward have played a major role in American culture as prophets and pedagogues of individual control of the body and health. In the antebellum United States, disease and disability came to be regarded as resulting from violations of the laws of nature. But those laws were readily comprehensible. It did not require advanced medical or scientific training to know them. The rules of good health were accessible to all. Because those rules were accessible, good health and fitness became moral imperatives. Individuals usually achieved them not accidentally, or providentially, or through esoteric knowledge, but simply through will power. Most persons could choose good health or reject it.[26]

Health and fitness thus often came to be taken as indicators of the appropriate exercise of the sovereignty of the self. They were made measures of a suitably American character. Antebellum "reformers assumed that a person could not behave in a morally responsible fashion unless his or her body was unfettered" from slavery "and uncorrupted" by bodily *infirmity*.[27] The assumption that disability corrupts one's capacity for responsible choices continued with the emergence of scientific medicine in the late nineteenth and twentieth centuries. Medical practice ostensibly forbears moral judgments against its patients, depicting disease and disability as biological processes, not divine chastisements. But in fact, moralizing about illness and disability persists, embedded in medical and societal discourse.[28] Sometimes this involves attribution of moral blame, for instance for contracting AIDS or acquiring a spinal cord injury while driving drunk. If traditional Western cultures took health or illness as signs of God's favor or displeasure, modern American culture has come to regard them as emblems of fulfillment or failure in meeting the requirements of democratic individualism. Since ill health supposedly results from individual negligence in following the principles of proper living, it is a distinctively modern form of moral failure: it is delinquency in the practice of individual self-control.

Twentieth-century medicine and allied social services also operate on a more far-reaching moral premise: the assumption that illness and, even more so, disability incapacitate individuals from participating in the democracy of free choices. Even if individuals are not culpable for their physical conditions, disabilities render them incompetent to practice the sovereignty of the self. So, whether or not they are morally blamable or the hapless victims of accidents or disease processes, they are unfit for full and authentic citizenship. Disability evidences unwillingness or incompetency to practice self-determination.

As a result, in American culture, personal health not only has affected the lives of individuals, it has far-reaching consequences for society. Insofar as impairment manifests the moral shortcomings of individuals, it exposes a negligence that threatens the viability of American freedom. Insofar as disability is a misfortune that befalls ill-fated souls, it subverts the very idea of a society of individuals in control of their personal destinies. Either way, the health of individuals will impede or perhaps even sabotage American social progress. Any dereliction of personal sovereignty, any incapacity for self-determination, calls democratic individualism into question. The presence of impairment raises a terrifying prospect: human beings may not be in control of their destinies after all. Disability imperils the American myth of the sovereignty of the self.

The fear evoked by the presence of people with disabilities has produced two simultaneous and predictable responses: they have been stigmatized, and they have been subjected to relentless exertions to fix them.

Stigmatizing disabled people has been a means of avoidance for the American majority whose identities, status and validity have been built on the myth of personal autonomy. Devaluation of people with disabilities has constituted an additional dichotomy that distinguishes the socially valid from the invalid. On one level, the dichotomy based on disability parallels the dichotomy based on race. Like racial prejudice, disability bias springs in part from what James Baldwin called the "social panic" of Euro-Americans, their "fear of losing status, [which] really amounts sometimes to a kind of social paranoia."

> One cannot afford to lose status on this peculiar ladder, for the prevailing notion of American life seems to involve a kind of rung-by-rung ascension to some hideously desirable state. If this is one's concept of life, obviously one cannot afford to slip back one rung. When one slips, one slips back not a rung but back into chaos and no longer knows who he is. And this reason, this fear, suggests to me one of the real reasons for the status of the Negro in this country. In a way, the Negro tells where the bottom is: *because he is there*, and *where* he is, beneath us, we know where the limits are and how far we must not fall. We must not fall beneath him. We must never allow ourselves to fall that low ... I think if one examines the myths which have proliferated in this country concerning the Negro, one discovers beneath these myths a kind of sleeping terror of some condition which we refuse to imagine. In a way, if the Negro were not here, we might be forced to deal within ourselves and our own personalities, with all those vices, all those conundrums, and all those mysteries with which we have invested the Negro race.[29]

Baldwin's insight about the origins of racial caste can help explain the fabrication of the disability caste. Disability too has functioned as a marker of where the bottom is in

American society. Disabled people too have been invested with myths that have enabled the majority to avoid facing their own "condition." In the latter half of the twentieth century, the disability caste has become even more necessary. The civil rights movements of racial minorities and of women too have made it increasingly difficult to use belief in an inferior racial caste or a subordinated sex as a means of maintaining the myths of classlessness and boundless opportunity, or of quieting the terror that one's status might plummet and one's identity might dissolve into chaos. At the same time, the myth of the self-contained, self-sufficient American individual more and more has clashed with contemporary experience. Americans cling to visions of absolute personal autonomy and unlimited individual possibility while, it seems to many of them, their power over their individual lives evaporates like a mirage.

As Baldwin pointed out, what human beings fear within themselves, they often attribute as the exclusive traits of some group they define as the opposite of them, their antithesis, the Other. White people have "need[ed] the nigger" to embody the traits that whites cannot tolerate within themselves. At the deepest level of American perception, "'the Negro problem,'" contended David Brion Davis, "meant that blacks are associated metaphysically with everything that compromised or stood in the way of the American Dream—with finitude, failure, poverty, fate, the sins of our fathers, nemesis. In short, with dark reality."[30]

On late-twentieth-century American telethons, disability has implicitly been offered as a replacement for race. People with disabilities are ritually presented as the new mudsill, the bottom of the social ladder below whom "we" must never allow ourselves to fall. The myths about "the disabled" propagated by telethons reveal little about the daily lives of people with disabilities, but these phantasms do betray the night terrors of those who prefer to think of themselves as "able bodied," as whole. The myths assure that "they," not "we," are dependent, helpless, incomplete, inauthentic. This prospect of restricted powers terrifies Americans, because it means not just loss of control, but loss of social validity within American society, loss of an American identity. Anyone who depends physically on others to carry out daily activities is seen as incapable of fulfilling the requirements for full membership in America. People with disabilities provoke anxiety and revulsion because they are defined as literally embodying that which Americans individually and collectively fear most: limitation and dependency; failure and incapacity; loss of control and loss of autonomy; at its deepest level, finitude, confinement within the human condition, and subjection to fate.

To avoid confronting these fearsome inner and social demons and to protect their own social validity, nondisabled Americans must see themselves as autonomous, potent, in control. One means of doing so is to display oneself as a giver. In America, it is not only better to give than to receive, it is a social necessity.

Thus, in America, giving must be public. It cannot be secret. Secretiveness would defeat one fundamental purpose of donating to help "the less fortunate." Contribution must be conspicuous for it to demarcate the radical difference between socially valid Americans and their counterimage, the invalidated, disabled Others.

But it is not enough to define people with disabilities as the inversion of authentic American identity. Merely invalidating them cannot adequately reassure those who are, for the moment, "healthy," because disability differs from race in one major respect: although white people cannot turn black, "healthy" people can and sometimes do get sick or become disabled. As the telethon hosts endlessly remind viewers, you or someone you love might in an instant be transformed—and invalidated. So, to sustain the myth that Americans control their destinies, the ritual invalidating people with disabilities must also attempt to revalidate them and thus reiterate the capacity of Americans to master fate.

At the beginning of the 1994 UCP Telethon, Dennis James explained that a few days earlier he had flown from Los Angeles to New York. He and his wife and son had just gone through the devastating Northridge earthquake. His house was in shambles. So was his son Brad's. On the flight east, he had reflected on "how unpredictable life can be, and how the forces of nature are at times so unexpected and so unaccountable. Now the flight to New York," he said, "gave me a chance to think, to think a lot about the reason why my family and I came to New York to do this annual telethon. It's a chance to once again meet, marvel, and appreciate the accomplishments of youngsters and adults who are disabled by cerebral palsy. When we see these accomplishments, I realize that it is literally within our power to do something about a force of nature which contributes to the birth of a brain-damaged child. Now we can't do anything about the force of an earthquake, but you can see what can be done about cerebral palsy's force. You'll actually see children, young people and adults who due to brain damage would have had a limited future, but because of the previous forty-two telethons ... [you] have helped almost three generations to a maximum fulfillment of life."

The following year, James made the point again. He reminded the audience that last year just before the telethon the earthquake had hit Los Angeles. Now southern California was recovering from torrential rains, and there had been a devastating earthquake in Kobe, Japan. "It points out how unpredictable the forces of nature can be," he mused. "Now look, I'm not comparing an earthquake or a flood to the birth of a brain-damaged child," which was, of course, exactly what he was doing. "But the emotional trauma, the need for help and support, as in the case of California, our recovery shows me that we do have the power to do something about the force of nature, even with the birth of a brain-damaged child. When we meet the children, the young people and the adults, with cerebral palsy, you'll be thrilled to see their levels of accomplishment. Some who couldn't walk will walk this year. Some who couldn't talk will talk this year. Because of you." "Able-bodied" donors could reassure themselves; they could still master fate.

In a sense, a disability is more fearsome than an earthquake. An earthquake lasts a matter of seconds, and after that one can begin to rebuild. But disability is viewed as an ongoing catastrophe, a disaster that never stops. How can one build an American life on the shambles continuously being made by it? And given the American belief in the connection among health, personal sovereignty, and qualification "to participate in a democracy of free choices," disability endangers things more essential than property or even life. It imperils identity and status.

In the late twentieth century, seemingly intractable social problems have left many Americans feeling even more impotent than they feel when confronting natural disasters. At least after an earthquake or a hurricane one can dig out and rebuild. Social ills often seem beyond anyone's ken or control. "When we read the newspapers or watch the news on TV," observed a Chicago-area UCP host in 1995, "we sometimes feel overwhelmed by problems that seem to have no solutions. It's a terrible helpless feeling." But people with disabilities can serve as vehicles to defeat that sense of helplessness. "United Cerebral Palsy offers everyone who wants to make a better world a way to solve problems that can be solved ... Make it a better world. We can."

The medical model of disability presents disabled people as a means for Americans to escape the mood of futility and fatalism that has overtaken them. In a moment when the myth of the sovereignty of the self and of American dominion over destiny is under threat, the "power to do something about a force of nature," disability, reassures Americans that they can still transcend the human condition. Thus, fixing disabled people has become a cultural imperative. Americans can still bring fate to heel and master human destiny. Just as the telethon ritual reassures them about the viability of public virtue and moral community, it revalidates their American identities. All they have to do is take people with disabilities and make them over.

Endnotes

1   Gordon Wood, *The Radicalism of the American Revolution* (New York: Vintage, 1992); J. R. Pole, *The Pursuit of Equality in American History* (Berkeley, CA: University of California Press, 1978).

2   Jack P. Greene, "The Limits of the American Revolution," in *The American Revolution, Its Character and Limits,* ed. Jack P. Greene (New York: New York University Press, 1987), 6–12.

3   Joel Kovel, *History and Spirit: An Inquiry into the Philosophy of Liberation* (Boston, MA: Beacon Press, 1992), 92.

4   Scott M. Cutlip, *Fund Raising in the United States, Its Role in America's Philanthropy* (New Brunswick, NJ: Rutgers University Press, 1965), 120–21.

5   Easter Seals Telethon 1989, Los Angeles segment.

6   Schools that sponsored hop-a-thons profited too. They got items like playground equipment.

7   Mt. 6:2, 4 Revised Standard Version.

8   James B. Simpson, *Simpson's Contemporary Quotations* (Boston, MA: Houghton Mifflin, 1988), 243, quoting from *Washington Post,* 15 November 1979.

9   On the 1994 Arthritis Telethon, cohosts Crystal Gayle and Sarah Purcell read from cards the names, geographical locations, and amounts promised by phone-in pledge makers, while Fred Travalena read the names, amounts donated by individuals, organizations, small businesses, and locations from a huge video screen. UCP had a series of revolving national announcers sitting in a "sky booth" who read the same information from pledge cards. On UCP's New York segments, labor leaders read the names of various donors and contributing union locals.

10 Editorial, *Chicago Sunday Jewish Courier,* 18 February 1923, quoted in Lizabeth Cohen, *Making a New Deal, Industrial Workers in Chicago, 1919–1939* (New York: Cambridge University Press, 1990), 59–60.

11 John Lear, "The Business of Giving," *Saturday Review,* 2 December 1961, 63, quoted in Cutlip, *Fund Raising,* 202; John R. Seeley et al., *Community Chest: A Case Study in Philanthropy* (Toronto: University of Toronto Press, 1957), 396, quoted in Cutlip, *Fund Raising,* 530; Cutlip, *Fund Raising,* 335–36.

12 David Brion Davis, "The American Dilemma," *New York Review of Books*, 16 June 1992, 13.

13 Ibid., 13.

14 William Roth, "Handicap as a Social Construct," *Society* 20 (March/April 1983): 56–61.

15 Edward D. Berkowitz, *America's Welfare State, from Roosevelt to Reagan* (Baltimore, MD: Johns Hopkins University Press, 1991), 91–93, 169; Theda Skocpol, *Protecting Soldiers and Mothers: The Political Origins of Social Policy in the United States* (Cambridge, MA: Harvard University Press, 1992), 118–20, 141–43, 148–51, 155–57, 467–68.

16 Easter Seals Telethon 1992.

17 James Baldwin, "The Discovery of What It Means to Be an American," in *The Price of the Ticket, Collected Nonfiction, 1948–1985* (New York: St. Martin's/Marek, 1985), 175.

18 Quoted in Wood, *The Radicalism of the American Revolution*, 135.

19 James Baldwin, "Down at the Cross, Letter from a Region in My Mind," in *The Price of the Ticket, Collected Nonfiction, 1948–1985* (New York: St. Martin's/Marek, 1985), 371.

20 James Baldwin, "In Search of a Majority," in *The Price of the Ticket, Collected Nonfiction, 1948–1985* (New York: St. Martin's/Marek, 1985), 231.

21 Robert H. Wiebe, *The Opening of American Society, from the Adoption of the Constitution to the Eve of Disunion* (New York: Alfred Knopf, 1984), 321.

22 Ibid., 327, 339.

23 Historians have omitted able bodiedness from the formulation of notions of American citizenship and identity, though it is often implicit. For general explanations of this formulation see Linda K. Kerber, "The Revolutionary Generation: Ideology, Politics, and Culture in the Early Republic," in *The New American History*, ed. Eric Foner (Philadelphia, PA: Temple University Press, 1990), 29; Wood, *Radicalism of the American Revolution*, 56, 178–79.

24 Wiebe, *The Opening of American Society*, 321–22.

25 Baldwin, "In Search of a Majority," 231.

26 Wiebe, *The Opening of American Society*, 160–63.

27 Ronald G. Walters, *American Reformers 1815–1860* (New York: Hill and Wang, 1978), 145.

28 Irving Kenneth Zola, "Medicine as an Institution of Social Control," *Sociological Review*, n.s. (November 1972): 491–92.

29 Baldwin, "In Search of a Majority," 232–33.

30 Davis, "The American Dilemma," 14.

CHAPTER 10

Patients at Work:

Insane Asylum Inmates' Labour in Ontario, 1841–1900

Geoffrey Reaume

In 1879, the provincial inspector of insane asylums for the province of Ontario, John W. Langmuir, wrote that to "implant and cultivate in that class of patients a taste for work ... is of infinitely greater importance, than any other portion of Asylum work and supervision."[1] When he made this statement, Langmuir was laying the groundwork for the intensification of patient labour which would see an increase in the rate of patient labour at Ontario's mental institutions from one-third in the late 1870s to 75 per cent of the entire inmate population by 1900.[2] The motives that influenced this policy were rooted in both Anglo-American ideas of work as therapy and the need to pay for the maintenance of more mental institutions in the province in the second half of the nineteenth century.[3] With increasing costs, administrators advocated the increased participation of unpaid patient labourers, a policy that literally paid off by saving untabulated thousands of dollars for the province. This chapter will focus on what patient labourers actually did and how many were engaged in what was called "employment," even though they were not paid. While at the beginning of the period, the level of work in Ontario's insane asylums was barely perceivable (insofar as the sources are able to tell us), it rose in a steadily growing crescendo of activity during the next six decades.

Before I discuss the actual nature of the toil done by patient labourers, it is necessary to address the rationale for work therapy as part of moral treatment from the perspectives of asylum operators. As James Moran and Steven Cherry have shown in reference to nineteenth-century proponents of moral treatment in Ontario, Quebec, and England, doctors provided a physiological basis for their claim that putting patients to work helped them to recover their sanity. Physical exercise brought about by certain types of work, such as agricultural labour or working in a laundry, was viewed as an essential way of redirecting a person's "alienated mind" from their troubles onto the task at hand. As well, doing regular, steady work would supposedly lead toward regular, steady, and above all, rational habits and away from mad thoughts. A good diet was essential to this work regimen, all of which, it was argued, would help to improve a person's physiological functions through invigorated brain activity and a healthier flow of bodily fluids which physical labour could help to regulate.[4] As Yannick Ripa has written in regard to women inmates in nineteenth-century France, from the asylum officials' point of view, the rationale for work was that it "focused attention on the concrete tasks of everyday life and dispelled their fantasies."[5] Physical and mental health were therefore linked with the positive reinforcement of each, leading to a sane mind. That was the theory. Of course, there were other ideas that motivated this work, as the writings of provincial asylum superintendents reveal. As will be seen below, the reality of patient labour and the impetus for pushing it forward on a wide scale in Ontario as the nineteenth century wore onward was quite different from the theory that justified it.

The Early Years: 1841–1860

For most of the initial decade of this study patient labour is not well documented. Between 1841 and 1850 the first Provincial Temporary Lunatic Asylum operated in Canada West, or Ontario, as the province was named after 1867. It was located in various facilities in Toronto. The first superintendent, William Rees, wrote in 1842 that it was his desire to implement "medical and moral treatment" in the treatment of insane asylum patients, who at that time averaged thirty-six men and women. Though he refers to their being engaged in "labours of various kinds," nothing is specified beyond fishing along the shore of Lake Ontario in the company of an attendant.[6] While evidence for patients' labour during these early years is scant, what evidence does exist reveals a practice that would reoccur in years to come: using asylum inmates to help get a new institution ready for later arrivals. In October 1849 male patients from the Temporary Asylum worked on making the grounds level at the new permanent provincial asylum in Toronto, several months before the first patients arrived in January 1850.[7]

From this time on, a more detailed picture begins to emerge of patients' labour in Ontario. Superintendent John Scott's words would be repeated time and again by asylum administrators over the next fifty years when he wrote in the annual report for 1850, "As a general rule, all who are capable are kept employed." He also defended the use of patients' work in words that would be echoed down the years by his successors. When he claimed that it was beneficial, not exploitative, the intent was to consider this practice a benign form of moral therapy: "In no case is labour made compulsory or painful, the patient who at first may be averse to work, becomes persuaded by his attendant, or stimulated by the example of others to make a beginning and in a very short time realizes the advantages and pleasures resulting. It is to be understood that the labour of patients is not reckoned on as a source of gain or profit, but simply as a means likely to promote their well-being of body and mind."[8] The prevention of "idleness," as Andrew Scull has noted, was a "leading principle" of moral treatment.[9] Individuals who went against this basic premise were duly criticized in annual reports and, one assumes, in person.

Those who did not work were described as "indolent and moping." Whether they objected to not being paid is impossible to know. However, the moralizing judgment toward patients who were capable of work but did not do it is clear from the earliest report and permeates much of this history. Patients' labour in 1850 included "cutting and preparing firewood"; kitchen, laundry, and ward work; male patients mending their clothes; and among women, needlework. Indeed, one report boasted that "among the females many are excellent needle-women and are so industrious as to perform all the work required in this Institution." When conditions allowed, forty to fifty men—about a third of all male patients—"engaged in digging, levelling, draining and in cultivating a large crop of vegetables." As an added incentive, coffee and bread were provided to patient field labourers around three in the afternoon.[10] Use of incentives, or bribes, to get people to work was not unusual. Ellen Dwyer had recorded the use of similar tactics in New York State's Willard Asylum during the nineteenth century.[11]

It is hard to imagine what incentive might have been used to get patients to do one particularly odious job a few years after the permanent asylum opened in Toronto. During the year 1853, diarrhea and dysentery frequently affected the patient population. The source of this recurring health problem was discovered to be a huge cesspool that had accumulated for several years underneath the basement floor as a result of a faulty drainage system. From November 1853 to January 1854, Joseph Workman, the recently appointed superintendent, had male patients clean it up. It was in an underground area measuring six hundred feet long by thirty to sixty feet wide with the sludge measuring three to five feet in depth. The work was done under the direction of attendants and included the removal of "several hundred cartloads" of what Workman later wrote of as "reeking filth." According to the superintendent, the "tedious, tiresome and sickening work" was done by "hard-worked lunatics." New gravel and drains were laid so that waste from the laundry, kitchen, and elsewhere would no longer collect beneath the asylum basement. This episode reveals how patients' working conditions could, at times, have been anything but "therapeutic." Though the superintendent reported that he had delayed this work until the cold weather to lessen the chance of the spread of disease, Workman reported that "the health of the inmates ... [and staff] ... was much affected" during the cleanup operation.[12]

In contrast to the cesspool cleanup, the benefits of outdoor labour were repeatedly emphasized. Most of this work would have been reserved for males. While statistics are absent for most of the 1850s about who did what, a reference to "the want of employment" for men patients during the winter indicates that alternative indoor jobs were not yet available for most of them. Nevertheless, by the mid-1850s some twenty to thirty patients of both sexes worked daily in the sewing room, where their work was overseen by a seamstress and a tailor. This work saved the asylum money by having all the "needlework" and men's coats made on the premises.[13]

While gender-specific tasks are mentioned in these early reports, one such example was quite unusual for an insane asylum: caring for a newborn baby. A baby boy was born under dreadful conditions to asylum inmate Catherine L. on 11 June 1856. This baby was taken from the mother and was looked after with "great tenderness" by the matron and nurse, who were "aided by a female patient."[14] How long this arrangement lasted is not stated; nor is there information about what eventually happened to mother and baby. The fact that a woman patient helped to care for this baby is evidence of how some asylum inmates took on nursing duties.

The use of patients as unpaid supplemental staff was practised elsewhere during the nineteenth century. Yannick Ripa has noted that in French asylums staff would occasionally use the "healthiest patients" to assist them in supervising other inmates at work. At the Pennsylvania Hospital for the Insane, Nancy Tomes records how some patients watched over fellow patients to ensure that they followed regulations on the ward.[15] In short, some patients were put to work as unofficial attendants, responsibilities that would have given them a degree of power over their peers, creating a "hierarchy" among inmates, as Ripa observes. The absence of any reference to this happening with any frequency in the Ontario records from the same period suggests that this was not a typical job for most patients. Instead, more common forms of physical work were emphasized.

Unquestionably, it was male farm labour that was repeatedly stressed by asylum officials during the 1850s as being most valuable from both a therapeutic and a financial perspective. This was so even though it was also claimed that more land was needed to realize the full potential of patients' agricultural labour.[16] The first clear statistics of how many patients worked overall during this period were offered by Joseph Workman for 1858. Noting that more patients could have been put to work if the means were available—that is, a larger farm—he observed that there were 196 "industrious" asylum inmates in Toronto, 41 per cent of the total. Workman boasted: "I do not believe there is any Asylum on this Continent in which so large an amount of work is done by the patients; indeed I have seen few that will compare advantageously with it."[17] The following year, the composition of this workforce changed in a way that reveals much about the value of patient labour to the provincial asylum system.

In 1859, to alleviate overcrowding at Toronto, a branch asylum was opened in Amherstburg, in the southwestern part of the province near Windsor. It was situated in the unused British military barracks at Fort Malden, along the bank of the Detroit River, and was thus called Malden Asylum. In order to get it ready for later occupants, "twenty of our most industrious" male patients were sent on 14 July 1859 to Malden with Dr. Andrew Fisher, the superintendent. Workman wrote that the "change produced by the removal" of these patients from Toronto "has been very palpable ... but I trust that our new stock will, under careful and kind treatment, soon present sufficient material to recruit our working forces."[18] As will become evident in later reports, Workman was one of many in the asylum bureaucracy who used the rhetoric of moral treatment as a recruiting mechanism for their own internal economy needs. Indeed, Dr. Fisher clearly regarded these patient labourers very highly when he wrote: "Each of these patients would perform as much work as an ordinary labouring man, and their loss must have been seriously felt at the [Toronto] institution."[19]

The work of these male patients was so "energetically" pursued that within three months a larger group of both men and women patients was sent from Toronto to live at the Malden Asylum. In what would become a frequent refrain over the next forty years, the use of unpaid patient labour was lauded by officials for saving the public money.[20] Using work therapy as cheap labour was also mentioned in published reports during the late 1850s at the Norfolk Lunatic Asylum in England.[21] Thus asylum proprietors on both sides of the Atlantic were not shy about stressing how supposedly therapeutic benefits of work for patients could also benefit the finances of mental institutions.

Work completed by patient labourers at Malden during the early months of its operation included preserving and repairing the main buildings; developing a drainage and water-supply system; installing new "water-closets," window guards, baths, furnaces, boilers, roofing, and eaves; fencing in fifty-eight acres of asylum farm land; grading surfaces; planting trees; and driving wooden piles into the Detroit River behind which stones were placed to create a stronger breakwater defence against soil erosion. Agricultural work also quickly became a prime feature of this facility. This is hardly surprising given the emphasis on this type of outdoor work under the tenets of moral treatment and the fact that this part of Ontario has some of the most fertile soil in the province. As men worked outside, women worked inside, making over 1,400 items in 1860 ranging from quilts to chemises to window blinds.[22]

While patients toiled to get the Malden property into shape for their peers, building a new asylum from the ground up was part of the work of another group of inmates. In Kingston, efforts were underway to construct a permanent asylum for people found to be criminally insane. Ordinary convict labour was used for much of this work, though there are also references to criminal "lunatic labour" being used for "bricklaying, painting, glazing" as well as farm and garden work.[23] Still other patient labourers elsewhere worked to build brick walls around the grounds upon which they lived. In 1860, ten years after it opened, permission was granted by the Provincial Board of Inspectors for "the work of building the wall to enclose the Asylum at Toronto, a work in which the patients themselves have been employed."[24] What more poignant example of patient labour can there be than that of insane asylum inmates building the very walls behind which they were confined?

Malden and Orillia Insane Asylum Patient Labourers During the 1860s

The most consistently detailed reports on patient labour in Ontario during the 1860s concern the Malden and Orillia insane asylums.[25] Both these facilities closed in 1870 after eleven and nine years of operation, respectively. A brief survey of patient labour at these two smaller institutions provides a good idea of the amount of work done by a relatively small labour force prior to any central directive being extensively pursued across the province on this issue. Keeping statistics on patients' overall labour was left to the whim of the superintendent during the 1860s, with the result that detailed data on the entire working population is sporadic, though there is some useful information. In 1861 it was reported that out of 196 patients at the Malden Asylum, 89 people, or 45 per cent, were "industrious," while the rest were listed as "idle."[26] By the end of the decade, the number of patient labourers at this facility oscillated between a low of 25 per cent of 208 patients in 1868 to 84 per cent of 159 people within the following year. It is hard to know how reliable these figures are. In the very same report that clearly tabulates two-thirds of all males at Malden as employed, Superintendent Henry Landor wrote that an average of half were "daily doing something." He further subdivides this group into two-thirds "working in the proper sense of the word," while the remaining third of male working patients do "slight things."[27] However, as will be evident below, there is no doubt as to how valuable this labour was.

The Orillia Branch Asylum, housed in an old hotel, was located on far less property than any other facility—six to eight acres along Lake Couchiching. Thus there were a smaller number of patients to work a smaller property. But work they did. The only patients' labour statistics for Orillia during the 1860s were for 1862, when 30 per cent of 128 patients were listed as working—40 per cent of the males, 32 per cent of the females.[28] At both facilities, women patients did sewing and knitting, mending all the clothes and creating thousands of new articles. Perhaps the most unusual items that female inmates at both Malden and Orillia made were straitjackets—six of these out of 1,639 articles made at Malden in 1861. During the first five months of Orillia's operation within that same year, when 25 women were housed there, they, along with female staff, made: 112 quilts, 128 sheets, 98 bed ticks, 86 pillow ticks, 219 pillow slips, 49 dresses, 65 cotton and flannel shirts, 92 cotton and flannel chemises, 76 cotton and flannel petticoats, 11 tablecloths, 25 pairs of socks, six stocking pairs, 46 women's caps, seven towels and rollers, 12 night gowns, five straitjackets, and 400 gallons of soft soap.[29]

In 1863, women at Orillia made more than 3,000 gallons of soft soap, 800 pounds of hard soap, and 50 pounds of candles.[30] These lists grew longer as the decade wore on; so much so that the Orillia superintendent was not exaggerating when he wrote in 1869, "Independent of the list of articles as given above, the mending and repairing allow little idle time for either nurses or patients."[31]

The list of jobs done by male patients at both Orillia and Malden during the 1860s is similarly extensive, and in the latter instance it included building the medical superintendent's residence. Patient labourers also built a laundry and bakery in 1861 at Malden; it still stands today, over 140 years later, as the interpretative centre and museum for Fort Malden National Historic Site, though the history of the people who built it is nowhere acknowledged within its walls.[32] The following list is a typical example of patients' labour recorded at these largely forgotten insane asylums from the 1860s. In addition to plastering, painting, carpentry, and laying floors, making benches, tables, cupboards, ladders, picture frames, a pantry, and a water-stand, creating new openings for doors and fireplaces, glazing lights, and shingling, twenty "industrious" men patients and their "keeper" at Orillia in 1862 also worked on the farm, built fences and a piggery, laid drains, paved

787 yards of farmyard, and made a 76-yard-long road, among other things.[33] Farm and garden produce at Malden was especially plentiful and profitable, with twenty-two items listed for 1862 valued at $1,645.45. The value of this yield rose to $3,000 by 1865. So successful was the Malden farm that residents had more grapes than they could consume; so the grapes were ground down and made into wine, "which will be fit for use in a year or so."[34] The same year, patients contributed to saving the Malden Asylum from being burnt down when they helped to operate the asylum fire engine, in which they had been trained in case of emergency.[35] As will become increasingly evident, beside saving buildings, patients also saved the asylum a good deal of money, even though officials offered contradictory views on how much they valued patient workers.

The Value Placed on Insane Asylum Inmate Labour During the 1860s and 1870s

The abilities of patient labourers were acknowledged by provincial authorities. However, this acknowledgment also proved patients were better workers than could sometimes be claimed, thus leaving asylum proprietors open to charges of exploitation for not paying them. James Moran has noted that at Quebec's Beauport asylum in 1849, the family of patient Jean Dupont charged that this man was "kept in the asylum in a state of 'slavery' because he was a good worker whose labour was of great value to the institution." He was subsequently released though asylum officials defended themselves by claiming that asylum inmate labour "does not pay."[36] In France exploitation charges included reference to the tiring nature of inmate labour and the primacy given to saving money as being more important than therapeutic benefits for patient workers.[37] One way around this charge of exploitation was praising individual workers while making general statements about the whole group. Yet evidence of patients' unpaid labour that contributed significantly to keeping provincial asylums operating clearly undermines broad statements about their supposed unreliability. After listing the immense amount of work they did in 1862, Orillia superintendent John Ardagh claimed these same workers were "fickle and whimsical," though his own reports and those of his contemporaries offer a different picture. In 1863 the floor of the Orillia laundry was in need of serious repair: "One of our patients, a mason, undertook the task of remedying it," with the result that it became "an excellent floor, hard and durable."[38] A year later Ardagh wrote of a male patient who was in charge of the men's dining room as being "more exacting with rules than if he were a paid attendant, and his assistants obey his rule and order."[39]

Rockwood Asylum superintendent Litchfield paid tribute to the labour of four patients judged criminally insane, about whom he wrote that "the value of their services to the Institution cannot be questioned." One of these men, a sixty-year-old cook who reliably served all meals to fellow patients, assisted by "insane attendants," was described thus: "I do not know where it would be possible to get paid labour to execute the work so well."[40] The savings to the public by getting patients to do so much of this work within the asylum is repeatedly stressed in annual reports during the 1860s, a clear indication that officials recognized how they could use "therapy" to their own financial benefit. Indeed, hiring outside help was seen as a waste of money when so many free patient labourers were around to do the job. For part of 1862 a tailor was employed at Malden, but this post was "abolished" when Superintendent Fisher realized it "did not pay"; thereafter all clothes for male patients were made by women patients "and the saving thus effected has been considerable."[41] By the end of the decade the Malden Asylum steward calculated the worth of two asylum patient farm workers as the same as one paid employee. With the value of farm produce more than meeting their expenses, they were able to realize "a very handsome profit." Patients laboured two thousand days on the farm the preceding year, six hours per day; at the unpaid rate of 50 cents for "ordinary day labour," the overall annual value of their work was estimated at $1,000.[42]

Although they were unpaid, an occasional "privilege" to asylum patient workers was recorded. Malden Asylum working patients, presumably men, were given beer to supplement their diet.[43] When it was time for some of these same inmates to move to a new asylum, fifteen to twenty of those who were considered among the most trusted inmates were sent to the London, Ontario, asylum farm to plant spring crops in 1870. Half a year later this facility opened, after which the Malden Asylum was closed and the remaining patients were transferred to this new institution.[44]

Within two years, just over half of the 496 patients were toiling away in the farm, garden, shops, and wards of the London Asylum, a steady figure into the mid-1870s.[45] Yet these numbers "give no adequate idea of the amount of work done," according to Superintendent Henry Landor, who was out to prove wrong a claim that patients under his charge were too "idle."[46] To assist with accomplishing this goal, a London Asylum bylaw had earlier stipulated, "[p]atients must be employed as much as possible," and attendants who "heartily" carried out this task would be looked upon more favourably by their employers.[47] Evidently, the results were very satisfactory for more than just the presumed goals of moral therapy. For the year 1874, Landor reported, "Everything is charged for and against, except labour of patients, which, of course, is abundant every year and tells strongly in favour of our balance sheet."[48] Inspector J. W. Langmuir also had an eye on the balance sheet, though he expressed his suspicions about patient labour as well when he wrote during the early 1870s that "all who are not mentally incapable of labour, are sufficiently sane not to care about working without wages."[49] As will be seen, these suspicions did not get in the way of a massive patient labour program that he advocated a few years later.

By the late 1870s there were four independent provincial insane asylums operating in the province—Toronto (1841), London (1870), Kingston (known as Rockwood from 1856 until it was transferred from federal to provincial control in 1876), and Hamilton (1876)—as well as one asylum for the "feeble-minded" in Orillia (1876).[50] With the establishment of a larger network of asylums than had ever before existed in Ontario, provincial authorities, in particular Inspector Langmuir, became noticeably more insistent about promoting the "Employment of Patients," a category that came to be systematically reported for each facility in every annual report beginning in 1879 and which continued to be reported until 1907. Thus the most detailed information for this study comes from this later period. Langmuir's emphasis on economy and efficiency was first felt in asylum laundry departments, which by 1878 had switched from hand to mechanized labour at all facilities.[51] Reduced laundry costs were realized by speeding up and increasing the volume of cleaning clothes as well as the fact that this mechanization resulted in two laundry maids losing their jobs to machines that unpaid patient labourers could operate at the Toronto Asylum.[52] Not only was it important to economize with unpaid patients' labour inside the asylum, but it was essential to economize in outside work as well. In 1879, Langmuir noted that provincial patient farm and garden labour "very materially reduced the cost of maintaining Asylums" in this particular year to the tune of $32,490.62.[53] So that his point would not be lost on medical officials, he continued: "It is clear therefore from the standpoint of public economy, and leaving out of the question the beneficial and healthful results accruing to the insane from land cultivation, that as large an area of land should be attached to asylums as can be profitably worked."[54]

A few years earlier, Superintendent Landor of the new London Asylum had also put a price on the value of this type of patient labour. Though he claimed that three working patients were the equivalent to one paid labourer, he nevertheless wrote in 1871 that the farm and garden work which patients had done that year "yielded more than double the cost of cultivation."[55] Several years later the bursar of the London Asylum estimated that five agricultural patient labourers were worth one paid worker, which he estimated saved the asylum $3,425.26 in the farm and garden category.[56] In 1878 the newly appointed London Asylum superintendent Richard M. Bucke said asylum patients only did half the work of "a sane person," though "still the aggregate amount of work done by the patients in a year at this Asylum is enormous."[57] Thus during the 1870s, patient labourers' worth, compared to ordinary paid work, was rated by provincial asylum officials as being in the range of two-to-one, three-to-one, and five-to-one. All of this number crunching, however variable, indicates that patients' labour was clearly recognized as being of prime economic benefit in keeping costs down, even while the operators of the asylum undervalued their unpaid workforce in relation to hired workers. It is notable that the practical effect of getting paid for one's work is not mentioned in these calculations as having had any influence on the level of output by patient labourers in contrast to regularly paid employees.

This devaluing of patients' labour compared to that of non-patients reached perhaps its most extreme form when the prospect of inmate help in one area was noted as being almost tantamount to a public health threat. In 1875 London Asylum superintendent Landor wrote that while patients were all right to clean up after the cooks and baker, they should not entertain any culinary ambitions, for "I decidedly object to eating or making others eat food prepared by patients."[58] No other asylum superintendent expressed similar "gastronomical terror" of patient food preparation during the period examined here.

In spite of this sort of occasional reluctance to employ patients in certain jobs, there is no doubt that Langmuir's entreaties to economize with an increase in patient labourers reached receptive ears among asylum superintendents by the late 1870s. In 1877, J. W. Wallace of Hamilton Asylum reported that an average of twenty male patients worked daily in a quarry "breaking stones for the roads," as well as on other outside jobs. A year later he wrote that "all the tailoring, dressmaking, mending and darning for the Asylum" were done by women patients who also worked in the laundry and kitchen, while men patients farmed, shovelled coal, did landscaping, and continued to work in a nearby quarry.[59] However, this was not enough, for he wrote, "I hope in a short time to have a stronger force of working patients."[60] As the next two decades would reveal, this creation of a "stronger force of working patients" was pursued as never before throughout all provincial asylums in Ontario as pressure was exerted on asylum superintendents to cut costs for an ever-expanding asylum inmate population.

The Intensification of Patient Labour in Ontario, 1880–1900

Statistics taken from five sample years between 1880 and 1900 reveal a wide variation in how many patients were employed at each facility (see table 10.1). However, by the mid-1880s there was one figure that stayed consistent: never less than 70 per cent of patients were working at all provincial insane asylums combined (these figures do not include the Orillia Asylum for the Feeble-Minded). Thus, in the six years since Inspector Langmuir's call for the widespread use of patient labour in 1879, the provincial rate had climbed over 100 per cent from one-third to over two-thirds by 1885, or 74 per cent. These figures are reflected in the operation of individual asylums. The London Asylum was consistently in either first or second place in overall patient employment during this period, with the largest proportion of patient workers—95 per cent—recorded in 1885, an increase of almost twice the ratio of only five years before. Superintendent Bucke noted in his report that patients worked "most of them nearly every day, during the year, exclusive, of course, of Sundays."[61] Eventually, the overall patient labour rate at London stabilized in the upper 70 to low 80 per cent range during the 1890s. London also had the largest farm operation of all the institutions then in existence—two hundred acres, plus a twenty-acre garden.[62] Thus Langmuir's call to use patients as agricultural labourers was able to be efficiently implemented at this facility, which was situated on prime farm land.

Yet even at an asylum such as Kingston, which had poor agricultural land and so was less successful in implementing farm labour, statistics show that there was more than enough work to be found for inmates. This included having male patients clear rocks from their "rough" farm land.[63] Except for 1895, Kingston competed with London for

TABLE 10.1: Asylum Inmate Labour in Ontario, 1880–1900

1880		Toronto	London	Kingston	Hamilton	Mimico	Brockville	Average
Days worked by gender as percentage	M	52.5	50	62	29.5	–	–	48.5
	F	47.5	50	38	70.5	–	–	51.5
No. of patients who worked		225	445	268	115	–	–	1053
% of total		30	49	54.5	20	–	–	39.5
1885								
Days worked by gender as percentage	M	47	48	49	50	–	–	48.5
	F	53	52	51	50	–	–	51.5
No. of patients who worked		469	983	488	371	–	–	2311
% of total		57	95	87	51	–	–	74
1890								
Days worked by gender as percentage	M	62	51	48.5	57	–	–	54
	F	38	49	51.5	43	–	–	45
No. of patients who worked		504	802	669	790	–	–	2765
% of total		52.5	76	84.5	75.5	–	–	72

TABLE 10.1: Asylum Inmate Labour in Ontario, 1880–1900 (continued)

1895								
Days worked by gender as percentage	M	32	47	51	52	59.5	49.5	48.5
	F	68	53	49	48	40.5	50.5	51.5
No. of patients who worked		772	966	549	861	398	136	3682
% of total		89	82	76	77	54.5	65	76
1900								
Days worked by gender as percentage	M	41	51	52.5	51	45.5	51	49
	F	59	49	47.5	49	54.5	49	51
No. of patients who worked		580	924	537	899	546	392	3878
% of total		68	80	82.5	78	77.5	61	75

Sources: All figures are from the annual report for each year and have been rounded off to the nearest decimal point. The numbers of patients who worked are not broken down by gender in the annual reports. All averages are based on the category "Total number of Asylum registers and actually under treatment in each Asylum" and not the lower "Number of patients remaining in Asylums on 30th September," as this latter figure does not include all patients resident for a given year, while the earlier one does.

either first or second place between 1880 and 1900 in the proportion of patients employed among Ontario's provincial asylums. Not having a good farm was no impediment to the employment of patient labourers. The increase in patient labourers at Hamilton was in some ways even more notable. The proportion of employed patients rose two and a half times between 1880 and 1885 and almost four times in ten years, from 20 per cent in 1880 to 75.5 per cent in 1890. Superintendent Wallace's goal of creating a stronger workforce was realized during his tenure and under his successor, James Russell, when Hamilton went from the smallest workforce among Ontario's insane asylums to a consistently strong third place by 1890. This pattern continued in 1895 and 1900, when there were six insane asylums operating in Ontario.

Overall work among patients at the Toronto Asylum was much less stable, rising from 30 per cent in 1880 to just over half in 1890, when it was last among four provincial insane asylums, to a peak of 89 per cent by 1895, the highest rate in the province. This rate declined by 1900, however, when there were just over two-thirds of patients working, making Toronto fifth out of six insane asylums. This generally lower rate was due to the objections of relatives of paying patients who did not want their family member working, since it was viewed "as derogatory to the social status of the patients."[64] But some of them did work. Since 89 per cent of the patients were employed at Toronto in 1895, some had to be from among the paying patients, who made up 37 per cent of the asylum population, the highest ratio in Ontario, with London's paying population next in line at 20 per cent.[65] Unlike at other facilities, this high rate of private patients in Toronto had been identified since 1883 as an obstacle to raising the number of working patients there.[66]

Thus it is not difficult to surmise that it was the poorest class of patients who contributed most to the internal economy of provincial asylums. Yannick Ripa reached a similar conclusion in her study of madwomen in nineteenth-century French asylums, where the poorest class of patients was recorded at that time as comprising "the majority of productive workers."[67] Studies of the Toronto and London asylums reveal these class biases in another way. Greater value was placed on lower-class patients who worked than on inmates who did not work regularly or who did no work at all.[68] Favouritism was also practised toward working patients at the asylum in London where "privileges are given to patients who work, and withheld from those who do not," and at the Toronto Asylum, where there was "bribing with something of a trifling nature," such as tea, coffee, and tobacco.[69] Between 1880 and 1900 the figures remained fairly stable for the number of public charges in Ontario's insane asylums—87 per cent in 1880 and 85 per cent in 1900.[70] Thus the vast majority of people who worked as patient labourers in Ontario were "free patients." This term became something of a misnomer, since it became increasingly clear that officials expected most of them to pay for their room and board as well as to reduce costs to the province through their own toil. Thus, the poorer the patient, the more work he or she was expected to do. Nineteenth-century middle-class views, which judged a person's worth by whether she or he was a good, reliable worker, was very much part of moral therapy during this period and influenced how the abilities of asylum patients were characterized.[71]

Without any doubt, the cheap labour and high-quality working abilities of insane asylum inmates saved provincial asylums a bundle of money. The per capita cost to the province of maintaining patients in Ontario's asylums was repeatedly referred to by administrators as being quite low; in fact, they boasted about how low maintenance rates were, clearly indicating how much was saved through patient labour. The average weekly maintenance rate for patients during the last decades of the nineteenth century was reported at Kingston as ranging from $2.32 in 1878 to $2.61 in 1895, when Superintendent C. K. Clarke wrote that "the maintenance rate is exceedingly low" and, he cautioned, should not be reduced further.[72] At the London Asylum, R. M. Bucke reported in 1885 that "the large amount of labor done by the patients is now beginning to tell upon our maintenance rate ... [T]he labor of the patients has been made to effect more or less saving." After listing various savings produced by patient labour, Bucke wrote that the "large decrease in the maintenance rate" was not all due to patient labour but was also because of various cost-cutting measures, such as lower consumption of meat and flour as a result of the large amount of vegetables on hand—which, he neglected to add, were produced by patients.[73]

Perhaps the best evidence of the bargain that free patient labour provided to provincial asylums was offered by figures from the Hamilton Asylum. Superintendent Wallace wrote in 1885 that this included "food, clothing, furniture, repairs and ordinary alterations of buildings, and all salaries and wages." Over a twenty-year period between 1880 and 1900, the average weekly maintenance rate for patients at Hamilton rose from $2.16 to $2.26. Like Bucke at London, Superintendent Russell at Hamilton connected these low maintenance rates to patient labour when he wrote about the 1891–95 period: "[D]uring the five years we had been doing a heavy amount of work ... our average yearly per capita cost was $120.31, or a weekly rate of $2.31. With such results as these I had no hesitation in deciding that we were certainly discharging our proper function and doing it by the most economic methods." Five years later he wrote that the average per capita cost per patient from 1896 to 1900 was $2.24 per week, and he concluded: "The expenditure is far below that of asylums in Britain, Europe and America."[74] Free insane asylum inmate labour, then, was very profitable for the province.

For the patients who toiled away for no compensation, their place of work within the asylum was greatly influenced by gender. For the most part, as in earlier decades, men and women continued working in sex-segregated jobs. This pattern was also typical of asylums outside Ontario during this period. In the United States, Britain, and France as well as elsewhere in Canada, the gendered division of labour in asylums was a standard feature of patients' labour.[75] The gendered nature of asylum inmate labour in Ontario during the period examined here is therefore not surprising. Nevertheless, the extent and significance of their labour deserves far greater attention than has been given in most asylum studies. Women were concentrated in doing indoor domestic work, such as sewing, knitting, and kitchen and laundry work, as well as cleaning the ward. Men were also recorded as doing kitchen work and cleaning on the ward, which is not surprising given that they lived in sex-segregated institutions. Indeed, keeping men and women separate within the institution was extended to the workplace as a matter of policy, and in one instance where this was not done, it was cause for concern. In 1900 Superintendent N. H. Beemer of Mimico Asylum wrote in regard to the laundry that "the incidental intermingling of so many male and female working patients is not entirely free from an element of danger even under the strictest possible supervision." So he recommended structural changes to the workplace that would keep the two sexes apart.[76] Interestingly enough, the laundry appears to be the only area in asylums where the sexes worked together, at least for a time. At the Norfolk Lunatic Asylum in England the laundry became a women-only workplace in 1888 after a female inmate became pregnant on the job site.[77] While some men were employed in laundry jobs, most of this work was done by women: 79 per cent at Hamilton in 1885, 69 per cent at London in 1890, 88 per cent at Kingston in 1895, and 76.5 per cent at Mimico in 1900, where it was reported that eighteen patients processed 270,392 laundry articles during that year alone.[78]

This predominantly female patient labour also cut down costs by allowing administrators to get rid of hired staff to do jobs that patients did for no wage, as in the London Asylum. Superintendent Bucke reported in 1885: "Some saving has been effected by dispensing with hired labor in the sewing-room, the patients now doing nearly the entire sewing of the institution, and the entire knitting."[79] At the time that this report was made, all of the sewing-room work and mending was done by women patients, and women inmates were also reported to have done 98 per cent of the knitting at London that year.[80] The sewing work included making 9,100 new items and repairing 50,289 other items, from blankets to blouses. In addition, 2,102 stockings, socks, mitts, and cuffs were knitted at the London Asylum in 1885.[81] Similarly, women patients were reported as having done nearly all the knitting of stockings at the North Wales Asylum in Britain during this period.[82] Thus Ontario was hardly alone in using moral treatment as a form of cheap labour. Women were also employed as domestic servants for asylum officials, as occurred at the Brockville Asylum in 1900 where two women patients worked an average of 230 days each in the "officers' quarters."[83]

As before, men continued working outdoors. Landscaping, ditch digging, and large-scale construction work were a part of this routine. In Hamilton it was reported in 1880 that "[a] drain has been constructed for the cellar of the Farmer's house, necessitating an excavation from four to six feet deep, and upwards of eight hundred feet long. This work has been done entirely by the labour of patients."[84] This heavy work was not at all unusual. A report from the same asylum fifteen years later states: "A new kitchen has been built at the farmer's house, also a kitchen at the gardener's house. The work on the last two buildings, including a cellar to the farmer's kitchen, was done entirely by asylum labor. The excavation for the foundation of the infirmary and kitchen at East House was done by patients' labor. The patients quarried all the stone, and the sand and stone were all hauled by asylum teams. The mason and carpenter work done by our own labor has been especially effective in building and repairing and has effected a large saving in work, which would otherwise have been done under contract."[85]

Male patient construction labour also quite literally built and rebuilt the institutions in which asylum inmates lived, a practice carried on from the beginning to the end of the period examined here. A sixteen-hundred-foot boundary wall, averaging sixteen feet in height on the east and west sides of the property, was rebuilt with patients' labour at Toronto Asylum in the years 1888–89.[86] To help relieve Toronto's chronic overcrowding, Mimico Branch Asylum was opened on the shore of Lake Ontario in 1890 and became independent two years later. It was five miles from the older facility. Before it was opened, male patients were sent back and forth the same day in 1888 to work on the farm. However, this was not a practical way of getting the work done. So, beginning in 1889, the first occupants of the soon-to-be-opened institution were ten male patient labourers and two attendants who were sent out from Toronto Asylum in 1889 to begin to get it ready for the later influx of inmates.[87] During the next few years, male patient labourers helped to build and maintain many of the buildings they and others would live and work in at Mimico, including the large "cottages" that housed up to sixty patients, the superintendent's residence, an Assembly Hall (which doubled as a chapel), storage facilities, sidewalks, and pavilions along the lakeshore. Patients also levelled rough ground for a 150-yard-long cricket oval.[88] Superintendent Beemer boasted in 1897 that the carpenter who directed patients in building the Assembly Hall "proposes to finish the whole structure without any hired help."[89] The skills of these patient labourers who built the boundary walls for the Toronto Asylum and who constructed the buildings and levelled the grounds at Mimico Asylum are still very much in evidence today, more than a century after they completed their work.[90]

One particularly unusual aspect of Mimico was the creation of "subways" underground to connect buildings. In 1891 three male patients worked 517 days in this subterranean world, either moving items from place to place or repairing leaks; by 1899 seven male inmates had accumulated 2,509 days as "subway" workers.[91] Upstairs, patients helped to bake a daily average of 180 loaves of fresh bread at Mimico, the quality of which was reputed to be "everything that could be desired"—a far cry from the "gastronomical terror" of patients' food preparation noted earlier at the London Asylum.[92] Indoor work by men included skilled jobs such as shoemaking, tinsmithing, and tailoring as well as painting both inside and outside the asylum.[93] Skilled artisans could also be put to work in an attempt to improve the appearance of the institution. At the Kingston Asylum the work of patient Peter M. was on display for all to see: in 1895 he cut "a beautiful stone basin," 46 feet long by 20 feet wide, as a fountain in front of the hospital.[94] This fountain too still exists, though without running water. Similarly, other male patients were put to work creating "ornamental gardens" at the London and Hamilton asylums.[95]

In the midst of all this toil by asylum inmates, Toronto Asylum superintendent Daniel Clark expressed reservations in 1885 that too much emphasis was being placed on patient labour.[96] Yet this concern was not taken up elsewhere, even at Toronto, where Clark remained in charge until 1905, as reports from the following years clearly indicate. Instead, enthusiasts such as London superintendent Bucke wanted to go even further. He suggested that a "work colony" be established in the wilds of Ontario, the purpose of which would be to employ the increasing number of patients whom he felt were sure to arrive on the doorsteps of asylums in the years to come. It would "earn its own living" through full-scale patient labour of never less than 80 per cent inmate workers at any time.[97] This scheme did not go anywhere, but it indicates how much medical officials were looking for ways to exploit patients' labour to the maximum benefit of saving the province money. So pervasive and open was this attitude that Superintendent Russell of the Hamilton Asylum proposed formalizing the reality of what asylums had become by a name change from "Asylum for the Insane" to "The School of Mental and Manual Training."[98] This name change did not happen, but the extent of the valuable unpaid work patients did is not in doubt.

In 1900 three-quarters of provincial insane asylum patients in Ontario were employed at their place of residence, and during the previous ten years 75 per cent had been so occupied.[99] These figures clearly indicate that inmate labour had become a central part of institutional life throughout the province and was essential to the internal economy of the mental hospital system. Ontario officials were not any different from their counterparts elsewhere when it came to using patient labour for economic self-interest, while claiming it was "therapy."[100] While asylum inmates in some places, such as nineteenth-century France, were unevenly paid for their labour, this did not happen in Ontario during the same period.[101] At the same time as the province's asylum patients did not get paid for their work, convicts in the prison system were being compensated. Ordinary convict labourers in Kingston were paid 30 cents a day, while convict tradesmen received 40 cents daily. In Kingston in 1859, three hundred convicts were paid at the higher rate for their labour.[102]

One patient, David M., who "does all the blacksmithing" for the Kingston Asylum, did have his $10 travel expenses paid in the late 1890s to go home for an occasional visit to see his family. This reimbursement was agreed to on the basis of his "general and mechanical usefulness" about the asylum.[103] After 1900 there are no further letters about it until 1904, when the inspector wrote the asylum in response to its latest request for travel money for this man: "I am instructed to say that the payment of any sum to patients for services rendered cannot be considered by the Department."[104] Having provided a brief precedent for some kind of compensation in lieu of services, the inspector put a stop to it. It would be the late twentieth century before compensating psychiatric patients for their work became a much more controversial issue in the wider community.[105]

Conclusion

There is no escaping the fact that having patients work to economize within the expanding provincial asylum system was the central purpose behind the escalation of patient labour in late nineteenth-century Ontario. The constant emphasis of this point in published reports makes the rationale explicit, even while some officials continued to claim that washing literally hundreds of thousands of pieces of laundry, knitting and sewing thousands of pairs of items, doing domestic work for asylum officers, digging ditches that were hundreds of feet long, planting crops, hauling rocks, and constructing brick walls, all by unpaid, insane asylum inmate labourers, was, in fact, therapy. Langmuir's successor, Inspector Robert Christie, wrote in 1896 that "the present condition of the institutions ... indicate[s] their advanced and improved state ... These have been done largely by institution labor, and the employment of patients ... The benefit patients derive from this cannot be overestimated, and if outside labor were employed, it is obvious that the expenditure would be largely increased."[106] In essence, this is no different from what R. M. Bucke had stated so simply eighteen years before in 1878: "Every patient who is fit to work is asked to do something, both for the sake of the patient and for the sake of the Asylum."[107]

The twin goals of saving money for the province and "benefiting" patients through unpaid work "therapy" allowed asylum officials to exploit people who were in no position to contest their unpaid status. There is a hint of patient agency in references to trusted workers almost always as male employees during this period, as with the farm labourers sent from Malden to the London Asylum in 1870 or the men who went to prepare the Mimico Asylum for habitation in 1889. Their trusted status was directly related to their work performance, and it indicates how this group of male patients was able to secure a greater variety of work, especially outside jobs, than was ever available to many of their peers, particularly women patients. Yet even here this privilege should not be exaggerated: digging ditches and hauling rocks would not have been fun. For all patients, both men and women, the work they did depended on the needs of the asylum and what type of work they could do.

In 1868–69, Henry Landor wrote that it was a good policy to employ patients in the same job that they had had before entering the asylum.[108] This approach allowed for the most efficient use of asylum labour. It also reflected the theory of early proponents of moral treatment at the York Retreat in Britain, who believed that it was important to provide work to patients based on their past abilities and existing preferences. According to Anne Digby, "This would not only revive the technical skills of earlier employment but also strengthen the moral faculties."[109] The reality of putting this theory into practice, however, has to be held up against the constant refrain of saving money, which was cited over and over as the main reason for the employment of patient labourers, even before the intensification of labour began in the last two decades of the nineteenth century. As the reports indicate, this policy was put into practice quite effectively—for the asylum operators.

It can be argued that destitute public patients who paid no fees were getting a good deal by working for what would otherwise be free room and board in an insane asylum. However, when their situation is compared to that of unskilled day labourers who toiled outside the asylum during this same period, there is a very significant difference in patients' ability to find work and "negotiate," such as it was, with an employer. Day labourers had far greater freedom of movement than did insane asylum inmates to choose where to look for work. They also had far greater opportunity to organize opposition to their exploitation by striking for better wages from their overseers, though of course they did not always succeed.[110] It is also important to note that skilled workers such as Peter M., who cut the ornamental stone basin at the Kingston Asylum, and many others who toiled in asylum workshops would have received a wage for their skilled labour out in the community. They would also have had far greater bargaining power than day labourers with an employer who was not paying them any wages at all. Indeed, in 1900 a copper company inquired at the Toronto Asylum whether one of its recently confined employees, forty-three-year-old coppersmith James W., could be released as the company was in desperate need of his skilled work. Superintendent Clark informed the company that Jim was not well enough to be discharged. As it turned out, Jim was never released. Instead, he worked with the asylum tinsmith until his death in 1928.[111] Had he been working out in the community, this coppersmith would have earned far more than the equivalent of room and board in an insane asylum. Yet neither skilled nor unskilled workers received a wage of any kind in Ontario's asylums. In short, there was an "equality" of wage discrimination, if nothing else, for all classes of inmate labourers.

In her study of the Willard and Utica asylums in New York State, Ellen Dwyer noted that some patients and friends protested that, far from getting a good deal with free room and board, they felt that people who had been involuntarily committed to an insane asylum did not owe the state anything.[112] This is an essential point to consider when examining this topic. Poor patients, who made up the vast majority of labourers in Ontario's asylums, were not given a choice of where they were to be "employed," unlike day labourers who were not confined behind brick walls. Yet, as has been noted elsewhere in this article, the same state that chose to confine mad people in nineteenth-century Ontario did provide compensation to penitentiary convict labourers. In addition to the many other restrictions a diagnosis of insanity brought, it prevented workers from getting the most basic entitlement they would have received out in the community, a wage for their work.

Ellen Dwyer has concluded that at the Willard Asylum "economic considerations tended to override therapeutic ones ... Clearly employing the largest number of patients for maximum profits was Willard's primary objective."[113] Indeed, this same point can not be emphasized too much as it relates to Ontario's public insane asylums during the nineteenth century. Moral "therapy," when stripped of its therapeutic veneer, was in reality a public works program run on the "free" labour of people confined in insane asylums. As the nineteenth century wore on, it becomes clear from reports of asylum officials that the use of unpaid patient labour in Ontario between 1841 and 1900 was ultimately influenced more by economic factors than by the therapeutic claims of medical officials.

Endnotes

1   Archives of Ontario, "Annual Report of the Inspector of Asylums, Prisons and Public Charities," 1879, 20. Note: All annual reports (AR) cited below are in the Archives of Ontario (hereafter AO). They were usually published the year following the period reported. All AR dates below reflect the year being reported, not the year of publication, unless otherwise indicated for pre-1859 reports. From 1859, when reports were published in separate volumes, only AR and year will be cited, except when no pages numbers were printed, in which case the specific asylum issuing the report will be indicated.

2   Langmuir noted that though one-third of patients worked, some did less work than others: AR, 1879, 19. In 1900 Inspector Christie wrote that 76 per cent of patients worked in Ontario's insane asylums and that 75 per cent had done so during the previous ten years: AR, 1900, xiv. However, statistics for the year 1900 show that he made an error in calculation of less than 1 per cent, as 3,879 working patients out of 5,149 insane asylum inmates equals 75.31 per cent. These figures do not include the Orillia Asylum for the Feeble-Minded. For data, see AR, 1900, xvi–xvii, xxxvi–xxxvii.

3   The history of moral therapy is a well-trodden field, though few historians have delved in detail into exactly what it was that asylum inmates did over an extended period of time in the jobs assigned to them. Most of the focus has been on the ideas behind moral therapy, as opposed trying to grapple with patients' labour as a worthwhile subject in itself. In addition to sources cited elsewhere in this article, one of the standard studies on this topic is Anne Digby, *Madness, Morality and Medicine: A Study of the York Retreat, 1796–1914* (Cambridge: Cambridge University Press, 1985). Canadian studies that address aspects of this topic include Cheryl Krasnick Warsh, *Moments of Unreason: The Practice of Canadian Psychiatry and the Homewood Retreat, 1883–1923* (Montreal and Kingston: McGill-Queen's University Press, 1989); Geoffrey Reaume, *Remembrance of Patients Past: Patient Life at the Toronto Hospital for the Insane, 1870–1940* (Toronto: Oxford University Press, 2000); and James E. Moran, *Committed to the State Asylum: Insanity and Society in Nineteenth-Century Quebec and Ontario* (Montreal and Kingston: McGill-Queen's University Press, 2000).

4   Moran, *Committed to the State Asylum*, 92; Steven Cherry, *Mental Health Care in Modern England: The Norfolk Lunatic Asylum/St. Andrew's Hospital c. 1810–1998* (Suffolk: Boydell Press, 2003), 66.

5   Yannick Ripa, *Women and Madness: The Incarceration of Women in Nineteenth-Century France*, trans. C. Menage (Cambridge: Polity Press, 1990), 125.

6   AO, AR, 1842, *Journals of the Legislative Assembly of Upper Canada* (hereafter JLAUC), vol. 2, appendix U. Reports for 1845–48 make no reference to patients' labour: AO, 1849, JLAUC, vol. 8, appendix 3, QQQQ.

7   AO, RG 10, MS 640, 20-B-5, vol. 2, [Commissioners'] Minute Book, 13 October 1849. Cited in Pleasance Kaufman Crawford, "Subject to Change: Asylum Landscape," in E. Hudson, ed., *The Provincial Asylum in Toronto* (Toronto: Toronto Regional Architectural Conservancy, 2000), 71–3.

8   AO, First Annual AR [1850], JLAUC, vol. 10, appendix C, 1851.

9   Andrew Scull, T*he Most Solitary of Afflictions: Madness and Society in Britain, 1700–1900* (New Haven: Yale University Press, 1993), 150.

10 AO, First Annual AR [1850], JLAUC, vol. 10, appendix C, 1851.

11 Ellen Dwyer, *Homes for the Mad: Life inside Two Nineteenth Century Asylums* (New Brunswick, NJ: Rutgers University Press, 1987), 133.

12 AO, JLAUC, 1854–55, vol. 13, appendix H [AR, 1853–54]; Joseph Workman, "A Description of the Pestilent Condition of the Toronto Lunatic Asylum in 1853, and the Means Adopted to Remove It," *The Sanitary Journal* 2, 1 (January 1876): 1–6. Certain details regarding physical dimensions vary between these two sources. Thanks to John Court, archivist, Centre for Addiction and Mental Health, Toronto, for providing me with a copy of the 1876 article.

13 AO, JLAUC, 1856, vol. 14, appendix 2 [AR, 1855].

14 AO, JLAUC, 1857, vol. 15, appendix 12 [AR, 1856]. This reference is in an 8 July 1856 report of Workman, who is responding to charges of abuse of this woman patient, Catherine L., who was three months pregnant upon admission. The Commissioners supported the superintendent's views.

15 Ripa, *Women and Madness*, 109–10; Nancy Tomes, *The Art of Asylum-Keeping: Thomas Story Kirkbride and the Origins of American Psychiatry* (Philadelphia: University of Pennsylvania Press, 1994), 207.

16 AO, *JLAUC*, 1857, vol. 15, appendix 12 [AR, 1856]. See also AO, *JLAUC*, 1857, vol. 15, appendix 12 [AR, 1856]; *JLAUC*, 1858, vol. 16, appendix 9 [AR, 1857].

17 AO, *JLAUC*, 1859, vol. 17, appendix 11 [AR, 1858].

18 AR, 1859, 46. An earlier branch asylum was opened in Toronto in 1856, known as the University Branch, which operated until 1869. The Malden Insane Asylum was a branch of Toronto Asylum from 1859–1861 and an independent facility from 1861–1870.

19 AR, 1860, 97.

20 AR, 1859, 46; AR, 1860, 84. See also Fisher's comments in this regard in his Malden Asylum report for 1860, 100. Besides saving money, he also valued patient labour as inducing discipline, a reference to moral treatment concepts.

21 Cherry, *Mental Health Care in Modern England*, 66–7.

22 AR, 1860, 96–100.

23 AR, 1859, 79; AR, 1861, 163.

24 AR, 1860, 10. Portions of this 1860 boundary wall still exist and are therefore the oldest surviving evidence of asylum patient labour in Ontario. Efforts were underway when this chapter was written to preserve this wall and remember the people who built it on the grounds of the present-day Centre for Addiction and Mental Health, Toronto.

25 Including branches, Ontario asylums in the 1860s were the following: Toronto, University Branch, Malden, Rockwood (federal ownership), and Orillia. Workman reports little about patient labour at Toronto for the 1860s.

26 AR, 1861, 112. Males comprised 48 per cent and females 41 per cent of Malden patient labourers.

27 AR, 1868–69, 60, 73. The huge difference between the 1868 and 1869 force of patient labourers is likely due to the change in superintendent in July 1868. Fisher left and Landor took over, having found the Malden Asylum, except the farm, in a state of neglect and collapse. Patients did an enormous amount of work getting the place back into shape. For reference to the problems of statistical interpretation regarding patient labour, see Dwyer, *Homes for the Mad*, 133.

28 AR, 1862, Orillia Branch Asylum [no paging].

29 AR, 1861: Malden, 115; Orillia, 123. How many women patients worked out of 25 at Orillia is not specified.

30 AR, 1863, 62.

31 AR, 1868–69, 80.

32 AR, 1861, 117; Malden AR, 1862 [no paging]. The author last visited this national historic site in August 2003. The only acknowledgment that this former British fort was for eleven years an insane asylum is a brief reference in a tourist pamphlet. The building housing the site's museum has wide-ranging displays about the fort's history during the nineteenth century, but in a telling omission, nothing is included about the people who built and laboured inside the very structure that is now a museum; nor is there any public interpretation about the history of the insane asylum period—yet another example of the hidden history of psychiatric patients that needs to be publicly acknowledged.

33 Orillia AR, 1862 [no paging].

34 Malden AR, 1862 [no paging]; AR, 1865, 59. Malden had sixty acres of cultivated land.

35 AR, 1865, Inspector E. A. Meredith's report, 10.

36 Moran, *Committed to the State Asylum*, 93.

37 Ripa, *Women and Madness*, 126.

38 Orillia AR, 1862 [no paging]; 1863, 60. The laundry floor measured 29 by 19 feet.

39 AR, 1864, 133.

40 AR, 1866, 130–1.

41 AR, 1863, 71.

42 AR, 1868–69, 71, 76.

43 AR, 1868–69, 74.

44 AR, 1869–70, 44; 1870–71, 73.

45 AR, 1870–71, 168; 1872–73, 177–78; 1874, 176.

46 AR, 1874, 168.

47 AR, 1871–73, 22.

48 AR, 1874, 169.

49 Inspector Langmuir's Report, AR, 1871–73, 25.

50 These dates can be found in AR, 1896, xi–xii.

51 Langmuir's emphasis on economy and efficiency can be found in AR, 1875, 18. Reference to the mechanization of provincial asylum laundry facilities can be found in AR, 1878, 26.

52 AR, 1877, 239.

53 AR, 1879, 21.

54 Ibid.

55 AR, 1870–71, 161.

56 AR, 1875, 237.

57 AR, 1878, 317.

58 AR, 1875, 226. Interestingly enough, at the Norfolk Lunatic Asylum in England during this same period, baking bread and brewing beer were not deemed appropriate jobs for patient labourers. See Cherry, *Mental Health Care in Modern England*, 67.

59 AR, 1877, 309; 1878, 348. No labour statistics are mentioned for 1878.

60 AR, 1878, 348.

61 AR, 1885, 66.

62 AR, 1880, 314.

63 AR, 1880, 335.

64 AR, 1894, 6.

65 AR, 1895, 35.

66 AR, 1883, 13–14, 66.

67 Ripa, *Women and Madness*, 107.

68 Cheryl L. Krasnick, "'In Charge of the Loons': A Portrait of the London, Ontario Asylum for the Insane in the Nineteenth Century," *Ontario History* 74, 3 (September 1982): 168–9; Reaume, *Remembrance of Patients Past*, 143–4.

69 AR, 1883, 86; AR, 1885, 45.

70 These figures do not include the Orillia Asylum for the Feeble-Minded, only the provincial insane asylums. When Orillia is added, there is no change of any note: the figures stay the same in 1880. In 1900 this figure increases by 1 per cent to 86 per cent of all inmates who were public charges. These figures were arrived at by adding the total paying patients in each year and then subtracting this number from the overall asylum population: AR, 1880, 18, 28; 1900, xvi–xvii, xlvii.

71 Andrew Scull, "Moral Treatment Reconsidered," in Andrew Scull, ed., *Social Order/Mental Disorder: Anglo-American Psychiatry in Historical Perspective* (Berkeley: University of California Press, 1989), 89–94.

72 AR, 1878, 330; 1895, 73. The maintenance rates for 1890 and 1895 are recorded in yearly figures, unlike for other years cited here. The weekly rate is thus calculated by dividing the yearly figure by 52 weeks to come up with the amount indicated.

73 AR, 1885, 66.

74 AR, 1880, 349; 1885, 114; 1895, 117; 1900, 87. The theme of low maintenance costs was also mentioned in the 1890 Hamilton Asylum report, where it was noted that "our expenditure is still low, and well within the appropriation in every department" (AR, 1980, 124). Though not part of this overall study, it is worth noting that at the Orillia Asylum for the Feeble-Minded (which opened in 1876, six years after the insane asylum there closed) Superintendent A. H. Beaton was especially pleased about how low the patient maintenance figures were for this institution. In 1895 he reported the amount was at a "low water mark" as it had dropped from a yearly per capita rate of $118.58 a year earlier to $105.18 that year, "a figure, I venture to say, that has never been equaled by any similar institution in the world" (AR, 1895, 213).

75 Gerald Grob, *The Mad among Us: A History of the Care of America's Mentally Ill* (New York: Free Press, 1994), 67; Dwyer, *Homes for the Mad*, 134–5; Anne Digby, "Moral Treatment at the Retreat, 1796–1846," in W. Bynum, R. Porter, and M. Shepherd, eds., *The Anatomy of Madness, Volume II, Institutions and Society* (London: Tavistock, 1985), 63; Cherry, *Mental Health Care in Modern England*, 67, 135; Ripa, *Women and Madness*, 109–10; Reaume, *Remembrance of Patients Past*, 139–42; Moran, *Committed to the State Asylum*, 83, 92–3.

76 AR, 1900, 114.

77 Cherry, *Mental Health Care in Modern England*, 135.

78 AR, 1885, 131; 1890, 91; 1895, 106; 1900, 126, 130.

79 AR, 1885, 66.

80 AR, 1885, 83.

81 AR, 1885, 90–1.

82 Pamela Michael, *Care and Treatment of the Mentally Ill in North Wales, 1800–2000* (Cardiff: University of Wales Press, 2003), 71.

83 AR, 1900, 149.

84 AR, 1880, 350.

85 AR, 1895, 122.

86 AR, 1888, 4; 1889, 5; 1890, 42–3.

87 AR, 1888, 4–5; AR, 1889, 6.

88 AR, 1891, 5; 1892, 10–11; 1893, 132, 156; 1894, 142; 1895, 159–60; 1896, 193–5, 224; 1897, 178, 207; 1898, 193, 222; 1899, 153, 173.

89 AR, 1897, 178.

90 Plans are underway to preserve and publicly memorialize the Toronto Asylum patients' labour and social history along the east and west boundary walls, which they re-built in 1888–89 (along with remaining portions of the 1860 patient-built south boundary wall) at the present-day Centre for Addiction and Mental Health, Toronto. The Mimico Asylum closed in 1979, when it was known as the Lakeshore Psychiatric Hospital. It is now part of Humber College, Toronto. A massive refurbishing campaign has made the old wards into classrooms and the Assembly Hall into a public arts and community centre. The cricket oval that was levelled by patients and one of the patient-built pavilions continue to be well used, while the superintendent's former residence housed people until recently.

91 AR, 1892, 134; 1899, 168.

92 AR, 1897, 179.

93 The statistical tables that list the "Employment of Patients," 1879–1900, identify these various jobs. For example, for Hamilton, see AR, 1890, 141.

94 AR, 1895, 74.

95 AR, 1880, 314; 1890, 124.

96 AR, 1885, 45.

97 AR, 1895, 39–42.

98 AR, 1895, 125.

99 For figures from 1900, see note 2 above.

100 Nancy Tomes, *A Generous Confidence: Thomas Story Kirkbride and the Art of Asylum-Keeping, 1840–1883* (Cambridge: Cambridge University Press, 1984), 285.

101 Ripa, *Women and Madness*, 110.

102 AR, 1859, 98, Report by D. McIntosh, Clark, Provincial Penitentiary, 31 December 1859; AR, 1860, 137, E. Horsey, Architect, Provincial Penitentiary, 21 January 1861.

103 AO, RG 63, A–I, vol. 135, file 4820, Kingston Asylum—Compensation to Patients, 1894–1904: Dr. Clarke to Inspector Christie, 15 June 1897; Inspector Christie to D. Miller, 16 June 1897.

104 Ibid. Inspector Christie to Dr. Clark; 27 July 1904.

105 Geoffrey Reaume, "No Profits, Just a Pittance: Work, Compensation and People Defined as Mentally Disabled in Ontario, 1964–1990," in S. Noll and J. Trent, eds., *Mental Retardation in America: A Historical Reader* (New York: New York University Press, 2004), 466–93. See also a recent report related to this issue: Arthur O'Reilly, *The Right to Decent Work of Persons with Disabilities* (Geneva: International Labour Organization, 2003).

106 AR, 1896, xxiv–xxv.

107 AR, 1878, 317.

108 AR, 1868–69, 61.

109 Digby, *Madness, Morality and Medicine*, 62.

110 Bryan D. Palmer, *Working Class Experience: The Rise and Reconstitution of Canadian Labour, 1800–1980* (Toronto: Butterworth, 1983), 72–3.

111 Reaume, *Remembrance of Patients Past*, 154.

112 Dwyer, *Homes for the Mad*, 133.

113 Ibid., 135. Dwyer also notes that this goal of putting patients to work on a large scale "enjoyed wide popular support" outside the asylum.

CHAPTER 11

Discipline and Dehumanization in a Total Institution:

Institutional Survivors' Descriptions of Time-out Rooms

Claudia Malacrida

This article reports on interviews with 21 institutional survivors who lived until the mid- to late-1980s in a total institution for the "training and care" of "mental defectives," operating in Alberta, Canada. The focus is on survivors' descriptions of Time-out Rooms, used to discipline unruly and escaped inmates. Foucault's theories about the disciplinary properties of modern society, the use of the gaze, technologies of the self, and scientific discourse are both supported and complicated by survivor narratives. In addition, the work of Erving Goffman is examined in terms of the process of dehumanization in total institutions. Ties between institutional practices and eugenics are speculated upon.

This article examines the narratives of 12 women and 9 men who are survivors of the Michener Center, a total institution for "mental defectives"[1] that has operated in the province of Alberta, Canada, from 1923 to the present day. Although these survivor narratives are specific to one institution, the Michener Center's practices of institutionalization and segregation reflected broader discourses and practices relating to science, eugenics and fitness in the West during the twentieth century. In this paper, survivor narratives covering experiences that occurred well into the 1980s are examined, with a focus on "Time-out Rooms," which were used to discipline misbehaving and runaway inmates.

Since the mid-1980s, historical, sociological and disability studies researchers have begun to expose the systematic institutionalization, degradation and eugenicization of disabled individuals in general, and developmentally disabled[2] people in particular, that occurred in the West during much of the twentieth century (McLaren, 1986; McLaren, 1990; Kuhl, 1994; Dowbiggin, 1995; Kevles, 1995; Proctor, 1995; Jones, 1999). Most of these histories exclude accounts from those who, having survived these practices, can tell us about the intimate mechanisms of disability oppression at its most profound level. Indeed, knowledge that comes from the positions or standpoints of those who are disabled is necessary to the construction of an emancipatory disability history (Wendell, 1996).

Survivors' stories also provide us with materials with which to examine theoretical understandings of difference and social control. In this paper, the work of Michel Foucault is played against survivor narratives, which complicate Foucault's claims about social control, embodied power, disciplinary versus punishment societies and power that is exercised through vision, visibility and the gaze. In addition, survivor narratives are examined against Erving Goffman's work on institutional life, and particularly against his ideas about the dehumanizing aspects of total institutions. Before engaging in an analysis of the interplay between these ideas and survivor narratives, I will provide a brief overview of the research project and a description of the Time-out Rooms.

Methodological Considerations

This paper is based on qualitative, semi-structured interviews with 21 former inmates of the Michener Center, a total institution for the "care and training" of individuals with developmental disabilities,[3] located outside of the town of Red Deer, Alberta, Canada. Research participants were recruited through a variety of agencies that provide services and support for individuals with developmental disabilities in the province of Alberta. The research participants are their own legal guardians, which is not necessarily representative of Michener ex-residents. Many individuals with developmental disabilities in Alberta are under the legal umbrella of the Office of the Public Guardian and do not have the ability to participate legally in social research without the permission of the Public Guardian. Although some efforts were made to reach participants through Offices of Public Guardians across the province, none of these facilitated the participation of their legal charges. This may mean that those who were able to participate in the research may be more independent and perhaps more intellectually capable than other possible interviewees. In turn, this may also mean that these survivor narratives reflect experiences in wards that were less oppressive than average; in the Michener Center, residents were segregated in wards according to hierarchies of disability, and it is likely that the survivors enjoyed better living conditions than others perceived as less intellectually competent.

For most interviewees, discussing the institution and its practices was conceived of as an upsetting, but necessary and important political and personal act. All participants were assured that they need not answer questions and that they could withdraw from the research at any time. Although many participants expressed fear about speaking out, none of these individuals withdrew or refused their participation. At the time of the interviews, individuals were asked whether or not they wished for anonymity in reporting research results; most preferred to be anonymous. For some survivors, however, naming themselves was important in terms of reclaiming an identity without shame. Thus, "Roy's" comments come from Roy Skoreyko, who, since leaving the Michener Center, has worked on behalf of institutional survivors and persons with developmental disabilities through his leadership role in the advocacy group, *People First*.

Institutionalization, Eugenics, Reintegration and Participants' Durations of Residency

It is useful to understand the relationships between the larger social context and some of the personal qualities of the survivors. The Provincial Training School (PTS) for Mental Defectives opened in 1923 in an imposing three-storey brick building, located in park-land outside of the small town of Red Deer, Alberta. Prior to its opening, children with intellectual disabilities either remained in their communities or were housed alongside individuals designated as mentally ill, in places like the Mental Hospital in Brandon, Manitoba, situated two provinces away. The PTS was seen at the time as a very progressive move because it segregated the "mentally retarded from the mentally ill," moved children closer to their families and purportedly shifted the focus of services from incarceration to education (Alberta Government Publications, 1985, p. 2).

The PTS's mandate was to engage in the work of "academic, vocational and personal development of retarded children and young adults" (Alberta Government Publications, 1985, p. 3), indicating that "trainees" would receive an education with the ultimate goal of a productive reintegration into society. Rhetoric concerning the training mandate of the institution and community reintegration persisted throughout Michener's[4] history: in the 1950s, the involvement of parent advisory groups resulted in "emphasis on increasing the trainee's independence" (p. 13), and in the 1960s, "program development produced a growing emphasis on resident training" (p. 14). Institutional rhetoric about training for "real" life aside, however, population figures for the institution indicate that residents remained in the institution for long periods, rarely returned to their communities, and their numbers grew steadily over the years. The institutional population peaked in 1969 with almost 2400 residents. In the 1970s and 1980s, through community and parent-driven advocacy efforts, deinstitutionalization began in earnest; by 1983 there were approximately 1600 residents, and in the year 1999, approximately 400 individuals remained (Alberta Government Publications, 1985; Michener Center Communications Officer, 1999). Most of the participants in this study left the institution between the mid-1970s to late-1980s as part of that deinstitutionalization movement.

Of the 21 individuals interviewed, the average age at admission was 12 years, and the average age for leaving was a little older than 27 years. In other words, the average person in this study spent *15 years* in the institution, and one person interviewed spent over 30 years inside. These lengthy stays do not support the institutional rhetoric of education and reintegration, but reflect practices that are more akin to lifelong internment, particularly when one considers that most of the individuals interviewed left the institution during a time of major shifts to communitization. Without this shift, we can safely assume that many of these individuals would have remained inside the Michener Center even longer, perhaps for their entire lives.

Language text

Eugenics and the Michener Center

While training and education were the given reasons for the institution's existence, eugenics concerns played an important role in establishing and sustaining the institution. During the first half of the twentieth century, a belief that "feeble-mindedness" could be attributed to poor genetic material prevailed in the minds of social reformers, government officials and medical and scientific practitioners (Smith, 1985; McLaren, 1986; McLaren, 1990). At the Michener Center, institutionalization, segregation and eugenics were intimately linked. The housing of "mental defectives" in a virtual fortress set at a distance from a small rural town, and the reportedly almost obsessive arrangements for sexual segregation within the Michener Center institution functioned as a covert form of eugenics; "defective" individuals segregated in these ways posed little risk of "polluting" the social body with their genetic material. More overt eugenics programmes also operated within the Michener Center; in 1928, just five years after the opening of the PTS, the Province of Alberta implemented the Sexual Sterilization Act and established the Alberta Eugenics Board. The Board regularly convened meetings at the Michener Center, and although things started slowly with "only" 16 sterilizations performed in 1930, by the time of the Board's closing in 1973, it was approving between 30 and 40 involuntary sterilizations per year, most of them on Michener residents (Alberta Government Publications, 1985; Park & Radford, 1998).

In addition to being deemed "mentally unfit," other categories of "impurity" are reflected in the demographic qualities of the study participants: of 21 participants, 11 were of Ukrainian heritage and three were Métis. In Alberta, Ukrainians were commonly derided as social misfits and second-class citizens, and Aboriginal persons (including Métis) continue to be treated with considerable prejudice. Beyond Alberta's borders, concerns about the troubling nature of both Eastern Europeans and First Nations People were clearly expressed in eugenics discourse in North America during the early part of the twentieth century (McLaren, 1986; McLaren, 1990; Dowbiggin, 1995). Thus, although this sample of participants is not representative of the general population at Michener, the participants' ethnic backgrounds do reflect circulating concerns about pollution and fitness that were embedded in eugenics discourse. Indeed, five of the twelve women and four of the nine men in this study stated that they had been involuntarily sterilized while residing in the Michener Center.

It is possible that eugenics concerns motivated the admissions of these survivors in other, more subtle ways. These individuals were often excluded from regular classrooms and were left to their own devices in communities that marginalized them. Indeed, concerns about truancy and delinquency were cited by three survivors as the imputed reasons for being admitted to the Michener Center. Thus, moral panics about keeping "problem" children off the streets and out of potential trouble may have led professionals to segregate such potentially "dangerous" (and vulnerable) young people from the rest of the community. The cordoning off of young people in this way also operated to preclude the possibility of their adult sexuality and reproduction in the community, again operating as a covert form of eugenics.[5]

Time-out Rooms

Time-out Rooms were an omnipresent means of exercising both reactive and precautionary control within the institution. From survivor narratives, it seems each unit in the Michener Center had at least one of these rooms; rather than being hidden away, the rooms were a part of the wards, within the sightlines of warders and other residents in each residential unit. Each room had a heavy, locked door with a small aperture through which instructions or food could be passed, and the inside of the room was fitted out with a drain in the middle of the floor and little else. A mattress would be dragged in at night for inmates to sleep on, to be removed in the morning to facilitate cleaning the cell. Inmates who were housed in the Time-out Rooms were typically naked, because staff feared that inmates might harm themselves by chewing at torn clothing or perhaps by trying to hang themselves (Anon, 2004). Furthermore, these rooms had a one-way mirror through which warders (and other inmates) could observe the individual being given a "Time-out," and in which the individuals inside could, no doubt, see themselves reflected.

All of the individuals interviewed for this project knew about the Time-out Rooms, speaking consistently about their uses and practices. According to participants, inmates were housed in Time-out Rooms as a result of resistance to daily institutional practices; acts of resistance included refusing to eat the food they were given, refusing to go to bed or wake up at the times they were told to, aggressive behaviour toward staff or toward other residents, or refusing to perform work duties as instructed. Above all, however, survivors noted that people were sent to the Time-out Rooms because of escape attempts. The detection of escape was a public event; its discovery would be heralded at any time of the day or night by wailing sirens and the hustle and bustle of ward searches and intra-institutional communications relating to the attempt. The combination of the sirens, the hubbub and the knowledge that those who attempted escape would inevitably end up in the Time-out Rooms comprised a powerful presence in survivor narratives about institutional life. Hence, Time-out Rooms were a central form of physical and psychological, reactive and proactive social control.

Michel Foucault, Bodily Discipline and the Gaze

Michel Foucault provides disability scholars with important tools for understanding institutional and embodied practices of social control in general, and the disciplinary practices attached to Time-out Rooms in particular. His theories permit us to see how bodily practices and visual power are implicated in institutional routines and undertakings. In Foucault's analysis of institutions, the physical layout of such places is never innocent or arbitrary; instead, vantage points, lines of surveillance, and the omnipresence of physical spaces like the Time-out Room are constructed in ways that can be read as discursive practices—the means through which a society's underlying ideas and values circulate and

WTF?!

are made material (Foucault, 1995). Thus, the Time-out Room's interior layout and its positioning within the institution give expression to institutional and societal norms about acceptable treatment for individuals in the Michener Center and, more broadly, for all individuals who are considered to be "less-than" normal. The rooms, with their vault-like qualities, express societal fears of those who are different; in this architecture, the unruly "defective" must "naturally" be contained, isolated and broken, and any acknowledgement of their human needs for comfort, safety or dignity is denaturalized.

Read

For Foucault, the body is the critical site upon which discursive formations are practiced. Societal values and knowledge, administered through discursive practices such as institutional routines, are written on the surfaces of individual bodies, in what Foucault termed bio-power[1] (Foucault, 1988a; Foucault, 1990). In Time-out Room practices, the inmate's naked body, placed in the room for all to view, is both a reflection and an expression of the kind of society in which such a body is positioned. In Foucault's model, the body, and particularly the body that is different or "less-than," has not been responded to uniformly across time and space; a careful observation of the ways that such bodies are handled or treated can provide us with insight into the workings of power and knowledge in a particular society. Thus, the Time-out Room, and its use on "less-than" bodies, reflects societal understandings about who is entitled to a minimum standard of decency and humane treatment, despite scientific or institutional rhetoric to the contrary. In other words, understanding the bodily practices of the Time-out Room can help us to understand the construction of non-humanness embedded in these institutional routines.

important bits

Since the Enlightenment, Foucault argued, the means of exercising bio-power in the West has shifted from the raw brutality of a punishment-based society to the use of discipline, in which routinized practices operate through the application of scientific knowledge to manage and contain what ultimately become docile bodies. To Foucault, the Enlightenment's benign advancements in prison reform and the asylum, for example, do not represent more humane or progressive ways of helping patients and inmates. Instead, these modern practices, informed by medical, psychiatric and criminological knowledge and professionals, actually operate to increase the pervasiveness of social control on increasingly docile bodies. Echoing Foucault's insights, the name and the design of the Time-out Room draws on the enlightened psychological discourse of behaviourism. Time-out Rooms were ostensibly used to "extinguish" bad behaviours through dispassionate and scientific means, with the goal of shaping inmates' behaviour in non-violent and controlled ways. As we will hear, however, survivors' stories about the daily practices of observation, exposure and surveillance that occurred in the Time-out Room clarify that these practices operated not only as benign and dispassionate means of extinguishing undesirable behaviours, but were in fact also coupled with more brutal and "unenlightened" punishments.

A final, important contribution of Foucauldian theory to understanding the Time-out Rooms rests in the metaphor of the gaze. In the clinic, the physician whose power

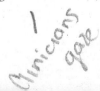
clinicians gaze

is drawn from his disciplinary knowledge is the observer whose gaze penetrates even beneath the surface of the patient's body, exposing not only the patient's disease or difference, but also providing evidence of the need for increased surveillance and expert intervention on the unruly body (Foucault, 1994). Foucault shows us that this gaze replaced brutality, as exemplified by the metaphor of the Panopticon—an ideal prison designed by Jeremy Bentham that promised a means of exercising power through the simple use of the gaze. From the Panopticon's central guard tower, the warder's gaze, which can be neither detected nor deflected by the prisoner, is the means through which bodily discipline is enforced. The effectiveness of the gaze as disciplinary force occurs to such extent that prisoners, engaging in "technologies of the self," preemptively discipline their own bodies, simply because at any time the warder *could* be watching (Foucault, 1988; Foucault, 1995). Indeed, as we will hear, these practices of gaze and technologies of the self are evidenced amply in the narratives of the Michener Center survivors, who have much to tell about the ways that power and expertise were supported through bodily management and visual penetration onto residents' bodies by staff and outside professionals.

Erving Goffman has also provided us with an analysis of "total institutions" that is fruitful to understanding the daily regimes of the Michener Center. Total institutions, to Goffman, are "a place of residence and work where a large number of like-situated individuals, cut off from the wider society for an appreciable period of time, together lead an enclosed, formally administered round of life" (Goffman, 1961, p. xv). He noted that life in such places is permeated with formal and informal practices designed to humiliate, degrade and deface the identity of the institutionalized person (pp. 20–21). The Michener Center was a total institution, serving a purportedly homogeneous "population" of "mental defectives," located on a large, self-contained farm outside of a small farming town in Alberta. "Residents" were often admitted to the Michener Center in childhood and literally spent decades there before having even a hope of discharge. In this setting, as Goffman might predict, processes of stigmatization operated as more than simple mechanisms of social control. Instead, institutionalized practices of humiliation and degradation operated to construct residents not only as individuals stripped of their former identity, but also as individuals who were stripped of their humanity. As we will hear in the survivors' stories, dehumanization seems to have been a central project in the daily rituals of the Michener Center, particularly in the practices of Quiet Room treatment.

Dehumanization can be an end in itself, by making the daily work of cleaning, bathing, feeding, housing and "training" inmates simpler for staff, who are no longer compelled to observe the decencies demanded by *human* inmates. When the daily chores attendant with "care" are constructed in such a way as to be aimed toward "non-humans," the niceties of privacy, respect and tenderness come to be seen as superfluous. Dehumanization—the facilitation of impersonal and unthinking care—undoubtedly occurred in the Michener Center, for many residents, the dehumanization process made possible abuse beyond the routinized brutality of total institutional life. In the narratives of Michener survivors, it becomes possible to imagine how the processes of dehumanization opened the way not only for careless and cruel daily practices, but also facilitated Michener's eugenics routines.

The Time-out Room: View from outside, View from within

As noted, every survivor in this study knew of and spoke about the Time-out Rooms, and the role of these rooms as an ever-present means of exercising control within the institution. Stan and Roy provide us with descriptions of the procedures for "admitting" a misbehaving resident into the Time-out Rooms that introduce us to contradictions between discipline-based modes of engendering social control and punishment-based methods in the practices of the Michener Center. Stan told me, "They would put you down on the floor in a 'sleeper.' It's like a headlock, and they put you to sleep and throw you in the Time-out Room ... It was scary, not nice. Had a window and glass, and a mat on the floor, and a drain in the middle." Roy concurred, saying, "They would put you in there in this room. You had no bed. You slept on the floor. They had windows ... people could see you walking back and forth. Some of them, they would put straitjackets on."

Stan and Roy's descriptions remind us of Foucault's Panopticon, with its deployment of the gaze as a disciplining arm of those in power. Like the Panopticon, the one-way mirror of the Time-out Room acted as a window to those who observed from outside, and it operated as the means through which warders could exercise constant and easy surveillance upon miscreants. Conversely, because Time-out Room inmates could not tell when they were being observed nor see who was outside, the one-way mirror acted as a visual reminder to inmates of the constant possibility of being observed. From these comments, it seems the Time-out Room did operate to create compliance and control through what Foucault would term "disciplinary" means—through observations of the self by others and through preemptive self-observations. However, Stan and Roy's comments allow us to see that in the Michener Center, there was more to social control than the disciplinary gaze. Instead, these comments convey that brute power, in the form of the straitjacket and the stranglehold, was a common and publicly displayed accompaniment to the behaviourist disciplinary control of the Time-out Room. Thus, rather than the smooth, rational, and impersonal surveillance-based power that Foucault imagined would take place in modern institutional orders, the stories these survivors tell us about the public violence and brute force of routine discipline at the Michener Center show us a more terrifying and chaotic picture of social control in action. Indeed, we can hear that both discipline-based or "modern" practices and punishment-based or "pre-modern" practices operated in concert within the institution.

Foucault also offers us the concept of bio-power with which to understand the circulation of power. Recall that, for Foucault, the body is the site upon which societal values and knowledge are inscribed through the practices of institutions and professions. In the Time-out Room, the rationality of science meets the unruly bodies of inmates who refuse to comply. From inmate descriptions, we can notice that the Time-out Room, despite its veneer of science, was also a means of displaying and reinforcing the "non-person" status of Time-out Room residents in particular, and perhaps of Michener inmates more generally. Glen, for example, described his experiences inside the Time-out Room as follows:

> The staff could look in from a window in the door but I couldn't see out of it. There was no toilet, and when I had to go, I had to bang on the door with my feet. But most of the time, no one would come, so I wet myself. I had to sit like that sometimes for hours until staff would come. That hurt my feelings.

This gentleman—naked, wet, and ignored—is not simply being treated with operant conditioning's sensory deprivation as a means of extinguishing undesirable behaviours. Instead, what Glen describes is systematic humiliation, enacted through bodily practices that would not be deemed fitting for someone "deserving" or fully human. The message of this kind of bio-power is that people like Glen are not part of the general social body, and hence have no claim to human rights or human dignity. Of course, Glen's descriptions also remind us of Goffman's claim that dehumanization is a central object of the daily routines and practices of total institutions (1961). This dehumanization, while making it "simple" for workers to handle inmates in unthinking and humiliating ways, also conceivably made it easier for the institution itself to treat inmates in ways that denied their human rights. In this way, the interactions relating to the Time-out Room can be imagined to extend beyond the walls of the immediate ward, connecting to broader practices within the Michener Center and its work with the Eugenics Board. In an institution where inmates were routinely conceived of as being less than human, and where this view was systemically upheld through institutional practices like the Quiet Rooms, it is possible to understand how other forms of routinized violence, such as involuntary sterilizations came to be seen not only as acceptable, but even as necessary accoutrements to institutional life.

Glen's description draws on Foucauldian notions of the gaze as a form of power and the use of spectacle as a disciplining force. Glen's comments build on Foucault's ideas, by reminding us that the added visual plane of the one-way mirror operates not only as a window through which outsiders view the humiliation of the inmate, but that the mirror also can provide the inmate with a view of himself that is both somber and humiliating. Thus, the views and perspectives represented in the actual construction of Time-out Rooms offer support and development of Foucauldian notions of the power of the gaze. In addition to their layout, the positioning of these rooms within the larger institutional setting is important to consider.

The Time-out Room: Spectacle, Prevention and Division

When discussing the Time-out Rooms, survivors noted that there was little secrecy or mystery surrounding the use of the space or the ways that individuals came to be incarcerated in them. The highly visible positioning of the rooms themselves, with one on each ward, typically as part of the "regular" hallway of resident rooms and within the sightlines of both the nursing stations and the public day-rooms of each ward, meant that residents of the institution could not avoid knowing about and seeing the Time-out Rooms. Furthermore, the sirens and flashlight searches that accompanied the internment of runaway residents into Time-out Rooms, and the struggles and straitjacketing that accompanied the internment of inmates with "bad" behaviour, meant that other residents could hardly ignore the violence attached to these spaces.

The public aspect of the Time-out Rooms' spatial designs is reminiscent of Foucault's punishment-type means of social control. Foucault tells us that, in pre-modern societies, punishments were enacted in highly visible public spectacles to warn the general public about what would happen to transgressors. While the Time-out Rooms, with their locked doors and windowed walls, at first glance seem to reflect a more private, disciplinary means of social control; nevertheless the public positioning of the space, and the often violent and noisy means by which inmates were admitted to the space in fact offered a spectacle of punishment to other inmates that let them know who was a "bad" inmate and the institutional response to inmates who resist. The spectacle of admission and the public positioning of the space offered all residents a visual performance of institutional might, evidenced by swift, brutal and unforgiving punishment for those who failed to comply with institutional regimes.

Survivors themselves acknowledged the cautionary or preventative qualities of Time-out Rooms. John, for example, noted that, "Some of the kids got put away on the side in this little place. In this dark room with a big window on the door. Sometimes they were there for 2 to 3 days." When I asked him whether that had ever happened to him, he emphatically noted, "No, I made sure I stayed out of trouble." For John, as for others, the architectural, spatial and physical aspects of the Time-out Rooms engendered preventative self-discipline and self-technologies, exercised in efforts to avoid trouble.

Recall Foucault's argument that technologies of the self are engaged in by individuals not only so that they can avoid social sanctions, but also so that they can come to think of themselves as good, deserving and worthy citizens (Foucault, 1988b). Drawing on Foucault, it is possible to understand that in John's description of himself as a person who "made sure [he] stayed out of trouble," there was more at stake than simply avoiding punishment. In addition, we can understand that compliance and avoiding punishment are ways that John can see himself as good, smart and unlike those who failed to avoid the stigma and brutality of the Time-out Rooms.

Divide and Conquer

Like John, most participants in this study were loath to admit to actually doing time in a Time-out Room, and they were remarkably unsympathetic toward those who did end up in them. Donna, for example, noted:

I never went to the Time-out Rooms, no. I would make sure I wouldn't get in trouble. So I could get out, you know? I thought that with my behaviour that sooner or later, I'd get out of Michener. I thought that I was the kind of person that knew what to do.

Donna's comments permit us to understand the cautionary value of the Time-out Rooms, and they also show how she was able to distance herself from her surroundings in several ways. First, she was able to provide herself with assurances that abuse and violation can actually be avoided in the institution. In the institution's chaotic and unpredictable environment, in which inmates had virtually no power over their days, their lives or their futures, the only power Donna was able to grasp was that which she wielded over herself. By telling herself that she was the kind of person who exercised positive behaviours, and by believing that these qualities would not only keep her out of Time-out Rooms but may even provide her with the ability to escape the institution, she could provide herself with assurances that institutional abuses could, and would, be avoided. Beyond Foucault's notion of technologies of the self that are aimed toward constructing a positive social self-concept, Donna's comments allow us to understand that such technologies offer the individual some real power—the power to avoid punishment, the power to imagine oneself as "in control" and the power to dream of another, better life.

Ironically, the power Donna deployed was not directed toward the institution or its workers, but instead maintained the *status quo* by engendering compliance and by reinforcing divisions amongst the inmates themselves. Donna's comments show us how institutional orders and self-technologies keep people from forming alliances amongst the oppressed. For her, the unruly co-resident is not seen as someone with a sense of justice or an enduring spirit, but she instead frames Time-out Room inmates as deserving of punishment or as individuals who simply do not know how to avoid it, unlike herself. This framing surely provided residents like Donna with assurances of personal power and safety in a place where both were in short supply, but it also precluded solidarity amongst inmates. Time-out Rooms seem to have functioned to divide and conquer through the construction of hierarchies amongst inmates.

Humiliation and the Gaze

As noted earlier, hierarchies within the institution were maintained through "grades" that separated wards according to the inmates' personal qualities. In addition, hierarchies were sustained through the use of the Time-out Rooms throughout the institution. This is reflected in comments like Donna's about those who were careless enough or foolish enough to "deserve" incarceration in the Time-out Rooms. The few descriptions provided by survivors who admitted to having spent time in Time-out Rooms provide us with some insight into how the rooms acted not only to "demote" inmates in the eyes

191

systematic use!
humiliation.

of others, but in their own eyes as well. When we recall Glen's description of being left unattended and incontinent, we can understand the Quiet Room as more than a form of discipline or punishment, or a vehicle to create divisions amongst inmates. Instead, Glen allows us to understand that the Time-out Rooms had another, central function, which was to humiliate and dehumanize its inmates. This perhaps explains why few survivors were willing to admit that they had ever experienced such humiliations, and why they spoke so harshly about individuals who had been in them.

Finally, Glen's description reminds us that the added visual plane of the one-way mirror operated not only to provide outsiders with a view on the inmate and her/his disgrace, but offered a view of the individual herself/himself that was both somber and shaming. Perhaps this self-view was as painful to inmates as was the knowledge that others could see them in their abject state. Glen's comments permit us to understand that the individuals who are the objects of their own gaze come to be seen as dehumanized, even to themselves.

Discussion

Survivors' descriptions of Quiet Rooms provide us with both confirmations and contradictions of Foucauldian concepts. Foucauldian ideas about punishment and discipline-based societies offer fruitful constructs for analysing the Quiet Room practices. Nonetheless, these ideas fall short of explaining the unruly, non-routinized brutality of the Michener Center when juxtaposed against the actual experiences described by those who lived in the institution. In addition to the use of science, routinization and the gaze in engendering institutional control, survivors describe both quotidian and extraordinary violence occurring in Time-out Room practices, and such brutality is more reminiscent of Foucault's pre-Enlightenment punishment model of social control than the disciplinary practices he theorized as the hallmarks of modernity. Foucault's concept of a historical transition from punishment-based social practices to discipline-based control is complicated in the survivor narratives, where both types of control are exercised simultaneously.

Furthermore, Foucauldian notions of technologies of the self can help us to understand why individuals might want to comply in the institution, why individuals in the institution distanced themselves from their fellow inmates, and how hierarchies and divisions were maintained within the institution. Drawing on survivor narratives sheds light on the personal power that can be gained when such hierarchies exist, and what gains can be had by individuals who seek to distance themselves from those who are suffering most from the order of things. Survivor narratives enable us to understand the terror and lack of control that prevailed in places such as the Michener Center, in turn making it possible to see how personal power could be obtained by individuals who told themselves that, given the right behaviours, they could remain safe and exercise some control over their lives.

Finally, Foucault's ideas provide tools for understanding the power of the spatial designs of the Rooms, their locations within the institution, and the ways that vision and visibility were organized to sustain power relations within the institution. Thus, the mirrored door, the viewing window and the hallways vista with the Time-out Room at its centre can be understood as means of exercising discipline through bio-power. These spectacles and views provided staff, fellow patients, and inmates themselves with specific and strategic perspectives, wherein the incarcerated individual can be seen and can become objectified and degraded. However, survivors' narratives move us beyond understanding the simple mechanics of space, vistas and the gaze. These survivor accounts provide us an added layer that permits an understanding of how such technologies of power can feel when one is at the receiving end of such visions, and they allow us to see that humiliation and dehumanization, rather than benign behaviourism in the form of operant conditioning, lie at the core of Time-out Room practices.

By drawing on Erving Goffman's work on stigma and institutionalization, it becomes possible to understand, if not why, then at least *how* dehumanization occurs. Goffman has provided us with an analysis of "total institutions" that can be used fruitfully in understanding the daily regimes of the Michener Center. Recall that for Goffman, total institutions are permeated with practices of humiliation, degradation and identity erasure (Goffman, 1961, pp. 20–21). In the Michener Center, and particularly in the Time-out Rooms, as Goffman might predict, institutional processes operated as more than means of discipline and control. Instead, institutionalized practices of humiliation, and degradation operated to erase the very humanity of the institution's residents.

Goffman's insights into stigma and dehumanization allow us to understand how the daily humiliations of institutional life facilitate further abuses, and Foucault's insights offer us the ability to understand the embodied aspects of social control and the ways that discipline relies on the penetrative gaze of experts. However, these theorists have also been criticized for the distanced and impersonal accounts they give of what are not simply processes of social control, but are instead horrific human experiences. Foucault has been assailed by feminist critics who note, for example, that "Foucault's is a world in which things move, rather than people, a world in which subjects become obliterated ..." (Hartsock, 1990, p. 167). [Nancy] Hartsock also notes that, although Foucault's theory is centred on the workings of power, his focus on the structure of discourse and discursive practices, rather than subject positions, leaves his analysis oddly devoid of insight into how oppression and power relations operate in the lives of living, breathing humans. Disability scholars have offered similar critiques of Goffman's perspective on social control, stigma and deviance. Tanya Titchkosky argues that Goffman's distanced reporting and observational style expresses a standpoint from the perspective of a presumed "we" who are "normal" who are observing and examining the ways that "abnormals" or "others" are stigmatized and managed (Titchkosky, 2000, 2003).

By asking institutional survivors to report on the practices within the institution, it is possible to move away from the distanced and objectifying standpoint of theorists or "normals," As Susan Wendell (1996) has argued, in order to develop an emancipatory knowledge of disability and its history, it is critical to examine disability oppression from the positions or standpoints of those who are disabled. When we listen to the narratives of disabled individuals themselves about their experiences of stigma, brutality, marginalization and social control inside the institution, we are offered far richer insights into the workings of power and the construction of difference than either Foucault's or Goffman's theories can provide. Instead, survivor narratives offer us a profoundly convincing personal and political argument against the institution's routine and systemic violence, and ultimately, against institutionalization itself.

Endnotes

1   I wish to make clear that this term is not my own, but reflects official language concerning the mandate of the Michener Center at the time of its opening in 1923, and for several decades thereafter.
2   In Canada, the term "developmentally disabled" is used to describe individuals with intellectual challenges; in the UK, "learning disabled" is more typical.
3   In 1973, in the midst of the shift away from institutionalization and the development of a community-living movement, a new swimming-pool complex was built on the premises, and the institution was renamed the Michener Center in celebration of Red Deer's most famous citizen, Roland Michener, a former athlete who became the Governor-General of Canada.
4   It must be noted, however, that institutionalization did not necessarily preclude sexual activity or reproduction for Michener inmates. In the interviews, three female survivors described witnessing incidents of sexual assault by staff, and two described roommates who were aborted when they became pregnant, all incidents occurring while these individuals were under segregated "care."

References

Alberta Government Publications. (1985) *Michener Centre: A history 1923–1983* (Edmonton, Canada).

Anon. (2004) Interview with ex-worker from the Michener Center.

Dowbiggin, I. (1995) Keeping this young country sane: C. K. Clarke, immigration restriction, and Canadian psychiatry, 1890–1925, *The Canadian Historical Review*, 76(4), 598–627.

Foucault, M. (1988a) The political technology of individuals, in: L. H. Martin, H. Gutman & P. H. Hutton (Eds) *Technologies of the self: A seminar with Michel Foucault* (Amherst, MA, University of Massachusetts Press).

Foucault, M. (1988b) Technologies of the self, in: L. H. Martin, H. Gutman & P. Hutton (Eds) *Technologies of the self: a seminar with Michel Foucault* (Amherst, MA, Massachusetts, University of Massachusetts Press).

Foucault, M. (1990) *The history of sexuality. Volume I: An introduction* (New York, Vintage Books).

Foucault, M. (1994) *The birth of the clinic: An archeology of medical perception* (New York, Vintage Books).

Foucault, M. (1995) *Discipline and punish: The birth of the prison* (New York, Vintage Books).

Goffman, E. (1961) *Asylums: Essays on the social situation of mental patients and other inmates* (Garden City, NY, Doubleday Books).

Hartsock, N. (1990) Foucault on power: A theory for women?, in: L. Nicholson (Ed.) *Feminism/postmodernism* (New York and London, Routledge).

Jones, R. L. (1999) The master potter and the rejected pots: Eugenic legislation in Victoria, 1918–1939, *Australian Historical Studies*, 113, 319–343.

Kevles, D. J. (1995) *In the name of eugenics: Genetics and the uses of human heredity* (Cambridge, MA, Harvard University Press).

Kuhl, S. (1994) *The Nazi connection: Eugenics, American racism, and German national socialism* (New York, Oxford University Press).

McLaren, A. (1986) The creation of a haven for "human thoroughbreds": The sterilization of the feeble-minded and the mentally ill in British Columbia, *Canadian Historical Review*, LXVII (2), 127–150.

McLaren, A. (1990) *Our own master race: Eugenics in Canada, 1885–1945* (Toronto, McClelland and Stewart Inc.).

Michener Center Board of Directors. (2001) Michener Board minutes, 1–11.

Michener Center Communications Officer. (1999) Private conversation concerning resident statistics.

Park, D. C. & J. P. Radford. (1998) From the case files: Reconstructing a history of involuntary sterilisation, *Disability & Society*, 13(3), 317–342.

Proctor, R. N. (1995) The destruction of "lives not worth living," in: J. Terry & J. Urla (Eds) *Deviant bodies: Critical perspectives on difference in science and popular culture* (Bloomington, IN, Indiana University Press).

Smith, J. D. (1985) *Minds made feeble: The myth and legacy of the Kallikas* (Rockville, MD, Aspen Publications).

Titchkosky, T. (2000) Disability studies: The old and the new, *Canadian Journal of Sociology*, 25(2), 197–224.

Titchkosky, T. (2003) Disability studies: The old and the new, in: T. Titchkosky (Ed.) *Disability, self, and society* (Toronto, University of Toronto Press Inc.).

Wendell, S. (1996) *The rejected body: Feminist philosophical reflections on disability* (New York and London, Routledge).

PART IV

Law and Social Space

Space, be it public or private, is socially organized and is, therefore, both ordered by and a producer of normative conceptions of who belongs, how to act, where to go, and how to get there.

Much of the organization of social space does not orient to the possibility of the presence of disabled people. Through this spatial oppression and exclusion it comes to seem as if it is normal for disabled citizens to be not present, let alone participants, in social space. Still, there are ongoing legal and political battles that confront the taken-for-granted exclusion of disabled people from a variety of social spaces. These battles are changing the conceptions of who "normally" belongs and where. The following two chapters address in very different ways the interrelation between law, space, and disability.

Human rights for disabled people have not and do not come easily. Indeed, in Chapter 12, Marcia Rioux suggests that the struggle for disability rights has an auspicious history in Canada and elsewhere. This struggle is part of the history of Canada and this history sets the stage for, as Rioux says, a social legal construction that acts as a barrier to full citizenship for disabled people even to this day. Rioux uses Canadian history as a way to analyze the struggle for disability rights and the involvement of the disability movement. She introduces an international understanding of disability that formulates it as a human rights issue. Social justice needs to be the orientation that society has toward disability and disabled people. Rioux demonstrates the difficulty that springs from attempting to orient to disability as a human rights issue and shows that this difficulty is embedded in the more conventional and "normal" societal ways of conceiving of disability. Society conventionally understands disability as a social development problem and thus as a problem of personal adjustment framed within a social context of charity. For Rioux, human rights and social justice aims are required as a prerequisite for a citizenry which includes disabled people in the various realms of social space.

In Chapter 13, Vera Chouinard argues that the social spatial marginalization of embodied difference, including disability, focuses on the issue of legal rights. The legal rights argument holds that social spaces are required to be accessible to disabled people since their inaccessibility marginalizes us. Chouinard presents a different, but related, way of understanding geography and social space. The social definition of social space, and the understanding of who belongs in these spaces and who does not, is often produced within what Chouinard calls "legal peripheries." She speaks of these spaces as the intersection of law as it is discursively represented or talked about and how law is lived. In this legal periphery, Chouinard says that the way the law is talked about and the way it is lived are fundamentally at odds. Neo-liberal democracy understands this discourse regarding legal rights as inclusionary and tolerant of diversity. Chouinard calls this approach "shadow citizenry" and demonstrates that life in this type of citizenry generates profound exclusion. Chouinard shows that it is within these spaces of "legal peripheries" that disabled people struggle politically and engage in the fight for human rights.

CHAPTER 12

Bending towards Justice

Marcia H. Rioux

Introduction

Political struggles for the rights of disabled people have an auspicious history in Canada as they do elsewhere. These struggles form part of the earliest political history of the country and set the stage for the social and legal construction of inequality that still acts as a barrier to full citizenship. Fortunately the nature of those political struggles is very distinct from the political struggles framed by the disability rights movement that has developed in the past 25 years.

In this chapter, I use early Canadian history as an introduction for looking at the nature of the current political struggle for change in which the disability rights movement is involved. I place that in the context of the evolving international norms and standards that frame disability as an issue of human rights and social justice, rather than social development and charitable aid. Recognising empowerment and control as central to the struggle for change, I argue that freedom is a fundamental right that has to be won to address the political disenfranchisement, economic disempowerment and social inequality that are the reality of disabled people universally. Being active participants in their own lives and in the transformation of their societies (that is, being free) is central to people overcoming the entrenched repression imposed by a model of caring for people. This challenges the current social and political lethargy that accepts the current position of disabled people as a natural state of affairs and the framing of the issues of disability as issues of services, income and care. Evidence of the changing nature of the struggle is found in Canadian law and jurisprudence in which the political struggle has clearly coalesced around freedom and agency.

Historical Struggles

As a political issue disability was evident as early as the mid-1700s in Canada. Britain, in its zeal to be rid of those deemed "undesirable," shipped them to the colonies. To Australia, they shipped the prisoners to populate that country and to get rid of them. In the case of Canada, they shipped what were termed "the poor, the indigent and the mentally and morally defective."

This led to some dissension in the early days in Canada. In 1766, a group of prominent citizens of Halifax, Nova Scotia (one of the eastern Maritime provinces), lodged a complaint with the English Lords of Trade and Plantations against an unimpeded influx to Nova Scotia of the "scum of all the colonies." He included:

> not only useless but very Bothersome to the Community, being not only those of the most dissolute manners, and void of all Sentiments of honest Industry, but also Infirm, Decrepit, and insane, as well as extremely indigent persons, who are unable to contribute anything towards their own maintenance. (Green 1986)

Two years later the citizenry voiced its concern that the so-called "scum" continued to place a heavy burden on a relatively weak economy, with a small population and a limited tax base (Franklin 1986). Accordingly, it sought legislation to prevent the immigration of disabled, infirm and other "useless" people into Canada.

In 1896, Dr. Bodington, the Medical Superintendent of the Province of British Columbia, on Canada's west coast, joined a growing number of those in the west who complained about the United Kingdom:

> ... shipping off to the Colonies weak minded young people who are unmanageable at home and unable to make a career for themselves, or earn a living.

On his own initiative Dr. Bodington shipped five such individuals back to England and urged the government to deport to the mother country "other chronic lunatics" (British Columbia 1897; British Columbia Assembly 1898).

The British government disallowed exclusory legislative bills in Nova Scotia and elsewhere because its own interest lay in the immigration of "such" people to its colonies. Indeed, Britain had given justices of the peace the power to sentence vagrants—including individuals with disabilities—to houses of correction until "the justices could place them out in some lawful calling ... either within this realm or his majesty's colonies in America" (*England, An Act to Amend and Make Effectual the Laws Relating to Rogues, Vagabonds, and Other Idle and Disorderly Persons, and to Houses of Correction*).

In 1895, Dr. Bruce Smith, the Ontario Inspector of Hospital and Charities, complained that the ever-increasing number of what he called "feeble-minded" in the province needed to be checked and prevented, and further:

> There is another point that must not be lost sight of and that is the fact that we are altogether too lax in regard to allowing undesirable immigrants to find shelter in this province. Too often ... mental and physical degenerates have been landed on our shores and have finally drifted, wither through mental, physical or moral deficiencies into one or other of our great public Charities. The majority of the feeble-minded girls, who

having fallen prey to some designing villain [by way of sexual intercourse] are sent to our Rescue homes, have only been a short time in this country.... (Green 1986)

These are not very illustrious early days in relation to disability in Canada. Some of the harsh words of the early settlers of our country can still be found today in the attitudes, laws, policies and programs that find their roots in the early rejection of disabled people—immigration procedures, sterilisation practices, pre-natal screening and selective abortion, institutionalisation, competency laws, education acts, medical care and triaging and others. But there have also been some significant victories. At the very least people are not still trying to ship disabled people out of the country. And relative to the goals of the disability rights movement, there are several legal cases and some social policies that suggest that the struggle for change is having an impact.

The nature of the struggle for change is not entirely clear. Alternative perspectives on the nature of disability, the political mechanisms to address disability, ethical imperatives invoked to justify actions directed towards disabled people, interpretations of the concept of disability, and disciplinary approaches to disability all impact on the way the struggle for change is manifested. There is not agreement on a singular, monolithic goal. To understand the move towards disability rights, as a political struggle, this article will first look at the emerging understanding of disability rights and then using some recent legislative action and legal decisions examine the way in which these reflect the way the struggle for change has evolved in Canada.

Shifting Paradigms

Over the past 20 years, the paradigm of disability has shifted from a medical welfare model to a human rights model. The rights paradigm recognises non-discrimination and equality rather than goodwill as the goals of the liberation and inclusion struggle. Inspired by other rights movements (race, religion, gender) of the 1960s and 1970s, disabled activists now see their disability in the same political context as black people view their race and feminists their gender. In particular segregation and institutionalisation, which have been the hallmark of disability policy, are seen in the context of racial segregation and apartheid. "Disability was reconceptualized by the activists as a different state of being rather than a tragic deviation from 'normalcy', and a social status vulnerable to discrimination by non-disabled persons" (Degener 1995). Empowerment and self-direction are accepted as key to achieving equality of opportunity and citizenship in society (Cooper 1999; Oliver 1990; Barnes 1994).

This reconceptualisation of disability, by the rights movement generally, by disability rights advocates and reflected in some government policies and programmes recognises disabled people's criticism of the medical and individualistic approach to defining disability. As an individual pathology, disability is seen as a physical, psychological or intellectual condition that results in a functional limitation. This means that it gets framed as an individual, rather than a society problem, and one that can be prevented or ameliorated through medical, biological or genetic intervention or through therapy, rehabilitation services and technical supports. But there is no leverage or argument that either the society or the environment needs to be changed if the problem rests in the individual as this paradigm suggests.

The model adopted by the disability rights movement is grounded in a framework of social pathology (Rioux 1997), and recognises and gives attention to the effect of the environment and the social structure on the consequent disability of an individual (ICIDH 1981). It recognises that disability is not only the result of the individual impairment, but is the result of interaction between individuals and the environment that is not intended or designed to enable participation (Roth 1983). It also recognises that the social causes of disability extend to the way in which social, economic and political structures contribute to disablement (Oliver 1990). The solution to the issues arising from disability is political. It recognises that beyond equal treatment or equal opportunity, notions of discrimination have to encompass the concept of "equal environmental opportunity" to enable disabled people to have opportunities equivalent to their non-disabled counterparts (Hahn 1993, 1997).

International Norms and Standards as Guidelines for the Struggle for Change

Internationally, in civil society, in state governments (Jones and Marks 1999) and within the United Nations system, there has been a reflection of this shift in paradigm. The emergence of international norms and standards relating to disability has carried with it the potential to transform an almost universal pejorative cultural resistance to the equalisation of opportunities for disabled people.

Following the designation of 1981 as the International Year of Disabled Person, the United Nations General Assembly adopted the *World Programme of Action concerning Disabled Persons* (1982). The *World Programme* identified as its goal the "full participation of persons with disabilities" in social life and development on the basis of equality. In 1993, the General Assembly adopted the Standard Rules on the Equalization of Opportunities for Persons with Disabilities (UN G.A. Res.48/96). The Standard Rules were important insofar as they supplement and provide greater specificity on the rights of disabled persons in light of conventional established rights. In 1998, the United Nations Commission on Human Rights adopted Resolution 98/31, Human Rights of Persons with Disabilities, reaffirming their commitment to the full participation of persons with disabilities in all aspects of life and to its promotion and application in international and domestic contexts.

Other international instruments articulating guidelines and standards on a range of disability-related issues include the 1975 Declaration of the Rights of Disabled Persons, the 1991 Principles for the Protection of Persons with Mental Illness and the Improvement of Mental Health Care, the 1993 Proclamation of the Economic and Social Commission for Asia and the Pacific on the Full Participation and Equality of People with Disabilities in the Asian and Pacific Region, the Tallin Guidelines for Action on Human Resources Development in the Field of Disability and the recent adoption of the Inter-American Convention on the Elimination of All Forms of Discrimination against Persons with Disabilities. These and other instruments are significant both in terms of their support for persons with disabilities, their value as authoritative interpretations of broad treaty obligations for disabled persons and for their potential contribution to the corpus of customary international law in the field of disability rights. The Standard Rules emphasise the goal of equalisation of opportunities as a fundamental concept in disability policy.

The principle of equal rights implies that the needs of each and every individual are of equal importance, that those needs must be made the basis for the planning of societies and that all resources must be employed in such a way as to ensure that every individual has equal opportunity for participation. Persons with disabilities are members of society and have the right to remain within their local communities. They are entitled to receive the support they need within the ordinary structures of education, health, employment and social services.

In addition, disabled persons are described as citizens with equal rights and equal obligations, who should receive assistance in assuming "their full responsibility as members of society".[1]

The most recent recognition of the status of disabled people is the adoption by the UN Human Rights Commission of Resolution 2000/51, which recognised disability as an issue of human rights. The resolution recognises that:

> ... any violation of the fundamental principle of equality or any discrimination or other negative differential treatment of persons with disabilities inconsistent with the United Nations Rules on the Equalization of Opportunities for Persons with Disabilities is an infringement of the human rights of persons with disability (para. 1).

The Commission in the Resolution invites all human rights treaty monitoring bodies to monitor the compliance of states with their commitments under the relevant human rights instruments and to include those with disabilities in complying with their reporting obligations to the UN (para. 11). The High Commissioner on Human Rights is called upon to work with the Special Rapporteur on disability of the Commission for Social Development, to examine measures to strengthen the protection and monitoring of human rights of persons with disabilities (para. 30).

This is the international context for social change in Canada. These are indicators that disability has been recognised as a legitimate issue of public concern. It also suggests that the political activism of the disability rights movement has had an impact. Further, there is recognition that the non-government sector speaking for disability includes disabled people themselves and not just their families or service providers or medical charities.

Control and Empowerment as Ends in the Struggle for Social Change

The struggle for social change is therefore a human rights struggle (Minow 1990).[2] It is about entrenching fairness, dignity, diversity and equality in societies. The development and administering of tests, classifications and medical evaluations are not central to that struggle. Providing services, while important, is not the essence of the political struggle but a means towards empowerment. However, it would appear that how to classify people's condition has received much more attention than the monitoring of human rights and the abuse of people's rights in their societies. Empowerment and control are central to the struggle and benchmarks against which to test policy choices, legal decisions and service models (Hahn 1997).

The litmus test about the struggle for change is, therefore, how much progress there has been to end the political disenfranchisement, economic disempowerment and social inequality that are the reality for disabled people. Providing services and care do not lead to empowerment. It is the right to choose—the right to self-determination that will lead to the societal transformation in which "difference [will no longer be considered] disruptive (if not threatening) and community involvement a luxury at best and an intrusion at worst" (Funderburg 1998).

Freedom as a Fundamental Right

The political question and the basis for the political struggle is related to the nature of empowerment. What prevents the exercise of rights? What constitutes the exercise of real freedoms? Amartya Sen, the winner of the 1998 Nobel Prize in Economics, argues in his recent book, *Development as Freedom* (Sen 1999), that:

> development[3] requires the removal of major sources of non-freedom: poverty as well as tyranny, poor economic opportunities as well as systematic social deprivation, neglect of public facilities as well as intolerance or overactivity of repressive states.

He explains that even with the unprecedented increase in wealth and material goods, millions of people living in rich and poor countries are still unfree. That is, they are unable to live as they would like. What people can positively achieve, he holds, is influenced by: economic opportunities, political liberties, social powers, the enabling conditions of good health, basic education and the encouragement and cultivation of initiatives, and the liberty to participate in social choices.

With adequate development opportunities, individuals can effectively shape their own destiny and help each other. They need not be seen primarily as passive recipients of welfare or charitable help. People can be active participants in the transformations that will change their lives and the societies in which they live.

Applied to disabled people, it is easy to see the non-freedoms that characterise their lives. They have none of the characteristics that Dr. Sen argues are essential to positive achievement. This is not, however, simply a case that they are poorer, are un- or underemployed, are more likely to be subject to abuse, are denied access to education in their community schools, are not given control over their own welfare assistance and so on. While these inequities in and reduction of health and well-being of disabled people need to continue to be addressed, there are other non-freedoms that require urgent attention.

It is the very essence of lives as "cared for" people and the contingent dependency that are the most important non-freedoms faced by disabled people. To be a passive recipient of services, income and care disempowers and depoliticises an individual. This includes the profoundly personal decisions of everyday life.

In some cases, not having the agency and autonomy to make decisions will not affect the immediate health of an individual. He or she may still have enough nourishing food and a good bed to sleep in, to be confident that no physical risk is encountered. But if the individual does not have agency, they are disempowered. And the consequence is a general acceptance that the disempowered disabled individual is a natural state of affairs. It is considered acceptable not to worry about the process if the end is achieved.[4] The end is argued to justify the means. But in fact, there is a demonstrated effect of having control of one's environment on the status of health and well-being. This provides a powerful argument for re-thinking some conventional assumptions. For example, there is a tendency to assume that if an individual needs support, then that need transforms him or her into a passive recipient of care thereby justifying the curtailment of freedom and choice. However, if as Dr. Sen would argue the end is empowerment, the end is freedom, then not empowering people is a contradiction of justice.

Freedom and empowerment also involve responsibilities that the individual has to be able to exercise. However, the substantive freedoms that people have to exercise their responsibilities are contingent on the personal, social and environmental circumstances. For example, a child who is denied the opportunity of inclusive elementary schooling in their neighbourhood school is not only deprived as a youngster, but is also disabled throughout life by not being able to do the things that rely on reading, writing, social skills and the curiosity that is learned in school. The adult who is not allowed to express their sexuality is not only denied the ability to have children but also the freedom to have the responsibility of a physically expressed emotional relationship. An individual who is placed in an institution or protective group home is not only deprived in terms of well-being but also in terms of the ability to lead a responsible life, which is dependent on having certain freedoms. "Responsibility requires freedom" (Sen 1999: 284).

Without the substantive freedom and capability to do something, a person cannot be responsible for doing it. So the struggle for change for disability rights advocates is for the opportunity for choice and for individuals to be entitled to make their own substantive decisions. This social commitment to individual freedom operates not only at the state level but also in other places, in community-based settings, in political and social organisa-tions, in NGOs and in the workplace.

Being protected from the freedom and empowerment needed to make choices and act responsibly is a common experience for disabled people. There is a great deal of informa-tion and knowledge about how to provide the maximum freedom for decision making. However there is a reluctance to use that information to enhance the freedom and rights that people have. There are a number of probable reasons. First, governments in many countries do not trust their own ability to set up appropriate accounting systems so that individuals with disabilities, rather than service agencies or charities, can be held account-able for determining needs and for managing the costs. Second, social values about dis-ability are still very negative, and conventionally people who are devalued are subject to controls on their freedom. Third, myths are still prevalent that suggest that freedom and responsibility of disabled people have to be curtailed for their own safety or for their best interests. It is a form of conventional paternalism based on the presumption of the dimin-ished capacity of the disabled person to understand his or her own circumstances. Fourth, there is a generalised fear about difference in many societies that leads to a perception that freedom to choose might be dangerous to society generally. Fifth, disability is viewed as a negative, abnormal state rather than simply diversity. In that context limitations on freedom and choice are interpreted as appropriate.

One of the important freedoms that people must have is the freedom to act as citizens who matter and whose voices count rather than living as recipients of state or charitable largesse. The struggle for change is to undermine, to attack the commonly held view that disabled people are simply patients or clients to whom benefits will be dispensed. It is to reinstate adults being in charge of their own well-being—to enable each individual to decide how to use their capabilities, no matter how those capabilities might appear to others. But the capabilities that a person does actually have depend on the nature of social arrangements, which is crucial for individual freedom. And that is where the state and society must take an active part in ensuring that the conditions for freedom, for choice, for empowerment are in place, as it is the state that has established the conditions that result in non-freedom.

There are both social responsibilities and individual responsibilities in achieving free-dom and empowerment. Social responsibilities include such mandates as: ensuring welfare is unhindered by regulations that restrict the well-being of people through where and how they live and who they live with; directly addressing blatant forms of discrimination, both direct and systemic; ensuring public accessibility to transportation, public services and places normally open to the public; gearing teaching to accommodate the diversity of students and maximise learning; providing people with the support they need to make decisions (for example, replacing incompetence proceedings with legislated supported decision making); and putting in place economic policies that provide opportunities for disabled people to work.

Individuals have a parallel responsibility to make choices about how they want to live their lives—about what job they want to take; about what educational facilities they enrol in and how they use the education they attain; about what use to make of the opportunities they have available to them. Freedom is then the empowered individual's right to make choices not within the narrow confines of externally defined limitations but within the full range of possibilities and within their own understanding of what well-being means to them. It includes both the right to make decisions and the opportunities to achieve those outcomes that are individually valued. Sen draws the distinction between the derivative importance of freedom (dependent on its actual use) and the intrinsic importance of freedom (in making an individual free to choose something he or she may or may not actually choose)—that is the process aspect of freedom and the opportunity aspect (Sen 1999: 292).

The Canadian Framework for Disability Equality Rights

Some recent legal cases in Canada provide insight into the nature of the political struggle of disabled people to have that freedom entrenched in law (Lepofsky 1997)[5] and policy; to establish human rights practices for disabled people; and to clarify what equality means. In each of these cases, the disability rights movement played a key role in decisions that recognised that the social change that was being pursued in the cases was about the freedom and agency of disabled people. The effectiveness of the struggle for substantive social change is reflected in these cases. These cases indicate that the courts are beginning to recognise the importance of the voices of disabled people and the manner in which they structure the injustice that they face.

Within the Canadian context, human rights protections for disabled people include both constitutional entitlements and federal and provincial statutory provisions.

Since the coming into force of the Canadian Charter of Rights and Freedoms in April 1985, Canada has had the distinction of a constitutional guarantee of equality rights for persons with "mental and physical disabilities." Section 15 provides:

1. Every individual is equal before and under the law and has the right to equal protection and equal benefit of the law without discrimination and in particular, without discrimination based on race, national or ethnic origin, colour, religion, sex, age, mental or physical disability.
2. Subsection (1) does not preclude any law, program or activity that has as its object the amelioration of conditions of disadvantaged individuals or groups including those that are disadvantaged because of race, national or ethnic origin, colour, religion, sex, age, mental or physical disability.

As a constitutional provision, this guarantee of equality rights applies to all levels of legislative authority in Canada. That includes law at the municipal, provincial and federal level, including taxation, immigration, education, health care and even human rights protections. For the past 15 years, section 15 has provided an important process for defining and clarifying the rights of citizens. It has provided a context in which the discourses as well as the legal and policy considerations of disability have gradually taken on an equality rights perspective. Since it covers both substantive and procedural rights under 15(1) and permits affirmative action under 15(2), it provides an authoritative instrument for challenging conventional thinking about disability as an individual deficit and advancing the alternative notion of disability as a social status. It also has provided the court the ability to determine the meaning of equality and to recognise notions of freedom and autonomy as elements of equality of outcome. In the first equality case to come before the courts (*Andrews v Law Society*, 1989), the Court adopted a contextual, effects-based approach that recognised disadvantage as central to the analysis of discrimination. For disabled people, this is important because that approach makes transparent the disadvantage produced by public policies or social practices that treat people exactly the same as their non-disabled counterparts result in the exclusion of disabled people.

The pressure from those in the disability rights movement and their allies in the equality rights movement that spurred the last-minute decision of the federal government to add *disability* to Charter section 15 is important to the history of the struggle for change that has taken place in Canada. It was evident even in the early 1980s that to redress the discrimination and inequality faced by disabled people required more than the existing human rights legislation. The federal government did not include a specific equality rights guarantee for disabled people in the original proposed patriation package in October 1980, although all the other listed groups were there as they are now. During the debate on the Charter of Rights and Freedoms between 1980 and 1982, when it was passed, the only new right to be added to section 15(1) was disability equality and that was done only after a significant debate on the merits of including it specifically, rather than as part of reading section 15(1) as an open-ended section:

> The federal government initially advanced the following arguments in opposition to the disability amendment. First, there was no need for a constitutional guarantee because statutory Human Rights Codes provided a better method for protecting disability equality. Second, terms like physical and mental disability were too vague and would pose problems for judicial interpretation. Third, the cost of providing equality to persons with disabilities was too high. Finally, disability rights might not have matured sufficiently in the mind of the public to justify their inclusion. (Lepofsky 1997; Lepofsky and Bickenbach 1985)

Those advocating for the disability amendment made the following arguments. "Disabled people constitute a significantly disadvantaged minority in Canadian society who are subjected to widespread discrimination in the public and private spheres, and who need constitutional protection" (Lepofsky 1997). Civil rights or anti-discrimination legislation, based on individual complaints, it was argued, did not provide adequate protection for the extent and type of legislative redress and change needed. Disability rights advocates argued, with respect to definition, that disability was no more difficult to define than other constitutional terms and there were definitions in the literature at the time that could be used. In other words, definition was not nearly so uncharted as some tried to make it out to be. The government was reminded of Canada's international obligations, particularly in the United Nations Year of the Disabled Person (UNDP). Disability rights advocates opposed any arguments about costs, reasoning that arguments about the cost of equality was inherently unjust and discriminatory in itself as it was not applied to any other groups being protected by the Charter provisions. They also argued that the cost of exclusion would more than compensate for the cost of inclusion. In the end, mental and physical disability were added as listed grounds for equality rights.

In subsequent cases under the Charter of Rights and Freedoms the Supreme Court has adopted a contextual, effects-based approach that recognises disadvantage as central to the analysis of discrimination (*Andrews v Law Society*, 1989; *Turpin v R.*, 1989). The court has enunciated constitutional equality principles that are of benefit to disability claims in a number of ways. First, the decisions have recognised that section 15 of the Charter is the culmination of Canada's legislative human rights tradition to secure full equality and full participation for disadvantaged groups who have traditionally faced discrimination. Second, section 15's prohibition against discrimination has been interpreted in the *Andrews* and *Turpin* decisions to encompass both direct discrimination and adverse effects discrimination. There is no requirement for plaintiffs to show that the discrimination was intentional. Third, the court in these cases rejected the equal treatment model of discrimination (Rioux 1994) in favour of an interpretation of equality that recognised that equality may require differentiation in treatment. Fourth, the court acknowledges that section 15 "... was intended to make real substantive changes to society" (Lepofsky 1997) and that the court can grant comprehensive remedies to advance equality "including requiring the spending of public money and the extension of benefits to previously excluded disadvantaged groups" (Lepofsky 1997: 291). Importantly the court placed statutory Human Rights Code legal principles into section 15, which gave constitutional importance to the early decisions and interpretations under the federal and provincial Human Rights Codes. Fifth, legislative bans on discrimination require an affirmative duty to accommodate the needs of discriminated against groups.

This perspective on Charter equality rights as well as a number of decisions by the courts on cases specific to disability rights, both before and after the Charter came in effect, set clear guidelines for the struggle for change that is ongoing. The outcome of equality requires more than the removal of physical barriers and adaptation of the current structures. Equality for disabled people is about achieving a barrier-free society in which disabled people can fully participate. In that context, it is about the re-structuring of society and its institutions so that the participation of disabled people is not an exception but inherent to the political, social and economic life. It is not an issue of assimilation but of recognising the inherent differences as a basis for ensuring equality and redressing discrimination. It involves freedom and empowerment. Examining a few of the legal decisions provides some insight into the outcome for disabled people.

Outcomes in Disability Cases

Even before provisions of the Charter came into effect there were several cases that set the standard for equality, for autonomy and for freedom as the fundamental entitlements of disabled people.

In a case before the Divisional [Provincial] Court of Ontario in 1982, the court rendered a decision in *Clark v Clark* (1982). The case involved an application by the father of Justin Clark for a declaration that his disabled son was mentally incompetent. Justin who had lived for 18 of his 20 years in an institution had decided to leave the institution and move to a supported living arrangement in his community. His father, fearful that Justin could not cope outside the institution, had initiated legal proceedings to prevent Justin from moving. The case was significant for a number of reasons (Rioux and Frazee 1999). First, Justin was the first person in Canada to testify at a trial using a Blissymbol Board to give legal evidence. Second, the judge presiding in the case rejected expert evidence based upon medical and psychological tests, choosing to place greater emphasis on Justin's own testimony and that of witnesses who knew him well as a person. Third, the case was decided in favour of Justin's right to self-determination:

> I believe a courageous man such as Justin Clark is entitled to take a risk.... With incredible effort Justin Clark has managed to communicate his passion for freedom as well as his love of family during the course of this trial.... We have, all of us, recognized a gentle trusting, believing spirit and very much a thinking human being who has his unique part to play in our compassionate, interdependent society.... I find and I declare Matthew Justin Clark to be mentally competent. (*Clark v Clark* 1982: 383)

In 1982, this was a significant decision and reflected the emergence in Canada of a changing perspective on disability and a different standard by which to look at the place of disabled people in society. The disability rights movement was beginning to be heard.

In 1986, the Supreme Court of Canada recognised the rights of disabled people in a decision related to the non-consensual sterilisation of a woman with an intellectual disability (*Eve v Eve* 1986). In 1976, a mother of a 21-year-old woman attending a segregated school in the province of Prince Edward Island filed for a court injunction to enable her to provide the consent for her daughter to have a non-therapeutic sterilisation. Eve's mother argued that her daughter could not cope with being a mother, that Eve was at risk of becoming pregnant and that therefore it was in her best interests to sterilise her.

The Supreme Court ruled that no one can legally be sterilised without personally consenting, unless it is a matter of medical necessity. There is no legislation in Canada that permits a third party (including parents, next-of-kin, the Public Trustee or the administrator of a facility) to consent to a non-therapeutic sterilisation on behalf of an individual who is unable to consent on her or his own behalf. Mr. Justice Laforest was unambiguous, when he held in the decision:

> ... it is obviously fiction to suggest that a [substituted decision] is that of the mental incompetent (sic), however much the court may try to put itself in her place. What the incompetent would do if she or he could make the choice is simply a matter of speculation.

This case, the first Supreme Court case in which people labelled with intellectual disabilities were given leave to intervene, addressed the fundamental nature of rights and agency. In Canada, as in many Western nations, laws have been put in place to protect those not in a position to speak for themselves, people with intellectual disabilities, people who are ageing and children. But in the process of "protecting," such laws often put disabled people in the position of having to prove that they are entitled to goods, services and opportunities that are considered rights for the non-disabled population. The result is that for many disabled people, rights become privileges to be earned. This legal model, which bestows rights as charitable privilege, emphasises benevolence and pity and puts in practice the exercise of control exercised through expert and professional decision making. The rationale for denying rights is paternalistic and usually argued from the perspective of the best interests of the individual concerned. This raises some fundamental questions about the basis of rights and claims by individuals to make their own decisions. It gives the authority in law to experts to decide who ought to be able to exercise their rights and to decide the criteria to exercise those rights. The court in the *Eve* case limited the *parens patriae* power, a beneficent, paternalistic area of responsibility, and argued that the right to procreate or the privilege to give birth is fundamental, thereby circumscribing the power of the state to an *a priori* restriction of rights based on disability.

Importantly, the case was not argued on the individual capacity of *Eve* but rather on the efficacy and fairness of substituted decision making and the exercise of fundamental rights. The case is not about disability, but about state or others' power over individual agency and autonomy.

In another decision relating to sterilisation, in which Leilani Muir sued the Province of Alberta for wrongful sterilisation while she was a resident of an institution 30 years before, she received a significant financial award in a court decision in 1995 in recognition of the damages she suffered: (1) resulting from the sterilisation, allowed by the law of that Province, at that time; (2) associated with the humiliating categorisation of being labelled a "moron"; and (3) connected with the improper confinement and detention in the institution and losses she suffered, including liberty, reputation, normal development experiences, enjoyment of life, civil rights, contact with family and friends and subjection to humiliation and disgrace, pain and suffering and institutional discipline.

The court in this case recognised that labelling in itself is a fundamental infringement of human dignity and the institution limited her liberty and other rights. It recognised that "care" does not extend to treatment that imposes loss of liberty, loss of privacy, cruel punishment or unauthorised drug experimentation.

In October 1997, the Canadian Supreme Court delivered a decision, hailed by the disability rights movement, that many commentators have suggested will require provinces to take positive measures to remove barriers which limit access to public services for disabled people. *Eldridge v British Columbia* (1997) involved a claim by three deaf applicants that the legislation governing health care services and hospitals in the province was discriminatory because it neither included sign language interpreter services as an insured service, nor required hospitals to provide sign language interpreter services. The court ruled that the government had violated the equality provisions of the Charter of Rights and Freedoms in its implementation of the provincial Medical Services Plan. "The court held that, in order for deaf persons to receive the benefit of medical services, they required communication with their doctors. Interpreters were not an ancillary service but an integral part of medical care. In providing a benefit scheme the state was obliged to provide the benefit in a non-discriminatory manner. Failure to provide interpreters meant that deaf people would receive an inferior quality of health care to hearing persons" (Mosoff and Grant 1999).

This decision is important for a number of reasons. First is the court's holding that "once the state provides a benefit, it is obliged to do so in an non-discriminatory manner." This is important because it gives recognition to the entitlement of disabled people to government benefits, an entitlement that is not discretionary or charitable. It recognises the status of disabled people to receive what others receive, as a claim and not as government largesse.

The second point that has relevance is the interpretation of equality that the Charter protects. The denial of equality in *Eldridge* arose from the failure of the government to take action (rather than the imposition of a burden). The discrimination arose from the adverse effects of a public benefit scheme that failed to provide the same level of service (adverse impact discrimination). The court held that:

> To argue that governments should be entitled to provide benefits to the general population without ensuring that disadvantaged members of society have the resources to take full advantage of those benefits bespeaks a thin and impoverished vision of s 15(1). It is belied, more importantly, by the thrust of this Court's equality jurisprudence.

The important principle here is that there is a positive obligation on the government to remedy inequality notwithstanding that the benefit scheme appeared neutral and the remedy meant that the government had to spend money.

The third issue of relevance is the importance and centrality that the court placed on reasonable accommodation as a "cornerstone" of ensuring equal benefit. The court included accommodation as a central element of section 15 and made clear in the ruling that it is the failure to provide reasonable accommodation that results in discrimination. It is not the disability.

The fourth issue of importance is the court's finding that "... governments should not be allowed to evade constitutional responsibilities by delegating the implementation of their policies and programmes to private entities." In other words, it gave a broader scope to the applicability of the Charter. To the extent that an organisation or private entity is providing a specific government objective the Charter applies to those activities or programmes. Who performs the activity is secondary to the activity itself in determining if it is a government service that is being performed.

The fifth issue of importance is the court's holding that effective communication is an indispensable component of the delivery of a medical service. This is important to recognising the systemic nature of the discrimination against disabled people and recognising that the discrimination cannot be redressed without changes to the definition of the services government provides. The court began its analysis with the recognition of the historical exclusion and marginalisation of disabled people:

> It is an unfortunate truth that the history of disabled persons in Canada is largely one of exclusion and marginalization. Persons with disabilities have too often been excluded from the labour force, denied access to opportunities for social interaction and advancement, subjected to invidious stereotyping and related to institutions. This historical disadvantage has to a great extent been shaped and perpetuated by the notion that disability is an abnormality or flaw. As a result, disabled persons have not generally been afforded the "equal concern, respect and consideration" that s. 15(1) of the Charter demands. Instead they have been subjected to paternalistic attitudes of pity and charity, and their entrance into the social mainstream has been conditional upon their emulation of able-bodied norms.

These cases reflect the direction in which the courts are headed in recognising discrimination, equality, empowerment, freedom, agency and full participation. It reflects the persuasive arguments that the disability rights community have made as *amicus curae* in each of these cases.

Conclusion

The struggle for change has, in itself, changed. It is no longer about better services in an unresponsive and ableist society. It is about equal outcome and entitlement, and about freedom and agency. Historically and legally it is possible to trace this evolution from exclusion to charity to service provision to freedom and rights. But it is not consistent. It is easy enough to find inconsistencies in legislation, in jurisprudence, in social attitude, and in practice. In many cases, there are different goals even within the same political jurisdiction and certainly cross-nationally. The continuing development of a strong disability rights movement and the legal entitlements that are being won in law courts do suggest however that the struggle for change is having an impact. Disability equality rights have found their way into recent international agreements and they are becoming a standard in jurisprudence in Canada. The voices of disabled people are being heard and given legitimacy. There is still a long way to go but some progress is being made. Martin Luther King, the leader of another great movement for social justice, once said: "The arc of history is long but it always bends towards justice." The urgency felt by those who live outside the boundaries of justice is palpable. But as they push, we can see the direction the arc is bending.

Endnotes

1   Standard Rules on the Equalization of Opportunities, Introduction para. 24–27. The *Standard Rules* in the preamble refer to other international instruments that are part of the legal framework for the human rights of disabled people notably *Universal Declaration on Human Rights*; the *International Covenant on Economic, Social and Cultural*; the *International Covenant on Civil and Political Rights*; the *Convention on the Rights of the Child*; the *International Convention for the Protection of the Rights of All Migrant Works and Members of Their Families*; the *Convention on the Elimination of All Forms of Discrimination against Women*; the *Declaration on the Rights of Disabled Persons*; the *Declaration on the Rights of Mentally Retarded Persons*; the *Declaration on Social Progress and Development*; and the *Principles for the Protection of Persons with Mental Illness and for the Improvement of Mental Health Care*.

2· Martha Minow maintains that a rights-based strategy has to be a part of any strategy for political empowerment.

3   He contrasts this foundational view of development as freedom with narrower views of development in terms of GNP growth or industrialisation.

4   The simplest example is the assumption that as long as one has food that has the basic nutrients it is not relevant whether one chooses it or where it is served. The fallacy of such an assumption seems self-evident.

5   For an evaluation of legal entrenchment of Charter rights in Canada see David Lepofsky's paper.

CHAPTER 13

Legal Peripheries:

Struggles over disAbled Canadians' Places in Law, Society, and Space

Vera Chouinard

Struggles against the socio-spatial marginalization of citizens disadvantaged by embodied differences such as race, gender, and mental or physical impairment often focus on issues of legal rights. In Western neo-liberal democracies such as Canada, as Blomley and Pratt illustrate, legal discourses help to map out who has a right to be where, who doesn't, and how conflicting rights in place, for instance between property-owners and their tenants, will be resolved. I explore a different but related facet of changing geographies of legal rights: namely, the socio-spatial production of legal peripheries or places in which law as discursively represented and law as lived are fundamentally at odds. These are places of "shadow citizenship and entitlement"—important to the cultural representation of neo-liberal democracies as inclusionary and tolerant of diversity, but lived as places of profound exclusion in which basic human rights are routinely denied. It is from such peripheral, disempowered locations that disabled Canadians are struggling to claim their places in law, society and space.

Embodying Citizenship: Disability Struggles in Canada

Over the past two decades, disabled Canadians have struggled against daunting odds to advance and assert rights to be included and participate in the same spaces of life as other citizens. Their struggles have been part of a global movement for the empowerment and civil rights of disabled people (Driedger 1987). The Canadian disability movement originated in Western Canada during the early 1970s, with the establishment of the first independent provincial organizations run by and for disabled people (rather than by rehabilitation professionals or charities). By the end of the 1970s, independent, consumer-led disability organizations had been established in much of Canada, making the disability movement national in scope (Driedger 1987; 1993).

Rights of mobility, physical access and equality under Canadian law were central to the political agenda of the disability movement. In a context in which disabled citizens were routinely denied access to many spaces of social life and thus suffered extremes of isolation, this liberal rights agenda spoke in a very immediate way to what it was like to be disabled in Canada. It spoke to hopes that greater spatial and legal equality of opportunity would enable disabled persons to fully participate in the life of the nation. And it addressed experiences of socio-spatial barriers to activism itself. The Coalition of Provincial Organizations for the Handicapped's (COPOH) second national forum on disability issues in 1979 was, for example, plagued by the same transportation problems it had been convened to address:

> The meeting took an ironic twist as about 100 people with various disabilities hassled with air and rail transportation while traveling to the Ottawa Forum. Three people with mobility handicaps, one person a wheelchair user, were refused taxi transportation at 2:00 a.m. at the airport. Another traveler from Ontario had to ride in the baggage car of a train because there was no seat in the regular coach where he could stretch out his legs. On top of this indignity, he still had to pay a full passenger fare! Blind people's guide dogs were put into the baggage area of the plane, thus traumatizing both the dogs and their owners. The guide dogs were so upset they had difficulty guiding for the first while in Ottawa. (Driedger 1987)

The agenda of the early disability movement appealed to liberal constructions of citizenship as equality of rights, rather than of socio-spatial outcomes. This discursive framing of disability rights issues had important implications for the politics of the movement. It meant that an agenda developed on the basis of masculine experiences of disablement was represented as a universal and inclusive one. Disabled women who challenged this agenda, by for example calling attention to how their rights to reproductive freedom were being denied in places of health care, found themselves silenced and relegated to subordinate, gendered roles such as note-taking (see Chouinard 1999). Disabled women thus learned that even within the disability movement their places would be especially marginalized ones.

Disabled women found themselves marginalized within spaces of feminist activism as well. Meetings were held in inaccessible places, and information and outreach efforts seldom included disabled women. When disability issues were a visible part of women's organizing, patronizing language and indifference to disabled women's concerns helped to put them in "their peripheral places"—at the margins of discussion and decision-making. Israel and Odette (1993, 8) relate one such experience:

> Able-ism is also reflected in the kind of language that non-disabled feminists use when referring to feminists with disabilities. For example, "you are so courageous" or "it's so nice that you were able to get out and come to this conference." ... Recently at a conference of 300 women addressing the issue of violence, approximately seven women attended the workshop held on disabled women's issues.... To the numerous disabled women who spend many hours preparing these seminars, the low numbers of non-disabled women participating in our workshops may be seen as sending a message about the importance of this issue within the larger context of women's issues.

Experiences of socio-spatial exclusion encouraged disabled women to develop separate spaces of organizing both through caucuses within disability organizations, and through the DisAbled Women's Network of Canada (DAWN) and its chapters. Here disabled women began to challenge the gender-specific ways in which ableist oppression was manifest in their lives: in debilitating norms of female beauty and vulnerability to violence and abuse for instance. The emergence of separate spaces of feminist disability activism was a response, in part, to the contradictions of liberal rights as represented and lived. Disabled women learned that they were not equal bearers of rights in practice—that no matter where they were and who gazed upon them the differences they embodied meant that they would be cast as "shadow citizens" whose rights to place and political voice would be denied.

Disabled women's struggles thus helped to reveal something that was difficult to appreciate from privileged positions within the disability and women's movements: that exercising rights is an embodied, geographically uneven, process which makes some citizens much more able to exercise their rights than others. This is an important lesson for rights struggles. For it reminds us that law is a slippery and contradictory realm of struggle, that it is whether, where and how fully we can exercise formal rights that matters, and that we ignore these lived geographies of rights at our peril.

Re-mapping Our Places in Society and Space: Gauging Victories and Defeats

As in other Western countries, the Canadian disability movement's accomplishments are often judged in terms of whether disabled people's places in law have become more or less equal to those of able-bodied citizens. This way of gauging "victories" and "defeats" reflects not only the liberal rights agenda of the disability movement, but powerful beliefs that legal institutions are the places through which socio-spatial justice is determined and realized. In these imagined geographies of rights, all citizens are guaranteed equality of rights irrespective of where or how they live, differences they embody, and how processes of differencing locate them in prevailing socio-spatial relations of power and oppression. Such mappings of our places in struggles for socio-spatial justice and inclusion blur the representational and the real, and make it difficult to contemplate the possibilities that rights as represented do not necessarily correspond to rights as lived, and that in practice justice is often denied to those who need it most.

In Canada, disability struggles have led to important changes in disabled people's formal human and citizenship rights. Rights to freedom from discrimination on the basis of disability have been enshrined in federal and provincial human rights codes and more recently in the *Canadian Charter of Rights and Freedoms (Constitution Act* 1982). Human rights codes and the Charter have provided bases for test case litigation, and allowed a body of case law to develop which generally upholds disabled people's rights to freedom from discrimination, and establishes legal remedies for discrimination on the basis of disability in spaces such as the workplace (Lynk 2000). Symbolically, these developments signal a liberal vision of a "just society" as one that is socially and spatially inclusive across diversities such as bodily differences. In practice, they signal that legal authority and power may deployed when disabled peoples' rights are violated, and this threat of legal force can in turn provide leverage in disabled peoples' informal struggles to assert rights (e.g., to accommodation of special needs).

Rights of mobility, access and inclusion have also been advanced through laws and judicial decisions upholding these rights in specific spaces of everyday life. Examples include federal aviation laws requiring disabled access to air transportation, the legal duty of employers to accommodate disabled employees under Canadian human rights law, and modifications of provincial building codes (since the 1970s) to include accessibility standards governing building features such as entrances, ramps, width of hallways and access to parking (*Ontario Building Code Act* 1992). Local governments are responsible for enforcing codes, and their impacts in terms of spatial access vary with regulatory practices, and local conditions such as construction activity. Codes such as Ontario's are also geared to the access needs of the stereotypical disabled citizen (i.e., the wheelchair user with mobility impairments). Limitations on the types of buildings subject to accessibility provisions further limits the efficacy of building codes in practice, as the *Ontarians with Disabilities Act* Committee (ODAC 1998, 4) notes:

> Many people commonly but mistakenly believe that all buildings must now be accessible to persons with disabilities because of the existence of laws called "building codes." The reality is that building codes only require that when a new building is constructed it be made accessible or that accessibility features be added to an older building when and if it is renovated. Who the disabled citizen is thus imagined to be (e.g., in terms of access needs) and where she or he is deemed entitled to exercise legal rights plays an important, albeit often unremarked, role in lived geographies of law, mapping rights into some places and not others, and making entitlement to rights in practice more socially and spatially uneven than we often assume.

Disabled Canadians have struggled against formidable odds for rights to inclusion in society and space. Given this struggle, and the fact that existing rights are under attack through measures such as cuts in funding to human rights commissions, it is vital that we critically assess the differences that legal rights are making and might make in disabled peoples' lives.

Making Sense of Our Places:
Shadow Citizens at the Periphery of Law, Society and Space?

To what extent have changes in legal rights enhanced disabled citizens' capacities to challenge their peripheral social and spatial places in Canada? We can start to answer this question by examining political and economic forces shaping their capacities to exercise existing legal rights in practice and in place.

Disabled people's economic places in society and space greatly limit their capacities to assert rights won under Canadian law. These locations, in the economic underclass (Barile 1993), are gendered ones, with disabled women especially likely to live in conditions of poverty, exclusion from paid work, and inability to cover costs of basics such as food. These are places of "shadow citizenship" in which rights enjoyed in principle are difficult or impossible to exercise in practice.

The economic consequences of being disabled in Canada are severe. Recent statistics show that this is especially so for disabled women. Poverty rates are high. In 1995, 36.2 percent of disabled women and 34.1 percent of disabled men in Canada lived in poverty (Fawcett 2000, section 1). In contrast, only 18.5 percent of able-bodied women and 15.6 percent of able-bodied men lived in poverty in that year. Unemployment rates are also high; for example, it is estimated that 74 percent of disabled women are unemployed in Ontario (DAWN Ontario 2000). When disabled women *are* employed it is in poorly paid positions; in 1994, over 65 percent of disabled women who worked full- or part-time in Canada fell into the two lowest earning quintiles, and 37.6 percent earned incomes less that $15,640 (Fawcett 2000, section 2). In contrast, 55 percent of able-bodied female workers and 30.9 percent of disabled male workers fell into the two lowest earning quintiles. Only 24.1 percent of able-bodied male workers were located in these low earning quintiles (*ibid.*).

Clearly then disabled women occupy especially peripheral positions in spaces of economic life such as local labour markets and places of paid employment. And this marginalization in turn limits their capacities to exercise legal rights. High rates of exclusion from paid labour mean, for example, that disabled women are especially unlikely to benefit from rights "victories" such as the legal duty to accommodate disabled workers. Exercising this right depends upon being employed in the first place and, as Fawcett (2000, section 2) notes, disabled women are usually last in the "job queue" (i.e., last hired, first fired). Further, it has primarily been workers who have acquired a disability while employed who have enjoyed the right to accommodation in practice (Lynk 2000). In this case, capacities to exercise employment rights are both place- and body-specific: dependent upon already being in a place of paid work and upon having entered the paid labour force on able-bodied terms.

Low incomes and exclusion from paid employment powerfully constrain disabled persons' access to the justice system. A disabled individual may be unable, for example, to afford the long and costly litigation required to enforce the Charter through court proceedings. Costs include lawyers and hiring expert witnesses to provide evidence. Disabled individuals are further disadvantaged by the fact that in Charter cases they are up against government opponents with litigation resources much greater than their own (ODAC 1998, 8). Enforcement of human rights codes is also an individual complaints-driven process that can be costly and lengthy. For disabled individuals who cannot afford to pay the only alternative is subsidized legal aid services, which often lack expertise in disability rights issues.

How are disability rights placed within the legal system and state, and what does this placement mean in terms of disabled people's capacities to exercise formal rights; for instance to protection from discriminatory practices? In answering this question, it is important to recognize that complaints of rights violations are not handled in a uniform way within the justice system and state, and that procedural and institutional variations in how complaints are resolved has a great deal to do with how effectively rights are protected in practice. Further, this uneven adjudication of legal rights is a key way in which differences in economic and political power have come to be inscribed within the justice system. In the contemporary Canadian context, it is clear that less weight is given to the human rights of marginalized groups such as the disabled in adjudicatory practice than to rights of more powerful groups such as property-owners or organized labour. Such discrepancies help to place those with human rights complaints in especially peripheral, disempowered positions in law, society and space.

In a critique of the complaints process established under the *Canadian Human Rights Act* and closely replicated under provincial human rights codes, Anand and Sharma (1999, 2–3) point out that, in contrast to adjudicatory bodies such as rental property tribunals or labour relations boards, human rights commissions have been granted sweeping powers to dismiss rights complaints without investigation and/or referral to a tribunal. These "gatekeeper" provisions have meant that human rights complaints may be summarily dismissed, thus denying complainants' rights to a hearing and access to the adjudication process.

Disparities in rights to hearings are a sobering reminder that socio-spatial inequalities in access to legal rights are in part reproduced through powers granted to judicial and quasi-judicial bodies, and that, in instances where particular rights are given relatively low priority (e.g., human versus property rights as in the above comparison), legislation and institutions may be designed and adjudication practiced in ways that seriously limit people's capacities to assert their legal rights. In the case of the Canadian Human Rights Commission, gatekeeper provisions have led to a majority of complaints being discontinued or dismissed prior to investigation. Anand and Sharma (1999, 2–3) report that: "Between 1988 and 1997, the Commission decided not to proceed with or to dismiss about two thirds of all complaints." Complaints of discrimination on the basis of disability represent a large proportion of cases filed with federal and provincial human rights commissions: 36.3 percent of all federal cases filed (Anand and Sharma 1999) and 25 percent of all cases in Ontario in 1998 (Ontario Human Rights Commission 1998). Disabled citizens are thus among those most likely to be adversely affected by high rates of dismissal.

Human rights commissions have experienced considerable fiscal (as well as political) pressure to exercise their powers of dismissal. As creatures of governments with limited commitment to enforcing human rights and with priorities such as deficit reduction, they have been vulnerable to constraints and cutbacks in funding which limit their capacities to adjudicate complaints and ultimately protect rights in practice. Kerzner and Baker (1999) note with respect to the Canadian Human Rights Commission that:

> Lack of funding has always been a problem for the Commission and in the last five years resources have been cut significantly. The Commission believes that financial restraint and program cutbacks are partly to blame for the obstacles it has encountered in dealing with complaints promptly even though the bulk of their funding is directed towards clearing up the backlog. They state that the inadequate funding does not permit the Commission to undertake the kind of systemic investigations and policy development it would like to do.

Barriers to justice, in combination with reductions in access to support services, such as paratransit, are making it more difficult for disabled Canadians to exercise their rights to participate in Canadian society and spaces of life such as the workplace. Persistently low rates of representation in the Canadian labour force, despite increases in availability over the past decade, suggest that employer resistance to hiring disabled workers remains stubbornly high, and that, moreover, systemic barriers to employment will remain in place unless employers are required to include disabled people in their workforces and penalized for discriminatory hiring and employment practices. From 1987 to 1997, the proportion of disabled people available for positions with private employers and crown corporations rose from 5.5 percent to 6.7 percent of the labour pool; however, their representation amongst paid employees rose only from 1.6 percent to 2.3 percent. Hiring rates were significantly lower, rising from only 0.6 percent in 1987 to 1.0 percent in 1997; indicating that increases in representation were primarily internal; that is, the result of existing employees who acquired disabilities (Kerzner and Baker 1999, 15).

Such persistent patterns of socio-spatial exclusion, and difficulties in enforcing human rights law through existing legal channels, have led to calls for comprehensive national and provincial disability rights acts (drawing for example on US and Australian models). As this paper suggests, however, legal acts alone will not ensure that disabled people's places as shadow citizens are fundamentally challenged. Changes in law and legal rights, for example provisions for class action suits against discriminatory practices affecting large numbers of disabled citizens and which thus, unlike individual complaints, have the potential to force the removal of systemic barriers, must be accompanied by procedural changes and initiatives aimed at empowering disabled citizens in and outside the justice system. These could include eliminating the current power of human rights commissions to deny complainants a hearing, mandatory employment and employment equity laws, and increased access to services such as paratransit and subsidized legal assistance.

Conclusions: Challenging Peripheral Places in Law, Society and Space

Disabled Canadians have fought long and hard for entitlement to basic human and citizenship rights, and equal protection of those rights. In doing so, they have helped to map out more formally equal places in society and space; places which in principle guarantee rights of access and inclusion without disadvantagement on the basis of bodily impairment. However, in practice disabled citizens' capacities to exercise legal rights are compromised by their peripheral places within law, society and space. These are embodied places of citizenship, in which differences of class, gender, race, sexuality and ability come into play in determining whether, where and how fully legal rights can be asserted in practice.

Among the lessons we can draw from these realities of disability rights in Canada is that it is important to examine not only how specific rights are written into and out of place, but also how different rights and rights claimants are placed in and against the legal system and state. Only then are we in a position to appreciate how, why and to what degree disabled Canadians continue to be denied their rightful place in society and space. And maybe then, as members of a country with a global reputation for leadership on human rights issues, we'll become determined to make the promise of legal rights and full citizenship a reality for disabled women and men. We should do so not only because the socio-spatial injustices which disabled Canadians suffer are a "national disgrace." We should also do it because these places of shadow citizenship will one day, if not now, be our own.

References

Anand, R. and Sharma, M. 1999 *Report on Direct Access to Binding Adjudication under the Canadian Human Rights Act.* Paper submitted to the Canadian Human Rights Review Panel 1 December, copy available from author

Barile, M. 1993 "Disabled women: An exploited underclass" *Canadian Woman Studies* 12:4, 32–33

Constitution Act 1982, *Canadian Charter of Rights and Freedoms*, part 1, section 15(1) and (2)

Chouinard, V. 1999 "Body politics: Disabled women's activism in Canada and beyond" in *Mind and Body Spaces: Geographies of Illness, Impairment and Disability*, eds R. Butler and H. Parr (London and New York: Routledge) 269–294

————. 2000 "Geographies of legal resistance: Legal clinic struggles to empower marginalized groups" *Historical Geography* 28, 108–133

Dawn Ontario 2000 (http://www.dawn.tyenet.ca) downloaded September 2000

Driedger, D. 1987 "Speaking for ourselves: A history of COPOH on its 10th anniversary" condensed version of her article in *Dialogue on Disability*, Volume 2 (Calgary: University of Calgary Press) http:/www.copoh.history.htm [as cited in Driedger, D. 1989 The Last Civil Rights Movement: Disabled People's International. New York: St. Martin's Press.]

————. 1989 *The Last Civil Rights Movement: Disabled People's International* (New York: St. Martin's Press)

————. 1993 "Discovering disabled women's history" in *And Still We Rise*, ed. L. E. Carty (Toronto: Women's Press) 173–187

Fawcett, G. 2000 "Bringing Down the Barriers: the Labour Market and Women with Disabilities in Ontario" (Ottawa: Canadian Council on Social Development)

Israel, P. and Baker, D. 1993 "The disabled women's movement 1983 to 1993" *Canadian Woman Studies* 13:4, 6–10

Kerzner, L. and Baker, D. 1999 *A Canadians with Disabilities Act?* Report prepared for the Council of Canadians with Disabilities, 14 May, available from the CCD, 926-924 Portage Avenue, Winnipeg, Manitoba (http//www/pcs.mb.ca/~ccd/cda.html) downloaded January 2000

Lynk, M. 2000 "Accommodating Disabilities in the Canadian Workplace" Paper presented to Labour Studies Program, McMaster University, copy available from the author, Faculty of Law, University of Western Ontario, London, Canada

ODAC 1998 *Making Ontario Open for People with Disabilities: A Blueprint for a Strong and Effective Ontarians with Disabilities Act* Report submitted to the Ontario Legislature by the Ontarians with Disabilities Act Committee, April 22

Ontario Building Code Act 1992 GENERAL O. Reg. 403/97, Ontario Regulation 403/97, amended to O. Reg. 278/99, http://www.gov.on.ca/MBS/english/publications/statregs/contents.html downloaded July 2000

Ontario Human Rights Commission 1998 *Annual Report* (Toronto: Queen's Printer)

PART V

Education, Technology, and Work

Education is often called the "great equalizer" and we can say this of technology and work as well. Disabled people are underrepresented in both education and in the workplace and are so because these two arenas of public life are largely inaccessible to those of us who are disabled. Technology, too, is often presented as the "great equalizer" in relation to disability. Voice recognition and speaking software programs, for example, are typically understood as technologies that allow disabled people to participate in many realms of public life, including education and work. But the matter is not as straightforward as that. Assistive technology is sometimes understood as "levelling the playing field" and thus as something that allows disabled people to be as "normal" as possible. Again, the matter is not as straightforward as that and the chapters in Part V explore the complex character of education, technology, and work.

In Chapter 14, Charles Miller, an Aboriginal person who is visually and hearing impaired, provokes us to think about literacy. By making use of his lived experience, Miller raises the issue of American Sign Language (ASL) and shows how it can be under-stood as a language distinct from the spoken word. Rather than conceiving of it as a mere translation of the spoken word, ASL is its own language steeped in its own culture. Edu-cation is not merely the acquisition of knowledge, since such a conception tacitly relies upon a "normal" learner. Miller demonstrates that being Aboriginal as well as visually and hearing impaired removes him, from the point of view of "mainstream society," from the region of normalcy. Education became, for Miller, an activity that led him toward normalcy while reminding him of his marginality.

In Chapter 15, Jacqueline Low explores the experiences of disabled students attending a large Canadian university. Disabled students must negotiate their way through university life since university environments, including versions of teaching and learning, are constructed and designed for non-disabled participants. Universities are not designed with disabled people in mind and this has consequences for disabled students when, unexpected as they are, they show up. One of the consequences of disability showing up, Low suggests, is that disabled students must negotiate both a disability and a non-disability identity as they move through university life. She says that these identities are inherently contradictory. Students reject their disability identities insofar as such identities are conceived of as deviant, thus generating isolation and constraining disabled students' interactions with others. And yet, disabled students must take on a disability identity, deviant as it is, in order to function in university. Such negotiation represents a movement between normalcy and abnormalcy.

Nancy Hansen and Chris Philo, in Chapter 16, explore the version of the body that appears in disability studies and disability geography. They provoke us to think about the impaired body in its materiality, as "flesh and bone," and its immediacy expressed in the appearance of disability in everyday places and in everyday practices. Hansen and Philo analyze the experiences of disabled women living in Scotland and in Canada. They speak of how these women negotiate their impairments in non-disabled spaces. Their emphasis is to shift the tension from wanting disabled people to "do things normally" to desiring disabled people to "do things differently." The point is that while doing things differently is not the normal way of doing things for non-disabled people, it is the normalcy of disability. In this way, Hansen and Philo disrupt our "normal" ways of thinking about normalcy.

In Chapter 17, Parin Dossa turns her attention to racialized disabled women. She explores testimonial narratives of racialized disabled women as a way to demonstrate the intersection of race and disability, especially as this relates to both education and work. No one is "just disabled." We live our disabilities in the midst of others and in the midst of our own race, gender, sexuality, and social class; we live our disabilities in and through our social locations. Dossa's work brings into relief subjugated knowledges that reveal how the state constitutes and reconstitutes racialized disabled women. She shows how the state continually constitutes racialized disabled women as marginal and can act to disqualify people from participating in the realms of both education and work. Through exploring the narrative of Fahimeh, Dossa shows how race and disability are continually reworked as a way to resist the stigmatization and marginalization of racialized disabled women. The margins are thus an occasion to reveal the workings of the centre. Dossa shows how marginality is not merely territorial but is, rather, a site of resistive practice.

CHAPTER 14

Visible Minorities:

Deaf, Blind, and Special Needs Adult Native Literacy Access

Charles Miller

As Ernestine and I walked up and down the length of the conference room at the Aboriginal Literacy and Learning Ontario Symposium, the audience saw two deaf or hearing-impaired individuals communicating, speaking with gestures. When people see this kind of communication they are often astounded and keep looking or staring at the talkers. It is an awesome experience for first-time onlookers. Often they are consumed with wonder about what is being said. We started our presentation at this Aboriginal Literacy Symposium using American Sign Language (ASL) as well as voice. But ordinarily when two people are signing they do not use their voices. That is why ASL is called a visual language. When a deaf person learns ASL or gets a cochlear implant, the world is reopened, whereas seeing ASL being spoken or signed may cause someone with normal hearing to feel shut out. Although this language is known as *American* Sign Language, it is also distinct to Deaf Native culture. It is a known language just like any other Aboriginal sign language before First Contact. The only difference is that ASL is not distinct to Aboriginal people, but to Deaf people in general and to those whose tongue is English. Deaf Natives in French-speaking communities speak French Sign Language (FSL), and there is also a distinct British Sign Language (BSL); ASL, however, is the predominant language used in English-speaking Canadian communities.

From my earliest recollection I was neither aware nor made aware by my parents that I was different from other children. However, by the time I reached adolescence, I noticed that my disability made me different from others. In other words, my parents did not single me out due to my handicap, but my disability slowed my academic education. My challenges became more and more apparent on a daily as well as yearly basis due to my limitations and the competitive nature of education. I did not want anyone to know I had disabilities, and my education suffered severely.

Eventually, I was able to enter a training program in a residential school, the Ontario School for the Deaf (OSD) in Belleville. I was just turning 16. Unlike children and youth who were forcibly "drafted" into residential schools, going there was my personal choice. I knew that on a reserve there really was not much help for people with my dual disabilities. I know this to be a fact although I did not live on a formal reserve; the city is like an "urban rez." Social acceptance among my deaf peers at OSD was difficult partly because

I was not classified as deaf, only partially impaired, and always because I was Aboriginal. Although I was isolated from my Aboriginal culture, I did have the opportunity to meet others who were hearing-impaired and became part of Deaf culture as a whole. I felt accepted on one hand, but isolated on the other due to their lack of cultural awareness of Aboriginal wholistic perspectives.

Many people in the hearing community try to dismiss the idea that Aboriginal language is the basis of our culture, but if they could understand that ASL is the basis of Deaf culture in ASL-speaking communities, they might begin to understand what traditional Aboriginal knowledge teaches: that language is the basis of culture. We are not talking about anything specific, but we are looking at a Deaf cultural language itself. This was one of the major comments that students in the deaf residential schools at the time made: Yes, we were allowed to learn and use our language, but only during our free time. We were not able to actually practice and utilize the language ourselves while in class. We were told to refrain from signing during class. This method of withholding our ability to speak hindered the process of our education.

The college almost had an uprising in terms of students wanting to have their language in the classroom. They taught us, yes, but always with oral speech. They imposed that rather than allowing students to speak their own deaf language. I suppose it was too much to be able to train the teachers to use sign language. Back then there was special training for the teachers on how to work with deaf students so that they could help the students in the use of speech and lip-reading from the spoken word. Nonetheless, those kids learned as they grew, learned ASL from the other kids. That is how they learned and developed a deaf culture as children and youth, the same way I learned it—from my own personal experience. In other words, I first learned ASL as a child would normally learn to speak a language, not from being taught from a book as some people learn it today. Over the years residential schools for the deaf have been phased out. The fact that there were some abusive situations helped in the move to having deaf children live at home as hearing children did. Parents started wanting their children to be at home with them.

Regardless of this, my ability to adapt was strong, and I graduated in 1971. However, I was still isolated because no services were offered with any elements of my Aboriginal heritage. This resulted in my following a path of alcoholism for 27 years. Fortunately, I eventually met a group of Aboriginal people like myself in Alcoholics Anonymous, and this helped me to make a change in my life's direction. Meanwhile, I was pleased to leave residential school behind me when I came to Toronto, yet the experience could not be left behind. Isolation and an unerring feeling of doom and despair followed me; this feeling is known today as *residential school syndrome*. It has continued within me although I have been traveling the healing path for many years.

I finally got my act together when I started working in the printing industry, as well as marrying my girlfriend, who is also culturally Deaf. Our home communication consists of ASL, English, and Native languages. ASL was my daughter's first language and English her second. English is my first language, ASL my second, Native my third. However, my wife uses only ASL. My daughter and I are not fluent in ASL or our Native tongue because we began learning it only six years ago. My daughter and I are fascinated by our Aboriginal culture, which we never dreamed of ever experiencing. We entered it by way of a challenge: an Aboriginal Elder urged my family not to isolate ourselves, but to come forward into the Toronto Native community. However, Karen, my wife of 29 years, has fallen into isolation—meaning she has no access to her deaf peers—over the past 10 years. However, this was her choice. As for me, I broadened my world with these three languages.

Although I have left the Deaf culture in the sense that I am culturally diverse, I continue to enhance my ASL signing skills. Because I am culturally diverse, I am able to bridge the gap for our Aboriginal people who need access to our traditional way of life. This bridging ability is why I am currently on the Translators Committee at Anishnabe Health in Toronto. It is also why I act as a liaison person who not only does outreach with other Native organizations, but who also works as a translator in the private sector. This includes such organizations as hospitals, shelters, courts, correctional services, sweats, doctors' appointments, housing, and so forth. The Translator Program has opened a large window of opportunity for me. I continue to enhance my career as a deaf/hearing translator across the greater Toronto area, in addition to acting as an advocate for urban Aboriginal people with disabilities who are in urgent need of culturally appropriate services.

Native deaf, blind, and deaf-blind persons, both on reserves and in urban centers, generally feel isolated, unaccepted, and unacceptable and often lack education. However, their voice and presence as a visible minority group is growing and becoming increasingly apparent. The barriers to the Sweet Grass Trail and living life to its fullest are numerous, but not impossible to overcome. Neither fetal alcohol syndrome and fetal alcohol effects (FAS/FAE), Usher's syndrome, residential school syndrome, nor any other challenges have been able to keep this Indigenous person down. I know how to move between communities, I have become productive, and I continue traveling the healing path of the Sweet Grass Trail.

Some people have asked me what would I propose now for Deaf Native people. This is a difficult question. Native education is regarded from a different perspective than mainstream education. Everything in the mainstream is defined by financial limitations: whether there is enough money for deaf, blind, and deaf-blind children's special needs to educate those children. Otherwise, those children have to go elsewhere, generally to an agency that addresses blind/deaf issues. And then again, it is also about money.

If there were to be a program that would reflect Aboriginal ways of learning for deaf, blind, and deaf-blind children, it would have to include all children. The major difficulty would be the language. Deaf children need ASL, FSL, or BSL. Blind children need Braille. Deaf-blind children need an intervening language, which is different again from ASL, FSL, or BSL. However, it is similar in that one uses one's hands to read or speak. There is no single language that could be used by all of these children. If such a program existed, to make the program unique it would have to include an Aboriginal language—or Aboriginal languages. There is currently no distinctly Aboriginal sign language because deaf languages are based on spelling out the words, and the spelling changes with the spoken language.

All the same, to go back to my above comment, our ancestors used forms of Native sign languages. The South Dakotas are bringing back their version of sign language when they speak, and so are some others. I bought a book on the subject by William Tompkins; the title is *Indian Sign Language*.

If anything is to be learned from this, it is that learning is a process that happens over time. I must have made a career choice five years ago when I was studying at George Brown College (or even 10 years ago). Starting in 1993 I began retraining through Aboriginal community training programs with a wholistic perspective and with formal postsecondary education. Today I have a new career working with the special-needs Aboriginal population who have the same disabilities as mine regarding their health issues. Presently I am contracted as a peer worker with Anishnabe Health of Toronto as an ASL interpreter. Finally, I am also a freelance ASL interpreter. The other day I found an essay I had written at George Brown, and even then I was talking about intervening for deaf, blind, and deaf-blind individuals. The questions I addressed were those that arose in the course of preparing for this symposium.

I wish to thank my friend Ernestine, who was my helper at the symposium. In a spirit of thanksgiving and in a prayer on behalf of all deaf, blind, and deaf-blind children, Ernestine and I wish to offer this prayer titled "The Native's Prayer."

Grandfather, Grandmother, hear me.
I am standing on Sacred Ground
Hear the drums beat forever.
I am holding the feather in my hand
And will never let go.
Here I am, carrying with me
The pains, griefs and isolation
Give me the strength and courage to go on.
I will be strong like the buffalos
Roaming the earth.
My spirit will fly with the eagles
To be free.
My heart will beat
Strong like the drum.
The Sacred Fire will never diminish in the distance.

—Singing Spirit, Ernestine LaCroix

Epilogue

After the Symposium I entered an Aboriginal literacy program at Council Fire Native Cultural Centre. It was a basic computer literacy program integrated with language literacy skills, and it enhanced my keyboarding skills. Now I can type without trying to see the keys, and this helps with my visual disability. Also, in the program I was learning the Oneida language. It did not matter which language I was learning. It did not matter if it was not my own. I learned things about the longhouse and other customs and cultural symbols of Hodenesonee peoples that added to my cultural diversity.

Dawn Antone, the Coordinator, was invited to participate in the Canadian Hearing Society Learning and Literacy Deaf Workshop. She and I participated in their conference—it was a way of putting the word out about Deaf Native literacy. I went with her, and at the conference they asked her, "Do you think that you could help Deaf people who are Native in the Literacy program?" Her answer was, "Only if Charlie was there." The point is that you cannot have a hearing person lead a Deaf Native literacy program any more than you can put a second-language speaker of any tongue to teach the language and culture. Such a person will not have the cultural grounding.

CHAPTER 15

Negotiating Identities, Negotiating Environments:

An Interpretation of the Experiences of Students with Disabilities

Jacqueline Low

Introduction

This paper explores the experiences of nine students with disabilities pursuing degrees at McMaster University. The analysis focuses on how these students negotiate disabled and non-disabled identities while negotiating the physical environment of the university campus. As a part of their every-day life at university, students with disabilities are engaged in rejecting deviant identities placed on them by others. These identities are reinforced by the isolating nature of an environment which constrains their interactions with others. At the same time, they must take on deviant identities in order to successfully function as "normal" university students.

It should be noted that Bogdan & Taylor (in Ferguson *et al.*, 1992) argue that an analytic focus on deviance obscures the fact that individuals with disabilities are seen as "normal" by those with whom they are in intimate relationships. However, I maintain that where relationships with non-intimates are concerned, students with disabilities are often labelled deviant (Goffman, 1963; Thomas, 1982). Accordingly, this paper focuses on how students with disabilities negotiate identities in the face of definitions placed on them by non-intimates in the largely impersonal world of the university campus. These three processes (negotiating environments, negotiating disabled identities and negotiating non-disabled identities) are necessarily interconnected and inherently contradictory (Thomas, 1982).

Method

Face-to-face unstructured interviews and a focus group were used as ways of generating data for this study. The sample was made up of interviews with nine university students with disabilities. Included in the interviews were students with varying degrees of mobility impairment, visual impairment, and one student with a learning disability. Of the students interviewed, three were male and six were female. Three were approximately 40 years of age and the rest were in their 20s. Only two of the students were non-white and they all came from lower-middle and middle-class backgrounds. With the exception of sex, these differences are probably reflective of the university population in general. No attempt was made to stratify the sample by sex, age, class or race as my intent was not to compare the experiences of different categories of students with disabilities, rather it was to explore the experience of students with disabilities in general. Also included in the sample were interviews with two members of McMaster's staff who serve students with disabilities and have disabilities themselves. While this sample cannot be considered exhaustive it shows the range of students with disabilities attending McMaster University and ensured that enough interviews were completed to show a repetition of many themes and patterns in the data (Glazer & Strauss, 1967). Small sample size is not ultimately problematic as this research is exploratory and my intentions are to build theory not generalize at the level of populations (Yin, 1989).

The interviews took place over a 3-month period from October through December of 1992. When most of the interviews had been completed a focus group was conducted organized around a selection of major themes which had emerged throughout the interviews (Morgan, 1988).

The data analysis followed a grounded theory approach and incorporated the assumptions of the interpretist perspective which sees "reality ... [as] ... created and social" (Ferguson *et al.*, 1992, p. 4). Contrary to the goals of description, prediction and control of the objectivist or positivist schools, the goal of this type of research is interpretive understanding of social situations (Ferguson *et al.*, 1992).

Some words about the nature of ethnographic research are in order at this point. I do not have a disability, hence my role in this study was restricted to that of the observer. While it is possible to seek empathetic understanding of the experiences of students with disabilities, it is not possible (except by extension) to participate in their world. Nevertheless, I have tried as much as possible to see the campus through the eyes of students with disabilities. On several occasions I travelled throughout the university with students and thereby had an opportunity to observe some of the environmental hazards they must negotiate in their day-to-day activities at McMaster. In addition, I have a certain amount of insider awareness (Douglas, 1976) into the world of physical disabilities as my mother has severe visual and mobility impairment. However, as interesting and informing as this kind of data can be (Becker, 1968), it is not to be confused with a perfect representation of the informants' point of view. Ethnographies are something different from merely an account from the informants' perspective, becoming something new in and of themselves. As Clifford & Marcus (1986) point out, "the historical predicament of ethnography ... [is] ... the fact that it is caught up in the invention, not the representation of cultures" (p. 2).

The Setting

McMaster University currently has a student body of over 22,000 full-time, part-time, continuing education, graduate and undergraduate students (McMaster University, Office of Public Relations, 1992). Of this total, approximately 150 are students with disabilities. The number of students with disabilities at McMaster University can only be approximated as not all students with disabilities make themselves known to the Ability and Access Office. It is likely that this figure under-represents students with concealable disabilities.

The campus is very large, covering 296 acres of land. There are 44 separate buildings totalling 362,322 square meters of floor space (McMaster University, Office of Public Relations, 1992/93). While some of these buildings are equipped with ramps and elevators, there are several older buildings equipped only with freight elevators and some which have no elevators at all. Several of the buildings are accessible solely through a basement passageway which restricts students with disabilities to underground travel (McMaster University, Equity and Access Center, 1991, pp. 30–33). Clearly, issues of accessibility and non-accessibility are more complex than merely the difference between using a ramp or climbing stairs.

> They slap a disabled sticker on a freight elevator and call the building accessible.... A building is only accessible if you can get in and use all the areas in it ... like the bathrooms ... like in Mills ... [library] ... it's accessible but I can't use the bathrooms ... you feel trapped once you're inside the building.

Through the Ability and Access Office McMaster University offers a variety of services to students with disabilities ranging from advance access to course materials and use of audio-visual aids to deadline extensions and extra time in which to write exams (McMaster University, Equity and Access Center, 1991, pp. 7–15). Again, practice is rarely as straightforward as policy. Several students told me of instances where they had problems making use of the services offered.

> Books are a problem ... most of the text books are available on tape but it's not always the right edition and so many people use them ... they're not always in the best condition ... all the workers in Mills are really accommodating ... it's not their fault.... Volunteers tape the books ... they're usually available in September but this year it was November.

In this particular study "the setting" is more than simply a place where interaction occurs. For students with disabilities, negotiation of the campus environment is a process inextricably linked to the processes involved in negotiating disabled and non-disabled identities.

Negotiating Environments

All students at McMaster must negotiate the physical environment of the university campus in their day-to-day activities, but students with disabilities face qualitatively different problems of mobility in their life on campus. Mobility is not only an issue of whether a student is physically able to climb stairs or walk across campus, it is also an issue of the amount of time and energy climbing and walking requires. Time is a resource that must be carefully managed if a student is to be successful at university, but students who rely on braces and crutches cannot run to make their next class.

> I get tired ... it takes me longer ... but I drive across campus ... I drive everywhere ...
> I'm lucky ... I guess for people who don't drive it's harder ... it must be really tough.

Students with visual impairments must at the very least slow down when they approach staircases. Those who use wheelchairs cannot take shortcuts and are restricted to the number of accessible entrances. Moreover, for students with visual or mobility impairments, the number of environmental hazards on the university campus multiplies.

When asked about mobility problems on campus one student with visual impairment quipped: "Well ... the construction ... I'm just waiting for that manhole with my name on it." Objects left obstructing corridors become barriers to movement or outright traps for students who can't see them or step over them. People can also serve as effective barriers for students with visual and mobility impairment.

> One of my pet peeves is bikes against the stair rails ... one time I bumped into a bike
> and it fell on me ... or when people sit under their lockers with their legs stuck out
> ... you'd think they'd say I'm here but they don't.

Ironically, structural additions to the campus and access to areas not open to other students (meant to increase accessibility) can be hazardous. For example, buildings considered accessible because they are equipped with a freight elevator are potentially dangerous.

> Most ... [students with disabilities] ... don't have the upper body strength I do ... or
> the balance and I can't lift the doors ... you know freight elevators have a door like
> a garage ... you pull it up ... if you let go it comes crashing down ... if you're in a ...
> [wheel] ... chair ... it could slice you in half ... it's just not safe ... I don't know anyone
> who uses them ... and this chair is so light that if I try to pull ... [the door up] ... I can
> flip backwards ... it's happened before ... I won't use them.
>
> The caf[eteria] isn't bad ... we can go there if you're willing to act as a break for me
> on that ramp ... [leading from the parking lot to the cafeteria] ... it's treacherous ... it's
> too steep and there's a curve halfway down and you're going so fast ... it's not safe.

That the campus is a particularly dangerous place for students with disabilities can generate fear.

> I got caught once ... only once in five years ... I was in the hall and a class was letting
> out ... I was facing the other way and I got caught in this sea of people ... I didn't
> want to speak out ... I couldn't say get out of the way ... I was scared.

Following landmarks is one of the strategies students with visual disabilities use in negotiating the campus environment.

> You count doors and then you know to turn ... you figure out the underground by
> sound ... the sound of the elevators ... the click of doors ... you know when it doesn't
> feel right ... you know it's the cafeteria because you smell the food.... You walk down
> a hall and you feel enclosed ... when you get to where the halls meet you feel open.

Despite their proficiency in using landmarks, location changes (a frequent occurrence on
university campuses) prove to be another hazard for students with visual impairment.

> Things move ... nothing's stable ... [classroom and office locations] ... it's disconcerting
> ... my husband does all the orientation for me ... he finds my classes.... Desks move
> ... I wish someone would tell me when they move the furniture.... You learn to be
> on your guard ... beware this setting changes.

While students with disabilities are by no means "helpless" (Thomas, 1982), given the
hazards and location changes ever present in the campus environment, they do at times
need help. Asking for and receiving help is more problematic than it might appear. Some
students with disabilities can be reluctant to ask for help and people without disabilities
sometimes may not offer to help.

> Independence ... [for people with disabilities] ... is pushed too far ... people end up
> floundering rather than asking for help ... I remember one episode when I was in
> an elevator with a professor and he said "I never know if I'm supposed to help or
> not" ... it's unusual that he asked ... most people don't ask ... they don't want to feel
> uncomfortable.

Just as the road to hell is paved with good intentions, help from others may bring students
with disabilities into jeopardy.

> I get into more trouble from people trying to help me than from people not helping
> ... they think they're helping by grabbing your arm and instead they push you down

the stairs ... you have to be careful who you ask for help and you have to tell them how to help you.

Another problem faced by students with visual and mobility impairments as they negotiate the campus environment is isolation. This isolation occurs on two levels; one subjective and one objective. On one level isolation is individually and subjectively perceived by students with disabilities.

> I'm dependent on rides ... [special transportation for people with disabilities] ... I'm afraid of being isolated ... out there at night out by the disabled door.... That's the door to Burke Science ... the designated area for Darts to come and pick us up.

On another level, students with disabilities are isolated in an objective sense when they are seen by others going in special doors, and in situations where they feel disorientated, unsafe and afraid. They are seen as moving slower and in situations where they have to ask for help. Areas on campus are acknowledged by others to be inaccessible to students with disabilities and they are seen as restricted to subterranean travel in the underground corridors. In their totality these things stigmatize students with disabilities, setting them apart from the general student population. For these students, the process of negotiation of the physical environment of the university campus is part and parcel of the process of negotiation of a disabled identity.

Negotiating Identities

It became clear early in the interviews that students with disabilities are engaged in two interconnected processes of identity negotiation in their lives on campus. Uppermost in their minds is negotiating a non-disabled identity. Their greatest desire is to be seen and treated as just another "normal" student. At odds with this process is that, at times, it becomes necessary for them to negotiate a disabled identity.

Disabled Identities

Over-emphasizing independence for students with disabilities can be counter-productive and can lead to situations where the expectations placed on them are inappropriate (Goffman, 1963).

> My very best friend has said that she doesn't see me as disabled ... but it can go too far ... people forget and they say things like "let's go for a jog" ... it doesn't work like that.

Likewise, in the classroom setting it may become necessary for a student to draw attention to his or her disability in order to have the same access to course material a "normal student" would have. One student told me: "Some profs don't understand ... they write things on the board and then point to them ... [but] ... I can't see." Furthermore, disabilities can sometimes prove instrumental in facilitating interaction with others.

> I don't like ... [guide] ... dogs ... they distance you from people ... people tend to pay attention to the dog and not to you ... you also miss the opportunity to make the friends you would by having to ask for directions.

These are examples of occasions where students with disabilities label themselves disabled. Far more common are situations where labels are placed on students by others. During each interview I asked students how they choose to be referred to (disabled student, student with a disability, etc.). Some responses referred to the pejorative nature of most labels placed on people with disabilities.

> I'll take blind over stupid ... people assume stupid ... disability is an umbrella label ... I don't find it offensive but it's negative ... I can't do this ... I can't do that.

A second type of response concerned the tendency of labels to change so rapidly that they become meaningless categories.

> I don't consider myself disabled ... things change ... it used to be disabled then person with a disability ... then mobility impaired ... mobility challenged.... The latest is differently abled but what does that mean?.... I mean we're all differently abled ... we all have different abilities it doesn't mean anything.

The indeterminate meaning of labels can have an homogenizing effect. According to one student: "Some professors think that all blind people are the same ... we're not." A further consequence is that these labels can result in the double stigmatization of students with disabilities: "If people know you're disabled ... even if there's nothing wrong with your hearing ... they speak louder." Finally, the meaninglessness of labels confuses others.

> It's confusing for people when you're not totally blind ... they don't understand.... Like ... [one] ... professor ... he would always ask ... "why can she do this and not that?"

Among the issues addressed in the focus group were the types of labels placed on people with disabilities. Aside from talking about the meaningless and misleading nature of labels, the members of the focus group discussed the socio-cultural meaning of recent changes in labels. In general the members were cynical about linking changes in labels to changes in the attitudes others have towards people with disabilities. Only one member felt that new labels represented positive change.

> *Member 1:* A professor called me differently abled.... What is that?.... The labels are changing.
>
> *Member 4:* [Laughing] ... I haven't changed ... I'm still blind ... they think they've done something for us.
>
> *Member 2:* I disagree ... people have changed the terms they use because they're becoming aware.
>
> *Member 1:* [Nodding in agreement] ... You have a point there.
>
> *Member 3:* Labels are changing their meaning.
>
> *Member 4:* [Interrupts and says sarcastically] ... Right ... dumb used to mean mute ... now it means stupid.

Whether a student is labelled disabled has much to do with the nature of their disability. It is not surprising that students with visible disabilities are more vulnerable to the labelling process than those with concealable disabilities. In Goffman's (1963) words, "visibility is crucial" (p. 48).

The visible nature of students' disabilities often constrains the way in which others interact with them. One student put it this way: "If you're in a wheelchair people have to look down at you ... they physically condescend to you."

The students I spoke with were also concerned that the visible nature of their disabilities restricts their sexual identities and limits their opportunities for developing romantic relationships.

> One of the biggest problems is how people view the disabled and their sexuality ... because I'm disabled I'm supposed to be asexual ... I was sitting in the cafeteria and at the table next to me was a girl and a couple of guys ... the girl was saying "I have this friend with spina bifida and she just had a baby isn't that great" ... and the guys ... one of the guys said "I could never have sex with someone like that".... That's the biggest problem ... boyfriends.... I worry about it ... is a guy ever going to be interested in me for me or is it just that they feel sorry for me?

In social interaction, students with visible disabilities must maintain a delicate balance between how they would like to behave and how others expect them to behave (Goffman, 1963). For example, a student who wears braces on her legs described how she was brought to task for what she felt was "normal" behaviour.

> I wear shorts a lot ... I don't even think about it and this girl said "I don't know how you
> can wear shorts" ... I said what do you mean and she said ... "I don't have too unattractive
> legs and I would never wear shorts ... how can you wear them with your legs?"

Students with visible disabilities also manage another sort of tension in their interactions
with others which arises out of situations where others misread the visual clues presented
by the person with a disability.

> I have cerebral palsy ... so my balance isn't very good ... sometimes you'll see me and
> I'll lurch ... people often think I'm drunk ... you know staggering around.

Understandably, students with visible disabilities frequently make efforts to conceal them
and those with concealable disabilities work to keep them hidden.

According to Goffman (1963), the difference between discredited and discreditable
identities is that the latter depends on the degree to which the individual can reduce stigma
by controlling disclosure of their deviant identity. For instance, some students make efforts
to appear "normal" by not displaying the props associated with students with disabilities.

> I try to appear as normal as possible ... I try not to be too conspicuous ... I don't carry
> all my tools around all the time ... I carry a small tape recorder ... a normal binder
> ... a normal watch ... I don't bring all my tools to class, they take up two seats ... the
> technology's bulky.... My braille writer ... my braille books.

Another student who had a concealable learning disability had more control than other
students over disclosure of his disability.

> If people want to think I'm a keener that's their problem ... I don't tell them any
> different.... If they approach me directly and ask about the computer I'd explain it
> to them ... I don't want to stand out.

One student said that she felt discrimination towards people with disabilities in the work
force obliged her to conceal the severity of her disability.

> When I first started looking for jobs I was upfront about how visually impaired I am
> ... I didn't get many interviews ... I became less up front and I got more interviews ...
> I wrote slight visual impairment on one application ... I got the interview ... when I
> went in I had the white cane.... He said "You never said you were blind...." I knew
> if I had told him he would have never given me a chance.

As Davis (1961) notes, having been labelled as potentially threatening "to the framework of rules and assumptions that guide sociability" (p. 125), students with disabilities set about "breaking through" this identity by actively negotiating a non-disabled identity.

Non-disabled Identities

If they weren't fully aware of it before, students with disabilities come face to face with their disabled identities when they arrive on a university campus amidst thousands of strangers. As Goffman (1963) points out, "normals really mean no harm; when they do, it is because they don't know any better. They should therefore be tactfully helped to act nicely" (p. 116). It is up to the student with a disability to help "normals" see them as "just ... any other student."

Davis (1961) argues that negotiating a non-disabled identity is a three-stage process of fictional acceptance, "breaking through" to normalized interaction, and institutionalization of the normalized relationship (pp. 125–131). The hallmark of the fictionalized acceptance stage is that "the interaction is kept starved at the bare subsistence level of sociability" (Davis, 1961, p. 127).

> They've been accepting for the most part ... they help me ... they treat me just like any other student ... they let me copy their notes if I ask them.

> I came here straight out of high school ... it was small and everybody knew me ... everybody accepted me ... for who I am ... the way I am and when I came here ... it's been rough.... I have acquaintances I can say hi to ... people I write essays with but as for seeing people off campus ... (she shook her head to indicate no).

Institutionalized acceptance of the normalized relationship centres around the difficulty of managing a non-disabled identity "in the face of the many small ... qualifications that must ... be made to it" (Davis, 1961, p. 130).

> Some profs use a lot of overheads ... one prof gave me large photocopies of all the over heads ... that was great ... he treated me like I was an individual who coincidentally couldn't see ... it was no big deal.... Helps to make it more normal ... that's real important for me ... to follow the learning process like everyone else ... with slight modifications.

However, as Davis (1961) cautions, "such amendments ... are ... underplayed in the early stages" (p. 130) as asking for concessions can interfere with the student's negotiation of a non-disabled identity.

> I try to be as normal as possible ... my rights shouldn't displace anyone else's ... I
> don't demand that the professors read the notes after they write them on the board
> ... I wait and ask someone to read them to me after class.

Tactics of Negotiation

Negotiating a non-disabled identity involves employing countless tactics of "breaking
through" to normalized relationships (Davis, 1961; Goffman, 1963). Among the tactics of
negotiation mentioned by students were: speaking out and increasing visibility, reasoning
with others, using humour, adopting aggressive or assertive attitudes, avoiding confrontations with others and distancing themselves from other students with disabilities.

In general, students saw speaking out as a method of negotiating a non-disabled identity. They also linked the concept of speaking out with the belief that increased visibility
of students with disabilities would promote the integration of students with disabilities
who would succeed them.

> It's the attitude I find hardest ... I find a lot of people are ignorant ... maybe it's
> because there aren't many of us ... [disabled students] ... here maybe if there were
> more of us here it would be different ... they wouldn't be so ignorant ... they would
> know better.

Although one student felt the issue of integration of students with disabilities into the
general university population was not so easily resolved. She argued that: "even though
there's more of us the stereotype still exists that the disabled belong at home."

Another strategy many students said they used in negotiating a non-disabled identity
was the tactic of reasoning with others. As one student put it: "I tell them my point of
view and I try to change their point of view." Although about half of the students said
that it wasn't their role to change everyone's attitudes.

> I don't blame them for making assumptions ... I am different ... provided they're not
> written in stone ... if I have to work closely with someone ... I try and talk to them
> ... I'd tell them ... it seems that you think this and this and this ... this is the way I
> see it ... if the person's not important to me I just let it be ... I'm not out to save
> the world ... people learn more through one-to-one interaction ... not in a selfish
> politically correct way.

People with disabilities often use humour as a means of negotiating a non-disabled identity (Davis, 1961; Goffman, 1963).

> You have to make jokes to get along.... Most people respond to humour ... as long as it's self-depreciating humour ... if I turn the joke on them they don't think that's funny ... humour breaks the ice ... it tells them it doesn't bother me why should it bother you.

However, humour doesn't always succeed. When reasoning and joking fail most of the students I spoke with said they adopt assertive or aggressive behaviours in negotiating their non-disabled identities. The students who mentioned this tactic always qualified their statements by saying they considered these sorts of attitudes to be inappropriate and ones which they reluctantly resort to.

> They say "sorry" ... "I didn't see you" ... I say ... [sarcastically] ... "I didn't see you either" ... one time I got really mad and I swore ... the words just came out ... it's not in my nature to talk like that but they just came out.

A few of the students who participated in the interviews adopted a fatalistic approach, believing the best tactic is avoiding confrontations with others. These students felt that confronting others about negative attitudes would further stigmatize them, interfering with their negotiation of a non-disabled identity.

> I'm not bitter ... if people have a problem with the disabled I'm not going to tell people they have a problem ... if someone was making fun of someone in a wheelchair I wouldn't say anything ... maybe if they were really being cruel I would but it's not my job to educate people ... if people notice I have a disability I say nothing.

Related to avoiding confrontation was an active disavowal of identification with other students with disabilities. For these students an important tactic in the negotiation of a non-disabled identity was distancing themselves from other students with disabilities. Students distance themselves from their disabled identities by expressing dislike for, attributing negative attributes to, and/or keeping physical distance between themselves and other students with disabilities (Goffman, 1963). The students who spoke with me were always careful to preface distancing remarks with the qualifier that they are not like other students with disabilities. They told me that other students with disabilities are too dependent, too self-centred, use their disability as a crutch or an excuse and/or cheat.

> I'm different from most other handicapped ... I want to blend in ... my rights should never be more important than anyone else's ... I never want to earn a handicapped A ... I'd rather have a B on my own steam.

Further evidence of this desire for distance was the lack of interest if not distaste students expressed towards the idea of a support group for students with disabilities. The reason they gave for their lack of interest can be divided into two general categories: (1) that they had better things to do and (2) they felt that it would be an unpleasant experience. One student: told me: "I don't know ... to tell you the truth I really wouldn't want that ... I think it would be just a lot of complaining." What is also plausible is that they felt membership in a group for students with disabilities would further constrain negotiation of non-disabled identities (Goffman, 1963).

Discussion

An irony of university life for students with disabilities is that many of their concerns: achieving academic success, making friends, expressing their sexuality, developing romantic relationships, etc., are the same concerns which occupy students without disabilities (Davis, 1961). Although given "the repressive nature of the relationship between the disabled and the rest of society" (Thomas, 1982, p. 20), the negative baggage visible disabilities can confer should not be underestimated.

Where identity formation is concerned, students with disabilities experience three negotiatory processes in their careers at university. They negotiate disabled and non-disabled identities while negotiating the physical environment of the university campus. These processes are interrelated and inherently contradictory. In order to achieve a non-disabled identity, students with disabilities must successfully negotiate a physical environment which in its inaccessibility isolates them from interaction with others, emphasizing their disabled identities. While Thomas (1982) convincingly argues that people with disabilities are no longer to be seen as passive and helpless, the students who spoke to me maintain that they sometimes do need assistance. Asking for help in negotiating the university environment is only one of the instances where students with disabilities must negotiate a disabled identity. The price they pay is that requests for help draw attention to their disabilities and consequently their deviant identities.

Also paradoxical is that in order to be seen as "normal," students with visible disabilities strive for independence and make efforts to reduce stigma by concealing their disabilities. Yet, in order to have access to the course materials and other rights of a "normal" student they must ask for concessions, thereby disclosing their disabled identities to their professors and/or classmates.

Furthermore, many of the tactics employed by students in negotiating non-disabled identities prove inconsistent. Tactics like speaking out on behalf of and increasing the visibility of students with disabilities on campus conflict with students' efforts to distance themselves from other students with disabilities. The popularity of the distancing strategy among these students indicates the degree to which they have identified with the "normal" population (Goffman, 1963). They have become the ultimate "other" to themselves. Yet all the students who spoke with me believe, at least on some level, they are objectively different from students without disabilities. According to one student: "I'd like to wake up one morning and be normal ... but that's not in the cards." Identification with the "other" interferes with development of the in-group solidarity Thomas (1982) maintains is essential to the social integration of people with disabilities.

Equally problematic is that many of the tactics students with disabilities employ in negotiating non-disabled identities: concealing disabilities, reasoning with others, avoiding confrontations with others, expressing aggressive and/or assertive attitudes or using humour, are strategies which operate on the individual level. It is questionable whether individual strategies alone can effectively challenge the deviant status of people with disabilities and promote social change.

The two tactics, which can be considered as acting on the socio-cultural level, increased visibility of students with disabilities and speaking out as a group, in this case, are also relatively ineffectual. First, it doesn't necessarily follow that increasing the visibility of a repressed group fosters integration of that group into the larger population; as continuing manifestations of racism and ethnic tension would indicate. Secondly, most of the students who participated in the interviews were loath to identify themselves with a group where membership is based on the presence of a disability. They expressed cynicism about employment equity programmes and were suspicious of the consequences of being characterized as a special interest group; believing this would have the effect of isolating them in a disabled sub-culture. However, it is possible that increased efforts on the part of university administrators to make universities fully accessible might alleviate those concerns and in the process enhance the undergraduate environment for all students.

Finally, the co-ordinator for students with disabilities at McMaster described how these students face a subtle form of social control which discourages them from organizing for change.

> The students often comment that there is no ... [lobby] ... group for them ... it really intrigues me ... they want one but no one wants to start it ... maybe it's because there hasn't been a central issue ... like access to galvanize them.... Maybe if we had an issue ... we're kind of in the middle here ... McMaster has done just enough so students don't organize.

Integration of students with disabilities into the general student population is not unlike the social integration of any group seen as deviant. Likewise, solutions to the problem of integration must necessarily be the same. While it is beyond the scope of this paper to suggest concrete strategies for change, I propose that future efforts must be aimed at the socio-cultural as well as individual levels of society.

References

Becker, H. S. (1968) *Sociological Work* (Chicago, Aldine).

Clifford, J. & Marcus, E. G. (1986) *Writing Culture: The poetics and politics of ethnography* (Berkeley, University of California Press).

Davis, F. (1961) Deviance disavowal: The management of strained interaction by the visibly handicapped. *Social Problems*, 9, pp. 120–140.

Douglas, J. D. (1976) *Investigative Social Research: Individual and team research* (Beverley Hills, Sage).

Ferguson, P. M., Ferguson, D. & Taylor, S. J. (1992) *Interpreting Disability: A qualitative reader* (New York, Teachers College Press).

Glazer, B. G. & Strauss, A. L. (1967) *The Discovery of Grounded Theory: Strategies for qualitative research* (New York, Aldine).

Goffman, E. (1963) *Stigma: Notes on the management of spoiled identity* (Englewood Cliffs, Prentice Hall).

McMaster University, Equity and Access Center (1991) *The Disabled Student: Faculty and student reference guide* (Hamilton, McMaster University).

McMaster University, Office of Public Relations (1992) *McMaster Fast Facts 1992/1993* (Hamilton, McMaster University).

Morgan, D. L. (1988) *Focus Groups as Qualitative Research* (Newbury Park, CA, Sage).

Thomas, D. (1982) *The Experience of Handicap* (London & New York, Methuen).

Yin, R. K. (1989) *Case Study Research: Design and methods* (Newbury Park, CA, Sage).

CHAPTER 16

The Normality of Doing Things Differently:

Bodies, Spaces, and Disability Geography

Nancy Hansen and Chris Philo

Introduction: Bringing the Disabled Body Back in?

The chapter contributes to an ongoing "retrieval" of the body in both disability studies and, more narrowly, disability geography. We develop a quite particular argument about what we term "the normality of (different bodies) doing things differently," seeking to offer a further strand in the project of fostering more radical and inclusive politics of accommodation energising Freund's (2001) thinking about "bodies, disability and spaces." The result is an essayistic paper, we admit, although we believe that the subtle "play" on words anchoring our overall argument is of some moment in the service of imagining other, more "hopeful ontologies" (as in Parr 2007) of disability *in* society. Our claims draw upon Nancy Hansen's in-depth research with a sample of disabled women living in Scotland and Canada, and shortly we will introduce that research and how we are borrowing from it here. To commence, though, we frame what follows by taking a brief critical "tour" through key debates within disability studies, mapping them across to how such debates have been reworked within the subfield of disability geography.

A recent collection of essays collected under the title of *Implementing the Social Model of Disability* (Barnes & Mercer 2004a) prompts a "taking stock" of what has been achieved through the adoption of the "social model" of disability in disability studies. Inspired by debates around the UN definition of disability from the early 1980s, criticism was directed at a prevailing "medical model" of disability that lodges disability in the apparently "damaged" body or mind[1] of an individual, inviting a personal narrative of "tragedy" followed by "heroic" efforts at self-adjustment. An alternative "social model" took shape, stressing not the individual but rather a wider society that fails to accommodate his or her impairment, thus demanding a critical stance on the underlying "ableism" of a non-disabled society that creates a world in its own able-bodied image. The social model, with its "emphasis on disabling social and environmental barriers ... contrasted with the ... orthodoxy that viewed disability as a 'personal tragedy', and disabled people as in need of care" (Barnes & Mercer 2004b, p. 2). Its chief foci became the structural forces leading to discrimination against disabled people in (capitalist) labour and housing markets, as linked with their being denied both basic civil rights and the opportunity to participate in the overall mix of economic, political, social and cultural activities supposedly available to everyone else (e.g., Abberley 1987; Oliver 1990, 1996). The social model became the foundation stone on which social-scientific disability studies matured during the 1990s, and in the process its theoretical co-ordinates broadened to include input from feminism, poststructuralism and postmodernism alert to cultural as well as political-economic "oppressions" of disabled people (Barnes & Mercer 2004b, p. 7).

These developments are well-known, and most commentators agree about the positive gains made by shifting perspective from the medical to the social model. Certain limits of the latter have begun to be registered, even so, not least because disability studies arrives at the seemingly odd position that the impaired body per se—in the specificity of its physical differences—ends up strangely evacuated from studies being undertaken. There is a deep-seated fear that any opening to the materiality of the impaired body will risk the return of the medical model (e.g., Hall 2000, p. 27), but others are less hesitant in insisting that bodies, and hence individual circumstances, experiences and narratives, must be centralised in a truly inclusive disability studies. Pinder (1995; cf. Shakespeare & Watson 1997) complains about the social model's "disembodied approach" wherein the "objective" features of someone's impairment (the lack of a limb, the paucity of sight, etc.) remain very much in the shadows of analysis, while there is a double-edge in Wendell's (1996) discussion of "the rejected body" (i.e., rejected both by society *and* by disability studies). Borrowing from work on the sociology of the body wherein bodily differences are brought to the fore, and where attention is paid to diverse embodied capacities for engaging with and acting in the world, Hughes & Paterson (1997) seek to retrieve "the disappearing body" in disability studies. Freund (2001, p. 689), meanwhile, though cautious about "over-emphasising" bodily difference, proposes that the way forward lies in a "social-materialist approach ... which locates mind-bodies in space." In such a vision, the specificities of individual impairments *do* matter, and must be foregrounded, but always in relation to the kinds of spaces that non-disabled people have created—and the sorts of time-space organisation of activities required by ableist society—which differentially, but rarely in a helpful manner, impact upon most cohorts of disabled people.[2]

This reference to space[3] allows us now to introduce the subfield of disability geography, which has been recognisable as such for about twenty years (Park *et al.* 1998) and boasts several book-length treatments (e.g., Imrie 1996a; Butler & Parr 1999; Gleeson 1999; Kitchin 2000) and journal theme issues (e.g., *Environment and Planning D: Society and Space* 1997; *Disability Studies Quarterly* 2001, 2004; *Urban Studies* 2001; *Canadian Geographer* 2003).[4] It encompasses a wide range of substantive concerns: some concentrating on physical accessibility and the difficulties faced by disabled people moving through streets, parks, shops, settlements and whole regions (e.g., Gant & Smith 1990, 1991; Golledge 1991; Vujakovic & Matthews 1994; Matthews & Vujakovic 1995); and others on social acceptability and the ableism of human-environmental design as linked to the stigmatising, patronising and demeaning of disabled people in everyday spaces (e.g., Hahn 1986; Imrie & Wells 1993; Butler & Bowlby 1997; Chouinard 1997, 1999; Kitchin 1998; Pain *et al.* 2001, Chap. 8; Valentine 2001, pp. 45–48; Mcfarlane 2005). The subfield has long appreciated the social model's critique of its medical counterpoint, most obviously perhaps in the exchange between Golledge (1993, 1996)—effectively mobilising the medical model and using his own personal experience (Golledge 1997) to authenticate claims—and Butler (1994), Gleeson (1996) and Imrie (1996b), all stressing the systematic "removal" of disabled people (and facilities serving them) from mainstream spaces of living, working and playing.

This being said, it can be argued that from the outset disability geography has retained a somewhat heretical stance with respect to a "pure" social model, always being prepared to keep bodily differences securely in the picture. Dorn (1994) emphasises the "spatial dissidence" between embodied impairments and the material organisation of social spaces, for instance, and he remarks that "[r]e-visioning disability as spatial dissidence highlights its physicality" (Dorn 1994, p. 3).[5] Gleeson (1993, 1998, 1999), meanwhile, adopts an historical-materialist framing of the demands imposed upon disabled people and their bodily (in)capacities by the varying "labour" expectations associated with different modes of production. What Hahn (1989) calls "the dynamics of human appearance," shaped by dominant visions of the idealised body shape, size and tone, has therefore never been far from the agenda of disability geography; while bodies as "things lived in," the immediate vehicles for a person's emotional, cognised and perhaps voiced encounter with the world, have also been at the fore. As Parr & Butler (1999, p. 21) write about the authors in their *Mind and Body Spaces* collection, "none ... would deny or dismiss the real, lived experience of changed/changing/painful/clumsy/immobile bodies." Hall (2000, esp. pp. 24–26, p. 28) explicitly addresses such considerations in disability geography, calling for the body in "its fleshy reality" to be part of the picture, not merely as a surface of contested representations or an inert object latched on to by social processes, but rather as the three-dimensional site where the biological and the societal fuse as, for instance, disabled people "persuade" their limbs and senses to "behave" in line with ableist expectations.[6]

As indicated, our goal is to continue this retrieval of the body in disability studies, as partially inspired by the example long set by disability geography. As also indicated, our discussion below draws upon—but does not provide a full reporting of—doctoral research undertaken by one of the authors. In this project, Hansen (2002) conducted in-depth interviews with 40 disabled women, 20 in Scotland and 20 in Canada, recruited through disability support groups, friendship networks and "snowballing," each following a rough guide of conversational topics, lasting between 30 minutes and two hours or more, and usually being held in locations familiar to the women.[7] Interviews were taped and transcribed, and transcripts were manually coded under a number of headings, with particular attention paid to both emerging commonalties and points of disagreement. Full details of these methods, their logistics and ethics are explained in Hansen (2002, esp. Chapter 4), together with an account of her own embodied experiences as a disabled researcher (see also Chouinard 1999; Anderson 2001), covering both the practicalities of interviewing and the sometimes fraught emotional dynamics full of tears and mutual disclosure. The outcome was a rich dossier of disabled women's experiences when "passing through other people's spaces," revealing how they cope with their embodied impairments in the often unforgiving socio-material environments of employment, education and community. More specifically, the women talked of feeling pressured to pass as normal, to perform[8] in a manner as closely corresponding as possible to an able-bodied way of doing things, all of which perpetuated a massive disjunction for them between the actual bodies that they inhabit and the bodies that they feel others think they *ought* to inhabit (in order to properly to occupy the spaces in question).

The "Wrong Body" in the Wrong Place

Part of the story for Hansen's respondents was the seeming unacceptability of their impaired bodies in many different societal contexts and public spaces. Almost as an extension of the infamous "ugly laws" once passed by US urban jurisdictions (Butler & Bowlby 1997, p. 420), and echoing Hahn's (1989) broader reflections on the constructed negative aesthetics of disability, much of this rejection is bound up with the visual appearance per se of the impaired body (Silvers 2002). Thus, impaired bodies—particularly ones that are much shorter or taller than prevailing norms (Kruse 2002, 2003), lacking limbs or perhaps having only "half-bodies," otherwise looking somehow "broken," "crumpled" or "disfigured" (Hawkesworth 2001)—have always risked being regarded as in some way sub-human, pre-human, "freak," "mutant," even "monster" (Leroi 2003), and viewed on the same feared continuum as illness and death (Michalko 2002a). Importantly, though, it is not only a matter of appearance, for what also comes into play are the differences of how impaired bodies *do things*, whether moving, gesturing, speaking, undertaking a task at work such as telephoning or typing, and so on. If people's comportment seems out-of-the-ordinary, being too slow or taking too long, involving "curious" jerks, postures or facial expressions, perhaps accompanied by "odd" sounds or smells, then the risk is that they become treated with suspicion or even hostility. The same outcome may arise if people depend upon artificial aids to enable their conduct, whether the use of a wheelchair, a seeing-eye dog, an electronic speech device or the like, such "implements" revealing somebody's mobility, visual or speech impairments.[9] Maybe disabled people are forced to account for these different bodily performances, too often they are shunned (i.e., ignored in a social event) or even formally excluded (i.e., sacked from a job), and they constantly feel pressure to perform as "normally" as they possibly can (i.e., to accomplish a doing of things that can pass muster as almost-normal).

Conversely, the non-disabled body is arbitrarily established as the "natural" way of appearing, being and doing, and everyday spaces (streets, parks, offices, schools) are effectively "naturalised" as ones to be inhabited and used by non-disabled people. Many kinds of bodies have arguably yet to "belong" in such places and it is as if their presence is treated as a form of trespass, unwanted or disruptive to silent conventions, thereby engendering an unfavourable reaction. Longhurst's (1994, p. 219; also 2001) study of pregnant women can be cited:

> [D]uring pregnancy in some places women find that their usual behaviours in public become increasingly socially unacceptable the more visibly pregnant they become. The familiar, the "everyday" of some places through the medium/experience/ physicality of their pregnant corporeality, can become unfamiliar zones in which they at times feel uncomfortable and unwelcome.

The case is even more problematic for disabled people whose bodily difference puts them beyond the range of "normal" varieties of embodiment, and who are indeed, in all sorts of ways on all sorts of occasions, made to feel that they are "out of place" in non-disabled spaces (e.g., Chouinard 1999, p. 150). Such spaces are rarely discussed in terms of how and why they *accept* the appearances and conducts of the non-disabled, nor in terms of what they offer to "the mobile," "the sighted," "the hearing" or "the able." The conformity of such spaces to the non-disabled remains almost entirely unquestioned, and in effect the non-disabled remain "unmarked" in much the same way that white people are commonly unmarked, set outside of racial or ethnic categories, in mainstream Western localities. Drawbacks are only perceived to arise when someone arrives who departs from such "natural" assumptions of not only embodied appearance but also comportment (Corker & Shakespeare 2002; Michalko 2002a).

The impression is left that mal- or under-performing impaired bodies should not "take up space," certainly not places unthinkingly conceived as non-disabled space, and Hansen (2002, esp. Chap. 7 on "community spaces") found many examples in her research. One is Lynda's:[10]

> Half-eleven in the morning, I have been in situations where they [strangers] have said to me "have you been on the booze already?" when I haven't! I don't drink now before I go to a pub or club because I have to have my wits about me when they [security people] say "you're not getting in, you're paralytic" [i.e., "paralytically drunk"], and I have to say to them "no I am not. I've got this, this and this" [Lynda has a neuro-muscular disability]. There have been a couple of times when they've asked my friends who I am with for confirmation of what I have said and they apologise to them not me (Lynda, Scotland, in Hansen 2002, p. 139).

Wider appreciation of Lynda's condition is lacking, and more broadly of the different kinds of comportment that a condition such as hers entails, and it is revealing that the knee-jerk coding of her body in the street or outside a club is that she must be intoxicated. What this example also illustrates is someone needing repeatedly to give voice to their disability, to explain it, so that her bodily difference can be accepted, albeit "on sufferance," by the non-disabled majority. A similar example—a subtle one perhaps, but included to indicate how conduct may "betray" impairment—is Joanne's:

> If go to the coffee shop, and say "can I have a cup of coffee?", then they will speak
> to me about different types of coffees, different sizes of cups, whatever, and I stand
> and look at them and I haven't a clue, and loads of times they must look at me as if
> I'm either thick, drunk or whatever, but as soon as I explain there is a problem[11] and
> "could they speak more slowly?", they will do it, well some of them will be fine and
> some of them don't have a clue they've got to do that ... I'm not complaining, I will
> have to continue to explain! (Joanne, Scotland, in Hansen 2002, p. 139).

While showing great fortitude, Joanne's impaired conduct does signal her difference, sufficient for some non-disabled people to regard her as out of place in the coffee shop, and it is telling, as in Lynda's case, that she is compelled continually to voice her impairment in explaining her (different) self.

On many occasions for disabled people the problem may be staring eyes,[12] often averted if the disabled person does try to make eye contact, alongside a pitying attitude towards someone's "imperfect" control of their bodily movements. Olive's experience of the gym is instructive:

> I go into the gym and I'm cumbersome moving from my chair to the machines and
> everything. You'll get certain people that will stare at you ... You'll get old ladies
> saying "what a shame," and you feel that you've got to be extra strong to put up with
> that. Nobody else would put up with that, they'd ... go up and say "what are you
> looking at, do you want a photograph?" (Olive, Scotland, in Hansen 2002, p. 137).

What can also happen is that pitying and patronising go hand-in-glove—Trudy (Scotland, in Hansen 2002, p. 143) complains about being constantly patted on the head: "I'm not a dog, don't pat me!"—fuelled by a chronic lack of expectation on the part of non-disabled people regarding the capacities of impaired bodies. It is largely assumed that the latter can achieve little by themselves: "I find ... that often in the general public, the expectation levels around the capacity of what a disabled woman or a disabled person is able to do are so limited" (Heather, Canada, in Hansen 2002, p. 141). An elision is made between physical and mental impairments, and Trudy (Scotland, in Hansen 2002, pp. 142–143) relates a chain of inferences made about her when she is out shopping, from "being in the wheelchair into somebody who was stupid," and she also recounts classic instances of non-disabled shop assistants asking if anyone is "with her" or talking very slowly to her, "like I was three." Reinforcing those of Lynda and Joanne, such experiences prompt the feeling of needing "to be extra strong" in order to combat the constant message that somehow "you" should not be there, that your mode of inhabiting the spaces in question—too clumsy, slow, spreading, sprawling, jerky—is plain wrong. What such a message effectively conveys, moreover, is underlying criticism of the different ways in which the impaired body occupies space and indeed time (a theme to which we now turn).

The Different Timings and Spacings of the Impaired Body

Understanding the embodied reality of disability in everyday life is crucial, and we need to ask about how the people concerned "notice" their impaired bodies when seeking to go about their daily business (going to work, attending classes, using shops, cinemas or parks, taking a child to the swings). Their embodied "art" of managing the time, space and speed realities of "doing" daily living demands more recognition than it usually receives, and Hansen's research furnishes detailed accounts wherein the most microscopic planning (of the timing and spacing) of (the seemingly most banal) activities is highlighted by her respondents. Examples to do with "domestic time and work space" (Hansen 2002, pp. 179–184) expose the complexity of simply getting up and preparing for a day at work or at classes:

> I usually have to get up at 6am to be ready and out the door at 7am to get my ride to work. It takes a lot of planning, I arrange what I'm going to wear the night before. I make my lunch, if I'm really organised the night before, and sometimes I have some of the clothes on [in bed] that I'm going to wear the next day, the night before, just to save me a bit of time in the morning (Heather, Canada, in Hansen 2002, p. 181).

> I have to go to bed really early, I have to rest as much as I can. I have to get up really early to get myself dressed and ready in time, and to be able to drive in the morning is quite difficult, as it's really painful driving in the morning, so I have to get up really early and get medicated really early on ... I waken [sic] up about 6.30am and take all the medication and I eat at 6.30,[13] and then I get up at 7.00am ... (Barbie, Scotland, in Hansen 2002, pp. 181–182).

These women underline the difficulties involved in deceptively straightforward activities such as dressing, which can eat up time for people with certain impairments, and—as in Barbie's case above—it is also evident that such activities, when hurried because of time constraints, can end up being painful and distressing. When this labour has to be combined with family duties, getting children up, washed, dressed, fed and off to school, which can be hard enough for non-disabled parents, then the time-space implications of being differently embodied are even more starkly revealed.

Hansen also recounts many examples of disabled people coping with the demands of "timing and spacing at work" (Hansen 2002, pp. 177–179; see also Pinder 1995; Freund 2001), exposing the "hidden geographies" (Dyck 1995) of small but deceptively important things such as the size of print, the positioning of furniture, the location of the toilets, the juxtaposition of offices, doorways, and so on. Spatial configurations relative to somebody's impairment are intimately connected to questions of temporality, since problematic spacings inevitably feed into people taking longer to complete activities than is "normal" or acceptable (to employers or colleagues). Thus:

> In the workplace ... [it] doesn't necessarily make those adjustments. I print out things larger ... it takes me longer to read things than ... normal people ... I have to make an adjustment for [my] eyes ... if people move things from me or they come at me too quickly, mostly a people interaction thing because I can adjust for stationary things ... People know not to move the garbage can in my office because I'm inevitably going to trip over it ... I don't have the eye-hand coordination that most people have because of the depth-perception issues, so when I'm drinking a cup of coffee I could slam the ... cup down and the next time I could miss it [the desk] completely ... (Candi, Canada, in Hansen 2002, p. 178).

> I certainly have sensed from early on that it probably isn't a level playing field in terms of some of the accommodations that I've needed. I often have to really persist, certainly in terms of getting a wheelchair-accessible washroom, it took about eight years for that to be completed. In terms of my office set-up, it's just a constant struggle to make sure that I have easy access to filing cabinets and assistance with portering, for example ... Your energy is being channelled in that area instead of, you know, being able to get back and do my work ... (Mary Lou, Canada, in Hansen 2002, p. 174).

Hansen's respondents relate a strong feeling of their only conditional acceptance in work, educational and other public settings, a phenomenon that she refers to as constantly being "on approval" (Hansen 2002, Chap. 8), which is all too frequently accompanied by a fear of *not* matching up to (ableist) expectations—by not being able to emulate the conduct of non-disabled counterparts in these settings—and of being in effect told to "go home" (being sacked, not having a contract renewed, failing exams and not being allowed to retake them).

Disabled people are often treated as though their way of doing things is disruptive to the "normal" speed, flow or circulation of people, commodities and capital because they "waste" more time and space than they should, maybe reducing profit margins.[14] Moving at a slow pace when boarding a train, bus or taxi or being slow in making a purchase acts as a hindrance to the "natural" rate of commerce:

> [T]hey [taxi-drivers] don't like taking disabled people in wheelchairs, they think we're a burden, and because a lot of us need the ramps down to get the wheelchair in, that makes it even worse because it takes longer ... so the longer they spend with you, the less money they are making ... So they tend to take their bad temper out on you and you get comments like, you'll go out ... on a rainy morning and they'll say, "why do disabled people want to come out in the rain anyway?" (Olive, Scotland, in Hansen 2002, p. 140).

The implications are arguably even more severe in the workplace itself when a disabled employee appears to be slowing down activity, thus being a drag on transactions, efficiency and productivity, debarring them from being the "fast subjects" demanded by the cutting-edge of capitalist enterprise (Thrift 2000). Audrey (Scotland, in Hansen 2002, p. 170) laments being "asked if [she] could type the same, as fast as the rest," while Camryn (Canada, in Hansen 2002, p. 170) talks about a constant sense of "feel[ing that] I'm under-performing ... that's not really anything that's said to me, that's just me, I do feel pressure." Various women remarked on feeling that they had to do *much more* than their non-disabled colleagues in order to be accepted as equals in the workplace, which could mean putting in more hours, completing more reports or thinking of more angles, just so that they avoid being regarded as "slow" workers (wherein "slow" can too easily become an assumption about mental as well as physical functioning). "I have to do my job twice as well to be seen as half as good," says Heather (Canada), while Stacey (Scotland, both in Hansen 2002, p. 170) confesses that "You feel that you have to prove yourself to be superhuman." It is possible to imagine the many knock-on effects for these individuals as they try even harder to cope with the timing and spacing of their embodied work tasks, the hope being that they can compensate for what they (are made to) feel are their deficiencies in this connection. At root, of course, the issue is that their different ways of doing things, the different spacings and timings of their embodied efforts at undertaking routine tasks in the workplace, homeplace or elsewhere, frequently remain unnoticed, under-valued or resented. Indeed, the differences here are often regarded as *in*sufficiently approximating what a supposedly "normal" person can achieve, irrespective of the fact that tasks do get completed, sometimes better than they would by a non-disabled person, but often at great cost to the ongoing physical and mental health of the people concerned.

Provisional Spaces; Corrected Bodies

Some societies more than others (see Komardjaja 2001) have begun to "accommodate" the "access" requirements of disabled people. Wheelchair ramps, accessible toilets, lifts (elevators), Braille signage and mini-coms (telephones accessible to deaf people) serve as visible signs of disability's growing place within the wider tracts of non-disabled space. The importance of these necessary accommodations in facilitating the physical access of disabled people into wider public places cannot be underestimated. What remains largely unrecognised, however, is that the terms of reference and the means of access have, as a rule, not been determined by disabled people but rather by non-disabled authorities. Governments spend large amounts of time and money counting, categorising and monitoring disabled people, documenting their differences (Titchkosky 2002), and yet the perspectives and experiences of disabled people in their own words—as in the previous sections of this paper—remain vastly unreported. Those disabled individuals who do speak out are often dismissed as "activists" or ignored, their opinions framed as anecdotal (Potts & Fido 1991; Michalko 2002b), and forms of access or accommodation that result from so-called "consultation" often remain tentative and superficial:

> Token efforts at cultural inclusion in many ways seem only to draw attention to the cultural absence of disabled women everywhere else. In the local spaces of everyday life, cultural practices contribute to oppressive living environments for disabled women. These practices include unsupportive professional and informal care-takers, invasive questioning by strangers, aversive reactions to the presence of the disabled in public spaces of various types and construction of local spaces which either exclude or segregate disabled users (e.g., government council chambers which lack disabled seating and sign language interpreters; local arenas and movie theatres which provide only segregated seating to wheelchair users) (Chouinard 1999, p. 151).

In short, there is an aversion to providing "space" for disabled people, and "reasonable accommodation" is often code for "minimum" as to nature, extent and cost in order that established speed, space and time patterns are not greatly disrupted (Kitchin 2000; Freund 2001; Michalko 2002a). This approach to disability appears as an add-on or an afterthought rather than as a *natural* or *automatic* part of the process, and economic viability remains at the forefront of decisions taken (Kerr & Shakespeare 2002). The spaces that are provided or modified in some way therefore remain distinctly provisional spaces, in which disabled people are "provisionally" allowed so long as they seek to inhabit, utilise and conduct themselves in these spaces as would a non-disabled person. They are indeed only there "on approval," to return to Hansen's phrase, and many disabled people once again feel "out of place," being left to explain or even to justify their presence under the most mundane of circumstances.

Accompanying the modifying of spaces, there is also a (far from tokenistic) approach that strives to "correct" the disabled body, to produce corrected bodies that fit in with the existing shapes and expectations of non-disabled space. Examples include everything from crutches and wheelchairs to artificial limbs (prostheses) and the promise of computerised inserts to make limbs and senses do what they cannot now do. In this respect, there is a "colonising" approach toward the impaired body, in that it becomes a site for interventions designed to convert it into something acceptable to the "colonising" power (non-disabled society). In the possible belief that the approximation of certain degrees of "able" can be engineered for disabled people, normalising or corrective measures are often presented as a "civilising" influence ostensibly for the betterment of the individuals at whom it is directed.[15] Here "civilising" equates with being able to fit in with expected comportments and time-space patterns of conduct, with medical intervention commonly perceived as the "civilising" agent (Hughes 2002) and those disabled individuals perceived as acquiring greater degrees of "ablebodiedness" being more readily accepted by the majority (at least in certain contexts: Michalko 2002a; Price & Shildrick 2002).

This situation is hardly straightforward, however, in that some technological adaptations comprise, as mentioned, visible stigmata that—so it is thought—a disabled person would happily discard if possible. Yet, for those individuals using these devices, they may provide mobility, freedom and independence, and it may even be an act of minor resistance to *continue* using them because doing so transparently singles out their conduct in the world as departing from non-disabled norms. One of Hansen's respondents speaks about the liberation that she feels in her wheelchair, thereby turning commonly held perceptions on their head:

> I started using a wheelchair ... because it was starting to be a real struggle getting in and out of the flat ... trying to balance on two sticks. I actually feel somewhat liberated having a wheelchair, although I have to plan where I'm going, making sure it's accessible, making sure there will be someone there to help me if I need it; and I can put my wheelchair in and out of the car if I absolutely have to but sometimes I don't feel like it, and I get help, so it has to be planned. But certainly in some ways I sometimes feel that developing a disability has allowed me to be more the person I really can be, because it's forced me to be more assertive. (Bev, Scotland, in Hansen 2002, p. 145)

Detailed body-knowledge arising here from "within" contests the corrected body approach, and may suggest quite other ways of responding to bodily difference, even to the point of assertively valorising the positive dimensions of being impaired and conducting life in harmony with, not kicking against, an embodied impairment.[16] Heather's case is similar, and shows an individual embracing not a wheelchair but crutches, not as a means to approximate non-disabled norms of movement but simply because crutches better served her goal of getting around for the purposes of living, working and "getting by":

> I remember when I was twelve I said ... "look I'm not going to walk the way other people do, but that doesn't mean I'm not going to get around, and that's OK"; and that was it ... I gave up practising to walk without my crutches because I knew that walking with crutches was a lot more comfortable for me, and it was OK with me,

and it gave me a lot more independence; and when I was walking *without* crutches I always felt that I ... looked like Quasimodo, which was not too cool (Heather, Canada, in Hansen, 2002, p. 136; emphasis added).

Tellingly, Heather refuses to pass as non-disabled, a decision that has actually enabled her to gain *greater* self-esteem, despite what non-disabled society might expect (i.e., that the more one can pass as non-disabled, the better one will feel about oneself).

Trudy's experience is also worth referencing, since it entails another form of resistance to the tyrannies of both the corrected body and the impulsion to pass as non-disabled:

> I'm supposed to try and walk as straight as I can, but that's because that's the normal way to walk, not because it will benefit me, so I did that for about a year and really struggled and when I finally asked ... "is there a purpose for me in walking like this?", they actually told me, "no it's just that's the way I should walk" ... So now ... I do a sideways walk, [my son] calls it my "crab walk," so I just walk like that and hang onto the walls, and I take quite a lot of seats ... but I've sort of adapted my way around (Trudy, Scotland, in Hansen 2002, p. 136).

Trudy's description of her motion illustrates a creative use of timings (lack of speed) and spacings (lateral movements and occupying "a lot of seats") that works for her. Like Heather, she has deployed her expert knowledge of her unique body, creating a distinctive style of personal embodiment, her "crab walk," which best conforms with her own requirements even if flouting standard practice. What these latter materials imply, moreover, is a rather different way of living with an impaired body, precisely not striving to "flatten it out" into a pale imitation of how non-disabled bodies look, move and do things.

Discussion: The Normality of Doing Things Differently?

Following from what has been written so far, the concluding argument is that disability geography (and disability studies more generally) is moving towards new ways of addressing the realities of the impaired body set within non-disabled space. In short, we must force ourselves to rethink the ways in which disabled people—in fact, all people, disabled or non-disabled—occupy worldly spaces of all kinds. Disabled people themselves can (and should) be consulted for fresh perspectives on how to "map" this thoroughly spatialised bodily terrain. Thus:

> [D]isabled women can build strength and determination to continue to fight for spaces in everyday life in which differences such as disability are not viewed as something to be "corrected" and avoided, but as part of the spectrum of human experiences that enrich all of our journeys through life and society (Chouinard 1999, p. 155).[17]

There is no magic solution, but we must confront the question about how much more could be accomplished if disabled people were better able to make their way in the world on their own terms. Much of their energy is spent trying to gain the "right" of passage; to cope with the negative attitudes, the poorly arranged surroundings, the constant fear of being "on approval" in non-disabled space: surely, much *more* could be achieved if this energy were expended in other, less negative ways.

These remarks are not supposed to deny that many disabled people encounter difficulties and hardships in living with their impaired bodies, certainly when fitting them into non-disabled space, and nor is it to deny that there is often a great deal of discomfort, fatigue, pain and attendant emotional states—despair, anger, regret—wrapped up in the normality of disabled existence (but the *same* is surely true for all of "us," whatever our physical or mental states). As a society, we have yet to develop a comfort level associated with impairment, fatigue and pain that ventures much beyond avoidance. Indeed, pivotal to what Michalko (2002a, esp. Chaps. 3 and 4), Wendell (1996) and others are writing is the need to attend to "suffering" in the lives of disabled people, but without the story being *solely* about "tragedy" which leaves no space for seeing—and perhaps empathising with—what it is that disabled people actually get on with doing. "[W]e must ... talk about how to live with the suffering body, with that which cannot be negotiated without pain, and that which cannot be celebrated without ambivalence," argues Wendell (1996, p. 179), but at the same time she calls for "a new concept of transcendence 'with body', which would involve feeling and knowing our connection to other lives, human history and society" (Wendell 1996, p. 178). What this implies is a sophisticated position that does not stop at accounts of bodily difference, difficulty and suffering, certainly not individualised accounts, but instead imagines a sustained dialogue between all sorts of people with all sorts of bodies—one might say a "conversation" of all humankind—wherein the normality of very different ways of human being, doing, relating and place-making is uppermost.

In this proposal, the realities of impaired bodies as experienced must be centralised, but always in a fashion rendering such realities as "extraordinarily ordinary." The issue becomes someone going about their business, and perhaps having to make adjustments that are greater than is true of some other people, but still on the same spectrum as what "we" *all* have to do in order to achieve anything. As one of Hansen's respondents puts it:

> To negotiate ableism, I think it's because people didn't understand, and I think that's the problem with the outside world, they don't understand what disability is, it doesn't mean that everything about you and your life and your head is disabled. I mean we've been given the wrong label, "disabled", it makes you sound as if there's something terribly wrong and I don't think there's anything wrong with disability, I ... see myself as getting around differently, I can't use my legs, so I use wheels, it's that simple (Trudy, Scotland, in Hansen 2002, pp. 181–182).

Part of the problem is that the disabled body cannot easily be the "ordinary body-of-functions" demanded by the capitalist West, and so it is entirely unsurprising to find many accounts couched in terms of how difficult it is for disabled people to cope with the things that they are expected to do by non-disabled society. What Michalko (2002a, esp. pp. 173–175) stresses, though, is the predominance of a "mimetic" model, wherein the focus alights upon the success or failure of disabled people in "imitating normality." What he proposes instead is an emphasis on the "ordinariness" of trying to do things, even if said things might be done differently in the process, perhaps more clumsily or slowly, with "unusual" body movements or using "unexpected" sensory cues. Hence, the focus should be less on disabled people striving to do things "normally," whatever that might actually mean, and much more on the simple, wholly unexceptional *normality of doing things differently*, and acknowledging, tolerating and maybe even (cautiously) celebrating the many and hugely varied ways in which things can be done. Intriguingly, Michalko (2002a, pp. 173–174) speculates that a heightened acceptance of this normality of doing things differently by disabled people comprises a thinking *with* disability, not just *about* it: one that might then assist in "mak[ing] a place for disability" with the capacity to disrupt "those places ready-made—usually by non-disabled others—for disabled people."

"I don't think there's anything wrong with disability, I ... see myself as getting around differently, I can't use my legs, so I use wheels, it's that simple": this is what Trudy says, and it stands as a mini-manifesto for us at the close of this chapter. It squares with Freund's (2001, p. 704) insistence that we need to envisage many more "spatial-motional-material possibilities" for accommodating bodily difference, and in the process to embark upon "many unexplored 'avenues' for comfortably accommodating a wide range of mind-bodies." This chapter nonetheless stirs in a crucial qualifier in helping to smooth through Freund's vision, and also as a further strand in the politically astute perspective of reframing disability politics suggested by the likes of DePoy & Gilson (2003). This qualifier is a deceptively simple insistence on registering the multitude of ways in which different bodies do (and can do) things differently. To our thinking, accommodationist agendas must be alert to such differences in the doing of things, treating the range here as wholly normal, and resisting banal assessments of "right" and "wrong" ways to get things done. Such a vision might herald a more fully fledged practice-based rather than narrowly function-based approach to the meeting of disability and environmental "design," one convened in recognition of the sheer diversity of practices—sometimes elegant and dextrous but sometimes awkward and cumbersome—integral to how humans of all kinds go about the doing of things in the world. Central to this vision is the proclamation that: "Imperfection is the essence of being organic and alive. Cardboard ideals of perfection are flat and pale by comparison" (Tollifson 1998, p. 106).

Endnotes

1   The social model has been most clearly articulated with reference to physical disability, and this chapter is primarily concerned with physical disability. Issues to do with "mental disability," including different strands of both mental ill-health ("mental illness") and intellectual disability ("mental handicap") are related, but not identical, and Beresford (2004, p. 219) suggests that we await the proper development of "a 'social model' of madness and distress."

2   At various points in what follow we will talk of *the* impaired body, in the singular, but we are well aware of the near-infinity of possible shapes, sizes, capacities, etc., of *real* impaired bodies.

3   Tellingly, Freund (2001) is influenced by disability geography, quoting Gleeson and Kitchin, and in effect he is importing ideas from disability geography back into disability studies, exposing the latter to new thinking about "bodies, disability and spaces."

4   There is a closely related literature on the geographies of chronic illness (e.g., Moss & Dyck 2005; Crooks & Chouinard 2006), wherein the complex entanglings of society, space and (the embodied effects of) illness are subject to sustained inquiry.

5   Dorn (1998) is particularly interested in those individuals such as the disabled activist, designer and architect Patty Hayes who are vocal-practical-political "dissidents," actively disputing the "disabling" built and social environment with which they are confronted. Many if not all disabled people are more everyday "dissidents," perhaps not as overtly politicised but still in effect "embodying" a political charge in how they are forced into "doing things differently" on a regular basis. This paper will exemplify precisely this point.

6   See also Worth (2005, pp. 21–24), who discusses the rise of what she here calls a "biosocial model," showing how contributions by scholars from both disability studies and human geography have fed into this development.

7   While Hansen was particularly concerned with the experiences of disabled women, bridging between disability studies and feminist theories, the gender dimension is of limited moment for the present paper. We suspect that similar findings would emerge for disabled men, although it is possible that they might be less troubled by the disjunctions under review, maybe feeling more empowered to be assertive of their "rights" to do things differently.

8   We could have developed a more theorised account of "performing" disability, maybe borrowing from the likes of Goffman, Butler and various works on performative geographies, but for the purposes of this chapter we stick with a straightforward discussion in which terms like "performance," "conduct" and "comportment" remain close to their everyday usage.

9   On occasion, it may be the use of such implements that "betrays" somebody's impairment, since many impairments are "invisible" to the immediate gaze, only becoming apparent through a person's dependence upon technologies of one form or another to enable their "normal" everyday conduct.

10 All names are pseudonyms.

11 Joanne has aphasia, which entails difficulties in understanding or "producing" speech as a result of brain damage.

12 Pain *et al.* (2001, p. 178) talk about the shift from "stairs" to "stares" in researching disability: i.e., from focusing on physical accessibility (how to deal with the obstacle of stairs) to considering social acceptability (how to deal with the intrusion of prying stares).

13 Some medication must be taken with food to prevent stomach damage.

14 Here we gesture to the historical-materialist critique of Gleeson (1998, 1999), who stresses how capitalist time-work disciplines, expectations and indeed contractual obligations so obviously militate against many disabled people whose impaired bodies simply cannot be made to "run" in accordance with such capitalist demands.

15 This is another manifestation of disabled people being perceived as sub-human in much the same way as "Aboriginal" peoples the world over have often been regarded as sub-human "savages" needing the Western "civilising" influence.

16 We are conscious of the dangers of recreating a kind of "heroic" narrative, but we feel that what is occurring here is rather different; it is not about "heroic" efforts against the odds to be just like a "normal" person, to do things "normally," but rather about individuals celebrating living with (not struggling against) their impairment. At the same time, though, we are wary of overplaying this argument, recognising that for many disabled people, perhaps especially those with acquired impairments, there will be regret, resentment and some measure of mourning for the lost non-impaired body. It would be wrong of us to suggest that all disabled people should be "comfortable" with, let alone celebratory of, their different bodies; just as it would be wrong to demand that any/all of "us" suddenly become "comfortable in our own skins."

17 The extent to which Chouinard would extend the same argument to disabled men is uncertain, and Hansen's own research did concentrate exclusively on disabled women; however, for the purposes of this chapter, the principle must be that the same argument can be so extended, even if we realise that the exact details of life as timed, spaced and voiced by disabled men will likely vary in important ways from those for disabled women.

References

Abberley, P. (1987), The Concept of Oppression and the Development of a Social Model of Disability. *Disability, Handicap and Society* 2, pp. 5–19.

Anderson, C. A. (2001), Claiming Disability in the Field of Geography: Access, Recognition and Integration. *Social and Cultural Geography* 2, pp. 87–93.

Barnes, C. & G. Mercer, eds. (2004a), *Implementing the Social Model of Disability: Theory and Practice.* Leeds: Disability Press.

Barnes, C. & G. Mercer (2004b), Theorising and Researching Disability from a Social Model Perspective. *In:* C. Barnes & G. Mercer, eds., *Implementing the Social Model of Disability: Theory and Practice,* pp. 1–17. Leeds: Disability Press.

Beresford, P. (2004), Madness, Distress, Research and a Social Model. *In:* C. Barnes & G. Mercer, eds., *Implementing the Social Model of Disability: Theory and Practice,* pp. 208–222. Leeds: Disability Press.

Butler, R. E. (1994), Geography and Vision-Impaired and Blind Populations. *Transactions of the Institute of British Geographers* 19, pp. 366–368.

Butler, R. E. & S. Bowlby (1997), Bodies and Spaces: An Exploration of Disabled People's Experiences of Public Space. *Environment and Planning D: Society and Space* 15, pp. 411–433.

Butler, R. & H. Parr, eds. (1999), *Mind and Body Spaces: Geographies of Illness, Impairment and Disability.* London: Routledge.

Canadian Geographer (2003), Theme Issue on Disability in Society and Space. *The Canadian Geographer* 47, pp. 383–508.

Chouinard, V. (1997), Making Space for Disabling Difference: Challenges to Ableist Geographies. *Environment and Planning D: Society and Space* 15, pp. 379–387.

Chouinard, V. (1999), Life at the Margins: Disabled Women's Explorations of Ableist Spaces. *In:* E. K. Teather, ed., *Embodied Geographies: Spaces, Bodies and Rites of Passage,* pp. 142–156. London: Routledge.

Corker, M. & T. Shakespeare (2002), Mapping the Terrain. *In:* M. Corker & T. Shakespeare, eds., *Disability/Postmodernity: Embodying Disability Theory,* pp. 1–7. London: Continuum.

Crooks, V. A. & V. Chouinard (2006), An Embodied Geography of Disablement: Chronically Ill Women's Struggles for Enabling Places in Spaces of Health Care and Daily Life. *Health and Place* 12, pp. 345–352.

Depoy, E. & S. F. Gilson (2004), *Rethinking Disability: Principles for Professional and Social Change.* Belmont, CA: Brook/Cole.

Disability Studies Quarterly (2001), Theme Issue on Disability Geography. *Disability Studies Quarterly* 21, pp. 1–134.

Disability Studies Quarterly (2004), Theme Issue on Disability Geography. *Disability Studies Quarterly* 24, pp. 313–444.

Dorn, M. (1994), Disability as Spatial Dissidence: A Cultural Geography of the Stigmatised Body. (MA thesis, University of Pennsylvania).

Dorn, M. (1998), Beyond Nomadism: The Travel Narratives of a "Cripple." *In:* H. J. Nast & S. Pile, eds., *Places through the Body,* pp. 183–206. London: Routledge.

Dyck, I. (1995), Hidden Geographies: The Changing Lifeworlds of Women with Multiple Sclerosis. *Social Science and Medicine* 40, pp. 307–320.

Environment and Planning D: Society and Space (1997), Theme Issue on Geographies of Disability. *Environment and Planning D: Society and Space* 15, pp. 379–480.

Freund, P. (2001), Bodies, Disability and Spaces: The Social Model and Disabling Spatial Organisations. *Disability and Society* 16, pp. 689–706.

Gant, R. & J. Smith (1990), Feet First in Kingston Town Centre: A Study of Personal Mobility. *Kingston Polytechnic, School of Geography, Kingston Accessibility Studies, Working Paper No. 2.*

Gant, R. & J. Smith (1991), The Elderly and Disabled in Rural Areas: Travel Patterns in the North Cotswolds. *In*: A. Champion & C. Watkins, eds., *People in the Countryside: Studies of Social Change in Rural Britain*, pp. 108–124. London: Paul Chapman.

Gleeson, B. (1993), Second Nature: The Socio-Spatial Production of Disability. (PhD thesis, University of Melbourne).

Gleeson, B. (1996), A Geography for Disabled People. *Transactions of the Institute of British Geographers* 21, pp. 387–396.

Gleeson, B. (1998), Justice and the Disabling City. *In*: R. Fincher & J. M. Jacobs, eds., *Cities of Difference*, pp. 89–119. New York: Guilford Press.

Gleeson, B. (1999), *Geographies of Disability*. London: Routledge.

Golledge, R. G. (1991), Special Populations in Contemporary Urban Areas. *In*: J. F. Hart, ed., *Our Changing Cities*, pp. 146–169. Baltimore, MD: The Johns Hopkins University Press.

Golledge, R. G. (1993), Geography and the Disabled: A Survey with Special Reference to Vision-Impaired and Blind Populations. *Transactions of the Institute of British Geographers* 18, pp. 63–85.

Golledge, R. G. (1996), A Response to Gleeson and Imrie. *Transactions of the Institute of British Geographers* 21, pp. 404–411.

Golledge, R. G. (1997), On Reassembling One's Life: Overcoming Disability in Its Academic Environment. *Environment and Planning D: Society and Space* 15, pp. 391–409.

Hahn, H. (1986), Disability and the Urban Environment: A Perspective on Los Angeles. *Environment and Planning D: Society and Space* 4, pp. 273–288.

Hahn, H. (1989), Disability and the Reproduction of Bodily Images: The Dynamics of Human Appearances. *In*: J. Wolch & M. Dear, eds., *The Power of Geography: How Territory Shapes Social Life*, pp. 370–388. London: Unwin Hyman.

Hall, E. (2000), "Blood, Brain and Bones": Taking the Body Seriously in the Geography of Health and Impairment. *Area* 32, pp. 21–29.

Hansen, N. E. (2002), "Passing" through Other People's Spaces: Disabled Women, Geography and Work. (PhD thesis, University of Glasgow).

Hawkesworth, M. (2001), Disabling Spatialities and the Regulation of a Visible Secret. *Urban Studies* 38, pp. 299–318.

Hughes, B. (2002), Disability and the Body. *In*: C. Barnes, M. Oliver & L. Barton, eds., *Disability Studies Today*, pp. 58–76. Cambridge: Polity Press.

Hughes, B. & K. Paterson (1997), The Social Model of Disability and the Disappearing Body: Towards a Sociology of Impairments. *Disability and Society* 12, pp. 325–340.

PART V: Education, Technology, and Work

Imrie, R. (1996a), *Disability and the City: International Perspectives*. London: Paul Chapman.

Imrie, R. F. (1996b), Ableist Geographers, Disablist Spaces: Towards a Reconstruction of Golledge's "Geography and the Disabled." *Transactions of the Institute of British Geographers* 21, pp. 397–403.

Imrie, R. & P. Wells (1993), Disablism, Planning and the Built Environment. *Environment and Planning C: Government and Policy* 11, pp. 213–231.

Kerr, A. & T. Shakespeare (2002), *Genetic Politics: From Eugenics to Genome*. Cheltenham: New Clarion Press.

Kitchin, R. (1998), Out of Place, Knowing One's Place: Space, Power and the Exclusion of Disabled People. *Disability and Society* 13, pp. 343–356.

Kitchin, R. (2000), *Disability, Space and Society*. Sheffield: Geographical Association.

Kitchin, R. (2001), Using Participatory Action Research Approaches in Geographical Studies of Disability: Some Reflections. *Disability Studies Quarterly* 21, pp. 15–34.

Komardjaja, I. (2001), New Cultural Geographies of Disability: Asian Values and the Accessibility Ideal. *Social and Cultural Geography* 2, pp. 77–86.

Kruse II, R. J. (2002), Social Spaces of Little People: The Experiences of the Jamisons. *Social and Cultural Geography* 3, pp. 175–190.

Kruse II, R. J. (2003), Narrating Intersections of Gender and Dwarfism in Everyday Spaces. *The Canadian Geographer* 47, pp. 494–508.

Leroi, A. M. (2003), *Mutants: On the Form, Varieties and Errors of the Human Body*. London: HarperCollins.

Longhurst, R. (1994), The Geography Closest in—the Body ... the Politics of Pregnability. *Australian Geographical Studies* 32, pp. 214–223.

Longhurst, R. (2001), *Bodies: Exploring Fluid Boundaries*. London: Routledge.

Matthews, M. H. & P. Vujakovic (1995), Private Worlds and Public Places: Mapping the Environmental Values of Wheelchair Users. *Environment and Planning A* 27, pp. 1069–1083.

Mcfarlane, H. (2005), Disabled Women and Socio-Spatial "Barriers" to Motherhood. (PhD thesis, University of Glasgow).

Michalko, R. (2002a), *The Difference That Disability Makes*. Philadelphia, PN: Temple University Press.

Michalko, R. (2002b), Estranged Familiarity. *In*: M. Corker & T. Shakespeare, eds., *Disability/ Postmodernity: Embodying Disability Theory*, pp. 175–183. London: Continuum.

Moss, P. & I. Dyck (2003), *Women, Body, Illness: Space and Identity in the Everyday Lives of Women with Chronic Illness*. Lanham, MD: Roman and Littlefield.

Oliver, M. (1990), *The Politics of Disablement*. London: Macmillan.

Oliver, M. (1996), *Understanding Disability: From Theory to Practice*. London: Macmillan.

Pain, R., M. Barke, D. Fuller, J. Gough, R. Macfarlane & G. Mowl (2001), *Introducing Social Geographies*. London: Arnold.

Park, D. C., J. P. Radford & H. H. Vickers (1998), Disability Studies in Geography. *Progress in Human Geography* 22, pp. 208–222.

Parr, H. (2007), *Social Space and Mental Health*. London: Blackwell.

Parr, H. & R. Butler (1999), New Geographies of Illness, Impairment and Disability. *In*: R. Butler & H. Parr, eds., *Mind and Body Spaces: Geographies of Illness, Impairment and Disability*, pp. 1–24. London: Routledge.

268

Pinder, R. (1995), Bringing the Body Back without the Blame? The Experience of Ill and Disabled People at Work. *Sociology of Health and Illness* 17, pp. 605–631.

Potts, M. & R. Fido (1991), *A Fit Person to Be Removed: Personal Accounts of Life in a Mental Institution*. Plymouth: Northcote House.

Price, J. & M. Shildrick (2002), Bodies Together: Touch, Ethics and Disability. *In*: M. Corker & T. Shakespeare, eds., *Disability/Postmodernity: Embodying Disability Theory*, pp. 62–79. London: Continuum.

Shakespeare, T. & N. Watson (1997), Defending the Social Model. *Disability and Society* 12, pp. 293–300.

Silvers, A. (2002), The Crooked Timber of Humanity: Disability Ideology and the Aesthetic. *In*: M. Corker & T. Shakespeare, eds., *Disability/Postmodernity: Embodying Disability Theory*, pp. 228–244. London: Continuum.

Thrift, N. (2000), Performing Cultures in the New Economy. *Annals of the Association of American Geographers* 90, pp. 674–692.

Titchkosky, T. (2002), Cultural Maps: Which Way to Disability? *In*: M. Corker & T. Shakespeare, eds., *Disability/Postmodernity: Embodying Disability Theory*, pp. 101–111. London: Continuum.

Tollifson, J. (1997), Imperfection Is a Beautiful Thing: On Disability and Meditation. *In*: K. Fries, ed., *Staring Back: Disability from the inside out*, pp. 105–122. New York: Plume.

Urban Studies (2001), Theme Issue on the Barrier-Free City (Disability and Urban Space). *Urban Studies* 38, pp. 231–376.

Valentine, G. (2001), *Social Geographies: Space and Society*. Harlow: Pearson Education.

Vujakovic, P. & M. H. Matthews (1994), Contorted, Folded, Torn: Environmental Values, Cartographic Representation and the Politics of Disability. *Disability and Society* 9, pp. 359–374.

Watson, N. (2004), The Dialectics of Disability: A Social Model for the Twenty-First Century. *In*: C. Barnes & G. Mercer, eds., *Implementing the Social Model of Disability: Theory and Practice*, pp. 101–117. Leeds: Disability Press.

Wendell, S. (1996), *The Rejected Body: Feminist Philosophical Reflections on Disability*. London: Routledge.

Worth, N. M. (2005), Current Discussions in Geographies of Disability. (MA thesis, University of Toronto).

CHAPTER 17

Disability, Marginality, and the Nation-State— Negotiating Social Markers of Difference:

Fahimeh's Story

Parin Dossa

Testimonial narratives of racialized women with disabilities bring into relief subjugated knowledge that reveal how the state constitutes and is reconstituted at the margins. Fahimeh's case example, drawn from a larger study on immigrant Muslim women in metropolis Vancouver, shows how women resist and rework the stigmatized labels of disability and race from their social locations at the margins. Our analysis of particular events and critical episodes show how Fahimeh, speaking in a collective voice, implicates the state to bring home the message that racialized persons with disabilities are human. Their humanness (desire for a just world) is affirmed through blurring of boundaries of the private and the public, and everyday life and state institutions. Fahimeh's testimonial shows that margins are not merely territorial; they are sites of practice that point to the makings of a just world.

Introduction

The state-of-the-art literature on disability calls for a paradigm shift from the disabled body to a disabling society. Demolition of social barriers, it is argued, would allow persons with disabilities to live "normally," which, according to a liberal democratic society, amounts to being productive and autonomous. While acknowledging the importance of this momentous shift, critiques have suggested three points of intervention (Butler & Parr, 1999; Corker & French, 1999; Kittay, 2001; Rapp & Ginsburg, 2001). First, an exclusive focus on disabling society renders invisible the lived reality of an impaired (different) body. Commenting on the workings of a centralist state with its long arm of legislation, Stiker notes that persons with disabilities "are designated so as to disappear, they are named so as to go unmentioned" (cf. Whyte & Ingstad, 1995, p. 8). Second, the social model of disability excludes persons with severe disabilities whose point of reference is not the market economy but sociality. Disability advocates have argued that the model of citizenship advanced by liberal democracies is limiting. Other than its fixation on rationality, independence and market productivity, liberalism does not valorize an alternative conception of personhood, as Kittay has expressed it. "We do not become a person without the engagement of other persons—their care, as well as the recognition of the uniqueness and the connectedness of our human agency, and the distinctiveness of our particularly human relations to others and of the world we fashion" (2001, p. 568).

Our third point of intervention comes from the work of racialized women with disabilities and their advocates. These women have argued that liberal democracies, with their normative and restrictive criteria of personhood, exclude markers of difference based on race, gender, class and disability (Bannerji, 1995; Razack, 1998; Thobani, 1999; Dua, 1999; Dossa, 2004). The process of exclusion is paradoxical: racialized women are desirable for their low-paid work in the lower echelons of the market economy. This form of exploitative "inclusion" requires that they be kept in their place (Othered) to sustain a labour pool (Creese, 1992). But Othering and marginalization are the very processes through which liberal democracies define their identities. Dualism of us and them, and the private and the public are integral to these democracies (Bannerji, 1993). Liberal democracies are then inclusive at one level and exclusive at another level. This contradiction creates in-between spaces where possibilities of progressive change may be explored.

Structural exclusion of racialized women with disabilities is more acute on account of the fact that they bear multiple markers of negative difference. They are not perceived to be productive members of society even at the lower echelons of the labour market. The role of a mother, a wife or a worker is not attributed to women with disabilities (Fine & Asch, 1988). They are relegated to the margins and rendered socially invisible. But margins must not be dismissed as being of no value.

Margins are commonly conceived of as a site where two scripts unfold: the workings of a liberal democratic state and its simultaneous undoing. This dynamic noted in the work of Das and Poole (2004) includes a third dimension revealing how women (and men) claim citizenship status and struggle for their rights. This dimension is not easily revealed; it is embedded in the nooks and crannies of everyday life and within spaces that are not evident. In their work on disabled women in New Delhi, Das and Addlakha (2001), for example, argue "that claims to membership and belonging within the [liberal] state may be enacted in everyday life in all kinds of dispersed sites" (2001, p. 512). One such site is domesticity. They note that domesticity along with kinship is narratively performed and it is through this act of performance that family members (the body-selves) break open the boundaries of the domestic world to engage with the state and its institutions.

Discourse on rights and social entitlements may then be looked at in-between the spaces of the domestic and the public.

In this chapter, I focus on the narrative account of a Canadian woman from Iran. My goal is to provide an example of how state institutions appropriate and are reconstituted at the margins. To document this process, where new imaginings and possibilities may be identified, I draw upon the narrative of one woman, Fahimeh. The narrative comes from a larger study on the everyday lives of Muslim women with disabilities in metropolis Vancouver, Canada.

Fahimeh's life spans two nation-states: Iran and Canada. At work are complex responses that emerge from in-between spaces, a site where both selective resistance and compliance to dominant norms and practices occur. It is important to note that gender is not a discrete unit of analysis. It is cross-cut by class, race, disability and other markers of difference. This cross-cutting requires a close reading of the lived reality of people, best captured through a focus on one woman (Dossa, 2004; also refer to Frank, 2000). Furthermore, a life story is at once personal and political, biographical and historical—a point noted by feminist ethnographers (Scheper-Hughes, 1992; Ong, 1999). A story then can assume a testimonial form that is politically charged. It is in this spirit that I present Fahimeh's story. Her story, like those of other women, spans the North–South divide, highlighting the different ways in which social markers of difference play out in particular contexts. It is important to note that in "a transnational postcolonial context, women struggle with new meanings attached to ethnicity, citizenship status and religion" (Collins, 2000, p. 9). Of interest are the intricate ways in which gender, class, race and disability converge to tell a larger story of oppression and progressive change. Fahimeh's narrative engages with the social construction of difference, state policy, social service provision or the lack of it as well as reconstitution of lives on the margins/borderlands, understood as a site of practice.

The Study

Fahimeh's story is among 16 that I had the privilege of hearing over the course of my field research (1992–2001) with two immigrant communities: East African and Iranian in metropolis Vancouver. Contacts with the two communities were established through grassroots level organizations and through networking. The women ranged in age from 25 years to 55 years. All the women except one were unmarried. None of the women were employed at the time of the study. Participants were interviewed two to four times in their homes or in cafeterias. Interview schedules included storytelling and semi-structured interviews, both of which reveal women's own experiences in the context of social, historical and economic relations. Each interview was about two hours long. I have not attempted to separate the narrative data from my interpretive analysis. To do so would have weakened our shared goal of "imagining alternative ways of thinking that will generate less oppressive relations" (Collins, 2000, p. 7).

The dilemma of voice has been addressed in the works of feminist scholars, largely from non-Western traditions. Occupying insider/outsider positions of being colonized and immersed in the dominant system, discursively and in practice, these scholars have put forward the analytical framework of situated knowledge. This means that we begin with the particular and explore its complex links with structural factors: political, social and economic. This process is carried out in collaboration with research participants, with a shared understanding of working towards social justice and equality. Our cognizance of unequal relations of power between the researcher and the research participants has led to a reflexive approach, requiring vigilance on two fronts. That we do not appropriate the voices of our participants in as much as this is possible—this remains a problematic issue—and at the same time we highlight structures of inequality using research tools at hand. It is this stance that has led me to blend research participants' takes on particular situations with my interpretations. This approach is not devoid of limitations as it carries possibilities of voice-appropriation. As Ong (1995) and Collins (2000) have argued, this problematic should not lead us to abdicate our responsibilities to interpret the data and provide larger contexts so that we can begin to address issues of structural inequalities.

My work on racialized Muslim women with disabilities is not from a distance. I was born and bred in Uganda. During the Asian exodus (1972), my brother was left behind on the grounds that the psychiatrist considered him as unfit for travel. He was diagnosed as "mentally challenged." He died a premature death resulting from lack of care. Furthermore, my work at a research institute on rehabilitation of developmentally disabled people in Alberta (1988–1991) brought home the multiple ways in which women, especially racialized women with disabilities, were rendered invisible. These two experiences have provided the impetus for this research.

Fahimeh is 50 years old and she joined her husband in Canada in 1991, along with her two sons. The couple's two older children (aged 18 and over) have remained in Iran owing to immigration restrictions. Fahimeh's leg was amputated in early childhood as a result of a car accident. The core of her story revolves around her struggle with and negotiation of her life in disabling settings in Iran and in Canada, respectively.

Telling Her Story[1]

> I was coming home from school when a car was reversing and hit my right leg. I did not feel anything at that moment and I just went home. I told my Mom what had happened. I had my dinner and I slept through the night. But from next day, I could not walk. My parents were not poor but they had not many resources, like a car. However, my Mom took me to a doctor who said that my leg nerve system was damaged and I should go to the hospital in Tehran to be examined closer.

In her account, Fahimeh reveals the contours of everyday life: going to school, eating dinner and going to sleep, aspects that we do not question unless they are subject to disruption. Probing of this reality makes us realize that discrete phenomena are indeed embedded in socio-economic and political contexts. The challenge here is to establish connections between the lived reality and the system. This is a difficult task as the system does not acknowledge its complicity in putting into place an ideology and practice that systematically disadvantages people on the margins.

Fahimeh's marginal (used interchangeably with "borderlands") location comes to light at the time of the accident. The rural residence of her family means that she does not have access to the urban-based infrastructure of services, a peculiarity of the Western model of development. Although Iran was not formally colonized, it was not free of longstanding Western intervention, owing to the country's rich oil resource (Sullivan, 1998). The fact that there was a hospital in the city and not in the fishing village where Fahimeh lived is paradoxical: not only are rural people deprived of the "benefits" of development—benefits that come at a cost—but they are internally displaced. This is because development projects undermine their subsistence base. Hence, at the time of the accident, Fahimeh's family was barely surviving. The larger scenario of lack explains why Fahimeh had to go to Tehran for treatment, but not without consequences.

Delay in getting to the hospital worsened her condition. Once in the hospital, her recovery was compromised because of the geographical distance between her home and the hospital. Over her two-year stay, "[m]y parents could only come once every six months. Doctors and nurses were my visitors. I had to stay in the hospital as we were far from the countryside so they did not have the budget to bring me back and forth." Upon her return to the fishing village, Fahimeh fell down. She was re-hospitalized. Owing to an overdose of anaesthetic, she went into a coma for a year and a half.

When Fahimeh returned home, she was not well accepted by her family. Not wanting to remain a passive victim of circumstances, Fahimeh decided to take matters into her own hands, taking one step at a time. First, she took up what was most readily available to her and that was sewing. This activity served two purposes: it helped Fahimeh to earn some money and it was therapeutic: "When I came back home, I had to control my shaking hands so I tried to learn sewing in order to control my hands. I wanted to learn sewing." Reflecting on her experience of how she taught herself to stitch and later embroider, Fahimeh said: "It was hard but I tried to help myself. I felt somehow that it was up to me to help myself, otherwise I would be a burden on my family." It is important to note how Fahimeh blurs the boundary between therapy and work, otherwise considered separate.

Fahimeh took the second step during the visit of a family friend from Tehran. This friend suggested that she could go to Tehran and work in a clothing factory. Fahimeh took this opportunity despite opposition from her father and her brother. "I left my parents' home because I could not take it anymore." She added: "I felt that I am pretty and my brain worked. Only my legs did not work so I tolerated all the hardships hoping that life would be better one day." Fahimeh left home at the age of 19. Soon after, she met her husband, Riaz, at a rehabilitation centre. The couple got married and raised four children—all boys. They were mentors to other wheelchair users. "I loved my son and my husband did the same. We both took care of him. We raised all our kids with love."

Fahimeh spent 50 years of her life in Iran. During this time, she reconstituted her identity in a way that did not amount to her assuming an essentialized label of disability, a social construct. She considered herself as a person who had lost the use of her legs but not her brain.

Fahimeh takes enormous pride in the fact that she not only survived but she brought happiness to her children. "My life is beautiful and I am happy that I raised four children who are also happy." Fahimeh did not wish to live as a helpless and a dependent person. Neither did she sit back and mourn when her husband joined an athletics team and travelled for eight years.

Fahimeh's life in a familiar social environment helped her to avoid wearing the label of disability as the sole marker of her identity. This meant that she knew how to capitalize on what was available to her and what sources to tap if she found herself in a dire situation. She worked towards creating a space where one's social worth is noted and one is counted as a person, counteracting the negative societal images of disability. This situation was reversed upon her migration to Canada. Though labelled as disabled, she was not entitled to access resources owing to compounded marginalization resulting from her being a disabled woman of colour. At work are negative markers of difference: race, gender, disability and class. The state, despite its welfare security system, does not serve disabled people well. Its scarce resources are distributed hierarchically, and also along a demarcated base line: the deserving (those who have the potential to be in the waged sector) and the undeserving (the opposite scenario) (Whyte & Ingstad, 1995). Racialized women with disabilities are placed at the bottom of this schema: they are the Other of the Other. "Neither a mother, nor a wife, nor a waged worker shall she be." This societal assumption renders her into a passive dependent situation. Fahimeh's life on the margins of society brings into relief both scenarios: the dominant system's dismissal of her life as a nobody and her own struggles to establish a place for herself and her family in Canadian society.

Ruptured Landscapes: Migration and Settlement

A major change occurred in Fahimeh's life when Riaz joined a disability athletes' team to travel around the world. On the Canadian leg of his journey, he applied for and was granted refugee status. This meant that Fahimeh had to raise the children on her own for a period of eight years—her youngest son was six years old when Riaz left for Canada. Fahimeh continued to take care of the family on her husband's savings and some money earned by her eldest son until such time when she received papers to migrate to Canada.

Her husband sponsored her and their four sons. Her two sons over the age of 18 did not qualify for immigration.

When Fahimeh came to Canada, she noticed that Riaz lived a simple life. He had a single self-made bed, a small dining table, some cutlery and some sports items. These were his personal belongings. Fahimeh was disappointed as she had heard that disabled persons were well looked after in Canada. Riaz was frustrated and despondent owing to social rejection, a poignant aspect of which was unemployment. "There was no kiss, no hug. I thought 'all right Fahimeh you have not been with him for eight years. Give him some time.' We slept that night on the same bed but nothing happened."

The following day, Fahimeh cleaned the house and made breakfast "and I asked him what he wanted for lunch. He had filled the refrigerator with food so I started right away to cook." Fahimeh did all the household work and the four of them lived in the bachelor suite for three months. Eventually "[w]e moved to that basement suite and after a while I talked to my husband. I asked him why he was so cold to me. It was hard on me. But I tried to talk to him. He would say: 'Leave me alone. Let me be as I am.'"

Fahimeh explained that in Iran, she and her husband used to go shopping and they ate out quite often. Sometimes they went to a cafeteria. But in Canada, her husband does not want to go out with her. He told her that they should both have married non-disabled people. He said: "Marriage of two disabled people is not correct. You face issues." "I said: 'What issues? I have faced all the issues in twenty-seven years of marriage and never complained. What is happening now?'" Fahimeh is sad that she and her husband do not go out together. "When I see other people go out, I feel depressed. Why not me?" Fahimeh stated that her husband is very conscious of them going out because he does not want the public to see two people—husband and wife—in wheelchairs.

Fahimeh's vulnerability, including spousal abuse (physical and verbal), is compounded by the fact that the outside world does not take any notice of her. She is isolated. Her sole contact at the time of the study was a social worker who had not made Fahimeh aware of the social services that she is entitled to. The social worker's indifference to Fahimeh's situation is a function of societal insensitivity to disabled women of colour (Razack, 1998; Dossa, 2004). Fahimeh is Othered on three fronts: she does not have the right skin colour, she is disabled, and she is a woman. Citing Williams, Collins' comments on Black women is relevant: "She belongs to a race that is best designated by the term problem and she lives beneath the shadow of that problem which envelops and obscures her" (2000, p. 3).

In Iran, Fahimeh had to cope with two markers of negative difference: gender and disability. But Fahimeh did not adopt a victimized position. Underlying her actions, such as establishing a family, is a vision of life where she reminds herself that being disabled does not mean that she has to take a back seat. This aspect is captured in her repeated comment to Riaz: "We do not have legs that does not mean that we do not have brains." Fahimeh takes pride in the fact that she raised four children from her wheelchair. This activity made it possible for her to claim the socially valorized role of a mother. It is through this status that she is able to subvert the stigmatized identity of a disabled woman. She refers to her life in Iran as "beautiful," despite struggles and an eight-year separation from her husband. Upon migration, Fahimeh finds herself in a socially vulnerable position, expressed on two fronts: the domestic sphere of abuse and the public sphere of indifference. Her race, class, gender and disability (the intersectionality paradigm) places her on the margins of the margins. Ironically, it is Riaz who captures societal attitude towards racialized persons with disabilities. To paraphrase: two people of colour should not be together in wheelchairs.

In *Disability and Culture*, anthropologists Whyte and Ingstad lay out the parameters for a comparative study of disability. They note that in the West, a centralist state plays a key role in framing our notions of disability. Here, disability becomes a marked group resulting in the creation of a paradoxical situation. On the one hand, they "are given a social identity, as citizens who have the same rights as others and should be integrated like ordinary people" (1995, p. 8). On the other hand, this homogenized integration denies disabled people the right to be different. This second stance is problematic, revealed in the paradox of disabled persons as being seen but not socially acknowledged. Compensating the disability difference through such measures as legislation and rehabilitation programmes renders disabled people socially invisible. What this comes down to is the denial and erasure of difference, compounded in the case of racialized women with disabilities.

A different scenario prevails in the global South (the non-Western world). Here, as Whyte and Ingstad have noted, there does not exist a homogenized viewpoint on impairment. "[T]he anomalies that may be seen as inhuman differ greatly from one society to another, and they do not correspond directly to biomedical definitions [read institutionalized] of impairment" (1995, p. 11). The authors contend that the non-institutionalized setting is more conducive towards maintaining personhood as in this setting "being a member of a family and having children are far more important to being a person than work capacity or appearance" (p. 11). When persons are primarily considered in relation to others, their personhood does not diminish to the same extent as in a situation where undue emphasis is placed on individual abilities and achievements.

Fahimeh's life in Iran may be considered in this frame. In the relatively non-institutionalized setting in Iran, she established herself as a mother and claims her personhood as opposed to being a non-entity. A different situation prevails in Canada. Here, it is social services that inform her quality of life, albeit within a scarce resource-base.

Racialized women with disabilities are marked as different. Their difference is not static; it is actively constructed in everyday life situations in relation to three dimensions. First, racialized women with disabilities are rendered socially invisible by a keep-them-out immigration policy. This means that the concerns of this group are not addressed by social services and, if they are identified every attempt is made to keep them in the private sphere through such strategies as making services inaccessible and withholding information that would improve their quality of life. Second is the political dimension that denies these women the rights and privileges extended to white/mainstream persons with disabilities. Institutional resources such as withholding of career and educational opportunities foster disenfranchisement. Finally the combination of disablism, class and race ideologies permeate the social system in such a way that persons with disabilities, though discriminated, are perceived to be white. This explains why disability organizations and advocacy groups do not substantively address concerns and aspirations of racialized women and men with disabilities.

The literature cited above substantively illustrates that race, as a marker of difference, must be considered in relation to the social constructs of gender and disability. Race is a factor in Fahimeh's life, as illustrated in the following examples. Riaz refuses to go out with Fahimeh as he does not want two "coloured" people to be seen in wheelchairs. Fahimeh has converted to Christianity so as to dilute her racialized status as a Muslim woman of colour. In her words: "It is good that I am seen with them [mainstream people]. Besides they will help me." Throughout the interview, Fahimeh was keenly aware of the fact that she does not receive services because she is from Iran (read different) and she does not speak English. This is part of the deficiency discourse attributed to immigrant women (Dossa, 2004). The following examples illustrate racism and disablism that Fahimeh experiences in her country of settlement.

The Wheelchair Incident

> They take forever to give me any kind of service. For example, once my wheelchair did not work. It took two weeks. I sat on the sofa for two weeks. I phoned the company and asked. They said "our workers are not here and they are on vacation. They will come later." When they came to take the wheelchair and repair it, it took two weeks. I could not go to school during that time. I could not get any work done. I just went to the bathroom every night and then slept the rest of the day.

Narrative scholars have informed us that people tell stories for two reasons: to give meaning to their experiences of suffering and pain, and to elicit the reader's response (Kleinman, 1988; Good, 1994; Das & Kleinman, 2001). Fahimeh, whose lifelong work has involved remaking a world from scratch, is determined to make visible an event that would otherwise go unnoticed—such is the force of societal silencing. Fahimeh brings home the impact of her two-week confinement, first through body language, and later through subversion of the script: disability equals dependence.

"I just went to the bathroom every night and then slept the rest of the day" suggests the level to which Fahimeh's body and through it her whole being is reduced. It brings home Frank's (1995) observation that the body does not speak, it begets speech. Space and time speak to the suffering that Fahimeh is subject to: she is grounded for two weeks and that also on the sofa. The irony is well stated: while other people (the paradigm citizens) are on vacation, an immigrant disabled woman (a lesser being) spends her time on the sofa. Fahimeh's use of the conversational mode is telling: "They said: 'our workers are not here ...'" It is society that is pathologized, not her body.

Fahimeh uses the wheelchair incident to show that she is not "dependent" and neither is she "disabled" in the way that society has constructed these categories. For her, not having a wheelchair means that she is not able to perform her domestic tasks; neither can she attend English as a Second Language (ESL) classes. In her words: "They should or could have lent me a wheelchair when they take mine away until mine is ready. In this way, a person would not be disabled of doing daily stuff." Fahimeh does not consider herself to be disabled; neither does she want to be racialized. "I wish they would know more about my country so that they would not consider me to be different."

Taking a Bus

The recurring nature of this incident requires that we use an active tense.

> Most of the bus drivers do not take you, some of them do. I have seen things. Most of the bus drivers are kind and human but some of them, because they do not feel like getting up from their seats and help a disabled person, they say wait and take the next bus. But I do not have that time. I have to get home and make dinner for my kids as my kids have come back home so they need me. I have anxiety and stress and want to come home. The bus driver does not know how stressed I am and the next bus causes me to be delayed by about two hours. I am late and am on the street for no reason. Yes, it has happened to me many times.

Once in the bus Fahimeh fastens her own seatbelt.

Fahimeh's re-telling of the bus driver incident(s) begins with the testimonial "you"— an inclusive genre—through which she brings the reader into her space. In other words, it is only after she has secured an audience that Fahimeh tells her story. It is important to note that she begins with positive words, "most of the drivers are kind and human." She does not want to portray herself as a victim; a second reading of her words reveals that them being "kind and human" is measured in the backdrop of unkindness and insensitivity. This double play of words serves her well. By not stereotyping all bus drivers as discriminatory, Fahimeh makes her story credible.

Fahimeh begins with a pragmatic stance, stating that the bus driver's reluctance to take her on board is due to him having to do some work—"safety" work. He has to get up from his seat, lower the front seat to make room for her wheelchair, and fasten a seatbelt around her. Fahimeh reverses this script and presents herself as not disabled, that is, not dependent. She states that he does not have to do any work. She puts forward her own definition: "I am a disabled person but I do everything on my own. I take care of myself," and this extends to the level where she would put the seat back in its *original* position. Furthermore, she lets the reader/her audience know that the bus driver's refusal to take her prevents her from preparing dinner for her children in good time. In the eyes of the society, she is a disabled immigrant woman who should not be in Canada. Fahimeh's awareness of this script is revealed by her intervening comment: "I am not a drain on the system. Give me any job and I will do it." In her own eyes, Fahimeh is a mother and a person who takes care of her children like any other woman. What is intriguing about her narrative is the way in which she uses the bus incident to foreground her humanity that social institutions, in concert with each other, have denied her.

"My Kids Are Hungry"

> About a month ago, I had a problem. We had nothing at home. No food and no money to buy food [that is, serve hot meals]. We had run out of money, and my husband did not let me tell anyone about this. Maybe someone could give us a small amount of money or help me somehow.

Upon the advice of a friend, Fahimeh sought the assistance of a financial worker. Fahimeh introduced herself: "I told her that we are a family and I said that 'we have not had any grocery for one week.' She said: 'we cannot help you or give you something.' I was sad and told her, 'what should I do now? My kids are hungry and need food.'" With much difficulty and a "lecture" on how she should spend her money, Fahimeh was finally able to get $80, cut from her next month's cheque.

> I went to an Iranian supermarket and bought food and vegetables. When my sons came home from school, they were happy and they told me: "How good that we have something to eat after two weeks." They said: "Thank you, Mom" and kissed me on the cheek.

Fahimeh renders a past event into the present by beginning on a temporal note: the incident happened a month ago. This shift is of fundamental importance as it subverts two dominant understandings. First, the past should be relegated to bygone days when racism occurred. We are now progressive and tolerant of difference (Bannerji, 1995; Razack, 1998). Second, discrimination and racism, encountered by Fahimeh, are attributed to the actions of particular individuals. Once we get rid of the "rotten apples," everything will be fine. This line of thinking is applied, for example, to police brutality towards First Nations and Black people (Razack, 1998). The fact that Fahimeh was not informed that she could turn to the system in times of emergency speaks to systemic and institutional racism. The system must be implicated for its failure to be fair and just; past discrimination has not disappeared, as Fahimeh informs us strategically.

A second narrative strategy that Fahimeh deploys is that of humanizing what is otherwise a bureaucratic setting. Once she steps in the office of the new financial worker, she introduces herself not as someone who has a disability but as a person who has a family. She then informs the worker that they have not eaten for a week. An unresponsive and unhelpful response ("We cannot help you") makes Fahimeh use a language that brings home the reality of her suffering: "My kids are hungry and need food." Fahimeh reaffirms her own dignity and sense of worth through portrayal of a human situation: she went shopping, she prepared dinner and fed her family, for which her children thanked her and kissed her. In what seems like a mundane account, the suffering and sense of crisis are not lost: her children kissed her as they got food after two weeks. Fahimeh succinctly reaffirms her competency as a mother, a wife and a worker: "The food lasted until the next cheque came." She leaves it to the reader to fill in the blanks: she stretched $80 for two weeks, feeding four mouths.

Concluding Note

Fahimeh occupies a marginal status within the Canadian nation-state, a liberal democracy where she has sought a new home, hoping to live a good life. But this goal remains unfulfilled. Observing her husband's life of bare minimum, she realized that her life will be filled with struggles that would entail securing resources for her family and affirming her identity as a person, and not as racialized woman with disabilities. She and Riaz had hoped to take up waged work but social service providers dismissed this goal as unrealistic. The latter's stance is attributed to the Canadian Immigration Policy that does not grant admission to racialized women and men with disabilities, except under special circumstances. Their exclusion is bolstered by disability, anti-racist and feminist scholarship that has given minimal attention to the lives of racialized women with disabilities (Dossa, 2005).

People on the margins (discursive and territorial), however, return the gaze to reconstitute their lives and map a world of possibilities. What is of interest is that the gaze returned does not take the form of romanticized resistance removed from the corridors of power. Margins exist within and outside the body politic and they constitute a site where the state is experienced and reconfigured. To appreciate this dynamic, we need to take note of the everyday world with its textured and nuanced interventions into the dominant discourse and practice, a point that has been noted particularly by anthropologists (e.g., Lock, 1993; Das & Poole, 2004). Let us revisit Fahimeh's testimonial account.

It was the disruption of Fahimeh's daily routine that brought home the connection between her/her family's social location and the "colonization" of Iran. The Western model of modernization did not benefit rural families, further impoverished by the foreign extraction of the country's rich oil resource (Farr, 1999). Fahimeh's accident then was not a personal affair confined to the discrete unit of the family: it had a politicized history.

Fahimeh takes on the socially valorized role of a mother to define herself as a woman in the wake of societal rejection of her body. She is able to lead a relatively normal life within the dispersed spaces of her community. Lack of state-based resources spares her the dilemma that persons with disabilities face in the West: entitlement to resources requires the adoption of an essentialized and stigmatized identity of disability (Whyte & Ingstad, 1995).

Through her testimonial narrative, Fahimeh subverts the stigmatized disability and racialized identity. She takes on the role of a mother at work (non-waged), and as a student attending ESL classes. By doing so, she engages the state at the margins, the space where her body is reduced to minimalist life. She presents herself as a woman, a mother and a "worker" who has a job to do. She is frustrated that the system (withdrawal of state services and lack of opportunity to undertake waged work) does not allow her to fulfil her role. By narrating critical episodes, she brings home the point that she is not disabled (read dependent). Failure of the system to provide for her is encapsulated in the incident, "my kids are hungry"—an incident that she reconfigures to show that she takes care of her family like other women.

Fahimeh's testimonial narrative reveals how we come to know about the workings of the state (its civil arm) at the margins. The latter are not only territorial spaces but are sites of practice where the state constitutes and is constituted by the subjects. Fahimeh's contribution in reconfiguring the state is to point out that borderlands and margins are not tightly constituted units, but areas where time-honoured dichotomies of the public and the private, and the able-bodies and dis-abled bodies (further marked through racialization and gender) do not hold water. The state is undone on the margins that it seeks to control and it is within the space of this undoing that Fahimeh affirms her identify as a woman and a mother—an identity that is denied to her by dominant discourse and practices.

Endnote

[1] I chose to focus on one woman for two reasons: (a) to facilitate a closer reading of a narrative; and (b) to recognize the collective endeavour captured in one voice. When marginalized people speak, they identify structured factors that shape their collective experiences.

References

Bannerji, H. (Ed.) (1993) Returning the gaze: Racism, feminism and politics (Toronto, Sister Vision Press).

Bannerji, H. (1995) Thinking through: Essays on Feminism, Marxism, and anti-racism (Toronto, Women's Press).

Butler, R. & Parr, H. (Eds) (1999) Mind and body spaces: Geographies of illness, impairment and disability (London and New York, Routledge).

Collins, P. H. (2000) Black Feminist thought: Knowledge, consciousness, and the politics of empowerment (2nd edn) (New York, Routledge).

Corker, M. & French, S. (1999) Reclaiming discourse in disability studies, in: M. Corker & S. French (Eds) Disability discourse (Philadelphia, PA, Open University Press), 1–12.

Creese, G. (1992) The politics of refugees in Canada, in: V. Satzewich (Ed.) Deconstructing nation: Immigration, multiculturalism and racism in 90s Canada (Halifax, Fernwood Publishing), 123–144.

Das, V. & Addlakha, R. (2001) Disability and domestic citizenship: Voice, gender, and the making of the subject, Public Culture, 13(3), 511–531.

Das, V. & Kleinman, A. (2001) Introduction, in: V. Das, A. Kleinman, M. Lock, M. Ramphele & P. Reynolds (Eds) Remaking a world: Violence, social suffering, and recovery (Berkeley, CA, University of California Press), 1–30.

Das, V. & Poole, D. (Eds) (2004) Anthropology in the margins of the state (Sante Fe, NM, School of American Research Press).

Dossa, P. (2004) Politics and poetics of migration: Narratives of Iranian women from the Diaspora (Toronto, Canadian Scholars' Press Inc.).

Dossa, P. (2005) Racialized bodies, disabling worlds: "They [the service providers] always saw me as a client, not as a worker", Social Science and Medicine, 60, 2527–2536.

Dua, B. (1999) Introduction: Canadian anti-racist feminist thought: Scratching the surface of racism, in: E. Dua & A. Robertson (Eds) Scratching the surface: Canadian anti-racist feminist thought (Toronto, Women's Press), 7–34.

Farr, G. (1999) Modern Iran (Boston, McGraw-Hill College).

Fine, A. & Asch, M. (Eds) (1988) Women with disabilities: Essays in psychology, culture and politics (Philadelphia, PA, Temple University Press).

Frank, A. (1995) The wounded story teller (Chicago, IL, The University of Chicago Press).

Frank, G. (2000) Venus on wheels: Two decades of dialogue on disability, biography, and being female in America (Berkeley, CA, University of California Press).

Good, B. (1994) Medicine, rationality, and experience (New York, Cambridge University Press).

Ingstad, B. & Whyte, S. (Eds) (1995) Disability and culture (Berkeley, CA, University of California).

Kittay, E. F. (2001) When caring is just and justice is caring: Justice and mental retardation, Public Culture, 13(3), 557–579.

Kleinman, A. (1988) The illness narratives: Suffering, health and the human condition (New York, Basic Books).

Lock, M. (1993) Encounters with aging: Mythologies of menopause in Japan and North America (Berkeley, University of California Press).

Lock, M. & Kaufert, P. (1998) Introduction, in: M. Lock & P. Kaufert (Eds) Pragmatic women and body politics (New York, Cambridge University Press), 1–27.

Ong, A. (1995) Making the biopolitical subject: Cambodian immigrants, refugee medicine and cultural citizenship in California, Social Science and Medicine, 40(9), 1243–1257.

Ong, A. (1999) Flexible citizenship: The cultural logics of transnationality (London, Duke University Press).

Rapp, R. & Ginsburg, F. (2001) Enabling disability: Rewriting kinship, reimagining citizenship, Public Culture, 13(3), 533–556.

Razack, S. (1998) Looking white people in the eye: Gender, race, and culture in courtrooms and classrooms (Toronto, University of Toronto Press).

Scheper-Hughes, N. (1992) Death without weeping: The violence of everyday life in Brazil (Berkeley, CA, University of California Press).

Sullivan, Z. (1998) Eluding the feminist, overthrowing the modern? Transformations in twentieth century Iran, in: L. Abu Lughod (Ed.) Remaking women: Feminism and modernity in the Middle East (Princeton, NJ, Princeton University Press), 215–242.

Thobani, S. (1999) Sponsoring. Immigrant women's inequalities, Canadian Woman Studies, 19(3), 11–17.

Whyte, S. & Ingstad, B. (1995) Disability and culture: An overview, in: B. Ingstad & S. Whyte (Eds) Disability and culture (Berkeley, CA, University of California Press), 3–37.

PART VI

Global Interconnections and Local Challenges

Disability experience together with disability studies does present challenges. At the same time, however, they also challenge. These challenges and this challenge are lived both globally and locally, which is explored in the following chapters.

Corbett Joan O'Toole, in Chapter 18, raises the issues of sexism and racism. The disability movement has a diverse membership and O'Toole interrogates the lack of analysis in relation to this diversity. The lack of such an analysis has disturbing consequences for disability studies. O'Toole argues for the inclusion of the analytic category of diversity in disability studies. Disability studies is a "white" enterprise and this is because it does not pay enough attention to the ways in which diverse identities intersect. An analysis steeped in intersectionality, argues O'Toole, provides for a richer understanding of disability and disability studies.

In Chapter 19, Anita Ghai speaks of the location of disabled women in both the women's and disability movements in India. She says that disabled women are absent in Indian feminism and ought to be included in feminist thought. This exclusion is foregrounded in what Ghai calls the existential reality of disabled women in the Indian scene. This scene also acts as foreground to positioning disabled women in the background of the Indian disability movement. Like O'Toole, Ghai points out the necessity of intersectionality in any analysis of disability.

Robert McRuer addresses identity and identification. In Chapter 20, he shows how we identify ourselves as living within social categories such as man, woman, disabled, queer, and so on, and we also identify with these categories. McRuer suggests that some identities such as disabled and queer are being deconstructed even as they are being formed. McRuer makes reference to the work of Lennard Davis and his suggestion that critical race theory, queer and feminist thought have inadvertently reinforced a reactionary identity politics. They did so even as they attempted to dismantle it. Davis suggests that disability transcends all categories of identity and difference and that all of us are united in disability. McRuer, however, says that if disability trumps all categories of identity and difference, this trope may then be understood as an act of colonialism. McRuer might also be suggesting that in the act of identification in multiple and messy ways, there might be something more going on than shoring up the boundaries of who belongs to political movements and cultural endeavours. Thus "queercrip" re-readings and re-interpretations of normate culture are also tied to the act of identification.

In the final chapter of this book, Carla Rice, Hilde Zitselsberger, Wendy Porch, and

Esther Ignagni raise the issue of women with facial and physical differences as this relates to conducting research that is community based and responsive to such communities. Even though there has been a growing discourse regarding diversity, dominant ideology still frames the body, including facial and physical difference, in a normal/abnormal binary. Biomedicine, for example, reinforces this binary by individualizing facial and physical differences. The authors suggest that public dialogue follows biomedicine and conceives of facial and physical difference as differences that should either be shunned or overcome. Postmodern and feminist perspectives, however, demonstrate how we construct a sense of our embodied self through the spoken and unspoken messages we hear from others about our lives. Rice et al. provide a way that facial and physically disabled women can reconstruct these messages as a way to build an alternative embodied self. Their work demonstrates how disability can be conceived of so as to generate an alternative to the normal/abnormal binary.

These final chapters can be read as offering a critical relation to the conceptions of disability that have been used by the newly emerging field of disability studies. By critically engaging these conceptions it is our hope that new, more diverse and complicated conceptions of and relations to disability become possible. Disability studies, too, is a space to rethink its normal conceptions of disability and in so doing pursue the promise of making new lives with and through our incredibly diverse ways of minding, sensing, moving, feeling, and speaking in the world.

CHAPTER 18

The Sexist Inheritance of the Disability Movement

Corbett Joan O'Toole

This chapter explores some of the inheritance of the disability movement and suggests areas for further analysis within disability studies. I address in particular the lack of analysis within the disability movement, specifically in terms of its diverse membership and how that narrowness has disturbing implications for disability studies.

The U.S. disability movement had many points of origin—from World War II veterans to the 1950s mothers of disabled children to the first Centers for Independent Living in the 1970s. But by 1980, the disability movement presented an image to the world as white people—primarily men, presumably heterosexual—who used mobility devices, most often wheelchairs. This standardized myth is not limited to the United States. Barbara Ryan quotes British writer Carol Thomas, who asserts that "men have dominated the disability movement in Britain, evidenced by a macho-like style in both the political arena and analytical debate. Because the social world is always gendered, a male-led movement centered on structural barriers to accessibility, particularly to work, has left out those related to domestic and family domains. In other words, the social disability movement is sexist" (2000, 4). As the disability movement has aged, the top positions have moved from being primarily white men to primarily white women, but there has not been any systemic interest in analyzing how disability might have a differential impact based on gender.

Furthermore, the U.S. disabled population is racially mixed. Numerous studies have shown us that as poverty increases, so does the number of people with disabilities. Neither poverty nor disability is equally distributed across racial and ethnic lines, and causal relationships exist between poverty (lack of adequate health care, of proper nutrition) and some disabilities. Although only 17.7 percent of the European American population aged 15 to 64 is disabled, 20.8 percent of the African American population and a startling 26.9 percent of the Native American population have disabilities (Bradsher 1996). The staff and leadership of the disability movement in the United States shows a very different pattern—almost completely white, middle class, and until recently, male. In each of the early historical shifts of the disability movement, however, women, people of color, gays and lesbians, and others who did not fit the proffered stereotype were active members. Evident in anecdotal accounts and early writings on the lived disability experience were representatives of all these groups who were important players doing important work for the community without public acknowledgment or equal rewards for their contributions.

The framework of disability during the 1970s produced many great achievements and outcomes—national legislation on disability rights, bringing people with disabilities to the living rooms of America, increasing public access, and increasing integration. These gains are an astounding tribute to years of dedicated hard work. And the hard work of these people, particularly the white men, has been extensively documented (Shapiro 1994). For example, the University of California at Berkeley's Regional Oral History Project undertook a massive effort to document the early history of the disability movement in Berkeley. The principal decision makers were all white and were part of the disability movement of the 1970s and 1980s. In November 2000, a conference was held to announce the completion of the project. Fifty-two people were chosen for this permanent tribute—their oral histories of the disability movement to "live forever as an insider's record of that important time." As Peggy McIntosh (1988) points out, "[white people are] given cultural permission not to hear voices of people of other races or a tepid cultural tolerance for hearing and acting on such voices." Sure enough, of the fifty-two people selected, forty-nine were white, two were African-American, and one was Hispanic. Among these participants, only one spoke about the roles that women played or the presence of lesbians within the early disability movement.

Research shows that those who have benefited the most from these advances have been those whose needs were the most parallel to the mythic disabled man (Fine & Asch 1988; Linton 1998). Citing Elizabeth Minnich, McIntosh writes, "whites are taught to think of their lives as morally neutral, normative, and average, and also ideal, so that when we work to benefit others, this is seen as work that will allow 'them' to be more like 'us.'" Potential funders are still reluctant to include diversity or outreach initiatives in either research or community efforts because of the overriding assumption that what is good for this mythic man is good for all people with disabilities (Garland-Thomson 1999). Research that focuses on, or significantly includes, disabled people of color is often marginalized by both funders and other disability researchers (Glenn 1995; Ford and Corbitt 1999).

The impact of the unwelcome, pervasive, perhaps even insidious, myth of the white, straight man in a wheelchair is evident in personal accounts, essays, and in the professional literature of disability scholars. People who have deviated from this mythic image often found themselves ostracized within the disability movement. One legacy of African American feminist, lesbian, mother, writer, cancer survivor/victim Audre Lorde is to name and claim the multiplicities and contradictions of our lives without shame. As Jim Davis-Rosenthal reminds us in "An Elegy for Audre Lorde" (1995), "The words we are still arguing over including—bisexual, heterosexism, [cancer], erotic; the words so many of us can't manage to include in the names of our organizations, our speech, our writing, appeared in her essays unproblematically [in the 1970s]. Her writing has been so important to so many people because she taught us to transform our silence into power because our fears will not prevent our deaths."

Even when collections on disability studies are put into annotated bibliographies, there is no standard format to reference intersecting issues or even a perceived need to inform the reader about the inclusion of diverse perspectives within the original collection. So authors' and editors' hard work is often obscured by subsequent chroniclers of the work—obscuring the depth of the writing that is, in fact, available on intersecting issues.

From my perspective as an activist for nearly thirty years, the disability studies movement has three consistent challenges: bringing the disability rights model into the academy; bringing an academic lens to disability; and providing useful information by, about, and for the disability community. Much of early disability studies focused on the first problem: how to move universities away from a medical model of disability and toward a disability rights paradigm. The writing in this area is extensive. Suffice it for me to say that this is an ongoing battle.

Gaining academic acceptance for the kinds of research encompassed by the term *disability studies* has proved just as problematic. In the early 1990s, Kirk MacGugan was pursuing a second Ph.D., this time in history. Her thesis proposal on the history of the disability rights movement from 1917 to 1947 was rejected because, in the words of her committee, "There is no disability history." Thankfully, subsequent disability studies scholars have proved them wrong. Nevertheless, any review of the attempts to do research on disability—AND having it viewed as a valuable academic contribution—is full of stories of struggle and arm-twisting.

The area that concerns me the most is the third prong: the need for disability studies to provide useful information by, about, and for the disability community. We all undoubtedly have stories from different disciplines about a researcher with an insider's perspective who provided an entirely new lens for challenging what was considered an existing "fact." I believe that any successful reframing of an oppressive idea or practice, without regard to discipline, will have a resounding and ultimately beneficial impact on people with disabilities. In discussing Carol Gilligan, Nancy Rice (2000) writes: "[her] work issued an implicit charge to researchers everywhere: be explicit in what the standard of 'normal' is taken to be and in how this is determined." Gilligan's challenge to "be explicit in what the standard of 'normal' is taken to be and in how this is determined" (2000) has deep resonance with disability studies. Our scholarship is often eager to challenge the medical model's definition of disabled people but is usually less eager to explore the larger tapestry of issues that relate to age, gender, race and sexual orientation.

When I first attended the Society for Disability Studies (SDS) meetings in the early 1990s, both the presenters and the audience were white. At the 2000 SDS meeting in Chicago, most of the presenters and audience were white and about 5 percent were people of color. At some previous SDS meetings, there were some presentations about disabled people of color—but these were almost always done by white, usually nondisabled presenters.

I understood this problem far better when I did a chart of what is being taught under the title "disability studies." It is both very exciting and very troubling to look at the programs and courses offered. Some sound remarkably similar to the courses offered as basic training for service providers in different fields. But there are some remarkable strides being made. Using information from the Winter 2000 issue of the *Disability Studies Quarterly*, and restricting my review to programs based in the United States or Canada, I found this pattern. Of twelve programs offered nationwide, only one has a specific focus to include women and disability issues and only one addresses specific issues related to people of color with disabilities (University of Hawai'i at Manoa). There are fifty-three classes offered at thirty-one universities. Of these, six classes address women and disability, six classes examine disability and race, and two discuss LGBT (lesbian, gay, bisexual, transgendered people) and disability (Kasnitz, Bonney, Aftandelian, and Pfeiffer, 2000). For me as a writer and activist on equity issues in disability, this is not an encouraging head count. It should be noted, however, that programs at Howard University and the Mississippi Institute for Disability Studies at the University of Southern Mississippi, neither of which was included in the *DSQ* article, do have specific goals to increase the participation of people of color in leadership and research roles. It will be instructive to monitor their activities and success in addressing those goals.

There is literature discussing how disability studies is like ethnic or women's studies but surprisingly little discussion of how disability studies is including women and people of color (Preston 2001). As one writer points out, "disability studies borrows from many fields and movements, including cultural studies, area studies, feminism, race-and-ethnic studies, and gay-and-lesbian studies" (Monaghan 1998). However, Rosemarie Garland-Thomson (2000) is often the lone voice reminding us that "disability can be included as a category of analysis that parallels and *intersects* [emphasis mine] gender, race, ethnicity and class." Bodies of literature found in many oppressed communities also document that when people outside the community do research, the results often miss important components of community life that can and often do directly influence the results. Studying disability without looking at the intersections of multiple identities results in a very limited perspective about who disabled people are and what they need. The Howard University Research and Training Center (2001) states:

> Very few instruments have been constructed and very little data exists which have utilized African Americans with disabilities as the exclusive data source. Often the research utilizes instruments that contain normative data based upon European Americans ... This data, at best, is often accepted as generalizable to African Americans and other minorities. However, the validity and reliability of the data is highly questionable and often limited in accurately describing the characteristics of this population.

Feminist disability scholars such as Harilyn Rousso, Rosemarie Garland-Thomson, Simi Linton, and Cheryl Green remind us that it is a mistake to think that the complexity of disability experience can be understood independent of other aspects of our lives.

I had a hard time finding disabled women of color that I admire that you would also know. A few women like Audre Lorde, mostly women who are either perceived as non-disabled or who became disabled later in life, will come to mind. But the voices of these members of my community—African American, Native American, Latina, and Asian American women who have lived with their disabilities for many years and who do not pass, while loud in my ears, are but whispers on the wind for the rest of society.

Do you know LaDonna Fowler, who is leading a struggle for recognition on tribal lands? Do you know Sylvia Walker, who runs a large research and training center that investigates the intersecting issues for disabled people of color? Do you know Atsuko Kuwana, who builds information bridges across the Pacific Ocean so that people in the United States and Japan know about each others' struggles? Do you know Kathy Martinez, who is probably the most successful organizer of disabled women's gatherings worldwide? These women, and thousands of others, remain invisible even in disability and women's studies. They are invisible because those of us with access to these academic gatherings have not formally acknowledged their work as vital to the survival and growth of our culture, as vital and as necessary as the efforts that we so passionately and proudly pushed forth in the beginning of the disability movement. We need to look at ways to support them, invite them to speak as equal voices and as keynote speakers, to publish their work widely and to commemorate their contributions to improving our lives and furthering our dreams—not as a one-size-fits-all covering but as a representation of the richly complex community that we are.

One of the great things about the history of disability studies is that it took the basic premises of the early disability movement and built on it. One of the worst things about disability studies is that it took the basic premises of the disability movement and built on it. We have to accept and refer to both aspects of our inheritance if we are to make the necessary changes for the growth of our community and for the future of our disabled children in all their diversity.

I want to end with the wisdom of some quotable women: Peggy McIntosh (1988) states: "Through Women's Studies work I have met very few men who are truly distressed about systemic, unearned male advantage and conferred dominance. And so one question for me and others like me is whether we will be like them, or whether we will get truly distressed, even outraged, about unearned race advantage and conferred dominance and if so, what will we do to lessen them." Simi Linton (1998) writes: "We have come out not with those brown woollen lap robes over our withered legs, or dark glasses over our pale eyes but in shorts and sandals, in overalls and business suits, dressed for play and work—straightforward, unmasked, and unapologetic" (3). And the final word from Audre Lorde: "I have come to believe over and over again that what is most important to me must be spoken, made verbal and shared, even at the risk of having it bruised or misunderstood" (Zami 2003).

Works Cited

Bradsher, Julie E. 1996. *Disability among Racial and Ethnic Groups*. Disability Statistics Center, Abstract 10.

Davis-Rosenthal, Jim. 1995 [Cited May 21, 2003]. An elegy for Audre Lorde, 1992. In *Standards* 5 (1). Available at: http://www.colorado.edu/journals/standards/V5N1/Lorde/jdrelegy.html.

Fine, M., and Asch, A. 1988. Beyond pedestals. In M. Fine and A. Asch, eds. *Women with Disabilities: Essays in Psychology, Culture and Politics*. Philadelphia: Temple University Press.

Ford, JoAnn, and Corbitt, Elizabeth. 1999 [Cited 2001]. Substance abuse: A strong risk, often overlooked. *Window on Wellness* (summer 1999). Available at: http://www.windowonwellness.com/back_issues/99summer/subAbuse/subAbuse.shtml. Accessed February 10, 2001.

Garland-Thomson, Rosemarie. 2000 [Cited September 10, 2002]. Incorporating Disability Studies into American Studies. Available at: http://www.georgetown.edu/crossroads/interests/ds-hum/thomson.html.

Garland-Thomson, Rosemarie. 1999 [Cited September 10, 2002]. The new disability studies: Tolerance or inclusion. *ADFL Bulletin*, 31 (1): 49–53. Available at: http://www.adfl.org/ADFL/bulletin/v31n1/311049.htm.

Glenn, Eddie. 1995 [Cited February 10, 2001]. African American women with disabilities: An overview. In *Disability and Diversity: New Leadership for a New Era*. Published by the President's Committee on Employment of People with Disabilities in collaboration with the Howard University Research and Training Center. Available at: http://www50.pcepd.gov/pcepd/pubs/diverse/glenn.htm.

Howard University Research and Training Center for Access to Rehabilitation and Economic Opportunity (HURTC). N.d. [Cited February 10, 2001]. Research Project 7: African Americans with disabilities: An ethnographic study. In *Overview of individual projects*. Available at: http://www.law.howard.edu/HURTC/overview.html.

Kasnitz, D., Bonney, S., Aftandelian, R., Pfeiffer, D. 2000. Programs and courses in disability studies at universities and colleges in Canada, Australia, the United States, the United Kingdom, and Norway. *Disability Studies Quarterly* (spring 2000) 20 (2). Center on Disability Studies, University of Hawaii at Manoa, Honolulu, Hawaii, and School of Social Sciences, the University of Texas at Dallas, Richardson, Texas.

Linton, S. 1998. *Claiming Disability: Knowledge and Identity*. New York: New York University Press.

———. 2000. Trans-Atlantic Commerce. *Disability & Society* 15: 699–703.

Lorde, Audre. 1997. *The Cancer Journals*. San Francisco: Aunt Lute.

McIntosh, Peggy. 1988 [Cited May 21, 2003]. Working paper 189, Wellesley College Center for Research on Women, Wellesley, Mass. Available at: http://www.alliancefordiversity.org/resources/article_privilege.html.

Monaghan, Peter. 1998, January 23. Pioneering field of disability studies challenges established approaches and attitudes. *Chronicle of Higher Education*. Available at: http://www.uic.edu/orgs/sds/articles.html#chron.

Preston, Paul. 2001. Review of *Illusions of equality: Deaf Americans in school and factory: 1850–1950* by Robert Buchanan. *Disability Studies Quarterly* 21.

Rice, Nancy. 2000. What is disability studies, and what does it have to do with facilitated communication? *Facilitated Communication Digest* 8 (2): 2–8. Available at: http://soeweb.syr.edu/thefci/8–2ric.

Ryan, Barbara. 2000 [Cited September 10, 2002]. Gender and disability from different angles. Review of *Female forms: Experiencing and understanding disability* by Carol Thomas. *Feminist Collections: A Quarterly of Women's Studies Resources* 21 (4): 4. Available at: http://www.library.wisc.edu/libraries/WomensStudies/fcmain.htm.

Shapiro, Joseph. 1994. *No pity: People with Disabilities Forging a New Civil Rights Movement.* New York: Times Books.

Zami, A Not-for-profit Collective for Lesbians of African Descent. 2003. [Cited May 21, 2003]. Available at: http://www.zami.org//lorderquotes.htm.

CHAPTER 19

Disabled Women:

An Excluded Agenda of Indian Feminism

Anita Ghai

Introduction

I must submit at the beginning that my understanding of the issues and related questions has been predominantly influenced by my own experiences as a disabled Indian woman advocating for the other disabled people in India. My initial engagement with the issue of oppression began as I negotiated my sociocultural and political positioning as a woman in a traditionally patriarchal society. A closer acquaintance with the developing intellectual discourse on feminism, especially in my own country, indicated how the movement that originated essentially as a response to oppression experienced by women excluded disabled women.

It was a painful and disillusioning realization to recognize that disabled women occupy a multifarious and marginalized position in Indian society, based on their disability and also on sociocultural identities that separate them into categories constructed according to such properties as caste, class, and residential position. Disabled women thus can have plural identity markers that make their daily experience perplexing and difficult. The recognition of such forces in my own existence, especially those that affect me because I am a disabled woman (Ghai 1998, 35), shifted my focus from the women's movement per se to the disability movement.

The disability movement in India has aimed its protest at the segregation and discrimination experienced by the disabled. My personal experience of the disability movement, however, indicated to me that the gender-based bias that women must contend with every day in patriarchal society also permeates India's disability movement. It is not as if disabled women have not resisted such marginalization. However, the task of locating the "self" under such conditions has been a daunting one.

To gain an insight into the issues confronting disabled women in India, I begin by looking at the general disability scene in India, and the dynamics of the feminist movement as well. I am aware that a Western audience may experience a sense of déjà vu with regard to many of the following arguments. All the same, these arguments are significant for an understanding of the specifics of Indian reality. Without getting into the debate of the areas of communality between a disabled woman in Washington, D.C., Toronto, or London, I restrict myself to a candid analysis of the experiences of disabled women in India.

The Indian Context and the Disability Movement

India, often described as an emerging superpower, has a population of one billion, out of which approximately seventy million are characterized as disabled. Public consciousness of the issues and concerns that affect the lives of those with disabilities is a fairly recent phenomenon. It was only in the forty-ninth year of India's independence that the first legislation advocating equal rights for disabled people came into effect. Though notified five years ago, the act still awaits proper implementation.

Notwithstanding the legislation, the State continues to be largely apathetic. Owing to a complete lack of public planning, responsiveness to any special condition such as disability is missing. Consequently, the physical environment is largely inaccessible and inconvenient. Dissemination of information in formats accessible to people with sensory impairments is very restricted. For instance, there is a single televised sign-language news bulletin per week for people with hearing impairments. The range of accessible reading materials for people with vision impairments also is extremely limited. The nonavailability of other assistive technology devices such as electrically powered wheelchairs at an affordable price adds to the miseries experienced by disabled people.

An example of indifference is the nationwide protests that people with disabilities had to engage in in order to be counted in the forthcoming census. Notwithstanding some small steps toward inclusion, the lives of disabled people remain mired in inhumane patterns of helpless cynicism, political inertia, and resistance to social innovation. In this climate, long-term solutions are neither sought nor found.

The State continues to rely on the voluntary sector for the provision of basic services for disabled people, although this sector, stretched beyond its resources, is unable to serve even a minuscule proportion of those in need. Needless to say, the disabled are relegated to the margins in every avenue of opportunity, be it education, employment, transportation, or any other significant life area. While disability advocates in the developed world have progressed from issues of service delivery and rehabilitation to an engagement with the multiple nuances/meanings of disabled existence, the developing world continues to agonize over securing the very basic elements that disabled people need to survive.

Thus, the meaning of disability in India is embedded in this basic struggle for survival. The predominantly elite, educated (and therefore privileged) group of disabled activists within the disability movement does not inquire into the subtle conceptual and cultural nuances that influence the nature of this survival. Most of the time, an agenda borrowed from Western counterparts lacks the reflexivity to analyze the Indian context in which disability is not a singular marker. In a scenario marked by widespread poverty, disability is not even perceived as a cause of vulnerability and total helplessness. As I argue elsewhere (Ghai 2001, 29), for poor families with a hand-to-mouth existence the birth of a disabled child or the onset of a significant impairment in childhood is a fate worse than death. It is truly the proverbial last straw on the camel's back, jeopardizing the entire family's existence.

The situation worsens because in addition to hopeless life conditions, disabled people often have to contend with cultural constructions marked by negativity and stigmatization. Within the Indian cultural context, disability implies a "lack" or "flaw" leading to a significantly diminished capability; images of the disabled also are associated with deceit, mischief, and devilry. Disabled people sometimes are depicted as suffering the wrath of God, and being punished for misdeeds that either they or their families have committed—a kind of penance or retribution for past misdeeds. Yet another strand of this cultural construction conceives of disability as eternal childhood, where survival is contingent upon constant care and protection. Here, the emphasis is on images of dependency, thereby reinforcing the charity/pity model. Consequently, charity and philanthropy have remained the predominant response to the predicament of disability. Even today, many institutions regularly receive food, old clothes, and money from society at large, which makes these charitable gestures not out of a sense of commitment to the issue of disability but as a response to a cultural expectation to do one's *dharmic* (religious) duty toward the needy, in the same spirit as one would give alms to beggars.

This "altruistic" paradigm is reflected in governmental policies, which until very recently looked at disability as a welfare issue. Even now, most government efforts are targeted at strengthening nongovernmental organizations without making any direct interventions. Western disability studies often fail to comprehend the reality of disability in India, which is marked by a complex amalgam of class, gender, and caste issues. Feminism with its emphasis on multiple oppressions is the key to guiding disability studies and research toward an understanding of the pluralities that characterize the experience of disability in India.

This list, though not exhaustive, illustrates the underpinnings of a negative cultural identity attributed to those with disabilities. Historically, alternative narratives have indicated instances where disabled people have been considered children of a "lesser god"—a status that provided spaces, in spheres of religious and metaphysical discourse, where the ability to transcend the body stands as a distinct possibility (Ghai forthcoming). By not acknowledging the centrality of physical body, these alternatives did provide the possibility for a dignified negotiation of difference. Even though assigning such a status to disabled people implied renunciation of their material bodies (in service to the god), such narratives did offer a metaphysic that was more humane than the oppressive lives that characterized disability. However, this option was largely available to disabled men only. That only few women could avail themselves of such alternatives was reflective of the patriarchal society, which viewed disability as an additional stigma beyond the stigma of being a woman. However, a position that provided such space historically may not have the same implications in present-day India. A recurrent change in the meaning of the body raises significant questions about the whole notion of transcendence of the body and its location in the patriarchal discourse.

However, contemporary constructions[1] (Miles 1999, 233) of disability in India do not draw systematically on historical and cultural research. They largely portray disabled

people as possessing a medical identity, perceived from a predominantly health and welfare perspective. This Western medical model, which focuses on the clinical dimensions
of impairment, dominates policy. For instance, the latest Indian human development
report states that "physical disabilities are genetic, biological and even birth defects and
future research must focus on the causes of such disabilities" (Shariff 1999, 148). Such a
policy stance makes medical intervention, without any regard for cultural analysis, the sole
instrument for addressing disability. The Indian milieu offers very little understanding of
the social model of disability, arguing that it is society that disables people with impairments, and therefore that any meaningful solution must be directed at a societal change
rather than at the individual. Rather than locating the disability in the body, the social
model conceives of disabled people as an oppressed group in society.

In its attempt to highlight the centrality of disability as an organizing principle of life,
and therefore to move it from the margins of social consideration, the disability movement has promoted sweeping generalizations about disability and handicap without regard
for differences in kind and degree of impairment, or different adaptations to impairment.
Consequently, the disability movement advances a few select agendas—mostly those that
address the concerns of middle-class men. As I have argued elsewhere, "The problem,
however, arises when their fight for 'disability rights' subsumes agendas that are visible
and significant only for the very privileged of the disabled. Concessions in air travel,
hotels, and special parking facilities, though undeniably necessary, are meaningful only
to a selected population of the disabled. The truth is that these issues do not resonate in
the lives of the majority of disabled who are further marginalized by virtue of their class,
caste, rural urban residence, and most strikingly, gender. What is and should be more
significant for them are the issues of education, employment, residence, technological
aids, and accessibility, to name a few. The reality, however, is that the majority of disabled
are still fighting to secure the 'bare minimum'" (Ghai forthcoming).

That there might be a gender dimension to disability has only recently been realized.
D. Das and S. B. Agnihotri (1999) indicate that the incidence of disability is intersected
(or influenced) by gender.[2] In the extrapolation of the available statistics, they have indicated that disabled women are marginalized much more than disabled men. Disability
legislation also adopts a gendered approach, with the result that out of twenty-eight chapters outlining various issues, not a single one addresses the problems of disabled women.
This approach reflects the general attitude toward disabled women in India in general.
In Hindi the phrase, "Women with disabilities" (*Ek to ladki oopar se aapahij*) means, "one
a girl, and that too disabled." This intermingling of disablement and gender marks the
reality of a woman with disability in India. Consequently, both congenital and acquired
disabilities for the girl child are seen as additional rather than initial liabilities. Opportunities for improving the quality of life of a disabled girl are virtually nonexistent. Already
living a life of subordination without education and employment, women can do without
the burden of disability. As a mother lamented, "Wasn't it enough that we have a hand

to mouth existence? Why did God have to add to punish us further by giving a Langri (crippled) daughter" (Ghai 2001, 31).

In a culture where being a daughter is considered a curse, being a disabled daughter is a fate worse than death. She has to contend with both her role as a daughter, when what was desired was a son, and with her disability. The desire for sons has to be understood in the context of the ritual value of sons as well as the social and economic burden in bringing up daughters (Johri 1998, 78). The construction of daughter as a burden is rooted in the cultural milieu that looks at daughters as *Parai* (Other). As Johri elaborates, "One of the religious duties of the father is Kanyadan, the unreciprocated gifting of the virgin, to the husband and the family. Giving dowry becomes a part of this ritual" (78). However, the implicit understanding in this practice is that whatever you are giving will be perfect. When she is offered, the disabled girl has to be compensated accordingly. If compensation is not possible, then compromises such as being married to a widower have to be made.

Disability in a son, on the other hand, though traumatic, will still be more acceptable as he does not have to be given away. While many authors have interpreted traditional texts such as *Manusmrti*, for the present purpose I follow the interpretation of Wendy Doniger and Brian K. Smith (1991, chap. 9).[3] Law 72, which states, "Even if a man has accepted a girl in accordance with the rules, he may reject her if she is despised, ill, or corrupted, or if she was given with something concealed," is followed by Law 73: "If anyone gives away a daughter with a flaw and does not mention it, that gift from the evil hearted daughter-giver may be annulled" (Doniger and Smith 1991, 205–206). Consequently, a culture in which arranged marriages are the rule inherently puts disabled women in a difficult position. However difficult, the possibility exists for "normal" women to resist this cultural arrangement, while disabled women confront an uphill task. Some disabled girls in the rich or middle class might be able to negotiate the difficulties inherent in arranged marriages, albeit with a great deal of compromising. Disabled sons retain the possibility of marriage, as they are not gifts but the receivers of gifts. Disabled as well as nondisabled men seek "normal" women as wives, and therefore participate in the devaluing of people because of disability.

The preference for a son in the larger Hindu community in India, in keeping with its religious philosophy, has now been coupled with technology that can provide a test to screen and determine the sex of an unborn fetus. The 1991 census counted 927 females to every 1,000 males in the Indian population. That was an all-time low level in the recorded female to male ratio, which stood at 934 females to 1,000 males in 1981. When the first count is made in 2001, a further decline is expected in the ratio, a reflection of the practice of aborting female fetuses (Krishnaji 2000, 1161). In a society where there is widespread female infanticide, aborting imperfect children will not cause any stir or rancor. This becomes clear in respect to the feminist campaign against amniocentesis as a sex-determination test. While there is an ongoing discussion of the ethical contradictions that prenatal sex testing poses for feminists, prenatal testing to identify and abort children at risk for disabilities does not get addressed (Menon 1996).

For disabled women themselves, these issues become secondary because cultural stereotyping denies them the role of motherhood. As elaborated by Sudhir Kakar, a psychoanalyst (1978, 56), whether a woman's family is poor or wealthy, whatever her caste, class, or religion, whether she is a fresh young bride or exhausted by many pregnancies and infants, an Indian woman knows that motherhood confers upon her a purpose and identity that nothing else in her culture can. Each infant born and nurtured by her safely into childhood, especially if the child is a son, is both a certification and redemption of her ability, role, and status as a woman. Disabled women are, however, denied the possibility of this fulfillment, as marriage and consequent motherhood are both difficult achievements in a socially restrictive environment. (It will be worth mentioning that single motherhood in the Indian culture has been the privilege of only very elite women. In general, having a child out of wedlock evokes stigmatization.) The denial of women's "traditional roles" to disabled women creates what Michele Fine and Adrienne Asch (1988) term "rolelessness," a social invisibility and cancellation of femininity that can impel disabled women to pursue, however hopelessly, the female identity valorized by their given culture but denied to them because of their disability.

A great deal of thoughtful work by Indian feminists analyzes the impact of the evaluative male gaze. However, the essential difference between being sexual objects and objects of the "stare" has not been understood. If the male gaze makes normal women feel like passive objects, the stare turns the disabled object into a grotesque sight. Disabled women contend not only with how men look at women but also with how an entire society stares at disabled people, stripping them of any semblance of resistance. Neither Indian feminism nor the Indian disability movement acknowledges that disabled women are doubly pinned by the dominant male gaze coupled with the gaze of the culture that constructs them as objects to be stared at.

In a culture where any deviation from a normally accepted archetype is seen as a marked deviation, the impaired body becomes a symbol of imperfection. The myth of the beautiful body defines the impaired female body as unfeminine and unacceptable. Disability is thus constituted as being profoundly of "Other" in our society. The roots of such thinking are found in Indian mythology: Lakshmana, brother of Lord Rama, cuts off the nose of Shurpanakha, sister of King Ravana, who is interested in him. That Lakshmana can only respond to what he defines as nonacceptable behavior by disabling the ugly female monster indicates how disability and desexing are equated in the Indian psyche.

This kind of reasoning is echoed in North Indian Punjabi culture, where, although girls are allowed to interact with their male cousins, they are not allowed to sleep in the same room. Disabled girls, on the other hand, are under no such prohibitions. This reflects what Harlan Hahn (Thomson 1997, 25) calls "asexual objectification," and also evidences the disregard of the dangers of sexual violation to which disabled girls are exposed. The assumption that sexuality and disability are mutually exclusive also denies that people with deviant bodies experience sexual desires and refuses them recognition as sexually typical despite their differences.

Indian feminist scholarship has looked at embodiment along the axes of caste, class, and historical phases such as the impact of colonization; however, the impaired body has not been considered as having analytical consequence. As Seemanthini Niranjana points out, "Focus on the body has been a symbolic one where the body is perceived as sign or code important to the extent that it is speaking about a social reality other than itself. Suggestive as it may be to speak of the body as representing encoded social meanings, as an image of society or even a metaphor for society, the question remains whether these perspectives can acknowledge the materiality of bodies, not merely as they are formed/ represented in a culture, but how they constitute the lived reality of persons" (1997, 106). Though this analysis takes up issues of cultural spaces and the female body, there is no mention of the disabled body.

This omission reflects a historical practice that continues to render the disabled invisible in a manner very similar to the invisibility experienced by blacks in a white racist society. As Robert Young (forthcoming) argues, "In a racist society it is necessary for the African-American subject to be rendered invisible in order to enable the Euro-American subject (whiteness) to preserve the illusion of autonomy, rationality and control" (cited in Erevelles 2000, 35). Erevelles's application of this analysis to disability pursues a similar argument. She says that a (nondisabled) subject, upon encountering its Other (the disabled subject) finds it necessary to suppress the memory of this deviant image in order to support the illusion of normalcy and wholeness. That these claims to normalcy or wholeness are themselves illusions becomes vividly apparent when one examines how constructions of a normative self are in fact predicated on the existence of the disabled Other.

It is ironic that feminists engaged with the issue of difference, united in their attempts to empower the powerless, and resolved to transform social inequalities have not picked up on the issues concerning the meaning of impairment for disabled women. While the disability movement's failure to acknowledge disabled women can be fathomed as reflecting the patriarchal character of a society it accepts and aims to be included in, at least within India, its disregard by the feminist movement, which claims objectivity through its theoretical deconstruction of oppressive social suppositions, is less understandable.

What is especially anguishing is that Indian feminist thought fails to recognize that the problematization of women's issues applies equally to disabled women's issues. In principle, some disabled women might have benefited from the activities of certain women's groups, but no documentation exists of specific instances. On the other hand, ample evidence abounds that disabled women are the victims of domestic violence and sexual violation. However, when the national Indian media gave widespread coverage to a story about a woman with cerebral palsy being abused by her father, women's groups gave no more than perfunctory response. Further, Indian feminist scholars have not attempted to develop theoretical responses appropriate to the situation of disabled women.

Only after major newspapers reported nineteen days later that fourteen mentally challenged girls were forced to undergo hysterectomies at Sassoon General Hospital in Poona

(a city in the state of Maharashtra) on 5 February 1994 did Indian women's groups intervene. Situated in a large rural community, developmentally disabled girls received care in
an institution in which they were prevented from wearing pajamas with drawstrings or
sanitary napkins with belts because it was claimed that the girls might use these to commit
suicide. While the girls were deprived of the means of managing their menstrual periods,
the boys were issued pajamas complete with drawstrings that could be used as a noose
much more easily than any sanitary napkin. Apparently, officials did not have the same
concern about boys committing suicide. To deal with the problem of menstrual hygiene,
the hospital decided to go ahead with hysterectomies. The protest of the women's groups
was invaluable because the operations stopped after the first fourteen girls. However, this
incident was not translated into a broader effort to open a dialogue about the enforced
sterilization of developmentally disabled women, which indicates that Indian feminists still
do not see women with disabilities as an important and enduring constituency.

While there is a strong emphasis on mainstreaming women's concerns for self-develop-
ment in the national policy document (Ministry of Women and Child Welfare 2000) on
empowerment of women, the paradox of a hierarchy within a hierarchy is evident because
discussions about certain groups of women considered lower class and caste, tribal, and
minority continue to be couched in "welfare" terms. Unlike Western countries, race is not
a significant distinguishing factor in India. Disabled women are not even mentioned in this
document that highlights a vision for the ministry of women and child welfare.

It is not as if no other issues have been neglected within Indian feminist discourse.
For instance, as Bhargavi Davar (1999) points out, mental health has not been a topic to
which feminist discourse has paid a lot of attention. Even Davar, however, fails to look at
the issue of disability when addressing mental health. Research on national mental health
studies omits discussion of women with disabilities, which reflects a presumption that
their mental health issues will "obviously be different" (IFSHA: A Report on Women,
Violence, and Mental Health, 1999). This reflects the skewed attitude of mainstream
feminists, who while sensitively exploring distress as a major component of a woman's
life experience, conveniently leave disabled women out of their focus.

It could be argued that by emphasizing this exclusion by feminists and women's
groups that I am ignoring the possibilities of resistance, which in the face of nonrecog-
nition can only be attributed to a sheer will to survive. Taking this into consideration,
I could argue that women with disabilities have formed support groups and are in the
process of challenging dominant constructions of disabilities. However, owing to the
absence of discussion among disabled people in general about differences in disabilities
and impairments, no group exists to collectively pursue the concerns of disabled women,
and thus to influence both the disability movement and the women's movement. Right
now the voices of disabled women are restricted to academic settings, where a double
oppression hypothesis is expounded. This hypothesis takes the standpoint that disabled
women experience a double disadvantage, as they fare worse than either disabled men

or nondisabled women socioeconomically, psychologically, and politically. Disability compounds their already marginal status as women.

Many feminist thinkers in the field of disability have objected to this "double disadvantage" approach since the literature does not empower disabled women. Says Jenny Morris,

> I always feel uncomfortable reading about our lives and concerns when they are presented in these terms. When Susan Lonsdale (1990) writes, "For women the status of 'disabled' compounds their status of being female to create a unique kind of oppression" (82), I feel burdened by the disadvantage. When Margaret Lloyd (1992) states that the issue for disabled women is "the dilemma of identity for an individual experiencing multiple disadvantage and oppression" (82), I feel a victim.... Such writings do not empower me. We have to find a way of making our experiences visible, sharing them with each other, and with non-disabled people, in a way that—while drawing attention to the difficulties in our lives—does not undermine our wish to assert our self worth (1996, 2).

While Morris is absolutely right in her stance, the problem is that even the double disadvantage hypothesis fails to produce concrete action as the outcome of the feminist discourse, and practice, does not move beyond tokenism and rhetoric. Feminism, which is cognizant of differences between women, is very similar to the struggle in India engaged in as a political movement. Both have had to fight continuously for mainstream feminism to acknowledge the dangers inherent in adopting the universal category of "woman"—and by default the exclusions of those living on the periphery and margins. Says Elizabeth Weed, "For those outside mainstream feminism, women's experience has never ceased to be problematic. The common ground of sisterhood long held as white feminism's ideal was always a more utopian than representative slogan. Worse, it was coercive in its unacknowledged universalism, its unrecognized exclusions" (1989, 24).

Indian disabled women experienced this exclusion when feminist theory and practice in India continued to ignore their experiential realities of discrimination, ignorance, and neglect. The feminists reinforced the construction of disabled women as being outside the hegemony of normalcy. Consequently, the much-needed political action has not been forthcoming. The resistance offered by disabled women has only led to a superficial acknowledgment of differences, with an implicit assumption that the core issue is gender. The perceived need is, therefore, to raise the gender issues presumably adequately enough to address all women's lives regardless of their backgrounds and differences. At least this recognition is responsible for the emergence of a discourse about difference; but I cannot ignore the reality that this discourse has not been able to effect much, if any, change—either in increasing acceptance of disabled women's concerns in social policy or in enhancing the quality of their lives. What could be the reasons for the failure of Indian feminists to acknowledge and empathize with the existential realities of disabled women? Although it is difficult to posit a clear answer to this query, my interviews with active leaders in the field offer insights into the reasons for this exclusion. In the following section, my aim is to share some of the concerns expressed by feminists and women's activists. However, before doing so, it is appropriate to briefly consider the situation of the Indian women's movement.

Reasons for Exclusion

The women's movement in India, according to Nandini Gandhi and Nandini Shah, has no beginning or origin: "It has always existed as an emotion, as an anger deep within us, and has flowed like music in and out of our lives and consciousness and actions" (1992, 15). Within the movement today many streams are based on ideology, class, or community, and rural or urban location all over India. The movement evinces deep concern for what are conceived as basic societal issues. These include poverty, class and caste inequalities, labor-related injustice, wages and employment, population technologies, *sati* (self immolation), dowry, and female feticide. With time, many other issues such as domestic violence, childhood sexual abuse, and sexuality have became dominant concerns of both feminist theoreticians in the academy and activists in the women's movement. The emphasis of Indian feminism has been not on the individual's issues but rather on collective issues with significant political ramifications. Nonetheless, the feminist agenda in India, as in other countries, has focused on a reconfiguration of gender constructions in society by questioning patriarchal norms. This has focused action on programs aimed at recasting the traditional gender roles.

The common thread in this attempt to reinvent gender identities has been the experience of oppression shared by all women. Ironically, the movement's exhaustive list does not include disability oppression, despite the fact that disability cuts across all categories and may be associated with the experience of many of the other oppressions against which the women's movement is fighting. One reason highlighted by theorists and activists alike has been that disabled women have not participated in the movement's meetings and actions. Consequently, accounts neither of their lives nor of their challenges to feminist theory have immediacy.

While this explanation may have some merit, it also underlines the inability of the feminist movement to consider what may prevent women with disabilities from actively participating in the movement's work. In a country where it is not unusual to develop structural amnesia with regard to a particular category of persons, there are few opportunities for disabled women to create an immediate presence and speak for themselves. Yet, the feminist agenda and the women's movement have not remarked on these conditions. Possibly, the experience of disability is imagined to be opaque, intransitive, and idiosyncratic. In the absence of a sustained discourse about disability in Indian feminist theory, the mistaken belief that biological impairment prevents people from evolving as full social, psychological, political, aesthetic, and cultural beings continues to prevail. Another feature of the many interviews carried out was the recurrent use of disability as an analogue for other kinds of limitations. For example, one respondent stressed that "being a woman is a biggest form of disability" (Bhasin 2000). Another observed: "Disability is like belonging to the lowest caste possible" (Bhattacharya 2000). There are several ways of understanding these analogies.

One option is to look at the sociocultural meanings ascribed to female bodies and those assigned to disabled bodies. Both are excluded from full participation in public and economic spheres; both are conceived in opposition to a norm that is assumed to possess natural superiority. Such comparisons can be both emancipatory and oppressive.

If the objective of invoking such comparisons is to understand the lived experience of different people and to grasp their authenticity, the potential is immense. However, if the categories operate only at a metaphorical level, such comparisons can lead to a total erasure of the category that is being invoked. It is true that analogy is a rhetorical device that is meant to enable the move from more familiar to relatively unknown terrain in order to understand how a set of relations evident in one sphere might illuminate the other. However, if a comparison or the parallel pits one set of the relations against the other, as is the case of women against disability, the strategic advantage of the analogy gets lost.

Without devaluing such metaphorical moves, I wish to focus on what gets "valorized" and "suppressed" in the process. My argument is that such analogizing results in a suppression of the harsh reality of the lives of disabled women limited by conditions much more difficult than usual to transcend. A shift from the theoretical/metaphorical to the material is essential to render visible the "cultural constructions" that have supported the currently flawed conceptualizations of disability and womanhood.

According to Nivedita Menon (2000), another, more fundamental, reason for the total absence of disability as an issue in the Indian women's movement—and the comparative lateness of its emergence in Western women's movements—could be that feminists all over the world have usually assumed "women" to be a category that is self-evident. That is, there is an unsupported assumption that all women, regardless of their differences from one another, have obvious shared concerns. This abstraction of "women" emerged from a feminist positing of "difference" as a challenge to the abstract category of "citizenship" which assumed masculinity as the norm. Up to the late 1970s, "sisterhood is global" seemed an unquestionable feminist truth. The challenges from women of color and other stigmatized and marginalized groups of women showed the category of "women" to be another abstraction, which in turn assumed the white, middle-class, heterosexual woman (without disability) to be the norm. In India, this kind of challenge has come from feminists of minority communities. The charge is that the women's movement has assumed the Hindu upper caste woman to be the norm, and this critique has emerged most clearly in the debates over the Uniform Civil Code (UCC). The debates were regarding the demand for a common set of personal laws that would apply to all religious communities in India. The opposition came from the belief that the emerging uniformity would essentially represent the voices of majority (which in this case was the Hindu women), thereby marginalizing the women from minority groups.

Menon, a vociferous activist in the women's movement and a political scientist by profession, feels that the invisibility of disability within feminism occurs because of mechanisms similar to those that have made women in general invisible in the larger society. But as a feminist who felt disturbed by the neglect of disability issues, she thinks that the movement has the potential to grow and change. Another reason for the failure to represent women with disabilities is that within the Indian women's movement there are far too many issues and far too few resources. Consequently, action has been oriented to the dramatic patterns that resonate in the lives of the majority of women who are able and normal, rather than to the minority who fail to exercise voice or agency. Notwithstanding these reasons, it is important to articulate the expectations that Indian feminism has aroused in disabled women. In the next section, I examine the possibilities evoked by these expectations.

Expectations from Feminism

Notwithstanding the current reality of the exclusion of disabled women within the Indian women's movement, I would argue that simply deciding to include them is insufficient. The problem cannot be resolved so easily by merely adding on disabled women as another category to the list of matters or kinds of issues requiring attention. Offering a feminist account of disabled girls is problematic because it requires including them in the discourse. However, writing a subject (for example, disabled women) into the ongoing discourse necessitates a certain exercise of power to construct that subject in some form, to give her shape, and to breathe life into her. This cannot be accomplished without knowing how she might construct herself.

This process thus requires certain reflexivity. To explore the possibilities authentically and adequately requires that the process have a dialogical character. It is vital that both feminist discourse and practice engage in a concerted dialogue with disabled women and the disability movement, so that a more inclusive theory as well as practice can emerge. To quote Mairian Corker, "It is often argued that theories are too complex for *ex post facto* explanation rather than for use by disabled people, they may lead to confusion and the paralysis of analysis. This is always a danger, if complexity of life is overemphasized, and if the need to understand fully is placed ahead of the need to act more effectively, because disabled people can be turned into interested spectators, rather than proactive participants of a strong social movement.... Theories which reduce or simplify disabled people's experience, particularly those which fail to conceptualize a dialogic relationship between disability and impairment can have the same effect" (1999, 639).

According to Corker, the resolution of these problems might come by following the example of Leonard (1997) in creating a paradigm of communication rooted in discursive strategies rather than structure. Failure to create these spaces even unintentionally does not alleviate the asymmetry of power relations. Feminist discourse has developed without disabled women taking a hand in shaping it. What now can be done about feminists' inattention to disabled girls and women, and how would feminist discursive attention look and read if, initially, they had been involved in its development?

Do we need a different kind of feminist theory to account for disabled women? As Rosemarie Garland Thomson observes (1997, 24), feminist theory can challenge the persistent assumption that disability is a self-evident condition of physical inadequacy and private misfortune whose politics concern only a minority of women. Feminist disability praxis would uphold women's right to define their physical differences and their femininity for themselves, rather than conforming to the social interpretation of their bodies. Such praxis could address some of the specific issues currently addressed by feminists, ones that might look different when seen through the lens of a disability perspective.

One matter that, though within the ambit of feminist thought, seems different from a disability perspective is the issue of caring for the mothers of disabled children in India. As I elaborate, "Although the stress of impairment impacts upon both the parents, it is usually the mother who bears the brunt of the child's disability" (Ghai 2000). Instances abound where women have been divorced, abandoned, or tortured because they have given birth to a disabled child. Given the preference for sons, even here blame of the mother is more severe in instances of a girl child. The fantasy of maternal omnipotence holds mothers responsible for providing the caring. Home care is usually the only option; there often is no question of choice. Indian feminists who have debated over the ethics of caring, and who are now in the process of initiating a debate over equality in caring (Davar 1999, 207), have not taken note of the conditions in which disabled people, and especially girls, are placed. Within the traditional Indian system, the mother has been a source of succor for the children, especially for girls with disabilities (Ghai 2001, 21). In the absence of social and community support, disabled women have relied largely on the caring provided by mothers, who undoubtedly have carried the extra burden. While it is perfectly justified to engage with their experiences of oppression in caring, the attempt to destabilize traditional notions in the absence of adequate alternative provisions might end up working against disabled women. In such a context, it will be worthwhile to engage with the cautionary note given by Anita Silvers that "far from vanquishing the patriarchal system, substituting the ethics of caring for ethics of equality threatens an even more oppressive paternalism" (1995, 52).

Another significant area where feminist questioning would be invaluable concerns the area of independent living as espoused by disability theorists in the West. In the absence of education, employment, infrastructure, and a social security system, autonomy is a formidable goal for women in India to attain, and more so for disabled women. The resolution of any issues concerning disability has to be in the context of the family and community. Indian feminists, with their grasp of the Indian reality, are equipped to devise options that can merge with the specific Indian context of the familial and the social.

One possible solution would be to apply Susan Bordo's view that the concrete experiences of exclusion have neither to be grounded in theory nor given a theoretical response. Rather, as new narratives began to emerge, the major task is to tell the story of diverse women's experiences in as truthful a manner as possible. The only requirement is to listen, to become aware of one's own biases, prejudices, and ignorance, so that a process of stretching the borders of what Minnie Bruce Pratt (in Bordo 1990, 138) calls the "narrow circle of self" can begin.

As Bordo explains, "No matter how attentive the scholar is to the axes that constitute social identity, some of the axes will be ignored and some selected" (140). An inescapable fact of human embodiment, as Friedrich Nietzsche pointed out, is that "... an eye turned in no particular direction, in which the active and interpreting forces, through which alone seeing becomes seeing *something*, are supposed to be lacking; these always demand of the eye an absurdity and a nonsense. There is *only* a perspectival seeing, *only* a perspectival knowing" (Nietzsche 1969, 119. Italics in original).

Perspectival knowing is never really pure. It is always influenced by our political, social, and personal interests. Even in acting on the desire to embrace our differences, we are unavoidably centric. Mere recognition of difference does not assure that we will construct an adequate representation of difference. Further, constant attention to difference might create and construct Others who are unheard of and therefore unfamiliar. As Michel Foucault reminds us, "Everything is dangerous—and every new context demands that we reassess the main danger" (1983, 232).

Thus, what is needed is not merely a strong commitment to create spaces where different voices can share their realities and be heard, but also an active integration of differences among and within women. However, for this possibility to become a reality, feminist discourse would need to go beyond a mere recognition of binaries. What is required is a consideration of multiple constraints that inhibit the articulation of difference. This task is an arduous and a complex one, especially when heterogeneity serves as a mere tool to hide homogenous understanding.

Endnotes

Special thanks are in order for the help, cooperation, and available insights of Anita Silvers, the generosity of Mairian Corker, the patience of Alexa Schriempf, and to all fellow feminists who spared invaluable time for interviews. I hope that this paper will initiate a meaningful dialogue within the Indian feminist community so that identity issues concerning gender and disability can evolve together.

1   Miles chooses not to reveal his first name.
2   The first names of Das and Agnihotri are not available.
3   *Manusmrti* consists of 2,685 verses encompassing representation of life in the world—how it is and how it should be lived. Manu is a fundamental text of the dominant form of Hinduism as it emerged historically. It provides the most influential construction of the Hindu religion and Indian society as a whole. A study of Hindu family

life, concepts of body, sex, attitudes to money and material possessions, politics, caste, and social practices, among many others, requires a knowledge of *Manusmrti*. For the present purpose, I follow an interpretation by W. Doniger and B. K. Smith.

References

Bhasin, Kamla. 2000. Conversation with author. New Delhi, 25 November.

Bhattacharya, Jaya. 2000. Conversation with author. New Delhi. 5 November.

Bordo, Susan. 1990. Feminism, postmodernism, and gender skepticism. In *Feminism/Postmodernism*, ed. Linda Nicholson. New York and London: Routledge.

Corker, Mairian. 1999. Differences, conflations and foundations: The limits to "accurate" theoretical representation of disabled people's experience? *Disability and society* 14 (5): 627–42.

Das, D., and S. B. Agnihotri. 1999. Physical disability: Is there a gender dimension? *Economic and political weekly* 33 (52): 3333–35.

Davar, V. Bhargavi. 1999. *Mental health of Indian women: A feminist agenda.* New Delhi: Sage.

Doniger, W., and B. K. Smith. 1991. *The laws of Manu.* New Delhi: Penguin.

Erevelles, Nirmala. 2000. Educating unruly bodies: Critical pedagogy, disability studies, and the politics of schooling. *Educational theory* 50 (1): 25–47.

Fine, Michele, and Adrienne Asch, eds. 1988. *Women with disabilities: Essays in psychology, culture, and politics.* Philadelphia: Temple University Press.

Foucault, Michel. 1983. On the genealogy of ethics. In *Michel Foucault: Beyond structuralism and hermeneutic*, ed. Hubert Dreyfus and Paul Rabinow. Chicago: University of Chicago Press.

Gandhi, Nandita, and Nandita Shah. 1992. *The issues at stake: Theory and practice in the contemporary movement in India.* New Delhi: Kali for women.

Ghai Anita. 1998. Living in the shadow of my disability. *The journal* 2 (1): 32–36.

———. 2000. Mothering a child of disability. *The journal* 2 (1): 20–22.

———. 2001. Marginalisation and disability: Experiences from the third world. In *Disability and the life course: Global perspectives*, ed. M. Priestley. Cambridge: Cambridge University Press.

IFSHA. A conference on women and sexual abuse. (Intervention for support, healing and awareness): C52, Second Floor, South Extension, Part II, New Delhi, India.

Johri, Rachana. 1998. Cultural constructions of maternal attachment: The case of a girl child. Ph.D. diss., University of Delhi, India.

Kakar, Sudhir. 1978. *The inner world: A psychoanalytic study of childhood and society in India.* Delhi: Oxford University Press.

Krishnaji, N. 2000. Trends in sex ratio. *Economic and political weekly* (April): 1161–63.

Leonard, P. 1997. *Postmodern welfare.* London: Sage.

Lloyd, M. 1992. Does she boil eggs? Towards a feminist model of disability. *Disability, handicap and society* 7 (3): 207–21.

Lonsdale, Susan. 1990. *Women and disability.* London: Macmillan.

Menon, Nivedita. 1996. The impossibility of "justice": Female feticide and feminist discourse on abortion. In *Social reform, sexuality and the state*, ed. Patricia Uberoi New Delhi: Sage.

————. 2000. Conversation with the author. New Delhi, 5 December.

Miles, M. 1999. Can formal disability services be developed with South Asian historical and conceptual foundations? In *Disability and development*, ed. Emma Stone. Leeds: The Disability Press.

Ministry of Women and Child Welfare. 2000. Policy document on empowerment of women. Government of India.

Morris, Jenny, ed. 1996. *Encounters with strangers: Feminism and disability*. London: The Women's Press.

Nietzsche, Friedrich. 1969. *On the genealogy of morals*. New York: Vintage.

Niranjana, Seemanthini. 1997. Femininity, space and the female body: An anthropological perspective. In *Embodiment: Essays on gender and identity*, ed. M. Thapan. New Delhi: Oxford University Press.

Shariff, Abusaleh. 1999. *India: Human development report: A profile of Indian states in the 1990s*. London: Oxford University Press.

Silvers, Anita. 1995. Reconciling equality to difference: Caring (f)or justice for people with disabilities. *Hypatia* 10 (1): 30–35.

Thomson, Rosemarie Garland. 1997. *Extraordinary bodies*. New York: Columbia University Press.

Weed, Elizabeth. 1989. *Introduction: Terms of reference. Coming to terms*. New York and London: Routledge.

Young, Robert. Forthcoming. *Invisibility and blue eyes: Towards a theory of African American subjectivity*. N. p. Revista Canaria de estudios Ingleses.

CHAPTER 20

We Were Never Identified:

Feminism, Queer Theory, and a Disabled World

Robert McRuer

Licia Fiol-Matta's *A Queer Mother for the Nation* is arguably one of the most important texts to emerge in the past few years from the interdisciplinary field of queer theory.[1] In a study of the Chilean Nobel Laureate Gabriela Mistral, Fiol-Matta demonstrates how Mistral's queerness—including a series of affairs with women, a non-normative gender presentation, and a spectacularly nonreproductive maternal identity—was deployed to abet state-sanctioned heteronormativity, patriarchy, and a racialized and racist nationalism. These discourses were consolidated, in other words, not in spite of but *through* Mistral's identifiable queerness. Fiol-Matta's text is important for many reasons, two of which I want to foreground. First, it makes explicit the fact that queerness has no *necessary* connection to progressive or radical political projects. Although arguably queer theory from its origins has demonstrated a sophisticated awareness that any discourse or identification can be appropriated, commodified, and made to serve dominant interests, Fiol-Matta fleshes out that awareness, providing in the process a provocative challenge to some of the more celebratory strands of queer theory or queer activism. Second, and related, her text implicitly participates in the larger critique of identity politics that has likewise animated queer theory from its origins, but that has become more urgent (and indeed much more common) as the normalization and heightened visibility of the past decade have focused perhaps more attention on tolerance of minoritized, identifiable, *contained* lesbian, gay, or even queer identities, rather than on a queer critique of structures of heterosexism, patriarchy, and homophobia.

Fiol-Matta's book can be understood as part of a larger critical shift toward what might be called postidentity theory and politics. The opening chapter of Lennard J. Davis's *Bending over Backwards: Disability, Dismodernism, and Other Difficult Positions*, for example, positions itself with a similar intent from the first line of the title: "The End of Identity Politics and the Beginning of Dismodernism: On Disability as an Unstable Category."[2] Postmodernity, according to Davis, has authorized a critique of virtually every grand theory or totalization; but it also has, in his estimation, prohibited a critique of minority identity:

> The one area that remained relatively unchallenged despite the postmodern deconstructionist assault was the notion of group identity. Indeed, the postmodern

period is the one that saw the proliferation of multiculturality. One could attach the shibboleths of almost any ground of knowledge, but one could never attack the notion of being, for example, African American, a woman, or gay. To do so would be tantamount to being part of the oppressive system that created categories of oppressed others. One could interrogate the unity of the novel, science, even physics, but one could not interrogate one's right to be female, of color, or queer. (12–13)

Davis then nods toward what he calls the "deconstructive worm of thought" that allowed for "performativity" and "social construction" to emerge as theoretical models within these movements, but somehow even these theoretical developments ended up undergirding the identity politics they were supposed to critique. As Davis argues, "the way out of the reductionist mode was to say that the body and identities around the body were socially constructed and performative. So while postmodernism eschewed the whole, it could accept that the sum of the parts made up the whole in the form of the multicultural, rainbow quilt of identities" (13). Postmodernism, in other words, almost did us in, but social constructionism and performativity kept us safe and allowed us to believe in identities that would always be part of the multicultural tapestry.

Since, for Davis, African American, feminist, and queer thought have inadvertently reinforced a reactionary identity politics even as they attempted to dismantle it, Davis argues that disability studies might provide a way out. As an emergent discourse, it is, apparently, less caught up in the tendency to rigidify that other movements exhibit. Rather than embracing an identity position or a crypto–identity position, disability studies could be at the vanguard of a new postidentity world. "Disability," Davis insists, "can be seen as the postmodern subject position"; indeed, the postidentity politics disability allows for can even replace postmodernism with what Davis calls "dismodernism" (14).

Of course, to some extent, what Davis calls dismodernism has been under construction for quite some time. A slightly different version of postidentity politics, not explicitly announced as such, emerges in the famous opening pages of Eve Kosofsky Sedgwick's *Epistemology of the Closet*, written a full decade before Davis's book:

Epistemology of the Closet proposes that many of the major nodes of thought and knowledge in twentieth-century Western culture as a whole are structured—indeed, fractured—by a chronic, now endemic crisis of homo/heterosexual definition, indicatively male, dating from the end of the nineteenth century. The book will argue that an understanding of virtually any aspect of modern Western culture must be, not merely incomplete, but damaged in its central substance to the degree that it does not incorporate a critical analysis of modern homo/heterosexual definition; and it will assume that the appropriate place for that critical analysis to begin is from the relatively decentered perspective of modern gay and antihomophobic theory.[3]

Sedgwick's claims can certainly be challenged on several levels. For one thing, the closet actually became available as a metaphor only in the second third of the twentieth century; furthermore, cultural anxieties about the New Woman, the mannish lesbian, and what Lisa Duggan has called "Sapphic slashers" suggest that the crisis Sedgwick pinpoints could as easily be indicatively female.[4] Nonetheless, *Epistemology of the Closet* accomplished a great deal, arguably rewriting contemporary theory in and through its grandiose claims that there is something queer at the center of "virtually any aspect of modern Western culture" and knowledge. What's important to note, however, is that this rewriting of contemporary theory is accomplished not from a space of identification, but from the space where identification unravels: the crisis of definition Sedgwick analyzes may have bequeathed us a culture obsessed with identity, but the whole point of the analysis is to demonstrate that such an obsession is historical. Implicit in the assertion that sexual identities appear at a particular moment to resolve (imperfectly) a whole series of cultural anxieties is the possibility that they can disappear. And, perhaps, the postidentity implication that their disappearance would be in the service of antihomophobic projects.

I would like to comprehend Davis's project similarly, but it seems to me that his postidentity rhetoric functions rather differently from Sedgwick's. "We can't go back to a relatively simple notion of identity," he writes. Furthermore, he argues, "I think it would be a major error for disability scholars and advocates to define the category in the by-now very problematic and depleted guise of one among many identities. In fact I argue that disability can capitalize on its rather different set of definitions from other current and known identities. To do this, it must not ignore the instability of its self-definitions but acknowledge that their instability allows disability to transcend the problems of identity politics" (23–24). As much as I take pleasure in the disabled world imagined by Davis, I would like for such a world to be realized through occupation and transformation of the world that compulsory able-bodiedness has made, not by a disability trumping and transcending other progressive theoretical projects, feminism and queer theory among them. Indeed, if a disabled world is achieved through trumping and transcending, it is hard not to perceive the projected moves as colonialist.

If we create our postidentity politics using a rhetoric of transcendence, several problems will result. First, we are more easily manipulated by an academic market always looking for the latest key (in other words, transcendence seems to offer a plenitude that cannot be sustained, only surpassed by the next potential explanatory key); second, and ironically given that Davis wants to stress instability, transcendence and the romanticism that generates a desire for transcendence ultimately rely on a coherence and harmony that exclude difference; and third and most important, the objects being transcended need to be, basically, inert. And indeed that is what we are offered: theoretical and activist projects hung up on identity, unable to think outside simplistic notions of identity, trapped in "the dead end of identity politics" (Davis, *Bending*, 29).

In the face of these quite serious charges, I confess that I see no choice but to take the decided risk of speaking for others. Even if somewhat playfully, then, let me go on record as saying this on behalf of feminists and queer theorists everywhere: we were never identified. Though it is definitely not what I mean, and though I do not think that the lament emerges from the most influential feminist or queer projects of the past few decades, I acknowledge that the assertion "we were never identified" could (and should) recall the lament that minority identities were just being formed even as they were deconstructed. Similarly, the assertion could and should recall our amazing, much-remarked on, and oft-feared capacity to labor undercover, working with and against various identities and identifications as we sabotage patriarchal and heterosexist institutions. What I really intend the assertion to signify, however, is twofold: (1) We were never identified in the sense that we were never reduceable to each other—the differences between and among feminists and queer theorists attest to vibrant, decades-long debates and disagreements about the cultures we would like to shape, transform, and inhabit; (2) we were never identified in the sense that we were never fixed with a simple, agreed-on, clearly demarcated identity, as in a police roundup that would pinpoint the culprit with a revelation that closes the case—"I think we can book her, Sergeant. Lock her up." Even when we were seemingly most committed to a definable identity, things were not so simple. "Gay is good," we insisted in the 1970s, insisting with the very next breath that "in a free society, everyone will be gay," thereby leaving fairly open, perhaps even yet to be invented, what *gay* actually would signify.[5]

We need a postidentity politics, but a postidentity politics that allows us to work together, one that acknowledges the complex and contradictory histories of our movements, drawing on and learning from those histories rather than transcending them. As queer theorist Alexandra Chasm writes,

> When it comes to choosing political allies, to committing material and psychic resources to a joint venture, it makes ... sense ... to choose trustworthy partners, people who share a vision, whether that vision is political, aesthetic, ethical, and/or otherwise social. It is also crucial to establish trustworthy techniques for coalition work, since trusting across identity proves so difficult. It would be foolhardy to ignore the role of identity, or to expect it to whither away, but it would be equally foolhardy to think identity politics can provide the basis for radical social transformation.[6]

Though both exhibit a will to postidentity, I find Chasm's rhetoric more effective than Davis's, for several reasons. First, Chasm demonstrates that feminists and queer theorists are aware of the troubles with identity. Second, and related, while critiquing identity politics, she acknowledges that identity is never simple (and it, like the condition of postmodernity, is not going away anytime soon, and if we want to effect radical change, we will have to somehow work with, through, and against it simultaneously). Third, although the instability of queerness has at times functioned as a direct answer or seeming corrective to identity politics, Chasm does not offer us a key. Queer theorists (and, perhaps most especially, queer rhetoricians) in general at this point are too aware of the fact that any discourse can be taken up, appropriated, redeployed in unexpected, problematic, even reactionary ways. That is, in fact, the central insight that founds a study like Fiol-Matta's *A Queer Mother for the Nation*. And, to reconnect this to disability studies, I would argue that *A Disabled Mother for the Nation* is imaginable, regardless of whether disability is understood as a stable identity or an unstable postmodern subject position. In other words, our identities, postidentities, words, and arguments are always, like it or not, appropriable. We cannot transcend that fact about language, about rhetoric; we cannot bend over backwards to theorize our way out of it. We can, however, continue to develop a rigorous vigilance as we struggle (in coalition) against interrelated systems of oppression.

Such a vigilance, it seems to me, is what Sedgwick's famous epistemology allowed for more than a decade ago. And although it is certainly polemical, to me *Epistemology of the Closet* does not supersede other projects; indeed, I take it as an invitation. Sedgwick writes that "an understanding of virtually any aspect of modern Western culture must be, not merely incomplete, but damaged in its central substance to the degree that it does not incorporate a critical analysis of modern homo/heterosexual definition," thereby invit-ing—as I see it—similar theses: we might now say, for instance, that an understanding of any aspect of modern Western culture must be considered incomplete if it does not incorporate a critical analysis of the crisis of able-bodied/disabled definition.

Regardless of whether Sedgwick can be critiqued for understanding the crisis of homo/hetero definition as indicatively male, I wonder whether, at the beginning of the twenty-first century, the crisis of able-bodied/disabled definition might be indicatively female, and, moreover, nonwhite. Perhaps it is an unlikely claim, given that an often-unmarked whiteness has arguably dominated disability studies to date. But as I read a text like Grace Chang's *Disposable Domestics: Immigrant Women Workers in the Global Economy*, a text not identified as a disability studies text, I wonder.[7] Disability identity as such never appears in *Disposable Domestics*, but the story Chang tells of some of the ways in which immigrant women of color are currently incorporated into a global economy is a disability story nonetheless. Financial crises, exacerbated by the structural adjustment programs of the World Bank and International Monetary Fund, have created a largely female, migrant workforce. In the United States and Canada, in particular, immigrant women of color have been transformed into what Chang calls a "super-exploitable, low-wage workforce to staff the nation's nursing homes, ever-increasing sweatshops, and middle-class households."[8] Anti-immigrant discourses and policies have worked to keep this workforce contingent, temporary, disposable, and far away from public services, including health care and education. Many of the individuals and groups Chang writes about are themselves elderly, sick, or disabled, even though they might never identify as such and even though—or, perhaps, precisely because—illness, disability, and age are often cause for termination where they are employed. When sixty-five-year-old Natie

Llever, for instance, was fired by Casa San Miguel in Concord, California, where she had been working as a certified nursing assistant, she was told, "You can no longer do this job because of your age. You are a sickly woman, and we want a young and strong worker for this job."[9]

Youth, strength, and ability, however, are commodities that are both desirable and, in Chang's words, "disposable" in regard to this workforce—long hours and hard labor ensure that a system that wants "young and strong workers" is always haunted by disability. I am not arguing that disability here be understood through a rubric of loss, lack, or pity; a disability identity politics has successfully challenged those able-bodied notions. I am arguing, however, that disability studies, in coalition with feminist, queer, postcolonial, and other movements, needs to develop new vocabularies for analyzing the postmodern subject position Chang writes about, a postmodern subject position that directly or indirectly (and problematically) enables all of us, given the foundational role an immigrant workforce plays in late capitalism.

Queerness has no *necessary* connection to progressive or radical political projects, and neither does disability identity or postidentity. Rather than identifying how any of the fields in which we work may provide a, or the, critical or theoretical key, we might do well to approach the question backwards: How does our own work generate not just solutions but problems? What issues are never identified in our fields and movements as they are currently constituted? Why? Who haunts the margins of the work that we do, the margins of the feminist, queer, and disabled worlds? What would an ongoing commitment to those spectral presences entail?

Endnotes

1 Licia Fiol-Matta, *A Queer Mother for the Nation: The State and Gabriela Mistral* (Minneapolis: University of Minnesota Press, 2002).

2 Lennard J. Davis, *Bending over Backwards: Disability, Dismodernism, and Other Difficult Positions* (New York: New York University Press, 2002). All future references to this work will be given parenthetically in the text.

3 Eve Kosofsky Sedgwick, *Epistemology of the Closet* (Berkeley: University of California Press, 1992), 1.

4 Lisa Duggan, *Sapphic Slashers: Sex, and Violence, American Modernity* (Durham, NC: Duke University Press, 2001).

5 See Allen Young, "Out of the Closets, into the Streets," in *Out of the Closets: Voices of Gay Liberation*, ed. Karla Jay and Young (1972; New York: New York University Press, 1992), 6–31, esp. 29.

6 Alexandra Chasm, *Selling out: The Gay and Lesbian Movement Goes to Market* (New York: Palgrave Macmillan, 2001), 236.

7 Grace Chang, *Disposable Domestics: Immigrant Women Workers in the Global Economy* (Boston: South End, 2000).

8 Ibid., xii.

9 Ibid., 93.

CHAPTER 21

Creating Community across Disability and Difference

Carla Rice, Hilde Zitzelsberger, Wendy Porch, and Esther Ignagni

Physical difference is looked at from the point that you would never want to have it happen to you. As if it's not something that you could possibly gain from. People need to understand that there are things to be gained from our experiences....

In our society, there are few positive images of women living with facial and physical differences and disabilities. While contending with discriminations faced by many women, women with physical differences and disabilities also are subjected to the stigma of a body which is perceived as not quite female (Garland Thomson, 1997), "less than whole" (DiMarco), and "not quite human" (Goffman, 1963). Women's experiences are directly related to western society's homogenized, naturalized, and patriarchal notions of body and appearance. Despite growing discourses about diversity issues, ideologies of the body remain embedded within binary oppositions of "normal" and "abnormal" (Davis, 1995, 1997). Physical differences and disabilities frequently are positioned as personal tragedy, a burden to self and others, deformity, and inferiority (Rogers and Swadener, 2001). Because of medicalization, differences in appearance and ability typically are interpreted as illness or disease. As a result, public dialogue and medical discourse tend to focus on physical difference and disability as something to be shunned or overcome (Zitzelsberger, Odette, Rice, and Whittington-Walsh, 2002).

People feel that you owe them an explanation because you don't look like everyone else. They ask, "What happened to you?"

Postmodern and feminist perspectives emphasize how body images and identities are produced and experienced through social interactions. Cultural meanings given to bodies become a basis for identity in interpersonal exchanges. People construct a sense of their bodily self from messages, spoken and unspoken, that they receive from other people throughout their lives. This occurs when they grasp how others perceive their bodies and understand the personal and social significance of these perceptions to their sense of identity and possibility.

One of the ways women with facial and physical differences and disabilities are marginalized in our society is through cultural and medical messages about the abject body, such as bodily fragility, dependency, contamination, and sickness, interwoven in their everyday interactions. Many experience negative or inaccurate perceptions about their bodies and lives, encountering judgmental comments, intrusive stares, and questions about their bodies (Keith, 1996). These are commonplace, occurring in interaction with family, friends, medical practitioners, strangers, and others.

Sometimes the way health care providers respond to me can have a big impact on how I feel about myself. If I hear words like "deformity" used to describe me then I feel really shitty.

Women with physical differences and disabilities frequently internalize negative judgements about their bodies and lives. They may have learned to view their body as inadequate, unacceptable, and a source of stress and anxiety. This can make it difficult for individuals to develop or maintain a positive sense of self and has important implications for physical and emotional health. For example, many women have experiences of health care interventions marked with a lack of privacy and respect, where difference or disability is the sole focus while other aspects of their identities and health care are not acknowledged (Leigh, Powers, Vash, and Nettles; Veltman, Stewart, Tardif, and Branigan 2001a, 2001b). Stresses involved in encountering negative perceptions can deter women's decision-making to access services in health care settings and can leave them feeling vulnerable in social situations (Nosek, Young, Rintala, Howland, Foley, and Bennett, 1995). At the same time, however, many develop creative strategies to navigate challenging interactions. Women tell how rejecting looks, critical comments, and intrusive touch are everyday experiences, yet they also speak of affirming messages that are features of their relational lives. Through interactions and connections characterized by support, validation, and affirmation, women come to understand and resist cultural meanings of their bodies that position them as "other" within social and medical discourses and relations.

I was objectified as a child. At eight years old, they stood me up against a wall in the cold to demonstrate how tall I was, and they were snapping pictures. I didn't start realizing that I was in textbooks until I was a teenager and I was really taken aback.... I went back as a teenager and destroyed all the pictures that remind myself where I was as a child.

In this chapter, we describe our involvement with *Building Bridges*, a project that examines everyday experiences related to the appearance and ability of adult women with disabilities and other body differences. We outline project activities such as workshops and art-making groups that have been designed to create opportunities for women to share stories, knowledge, and practical ideas with others who have similar concerns and experiences; look at the significant skills that they already use to negotiate stressful and challenging interactions; and build on their existing knowledge and skills together.

Impetus for Our Initiative

I have so much to say ... a voice muffled by the fears of others. I refuse to stay quiet. I will be heard.

In August 1999, *Building Bridges*, a partnership project of AboutFace International, the only organization in Canada providing services to persons with facial differences, and the Body Image Project, Sunnybrook and Women's College Health Sciences Centre, was developed. Supported by the Ontario Trillium Foundation, this project was created with, by, and for women living with facial differences, physical differences, and/or disabilities. Quotes and artwork embedded throughout this piece are the voices and images of women who have participated in the project.

A vital part of the project was the series of workshops held across Ontario from 1999 to 2004. Women who joined our workshops have included those with visible or hidden differences, such as women with facial and other physical differences or disabilities, which may be present at birth (such as spina bifida or cleft lip and palate) or acquired later in life through injury (such as a burn or spinal cord injury) or illness (such as facial cancer). Some women may not identify themselves as having a disability, however, there are often overlaps in issues regarding body and self-image.

I have learnt the benefits of having a cross-disability workshop. Not only did the participants become sensitive to issues of cross-disability but they learnt that their "community" is greater than they had previously thought. I believe that this awareness will create a stronger base for change in society.

Impetus for *Building Bridges* came from the recognition that there are few spaces for women to explore their subjective and social experiences of living with physical differences and/or disabilities. It was also recognized that there are few places for individual and group resistance to dominant views of body difference. Our objective in the *Building Bridges* workshops has been to provide a place for women to acknowledge their bodies and lived experience as sites of knowledge. The project builds bridges between and across participants' perceived differences and among established and emerging communities of those with disabilities and differences. Liminally situated between a mainstream health care institution and a grassroots community organization, the project also creates opportunities for building bridges between health providers and women with and without differences and disabilities. This is critically important. Active presence of women with disabilities and differences as facilitators gives hope that not all health providers accept conventional accounts of difference conveyed in training. In addition, women living with physical differences and disabilities have insights about operations of cultural meanings of body normalcy and body abjection within everyday life that position them as sites of knowledge for health providers and for all women.

We all have issues around appearance. Let's stop looking at each other like we're supposed to be something other than who we are and start realizing we are on this continuum of difference.

From Skill Development to Skill Discovery

The workshop sessions used individualized exercises, art making, journaling, small group work, discussions, and large group activities including drama and storytelling. Whatever the modality, a key aspect of our workshops and art-making groups has been the cultivation of a positive identity, not in spite of difference and disability, but through incorporating one's body difference into one's positive sense of identity.

Surgery is wonderful and it can give people new opportunities, but it is only part of the answer. You still need to find ways to be able to go out there and not let people's stares or comments stop you from doing what you want to do.

While we began workshop and support group sessions using traditional "skills development" and "solutions-focused" methods (Fiske, 1999; Metcalf, 1998), we increasingly adopted a "narrative approach" in our facilitation (Drewery and Winslade, 1997; White and Epston, 1989). This method is a therapeutic application of postmodern theory. Within health promotion, it has emerged as an effective approach for facilitating alternative meanings, identities, and worldviews excluded by dominant accounts and for fostering affinities and actions among marginalized people (Williams, LaBonte, and O'Brien, 2003). Facilitators working from a narrative perspective view participants as having expertise and skills in the challenges of living with body differences, but understand that this knowledge may be hidden by dominant stories that portray them as inadequate or incapable (Silvester, 1997). For example, individuals with disabilities and differences often hold important insights about their bodies, health care, needs, and lives that are derived from their everyday experiences but which may be devalued by greater authority given to expert knowledge. From our perspective, because a narrative stance views participants as possessing unrecognized skills in living with difference, it more fully supports them in discovering their own knowledges, and in building on capacities for action that may already work for them in their own lives.

A workshop facilitator sums up her perspective on the workshop process:

Speaking as a woman with a facial difference, I believe that it is essential that women living with disabilities/facial differences understand that being different is not only negative, but that it has many positive sides (i.e., empathy, strength, courage, etc.). Through the Building Bridges Program, the participants are reminded of what they already know and possess—their survival skills, their inner strength, their communication skills, and their ability to adapt to challenging situations. Women have lived this far in a society that condones attitudinal abuse, and in the workshop context are encouraged to look at the consequences of this abuse and to hone their knowledges derived from their experiences. We offer support so that women may become more comfortable with their bodies and their lives. Through our program, they understand that they are not alone.

Over time, we have reworked and refined our workshop method to encompass five strategies for helping participants discover and build on individual and communal knowledge and strengths: telling our stories; taking a not-knowing stance; asking purposeful questions; de-centering our expertise; and creating communities across difference.

Building Bridges Workshop Methods

What is positive for me about the group is to see that I am not alone and I can share my life experience with others.

Telling Our Stories

One of our most significant workshop methods has been use of storytelling within a group context. Storytelling invites description and explanation on the who, how, why, what, and then what (LaBonte and Feather, 1996). It enables women to see themselves as authors in their own lives. Most activities are designed so participants can look at what has worked well in social and health care interactions and what they could do differently. Through telling stories and witnessing storytellings, participants are able to remember and reclaim the knowledges and skills that they already possess, gain insights, and identify alternative actions in challenging situations. Others' reflections on their stories amplify participants' awareness of knowledge and skills they already use to handle difficult interactions. When women recognize the ways their stories resonate with each other, this creates movement, or new understandings of common experiences and new energy for action. Telling stories within a group context moves participants to recognize the collective knowledges and skills that are present within the group. Many women have commented that they have felt more empowered through recognizing their abilities to make choices and by expanding their choices within interactions.

When I was younger, how I got though those experiences was by developing a sense of humour.... I was tired of these solemn faces looking at my body. Why did I have to make them comfortable? But I did. That has always been the way that I approach the world in terms of dealing with some really difficult times.

Taking a Not-Knowing Stance

Using a narrative approach to group work, facilitators begin from the assumption that women in the workshop have knowledge, skills, and insights about moving through difficult situations, and that these knowledges can provide alternatives for actions. Narrative facilitators uncover people's stories by taking a curious or "not-knowing" stance, asking questions without having preconceived ideas or theories about what the outcomes should be (Drewery and Winslade, 1997). The facilitator's expertise lies in looking for the meaning and effects of problems in people's lives and listening for alternative stories, or examples of their responses and actions in constraining circumstances.

Facilitators use questions to assist participants in accessing what they know about dealing with difficult social and medical encounters and to share this knowledge within the group. For instance, those who have experienced a high degree of medicalization and institutionalization often have been placed in passive roles in health care interactions and given limited opportunities to share information with providers and others about their bodies, health, needs, and lives. This can undermine women's confidence and abilities to access and communicate their knowledge and to collaborate with others in their health care. In *Building Bridges* workshops, facilitators are influential not by imposing interpretations or making interventions that could reinforce participants' relinquishing of agency but through using their questions and reflections to guide women toward the knowledge and skills they have of their lives that are relevant to addressing the challenges at hand.

The exercises were ones that we could apply to everyday life. Also, looking at things the way others see them, was very valuable to me. Thus, I learned not to make myself the victim before I enter a situation.

Asking Purposeful Questions

A key aspect of the method is to support participants in recognizing and validating their own knowledges by the questions facilitators ask and the ways they phrase these questions. Rather than giving emphasis solely to the problem, this approach to asking questions stresses the multiple facets of each person that they bring when dealing with challenging clinical and other social interactions. The method assists participants in deconstructing oppressive identities and in claiming subjugated knowledges marginalized by dominant medical and cultural views. Questions facilitate generative processes of exploring other possibilities of embodiment and preferred accounts of selves.

A wheelchair can be seen as something positive. It's a tool that's liberating. I always thought of it as a prison on wheels. Now I see it gives me freedom.

De-centering Our Expertise

Facilitators have found that the more they "de-centre" themselves by not taking the expert role (White), the more participants in the group speak openly, and direct the focus according to their own interests, desires, and solutions. When facilitators are "de-centred," women are recognized as having expertise and "primary authorship status" over their own lives. Participants, not facilitators, hold knowledge and skills generated over the course of their lives that can become important tools for addressing the predicaments they face (White).

My goal was to see myself as a sexual and beautiful person. Now when people flirt with me, I accept it as a compliment and I don't automatically think that it's impossible for someone to flirt with me.

Creating Community across Difference

The facilitator's role is to build a collaborative group learning process. Group responses are structured to give participants the tools to witness, affirm, and inspire each other. While most participants are initially more conscious of differences within the group, openness to safely ask questions eventually sparks interesting conversations about people's affinities. Encouraging individuals to share with others who have similar concerns and experiences helps end feelings of isolation. This is important, as many people with differences and disabilities may have limited opportunities to learn or talk about their bodies and lives or examine possible intentions and actions within social situations.

It is fascinating how powerful we feel with each other's support; there's nothing like knowing we have shared experiences and outlook. I really think that since we have a social problem, having social support is part of the solution—both in the workshop and afterwards.

Within the workshop settings, participants have the opportunity through activities and discussion to question and resist cultural meanings related to their bodies that position them as "other" in interactions. Through seeing themselves as members of a group that is rejecting its position as marginal, many participants move to cultivating new or preferred views of their difference. As they revisit medical meanings received in clinical settings, collective recollection of past responses and actions often motivates women to revision the value and possibilities of living with disabilities and differences. While enhancing individual agency within and without health care situations, women develop connections that build bridges with other women and create commonality around physical difference and disability. This not only helps participants to challenge perceptions of themselves, but it builds a sense of community across physical difference and disability.

Importance of Facilitators with "Insider Knowledge"

In our culture we're all raised with the idea of being independent and being strong and especially people who have facial differences. I know a lot of times when I grew up I got these messages all the time, "oh you are so strong and coping so well." So that kept me from wanting to talk about any problems or issues.

In our workshops, women with physical differences and disabilities are facilitators. Having facilitators who can become part of the group, while remaining aware of group process, is highly effective. For example, many people with physical differences and disabilities have learned that they should not speak of the difficulties that they encounter in their day-to-day lives. Friends and family members often feel they have little experience to draw upon when responding to women confronting stressful and challenging interactions. It may be difficult for friends and family to know their loved one is experiencing daily intrusions they can do nothing to change. Consequently, when trying to discuss a troubling social moment, many women have encountered subtle cues suggesting that it was a topic best avoided. In communicating their stories to a facilitator and a group who also live with body differences or disabilities, women do not have to succumb to societal pressure to make their storytelling more palatable.

Facilitators who share their own challenges of living with a difference and/or disability can support participants to speak of painful situations and vulnerabilities. In this way, facilitators with "insider knowledge" can act as role models, mentors, and advocates (White). Participants in our workshops have commented on how comfortable they were made to feel by the facilitators and how much they appreciated the personal sharing by the facilitators.

I am so glad to have had this quality experience with a group of women of all ages and backgrounds. Their diversity made it a rich learning experience. Also, it is amazing that this was free! I value that the facilitators were women with physical differences.

THE CIRCLE CAN BE UNBROKEN

by Christene Rowntree

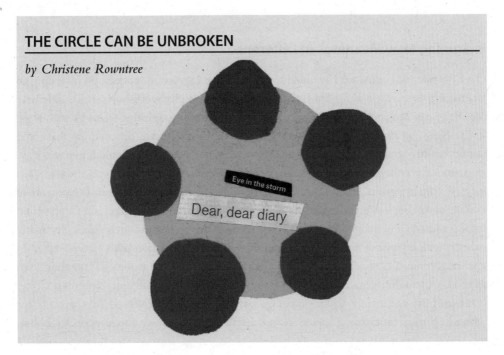

The colours and smaller circles represent the cycles of a woman's life. The yellow [of the large] circle means there is always something good in your life if you look for it, even though you might be living in the middle of a storm. The yellow also represents the warmth of the sun and joy and the good things in life like sitting on my balcony in the sun. The blue [of the smaller circles] represents the colours of the earth, which is life. The reason I chose felt for this piece is that felt is matter, it has texture; I felt paint was too calm for this piece.

Sometimes for me, my life is like living in the eye of the storm. Even though I don't cause the hurricane, there are people around me that *are* the hurricane. In the morning, some of the people that have to help me with my daily needs, are like a hurricane getting you up. "Good Morning Sunshine!" Their pace is so quick, and sometimes they come in really anxious. So that's what I meant by "Eye in the Storm"; my sense of space is gone.

The only time that I feel spiritual or alone is when I'm writing in my journal which explains the "Dear, dear diary" in my piece. Other people can just go drink a glass of wine and put their feet up to relax, but I have to have someone to help me to pour the glass of wine, so I can't escape the same way other people do. Keeping a journal is important for my sanity. It is my sense of privacy. I can use it to vent my anger when I have to. Before my CP got worse, I used to drive around when I needed to vent. I also use my journal as source material for the comedy that I write. I turn situations around and put it right back in their faces. I take things and turn them around and make them funny.

Imagining New Meanings of Difference

Over the past two years, we have held several creative expression workshops, including an art-making series called *Being and Becoming* and a photography workshop series entitled *See Me*. *Being and Becoming* featured four themes: love, sexuality, spirituality, and possibilities. In the *Being and Becoming* workshops, women were encouraged to do anything that came to mind relative to each theme with any of the art materials available, including paint, clay, magazines for collage, textiles, and other craft materials. The *See Me* workshop sessions focused on participants' examining, through photography, social and clinical moments of looking and being looked at; exploring what was concealed and revealed in interactions; and recollecting old and imagining new ways of seeing their bodies and themselves. For many women with disabilities and differences cameras have an association with pictures taken in medical settings. In *See Me* workshops, participants have the opportunity to take their own pictures, creating images that resonate with and reflect on their different senses of self.

In our art and image making groups, participants are introduced to a process for witnessing and participating in the group. Facilitators introduce this process by telling group members that it is not their role to give opinions, or place positive or negative judgements on other participants' art or images. As witnesses, their task is to engage with others about what they have heard and seen, and link and build on each other's expressions. Participants are also encouraged to reflect on what they have learned and/or how they have shifted as a result of viewing others' artwork and listening to them talk about their expressions of creativity. This approach helps facilitators and participants to shift from evaluating or interpreting the artwork to allowing themselves to be affected and moved by each other's art making. For example, one participant who created two clay sculptures of her body differences said about her art pieces, "my nose and my spine are issues that are very hard for me to look at." Once her pieces were done she expressed to the group: "it felt so liberating to feel the clay nose, and to trace my clay spine with my finger." Another participant who depicted a woman in a wheelchair voiced of her work, "that woman is in action, with her arm out showing movement."

In many images created throughout the sessions, the women illustrate how possibilities for their lives are constrained in some ways by body limitations. Yet, the more recurrent locations of the limitations they encounter are external barriers, including attitudinal and literal walls others have built to exclude them. Unlike traditional support group exercises that are highly structured, the creative processes women partake in are more fluid, without sharp beginnings and endings. Often participants undertake exploring possibilities for their bodies and lives in informal conversations as they pick out a paint colour or learn how to set up a shot with the camera. Comments from workshop evaluations suggest that while women view the art and image making as valuable, the most meaningful feature of these groups is the sense of connection they feel in sharing their images, artwork, and stories with other women. One woman wrote what inspired her most was "the joy" she felt in witnessing participants discuss their creative work, where others wrote that they were most moved by learning other women were dealing with similar issues.

Building Bridges creates an opportunity for shifts in meaning of difference and disability to occur. Shifting meanings of difference has important implications for increasing individuals' capacity to collaborate in their health, and for enabling them to expand their options and choices in challenging health care interactions. When women perceive health providers' increased openness to understanding their unique experiences of disability and difference, this enhances practitioner-client communication, comfort, and competency in clinical situations. The project does not deny the challenges of others' and our own perceptions of body difference, but it does open up the possibility to imagine. Imagining becomes a resource that allows women to make new meanings and create new connections through art, image, and metaphor, and in so doing, envision new images and interpretations of difference.

References

Davis, L. *Enforcing Normalcy: Disability, Deafness and the Body.* New York: Verso Press, 1995.

Davis, L. Ed. *The Disability Studies Reader.* New York: Routledge, 1997.

DiMarco, L. C. "Disabled Women Are Doubly Discriminated against." *Women's Education-Education Des femmes* 12 (2) (1996): 6–10.

Drewery, W., and Winslade, J. "The Theoretical Story of Narrative Therapy." *Therapy in Practice: The Archaeology of Hope.* Eds. G. Monk, J. Winslade, K. Crocket, and D. Epston. San Francisco: Jossey-Bass, 1997. 32–52.

Fiske, H. *Workshop in Solution-Focused Counselling.* Toronto: Office of Advanced Professional Education, University of Toronto, 1999.

Garland Thomson, R. *Extraordinary Bodies: Figuring Physical Disability in American Culture and Literature.* New York: Columbia University Press, 1997.

Goffman, E. *Stigma: Notes on the Management of Spoiled Identity.* Englewood Cliffs, NJ: Prentice Hall, 1963.

Keith, L. "Encounters with Strangers: The Public's Response to Disabled Women and How This Affects Our Sense of Self." *Encounters with Strangers: Feminism and Disability.* Ed. J. Morris. London: Women's Press, 1996. 69–88.

LaBonte, R., and Feather, J. *Handbook on Using Stories in Health Promotion Practice.* Ottawa: Health Promotion and Development Division, Health Canada, 1996.

Leigh, I., Powers, L., Vash, C., and Nettles, R. "Survey of Psychological Services to Clients with Disabilities: The Need for Awareness." *Rehabilitative Psychology* 49 (1) (2004): 48–54.

Metcalf, L. *Solution Focused Group Therapy.* New York: Simon and Schuster, 1998.

Nosek, M., Young, M., Rintala, D., Howland, C., Foley, C., and Bennett, J. L. "Barriers to Reproductive Health Maintenance among Women with Physical Disabilities." *Journal of Women's Health* 4 (5) (1995): 505–518.

Rogers, L., and Swadener, B. Eds. *Semiotics and Dis/ability: Interrogating Categories of Difference.* Albany, NY: State University of New York Press, 2001.

Silvester, G. "Appreciating Indigenous Knowledge in Groups." *Narrative Therapy in Practice: The Archaeology of Hope.* Eds. G. Monk, J. Winslade, K. Crocket, and D. Epston. San Francisco: Jossey-Bass, 1997. 233–251.

Veltman, A., Stewart, D., Tardif, G., and Branigan, M. *Perceptions of Primary Healthcare Services among People with Physical Disabilities.* Part 1, Access Issues. Toronto: Disabled Women's Network of Ontario (DAWN), 2001a.

Veltman, A., Stewart, D. E., Tardif, G. S., and Branigan, M. *Perceptions of Primary Healthcare Services among People with Physical Disabilities.* Part 2, Quality Issues. Toronto: Disabled Women's Network of Ontario (DAWN), 2001b.

White, M. *Intensive Training in Narrative Therapy.* Toronto: Brief Therapy Training Centres, Gail Appel Institute, October 21–25, 2002.

White, M., and Epston, D. *Narrative Means to Therapeutic Ends.* New York: W. W. Norton, 1989.

Williams, L., LaBonte, R., and O'Brien, M. "Empowering Social Action through Narratives of Identity and Culture." *Health Promotion International* 18 (1) (2003): 33–40.

Zitzelsberger, H., Odette, F., Rice, C., and Whittington-Walsh, F. "Building Bridges across Physical Difference and Disability." *Ways of Knowing in and through the Body: Diverse Perspectives on Embodiment.* Ed. S. M. Abbey. Welland, ON: Soleil, 2002. 259–261.

APPENDIX

Students' Resources:

Further Readings and Related Websites

Further Readings

The following suggested readings are not intended as an exhaustive list, but they provide a taste of the diversity of the field of disability studies while supporting many different research interests and directions.

Cultural Studies and the Humanities

Cohen, Jeffrey Jerome and Gail Weiss (Eds.). (2003). *Thinking the Limits of the Body*. New York: State University of New York Press.

Corker, Mairian and Sally French (Eds.). (1999). *Disability Discourse*. Buckingham: Open University Press.

Darke, Paul. (1998). "Understanding Cinematic Representations of Disability." In Tom Shakespeare (Ed.), *The Disability Reader: Social Science Perspectives*. London: Cassel Academic. 181–200.

Davis, Lennard J. (2002). "Bodies of Difference: Politics, Disability, and Representation." In Sharon Snyder, Brenda Jo Brueggemann, and Rosemarie Garland Thomson (Eds.), *Disability Studies: Enabling the Humanities*. New York: The Modern Language Association of America. 100–108.

Davis, Lennard J. (Ed.). (1997). *The Disability Studies Reader*. New York: Routledge.

hooks, bell. (1990). "Marginality as Site of Resistance." In Russell Ferguson, Martha Gevner, Trinh T. Minh-ha, and Cornel West (Eds.), *Out There: Marginalization and Contemporary Cultures*. New York: The New Museum of Contemporary Art and Cambridge: The MIT Press. 341–345.

Kuppers, Petra. (2003). *Disability and Contemporary Performance: Bodies on Edge*. New York: Routledge.

Linton, Simi. (1998). *Claiming Disability: Knowledge and Identity*. New York: New York University Press.

Mairs, Nancy. (1996). *Waist-High in the World*. Boston: Beacon Press.

Michalko, Rod. (2002). *The Difference That Disability Makes*. Philadelphia: Temple University Press.

Michalko, Rod. (1999). *The Two-in-One: Walking with Smokie, Walking with Blindness.* Philadelphia: Temple University Press.

Michalko, Rod. (1998). *The Mystery of the Eye and the Shadow of Blindness.* Toronto: University of Toronto Press.

Mitchell, David and Sharon Snyder. (2000). *Narrative Prosthesis: Disability and the Dependencies Discourse.* Anne Arbor: University of Michigan Press.

Paterson, K., and B. Hughes. (1999). "Disability Studies and Phenomenology: The Carnal Politics of Everyday Life." *Disability & Society,* 14(5): 597–610.

Sandalh, Carrier and Philip Auslander (Eds.). (2005). *Bodies in Commotion: Disability and Performance.* Ann Arbor: University of Michigan Press.

Siebers, Tobin. (2008). *Disability Theory.* Ann Arbor: University of Michigan Press.

Snyder, Sharon, Brenda Jo Brueggemann, and Rosemarie Garland Thomson (Eds.). (2002). *Disability Studies: Enabling the Humanities.* New York: The Modern Language Association of America.

Snyder, Sharon and David Mitchell. (2006). *Cultural Location of Disability.* Chicago: University of Chicago Press.

Sobchack, Vivian. (2004). *Carnal Thoughts: Embodiment and Moving Image Culture.* Berkeley: University of California Press.

Stiker, Henri-Jacques. (1997). *A History of Disability.* William Sayers (Trans.). Foreword by David T. Mitchell. Ann Arbor: University of Michigan Press.

Thomson, Rosemarie Garland. (1997). *Extraordinary Bodies: Figuring Physical Disability in American Culture and Literature.* New York: Columbia University Press.

Thomson, Rosemarie Garland (Ed.). (1996). *Freakery: Cultural Spectacles of the Extraordinary Body.* New York: New York University Press.

Titchkosky, Tanya. (2003). *Disability, Self, and Society.* Toronto: University of Toronto Press.

Wendell, Susan. (1996). *The Rejected Body: Feminist Philosophical Reflections on Disability.* New York: Routledge.

Williams, Gareth. (1998). "The Sociology of Disability: Towards a Materialist Phenomenology." In Tom Shakespeare (Ed.), *The Disability Reader: Social Science Perspectives.* London: Cassell Academic. 234–244.

Intersectional Approaches in Disability Studies

Butler, Judith. (1993). *Bodies That Matter: On the Discursive Limits of "Sex."* New York: Routledge.

Butler, Judith. (1990). *Gender Trouble: Feminism and the Subversion of Identity.* New York: Routledge.

Chivers, Sally. (2006). "Baby Jane Grew up: The Dramatic Intersection of Age with Disability." *Canadian Review of American Studies,* 36(2): 211–227.

Clare, Eli. (2001). "Stolen Bodies, Reclaimed Bodies: Disability and Queerness." *Public Culture,* 13(3): 359–365.

Corker, Marian and Tom Shakespeare (Eds.). (2002). *Disability/Postmodernity: Embodying Disability Theory.* London: Continuum.

Das, Veena and Renu Addlakha. (2007). "Disability and Domestic Citizenship: Voice, Gender and the Making of the Subject." In Benedicte Ingstad and Susan Reynolds Whyte (Eds.), *Disability in Local and Global Worlds*. Berkeley: University of California Press. 128–148.

Dingo, Rebecca. "Making the 'Unfit,' Fit: The Rhetoric of Mainstreaming in the World Bank's Commitment to Gender Equality and Disability Rights." *Wag.a.du: A Journal of Transnational Women's & Gender Studies*, 4 (Summer): 93–107.

Dossa, Parin. (2009). *Racialized Bodies, Disabling Worlds: Storied Lives of Immigrant Muslim Women*. Toronto: University of Toronto Press.

Ingstad, Benedicte and Susan Reynolds Whyte (Eds.) 2007. *Disability in Local and Global Worlds*. Berkeley: University of California Press.

Ingstad, Benedicte and Susan Reynolds Whyte (Eds.). (1995). *Disability and Culture*. Berkeley: University of California Press.

Kafer, Alison. (2003). "Compulsory Bodies: Reflections on Heterosexuality and Able-Bodiedness." *Journal of Women's History*. Vol. 15(3): 77–89.

Lorde, Audre. (1984). *Sister Outsider: Essays & Speeches*. Freedom, CA: The Crossing Press.

Mollow, Anna. (2004). "Identity Politics and Disability Studies: A Critique of Recent Theory." *Michigan Quarterly Review*. Vol. XLIII (2): 269–296.

Morris, Jenny (Ed.). (1996). *Encounters with Strangers: Feminism and Disability*. London: The Women's Press, Ltd.

Moser, Ingunn. (2005). "On Becoming Disabled and Articulating Alternative." *Cultural Studies*. Vol. 19(6): 667–700.

Parekh, Naidu Pushpa. (2006). "Gender, Disability and the Postcolonial Nexus." *Wag.a.du: A Journal of Transational Women's and Gender Studies*, 4. http://web.cortland.edu/wagadu/Volume%204/articles4.html (11/15/2007).

Pronger, Brian. (2002). *Body Fascism: Salvation in the Technology of Physical Fitness*. Toronto: University of Toronto Press.

Razack, Sherene. (1998). "From Pity to Respect: The Ableist Gaze and the Politics of Rescue." From *Looking White People in the Eye: Gender, Race and Culture in Courtrooms and Classrooms*. Toronto: University of Toronto Press. 131–156.

Roman, Leslie. (2004). "States of Insecurity: Cold War Memory, 'Global Citizenship' and its Discontents." *Discourse*, 25(2): 231–259.

Schaffer, Kay and Sidonie Smith. (2004). *Human Rights and Narrated Lives: The Ethics of Recognition*. New York: Palgrave MacMillan.

Shildrick, Margrit and Janet Price. (1996). "Breaking the Boundaries of the Broken Body." *Body & Society*, 2(4): 93–113.

Smith, Bonnie G. and Beth Hutchinson (Eds.). (2004). *Gendering Disability*. New Brunswick: Rutgers University Press.

Stone, Sharon Dale. (2003). "Disability, Dependence, and Old Age: Problematic Constructions." *Canadian Journal on Aging*, 22(1): 59–68.

Titchkosky, Tanya. (2007). *Reading and Writing Disability Differently: The Textured Life of Embodiment*. Toronto: University of Toronto Press.

Mad Studies

Beresford, Peter. (2000). "What Have Madness and Psychiatric System Survivors Got to Do with Disability and Disability Studies?" *Disability & Society*. Vol. 15(1): 167–172.

Beresford, Peter in the *Guardian*: www.guardian.co.uk/society/2005/jan/05/mentalhealth.guardiansocietysupplement

Bracken, Patrick and Philip Thomas. (2002). "Postpsychiatry: A New Direction for Mental Health." *British Medical Journal*. 322: 724–727.

Burstow, Bonnie. (1990). "A History of Psychiatric Homophobia." *Phoenix Rising: The Voice of the Psychiatrized*. Vol. 8(3&4): S38–S39.

Capponi, Pat. (2003). *Beyond the Crazy House: Changing the Future of Madness*. Toronto: Penguin Books.

Carten, Ron. (2006). *The AIMS Test, Mad Pride and Other Essays*. Vancouver: Keewatin Books.

Fanon, Frantz. (2004 [1961]). *The Wretched of the Earth*. New York: Grove Press.

Finkler, Lilith. (1997). "Psychiatric Survivor Pride Day: Community Organizing with Psychiatric Survivors." *Osgoode Hall Law Journal*. Vol. 35(3&4): 763–772.

Foucault, Michel. (1979). *Discipline and Punish: The Birth of the Prison*. Alan Sheridan (Trans.). New York: Vintage Books.

Foucault, Michel. (1975). *The Birth of the Clinic: An Archaeology of Medical Perception*. New York: Vintage Books.

Gofman, Erving. (1961). *Asylums: Essays on the Social Situation of Mental Patients and Other Inmates*. New York: Anchor Books.

Ingram, Richard. (2007). "Double Trouble." In Kimberly Myers (Ed.), *Illness in the Academy*. Purdue: Purdue University Press. 209–219.

Kleinman, Arthur, Veena Das, and Margaret Lock. (Eds.). (1997). *Social Suffering*. Berkeley: University of California Press.

Reaume, Geoffrey. (2002). "Lunatic to Patient to Person: Nomenclature in Psychiatric History and the Influence of Patients' Activism in North America." *International Journal of Law and Psychiatry*, 25(4): 405–426.

Reaume, Geoffrey. (2000). *Remembrance of Patients Past: Patient Life at the Toronto Hospital for the Insane, 1870–1940*. Toronto: Oxford University Press Canada.

Rosenhan, David. (1973). "On Being Sane in Insane Places." *Science*, 179 (70): 250–258.

Shimrat, Irit. (1997). *Call Me Crazy: Stories from the Mad Movement*. Vancouver: Press Gang.

Szasz, Thomas S. (1989). *Law, Liberty, and Psychiatry*. New York: Syracuse University Press.

Thomas, Philip and Patrick Bracken. (2004). "Hearing Voices: A Phenomenological-Hermeneutic Approach." *Cognitive Neuropsychiatry*, 9(1/2): 13–23.

Weitz, Don. (2008). "Struggling against Psychiatry's Human Rights Violations: An Antipsychiatry Perspective." *Radical Psychology*. Vol. 7: 1 www.radicalpsychology.org/vol7-1/weitz2008.html.

Social Model of Disability

Barnes, Colin. (1998). "The Social Model of Disability: A Sociological Phenomenon Ignored by Sociologists?" In Tom Shakespeare (Ed.), *The Disability Reader: Social Science Perspectives*. London: Cassell Academic. 66–78.

Barnes, Colin and Geof Mercer. (1997). *Doing Disability Research*. Leeds, UK: The Disability Press.

Barnes, Colin, Geof Mercer, and Tom Shakespeare. (1999). *Exploring Disability: A Sociological Introduction*. Malden, MA: Polity.

Barnes, Colin and Mike Oliver. (1995). "Disability Rights: Rhetoric and Reality in the UK." *Disability and Society*, 10(l): 111–116.

Barton, Len and Mike Oliver (Eds.). (1997). *Disability Studies: Past, Present and Future*. Leeds, UK: The Disability Press.

Charlton, James I. (2000). *Nothing about Us without Us: Disability Oppression and Empowerment*. Berkeley: University of California Press.

Finkelstein, Vic. (1998). "Emancipating Disability Studies." In Tom Shakespeare (Ed.), *The Disability Reader: Social Science Perspectives*. London: Cassel. 28–49.

Finkelstein, Vic. (1993). "Disability: An Administrative Challenge?" In Michael Oliver (Ed.), *Social Work: Disabled People and Disabling Environments*. London and Philadelphia: Jessica Kingsley Publishers. 19–39.

Gordon, Beth Omansky and Karen E. Rosenblum. (2001). "Bringing Disability into the Sociological Frame: A Comparison of Disability with Race, Sex, and Sexual Orientation Statuses." *Disability & Society*. Vol. 16(1): 5–19.

Leeds Disability Studies Archive, www.leeds.ac.uk/disability-studies/archiveuk/

Mackay, Robert. (2003). "'Tell Them Who I Was': The Social Construction of Aphasia." *Disability & Society*, 18(6): 811–826.

Oliver, Michael. (1996). *Understanding Disability: From Theory to Practice*. New York: St. Martin's Press.

Oliver, Michael. (1990). *The Politics of Disablement*. Hampshire, London: The MacMillan Press Ltd.

Priestley, Mark. (2003). *Disability: A Life Course Approach*. Cambridge: Polity Press.

Russell, Marta. (1998). *Beyond Ramps: Disability at the End of the Social Contract*. Monroe: Common Courage Press.

Thomas, Carol. (2004). "How Is Disability Understood? An Examination of Sociological Approaches." *Disability & Society*, 19(6): 569–583.

Thomas, Carol. (1999). *Female Forms: Experiencing and Understanding Disability*. Buckingham: Open University Press.

Disability Studies in Education

Barton, Len. (2006). *Overcoming Disabling Barriers (Education Heritage)*. New York: Routledge.

Barton, Len. (1998). "Sociology, Disability Studies, and Education: Some Observations." In Tom Shakespeare (Ed.), *The Disability Reader: Social Science Perspectives*. London: Cassell. 53–64.

Barton, Len and Felicity Armstrong. (2007). *Policy, Experience, and Change: Cross Cultural Reflections on Inclusive Education (Inclusive Education: Cross Cultural Perspectives)*. New York: Springer.

Connor, David. (2008). "Not So Strange Bedfellows: The Promise of Disability Studies and Critical Race Theory." In Susan Gabel and Scot Danforth (Eds.), *Disability and the Politics of Education: An International Reader*. New York: Peter Lang. 453–476.

Danforth, Scot and Susan Gabel (Eds.). (2007). *Vital Questions Facing Disability Studies in Education*. New York: Peter Lang.

Davies, Charlotte. (1998). "Constructing Other Selves: (In)Competences and the Category of Learning Difficulties." In Richard Jenkins (Ed.), *Questions of Competence: Culture, Classification, and Intellectual Disability*. Cambridge: Cambridge University Press. 102–124.

Erevelles, Nirmala. (2006). "How Does It Feel to Be a Problem? Race, Disability, and Exclusion in Educational Policy." In E. A. Brantlinger (Ed.), *Who Benefits from Special Education? Remediating (Fixing) Other People's Children*. Mahwah, NJ: Lawrence Erlbaum Associates.

Erevelles, Nirmala. (2005). "Understanding Curriculum as Normalizing Text: Disability Studies Meet Curriculum Theory." *Journal of Curriculum Studies*, 37(4): 421–439.

Erevelles, Nirmala. (2000). "Educating Unruly Bodies: Critical Pedagogy, Disability Studies, and the Politics of Schooling." *Educational Theory*. Vol. 50(1): 25–47.

Ferri, Beth and David Connor. (2006). *Reading Resistance: Discourses of Exclusion in Desegregation and Inclusion Debates*. New York: Peter Lang.

Freeman, Diane P. and Martha Stoddard Holmes. (2003). *The Teacher's Body: Embodiment, Authority, and Identity in the Academy*. New York: State University of New York Press.

Freire, Paulo. (1983). "The Importance of the Act of Reading." *Journal of Education*. Vol. 165(1): 5–11.

Gabel, Susan L. (Ed.). (2005). *Disability Studies in Education: Readings in Theory and Method*. New York: Peter Lang.

Gabel, Susan and Scot Danforth (Eds.). (2008). *Disability and the Politics of Education: An International Reader*. New York: Peter Lang.

Graham, Linda and Roger Slee. (2008). "Inclusion?" In Susan Gabel and Scot Danforth (Eds.), *Disability and the Politics of Education: An International Reader*. New York: Peter Lang. 81–99.

Lewiecki-Wilson, Cynthia and Brenda Jo Brueggmann (Eds.). (2008). *Disability and the Teaching of Writing: A Critical Source Book*. Boston: St. Martin's Press.

Linton, Simi, Susan Mello, and John O'Neill. (1995). "Disability Studies: Expanding the Parameters of Diversity." *Radical Teacher*. Vol. 47: 4–10.

Livingston, Kathy. (2000). "When Architecture Disables: Teaching Undergraduates to Perceive Ableism in the Built Environment." *Teaching Sociology*, 28(3): 181–191.

Michalko, Rod. (2001). "Blindness Enters the Classroom." *Disability & Society*. Vol. 16 (3): 349–359.

Peters, Susan. (2005). "Transforming Literacy Instruction: Unpacking the Pedagogy of Privilege." In Susan L. Gabel (Ed.), *Disability Studies in Education: Readings in Theory and Method*. New York: Peter Lang. 155–172.

Slee, Roger. (2004). "Meaning in the Service of Power." In Linda Ware (Ed.), *Ideology and the Politics of (In)Exclusion*. New York: Peter Lang.

Solis, Santiago, (2006). "I'm 'Coming out' as Disabled, but I'm 'Staying in' to Rest: Reflecting on Elected and Imposed Segregation." *Equity and Excellence in Education*, (39): 146–153.

Titchkosky, Tanya. (2005). "Disability in the News: A Reconsideration of Reading." *Disability and Society*. Vol. 20(6) (October): 653–666.

Ware, Linda (Ed.). (2004). *Ideology and the Politics of (In)Exclusion*. New York: Peter Lang.

Watts, Ivan Eugene and Nirmala Erevelles. (2004). "These Deadly Times: Reconceptualizing School Violence by Using Critical Race Theory and Disability Studies." *American Educational Research Journal*. Vol. 41(2): 271–299.

Ethics, Eugenics, Policy, and Law

Bickenbach, Jerome. (1993). *Physical Disability and Social Policy*. Toronto: University of Toronto Press.

Cadwallader, Jessica. (2007). "Suffering Difference: Normalization and Power." *Social Semiotics*. Vol. 17(3): 375–394.

Chouinard, Vera. (2003). "Challenging Geographies of Ableness: Celebrating How Far We've Come and What's Left to Be Done." *The Canadian Geographer* 47(4): 383–385.

Crichton, Anne and Lyn Jongbloed. (1998). *Disability and Social Policy in Canada*. Toronto: Captus Press Inc.

Diprose, Rosalyn. (2005). "A 'Genethics' That Makes Sense: Take Two." In Margrit Shildrick and Roxanne Mykitiuk (Eds.), *Ethics of the Body: Postconventional Challenges*. Cambridge: MIT Press. 237–258.

Driedger, Diane. (1989). *The Last Civil Rights Movement: Disabled Peoples' International*. New York: St. Martin's Press.

Enns, Ruth. (1999). *A Voice Unheard: The Latimer Case and People with Disabilities*. Halifax: Fernwood Publishing.

Gadacz, Rene. (1994). *Re-thinking Dis-Ability: New Structures, New Relationships*. Edmonton: The University of Alberta Press.

Jones, Ruth J. E. (1994). *Their Rightful Place: Society and Disability*. Toronto: Canadian Academy of the Arts.

Kerr, Anne and Tom Shakespeare. (2002). *Genetic Politics: From Eugenics to Genome*. Cheltenham, England: New Clarion.

Overboe, James. (2006). "Disability and Genetics: Affirming the Bare Life (State of Exception)." *Canadian Review of Sociology and Anthropology*. May. Vol 42(2): 219–235.

McColl, Mary Ann and Lyn Jongloed. (2006). *Disability and Social Policy in Canada*, 2nd edition. Toronto: Captus Press.

Murphy, Robert. (1987). *The Body Silent*. New York: W.W. Norton.

Patterson, Annette and Martha Satz. (2002). "Genetic Counselling and the Disabled: Feminism Examines the Stance of Those Who Stand at the Gate." *Hypatia.* Vol. 17(3): 118–144.

Pothier, Dianne and Richard Devlin. (2006). *Critical Disability Theory: Essays in Philosophy, Politics, Policy, and Law.* Vancouver: UBC Press.

Prince, Michael J. (2004a). "Canadian Disability Policy: Still a Hit-and-Miss Affair." *Canadian Journal of Sociology,* 29(1): 59–82.

Prince, Michael J. (2004b). "Disability, Disability Studies, and Citizenship: Moving up or off the Sociological Agenda?" *The Canadian Journal of Sociology,* 29(3): 459–467.

Reaume, Geoffrey. (2007). *Lyndhurst: Canada's First Rehabilitation Centre for People with Spinal Cord Injuries, 1945–1998.* Montreal and Kingston: McGill-Queen's University Press.

Scott, Robert A. (1969). *The Making of Blind Men: A Study of Adult Socialization.* New Brunswick: Transaction Books, Inc.

Shildrick, Margrit. (2005a). "Beyond the Body of Bioethics: Challenging the Conventions." In Margrit Shildrick and Roxanne Mykitiuk (Eds.), *Ethics of the Body: Postconventional Challenges.* Cambridge: MIT Press. 1–29.

Snyder, Sharon L and David T. Mitchell. (2006). "Eugenics and the Racial Genome: Politics at the Molecular Level." *Patterns of Prejudice.* Vol. 40(4–5): 399–412.

Taylor, Kerry and Roxanne Mykitiuk. (2001). "Genetics, Normalcy, and Disability." *ISUMA.* Vol. 2(3): 65–71.

Tremain, Shelly (Ed.). (2005). *Foucault and the Government of Disability.* Chicago: University of Michigan Press.

Zola, Irving Kenneth. (1993). "Self, Identity, and the Naming Question: Reflections on the Language of Disability." *Social Science and Medicine,* 36(2): 167–173.

Zola, Irving Kenneth. (1977). "Healthism and Disabling Medicalization." In Ivan Illich, Irving K. Sola, John McKnight, Jonathan Caplan (Eds.), *Disabling Professions.* London: Marion Boyars Publishers Ltd.

Related Websites

www.disabilityonline.com/

With over 2,000 links, Disability Online is a good resource and it includes a more cultural studies based set of disability studies links at:

www.disabilityonline.com/categories/crip_culture/disability_research/index.html

www.webring.com

Disability Studies WEB RING is the hub of disability studies information—searchable, this web ring provides access to many disability studies websites and resources.

www.ragged-edge-mag.com/

An on-line disability magazine—activist, artistic, political, and always interesting. USA based.

http://disstud.blogspot.com/

This website is hosted by Temple University. It is very in-depth, current, and fully communicates the vibrancy of the field as well as a lot of disability studies activity in the USA and beyond. This blog also tracks many other blogs and is very accessible. Disability World named the Temple University blog as number three on its "ten outstanding events, products and developments that impacted people with disabilities in 2006" list. www.disabilityworld.org/01_07/top10.shtml

http://whatsortsofpeople.wordpress.com/

What sorts of people should there be? is a broad, interdisciplinary, collaborative project in the humanities and social sciences that focuses on human variation, normalcy, and enhancement. By weaving together distinct philosophical, historical, and comparative threads through the establishment of a Canadian-based team of 44 researchers from 18 disciplines, this project will undertake innovative work on this topic at the interface of the humanities, biotechnology, and the social and health sciences. It will range from exploring the relatively unexamined history of eugenics in Canada (especially Western Canada) to understanding ideas about and policies concerning bioenhancement and normalcy in distinct cultural and national contexts, to engaging in more speculative, future-oriented reflection on emerging biotechnology and its entwinement with social planning and individual decisions.

www.disabilityworld.org/aboutus.html

Disability World is a unique international on-line magazine (e-zine) dedicated to advancing an exchange of information and expertise about the international independent living movement of people with disabilities. Published by the World Institute on Disability (WID) since 2000 and available only on-line, *Disability World* features a wide variety of news reports, international studies and research, new projects, interviews, book and film reviews.

www.disstudies.org/

The Society for Disability Studies (SDS) is an international non-profit organization that promotes the study of disability in social, cultural, and political contexts. Disability studies recognizes that disability is a key aspect of human experience, and that the study of disability has important political, social, and economic implications for society as a whole, including both disabled and non-disabled people.

www.disabilitystudies.ca/index.htm

The Canadian Centre for Disability Studies (CCDS) website is of importance to those who are interested in, working from, and are committed to a disability studies approach. Operated by members of the disability studies community, the CCDS is composed of those who identify as scholars and community members.

www.leeds.ac.uk/disability-studies/

The Center for Disability Studies (Leeds, UK) is host to the excellent resource of an archive of primarily social model publications organized by both subject and author. Leeds DS Archive: www.leeds.ac.uk/disability-studies/archiveuk/index.html

www.neads.ca/en/

NEADS is a Canadian-based National Educational Association of Disabled Students. NEADS hosts links including Canadian government disability-related web resources.

www.neads.ca/en/norc/other_sites/osi_gov.php
www.enablelink.org/

Links people with disabilities with a world of resources and provides a lot of Canadian content. Close to the mandate and interests of the Canadian government.

www.abilityinfo.com/index.html

A website for students who are studying in the field of disability, as well as professionals working within it. Canadian based.

www.hrsdc.gc.ca/eng/home.shtml

Human Resources and Social Development Canada provides information on disability issues.

http://library.lambton.on.ca/disability_resources.htm

Canadian-based website that provides comprehensive lists of disability information and resources.

www.bioethicsanddisability.org/Disability%20Studies.html

At Bioethics and Disability you will find many useful links for a critical relation to science, able-ism, and disability, including technology advancements.

http://media-dis-n-dat.blogspot.com/2008/09/cuny-offers-new-masters-degree-in.html

Reflections on media images of people with disabilities and disability issues.

www.disabilitymuseum.org/

Their mission is to promote understanding about the historical experience of people with disabilities by recovering, chronicling, and interpreting our stories.

www.h-net.org/~disabil/

H-Disability is a scholarly discussion group that explores the multitude of historical issues surrounding the experience and phenomenon of "disability." H-Disability was established in response to the growing academic interest and expanding scholarly literature on issues of disability throughout the world.

http://dha.osu.edu/

The Disability History Association. USA based.

www.udeducation.org/

Universal Design Education Online: Teach and Learn.

www.universaldesign.net/

Universal Design Network for Educators.

http://bccc.syr.edu/

"The Beyond Compliance Coordinating Committee (BCCC) is an organization consisting of Syracuse University students who are working to create and support a positive climate toward disability that values individual difference in all University settings."

www.independentliving.org/links/

The Independent Living Institute is a policy development centre specializing in consumer-driven policies for disabled people's self-determination, self-respect, and dignity. They host a good set of links ranging from accessible and universal design to jobs and research. A new bibliography is now hosted in the library of the Independent Living Institute: "Glimpses of Disability in the Literature & Cultures of East Asia, South Asia, the Middle East & Africa." A modern and historical bibliography, briefly annotated.

www.independentliving.org/docs7/miles200807.html
www.independentliving.org/docs7/miles200807.pdf

This bibliography lists and annotates 130 novels, short stories, biographies, literary criticism, and a few materials from philosophy, anthropology, and folklore in which disability, deafness, or mental disorders play a significant part, in East Asia, South Asia, the Middle East, and Africa. Available mostly in English or French.

Websites Related to Travel, Politics, Madness, Journals, and the Arts

www.RollingRains.com

The Rolling Rains Report.

www.rds.hawaii.edu

Review of Disability Studies and related blog: www.rdsinternationaljournal.blogspot.com.

www.mindfreedom.org/

MindFreedom International.

http://community.livejournal.com/no_pity/

No Pity (live on-line journal).

www.madstudentsociety.com

Mad Student Society.

www.disabilitylib.org.uk

Disability Liberty.

http://dsq-sds.org

Disability Studies Quarterly, open access.

www.rdsinternationaljournal.blogspot.com/

Review of Disability Studies: An International Journal.

www.autistics.org/

Autistics.org has a library catalogue of essays written by autistic people, a discussion forum, and links to other neurodiversity websites.

www.sentex.net/~nexus23/naa_02.html

No Autistics Allowed: Explorations in discrimination against autistics is a catalogue of Michelle Dawson's writings on autism and discriminatory practices in Canada.

www.mindfreedom.org/

Mindfreedom International vision: "Unite in a spirit of mutual cooperation for a nonviolent revolution of mental health human rights and choice. MFI is an independent nonprofit coalition defending human rights and promoting humane alternatives for mental and emotional well being."

www.psychiatricsurvivorarchives.com/

The Psychiatric Survivor Archives of Toronto is dedicated to ensuring that the rich history of people who have experienced the psychiatric system is preserved for our community and the wider community as a resource from which everyone can share and learn.

www.power2u.org/

The mission of the National Empowerment Center Inc. is to carry a message of recovery, empowerment, hope, and healing to people who have been labelled with mental illness. We carry that message with authority because we are a consumer/survivor/ex-patient-run organization and each of us is living a personal journey of recovery and empowerment.

www.freedom-center.org/

Freedom Center is a support and activism community run by and for people labelled with severe "mental disorders." We call for compassion, human rights, self-determination, and holistic options.

www.peoplefirstltd.com/

People First is an organization run by and for people with learning difficulties to raise awareness of and campaign for the rights of people with learning difficulties and to support self-advocacy groups across the country.

www.heavyload.org/about.html or http://stayuplate.org/about.html

Heavy Load is a current British punk music band composed of musicians with and without varying disabilities. They have recently used their music to launch a campaign called "Stay up Late." Frustrated with the tendency for their disabled fan base to go home much too early and ultimately miss out on their shows—since their support staff finish their work shifts at 9 pm—Heavy Load has begun a movement to demand their right to party. Their demands include: acknowledging and respecting the insider perspectives of disabled people in scheduling shows and venues; adjusting "normal" working hours to permit disabled people to participate in after-hours work and have social lives too; and refusing to allow fans' disability to prevent their inclusion in the audience. See how Heavy Load is an unconventional disability studies movement fighting to Stay up Late.

www.ldaf.org/

London Disability Art Forum. This website offers large, high-definition photos of disabled artists' work and an art disability culture blog written by Davie Watson, the editor of a magazine of the same name, which discusses happenings and issues in the art world from a disability perspective.

www.disabilityarts.info/

Disability Cultural Project. The aim of the organization is to further the cultural equality of deaf and disabled people/deaf and disability arts practice in the UK and internationally, and to evolve new approaches to the way these are delivered.

www.s4dac.org/

Based in Vancouver, Canada, the Society for Disability Arts and Culture (S4DAC) presents and produces works by artists with disabilities and promotes artistic excellence among artists with disabilities working in a variety of disciplines.

Copyright Acknowledgments